D1598218

CAMBRIDGE STUDIES IN EARLY MODERN HISTORY

Editors

J. H. ELLIOTT   H. G. KOENIGSBERGER

THE STATE, WAR AND PEACE
Spanish Political Thought in the Renaissance
1516–1559

CAMBRIDGE STUDIES IN EARLY
MODERN HISTORY

Edited by Professor J. H. Elliott, The Institute for Advanced Study, Princeton, and Professor H. G. Koenigsberger, King's College, University of London

The idea of an 'Early Modern' period of European history from the fifteenth to the late eighteenth century is now widely accepted among historians. The purpose of the Cambridge Studies in Early Modern History is to publish monographs and studies which will illuminate the character of the period as a whole, and in particular focus attention on a dominant theme within it, the interplay of continuity and change as they are represented by the continuity of medieval ideas, political and social organization, and by the impact of new ideas, new methods and new demands on the traditional structures.

The Old World and the New, 1492–1650–J. H. ELLIOTT

French Finances 1770–1795: From Business to Bureaucracy–J. F. BOSHER

The Army of Flanders and the Spanish Road, 1567–1659: The Logistics of Spanish Victory and Defeat in the Low Countries Wars–GEOFFREY PARKER

Chronicle into History: An Essay on the Interpretation of History in Florentine Fourteenth-Century Chronicles–LOUIS GREEN

France and the Estates General of 1614–J. MICHAEL HAYDEN

Gunpowder and Galleys: Changing Technology and Mediterranean Warfare at Sea in the Sixteenth Century–JOHN FRANCIS GUILMARTIN JR

Reform and Revolution in Mainz 1743–1803–T. C. W. BLANNING

THE STATE, WAR AND PEACE

Spanish Political Thought
in the Renaissance
1516-1559

J. A. FERNÁNDEZ-SANTAMARIA

PROFESSOR OF HISTORY
CALIFORNIA STATE UNIVERSITY, HAYWARD

CAMBRIDGE UNIVERSITY PRESS

CAMBRIDGE

LONDON · NEW YORK · MELBOURNE

Published by the Syndics of the Cambridge University Press
The Pitt Building, Trumpington Street, Cambridge CB2 1RP
Bentley House, 200 Euston Road, London NW1 2DB
32 East 57th Street, New York, NY 10022, USA
296 Beaconsfield Parade, Middle Park, Melbourne 3206, Australia

First published 1977

Printed in Great Britain by
Western Printing Services Limited, Bristol

Library of Congress Cataloguing in Publication Data
Fernández-Santamaria, JA 1936–
The state, war and peace.
(Cambridge studies in early modern history)
Bibliography: p.
Includes index.
1. Political science – History – Spain. 2. Spain –
Politics and government – 1516–1556. I. Title.
JA84.S7F47   320.5'0946   76-27903
ISBN 0 521 21438 6

A mi madre
A la memoria de mi padre
A la memoria de mi abuelo, Antonio Santamaria,
alcalde socialista de El Ferrol

Contents

Abbreviations   xi
Acknowledgments   xv

Introduction   1

PART I
MEDIEVAL CONSTITUTIONALISM, CHRISTIAN HUMANISM, AND
NEOSCHOLASTICISM (1516–1539)

1   The opposition to empire: Alonso de Castrillo   11
    The Habsburg succession   11
    Of gods and giants   15
    The revolt of the Comunidades   17
    Nature and the origin of political authority   23
    On citizens and citizenship   25
    Conclusion   31

2   Advocates for empire   35
    Introduction   35
    Alfonso de Valdés   38
    Juan Luis Vives and the concord–discord dialectic   49
    Conclusion   56

3   The discovery of America and the School of
    Salamanca: Francisco de Vitoria (1)   58
    Introduction   58
    The fons et origo *of political power*   63
    The function of the state and the end of civil society   68
    The secular order and the ruler   72
    *The Indian commonwealths of the New World
    and the perfect community*   75
    *On the lawful and the illegitimate titles for the reduction of
    the Indians*   80
    A brief excursus: Diego de Covarrubias   87

viii   *Contents*

4   Francisco de Vitoria (II)   97
    The international order: sovereignty vs. jus gentium   97
    The order of grace   100
    Vitoria on justice   104
    A critique of the Vitorian system   108
    Conclusion   113

5   The age of Erasmus on war and peace   120
    Introduction   120
    Saint Augustine   123
    Erasmian pacifism and the Neoscholastic doctrine of the just war 130
    Vives on concord and discord   144
    Christian humanism and conditional bellicism: Valdés,
        Rabelais and More   150
    Conclusion   158

                        PART II
        THE WANING OF ERASMIANISM (1539–1559)

6   Humanist foundations for a universal society: Juan
        Ginés de Sepúlveda (I)   163
    Life and times   163
    Stoic oneness, Aristotelian pluralism, and Saint Augustine's
        doctrine of the just war   169
    Vita activa *and* vita contemplativa   172
    Activity and the moral virtues   176
    On civile *and* herile imperium   188
    Civil society: citizens and citizenship   191

7   Classical humanism on the American Indians: Juan Ginés
        de Sepúlveda (II)   196
    Prudence, the ruler, and the laws   196
    The rationality of the American Indians   201
    The Indians and civil society   207
    The Indians and natural slavery   209
    On the nature and goal of the just war   214
    Democrates alter: *the just war and the New World*   220
    The proto-civility of the American Indians   231

8   On princes, counselors, and councils: Charles of Habsburg,
        Antonio de Guevara, and Fadrique Furió Ceriol   237
    The Carolinian instrucciones   237
    Mirrors of princes: Renaissance and Baroque   247
    Valdés' perfect prince   252

Contents

Guevara on the prince and his privado   254
The Vida del famosísimo Emperador Marco Aurelio, con el
   Relox de príncipes   260
The life and times of Furió Ceriol   271
El concejo y consejeros del príncipe: *the prince*   275
The concejo   280
The consejero   284
Conclusion   290

Bibliography   295
Index   309

Abbreviations

SOURCES

Apologia   J. Ginés de Sepúlveda, *Apologia pro libro de justis belli causis*, in *Opera* (4 vols., Madrid, 1780), Vol. IV.

CD   J. L. Vives, *De concordia et discordia in humano genere*, in *Opera omnia* (8 vols., Valencia, 1784), Vol. V. Also in *Obras completas*, ed. and trans. L. Riber (2 vols., Madrid, 1948), Vol. II.

CFM   Saint Augustine, *Reply to Faustus the Manichaean*, in 'A Select Library of the Nicene and Post-Nicene Fathers of the Christian Church', ed. P. Schaff (14 vols., Buffalo, 1887; New York, 1907), Vol. IV.

Cohortatio   J. Ginés de Sepúlveda, *Cohortatio ad Carolum bellum suscipiat in turcas* (Bologna, 1529), in *Opera*, Vol. IV.

Concejo   F. Furió Ceriol, *El concejo y consejeros del príncipe* (Antwerp, 1559). Also *El concejo y consejeros del príncipe y otras obras*, ed. D. Sevilla Andrés (Valencia, 1952).

COR   A. de Valdés, *Diálogo de las cosas ocurridas en Roma*, ed. J. F. Montesinos (Madrid, 1928). Also *Alfonso de Valdés and the Sack of Rome*, ed. and trans. J. E. Longhurst (Albuquerque, N.M., 1952).

DA   J. Ginés de Sepúlveda, *Democrates alter*, ed. and trans. A. Losada (Madrid, 1951).

DBI   D. Erasmus, *Against War*, ed. J. W. Mackail (Boston, 1907). Also in *Opera omnia*, ed. J. Clericus (10 vols., Leiden, 1703–1706), Vol. II.

DBP   J. Clichtove, *De bello et pace* (Paris, 1523).

DCD   Saint Augustine, *The City of God*, trans. M. Dods, in 'A Select Library'. See above under CFM.

DCR   J. L. Vives, *De Communione rerum*, in *Opera*, Vol. V. Also in *Obras*, Vol. I. See above under CD.

DI   F. de Vitoria, *De Indis recenter inventis. Relectio prior*, in *De Indis et De iure belli relectiones*, ed. E. Nys, trans. J. P. Bate,

	The Classics of International Law, gen. ed. J. Brown Scott (Washington, 1917). Also in *Relecciones Teológicas*, ed. and trans. L. A. Getino (3 vols., Madrid, 1933–1936), Vol. II.
DJG	F. de Vitoria, *De jure gentium et Naturali*, trans. F. C. Macken, in *The Spanish Origin*. See under DPC.
DLA	Saint Augustine, *The Free Choice of the Will*, trans. R. P. Russell (Washington, 1967).
Dominio	M. Cano, *De dominio indiorum*, ed. L. Pereña Vicente, in *Misión de España en América, 1540–1560* (Madrid, 1956).
DP	J. Ginés de Sepúlveda, *Democrates primus*, in *Opera*, Vol. IV. See also A. Losada's translation (Madrid, 1963).
DPC	F. de Vitoria, *De potestate civili*, trans. G. L. Williams, in J. Brown Scott, *The Spanish Origin of International Law. Part I: Francisco de Vitoria and His Law of Nations* (Oxford and London, 1924).
DPE I	F. de Vitoria, *De potestate Ecclesia prior*, in *Relecciones Teológicas*. See above under DI.
DR	J. Ginés de Sepúlveda, *De regno*, in *Opera*, Vol. IV. Also A. Losada's translation (Madrid, 1963).
EE	M. Bataillon, *Erasmo y España*, trans. A. Alatorre (Mexico, 1966).
Epistolae	J. Ginés de Sepúlveda, *Epistolario de Juan Ginés de Sepúlveda: selección*, ed. A. Losada (Madrid, 1966).
GP	F. Rabelais, *Gargantua and Pantagruel*, trans. J. Le Clerq (Modern Library, New York, n.d.).
IPC	D. Erasmus, *The Education of a Christian Prince*, ed. and trans. L. K. Born (New York, 1968). Also in *Opera*, Vol. IV. See above under DBI.
Letters	Saint Augustine, *Letters of Saint Augustine*, in 'A Select Library', Vol. I. See under CFM.
LW	F. de Vitoria, *De Indis recenter inventis. Relectio posterior (De iure belli)*, in *De Indis et De iure belli relectiones*. See above under DI.
MC	A. de Valdés, *Diálogo de Mercurio y Carón*, ed. J. F. Montesinos (Madrid, 1929).
MF	C. de Seyssel, *La Monarchie de France*, ed. J. Poujol (Paris, 1961).
Peccatum	D. de Covarrubias y Leyva, *Regulae peccatum, de regulis Iuris lib. 6 Relectio* (Salamanca, 1558).
Pol	Aristotle, *Politics*, Jowett edition.
Proposiciones	J. Ginés de Sepúlveda, *Proposiciones temerarias, escandalosas y heréticas que notó el doctor Sepúlveda en el libro de la conquista de Indias*, in A. M. Fabié, *Vida y escritos de don Fray Bartolomé de las Casas* (2 vols., Madrid, 1879), Vol. II, Appendix 25. The two volumes are numbers LXX and LXXI of the *Colección de documentos inéditos para la Historia de España* (CODOIN).

PQL   D. de Covarrubias y Leyva, *Practicarum quaestionum liber*, in
        Textos jurídico-políticos, ed. M. Fraga Iribarne, trans. A.
        Río Seco (Madrid, 1957).
QP   D. Erasmus, *The Complaint of Peace*, trans. T. Paynell, modern
        edition of W. J. Hirten (New York, 1948).
IIa–IIae F. de Vitoria, *Comentarios a la secunda secundae de Santo
        Tomás*, ed. V. Beltrán de Heredia (5 vols., Salamanca, 1932–
        1935).
TR   A. de Castrillo, *Tractado de Républica* (Madrid, 1958).

JOURNALS

AAFV   *Anuario de la Asociación Francisco de Vitoria*
AIA   *Archivo Ibero–Americano*
AS   *Acta Salmanticensia*
AST   *Annalecta Sacra Tarraconensia*
AUM   *Anales de la Universidad de Murcia*
BH   *Bulletin Hispanique*
BHR   *Bibliothèque d'Humanisme et Renaissance*
BHS   *Bulletin of Hispanic Studies*
BJRL   *Bulletin of the John Rylands Library*
BRAE   *Boletín de la Real Academia Española*
BRAH   *Boletín de la Real Academia de la Historia*
CD   *La Ciudad de Dios*
CH   *Church History*
CHM   *Cahiers d'Histoire Mondiale*
CNJ   *Cahiers de la Nouvelle Journée*
CT   *La Ciencia Tomista*
CuH   *Cuadernos de Historia*
CV   *Ciencia y Vida*
EA   *Estudios Americanos*
EHSE   *Estudios de Historia Social de España*
ES   *Estudios Segovianos*
HAHR   *Hispanic American Historical Review*
HLQ   *Huntington Library Quarterly*
HTR   *Harvard Theological Review*
JHI   *Journal of the History of Ideas*
JMH   *Journal of Modern History*
JWI   *Journal of the Warburg Institute*
MLR   *Modern Language Review*
MQR   *The Mennonite Quarterly Review*
RDP   *Revista de Derecho Público*
RecH   *Revue Hispanique*

xiv   *Abbreviations*

REDC	*Revista Española de Derecho Canónico*
REDI	*Revista Española de Derecho Internacional*
REP	*Revista de Estudios Políticos*
RF	*Razón y Fe*
RFH	*Revista de Filología Hispánica*
RFN	*Revista di Filosofia Neoscolastica*
RGDIC	*Revue Générale de Droit International Comparé*
RGDIP	*Revue Générale de Droit International Public*
RH	*Revue Historique*
RLC	*Revue de Littérature Comparée*
VV	*Verdad y Vida*

Acknowledgments

Although the shortcomings of this book are clearly the sole responsibility of the author, whatever merit it may possess is largely due to the care, interest, and scholarship of friends and colleagues.

It is difficult to find the words which would rightly measure the magnitude of my debt to Professor Gerald Strauss, whose kindness, encouragement, and learned guidance have been with me since my graduate student days. I am profoundly grateful to Professor Gerald S. Henig for his unfailing support and invaluable advice during the past five years. I would also like to express my special thanks to the editors, Professors John H. Elliott and H. G. Koenigsberger, from whose patience and excellent suggestions the manuscript itself greatly benefited. For their interest and encouragement I am indebted to Professors William A. Bullough, Lejeune Cummins, and Tom G. Hall.

Last but not least, I should like to acknowledge my lasting obligation to three friends: Mrs Lori Henig, who never failed to take an interest in the progress of the work; Miss Susan Shepard, whose patience and concern so often made the path easier; Miss Jennifer Henig, who since her coming has been a source of constant delight and happiness.

Introduction

Although all too often ignored by students of political thought, the Spanish contribution to the history of political ideas in the sixteenth century is not only impressive but 'up-to-date' enough to satisfy the most demanding among critics. All the themes which the age inherited from the medieval tradition and which constitute the composite heart of Renaissance political theory were extensively studied by the publicists of the Spanish school. To argue that their answers are largely based on a foundation of Stoic, Platonic, Aristotelian, Augustinian, or Thomist vintage merely confirms how much they have in common with their own age.

In addition the Spanish school concerned itself with a question prompted by the fact that at this juncture Castile strives to play three political parts at times drastically incompatible with each other: a modern state in its early evolutionary stages forced by the vagaries of dynastic arrangements into a framework of the medieval imperial idea, while simultaneously becoming the nucleus of a rapidly growing and new form of empire. The political theme created by these circumstances revolves around the role to be played by the individual and autonomous commonwealth, not as an isolated entity precariously surviving in a hostile and anarchic world but as a responsible member of an international community of sovereign states. The importance of this idea in the evolution of Spanish political thought from Vitoria to Suárez (1548–1617) is difficult to overestimate and in no small measure owes its origin to a phenomenon which in the early sixteenth century was privy to Spain alone: the political puzzle posed by the acquisition beyond the sea of extensive territories populated by a hitherto unknown group of nations enjoying impressive social and political organizations of their own. And this alone, aside from the other more familiar themes, is as important and legitimate a part of sixteenth-century political speculation as Erasmus' pedagogical efforts aimed at pointing the way leading to a better society; Bodin's underlying anxiety for the return of political order to civil war-torn France; or Machiavelli's attempt to draw conclusions conducive to the formulation of lasting political principles from the misfortunes of his beloved Italy.

The special character of Spain's political philosophy in the age of Erasmus, moreover, illustrates the shortcomings of an outlook – by no means entirely banished from the domain of Spanish history – which in its anxiety to uncover the foundations of modernity judges the past according to latter-day standards, and jettisons as obsolete whatever cannot justify its existence in terms of its own future survival. The internationalism of the Spanish school is a case in point. It is often described as a hopelessly antiquarian attempt to preserve an ideology doomed to be submerged by the rising tide of the emerging nation-state with its ruthless individualism deaf to universalist appeals. Alas, in this as in many other instances the man of the Renaissance, in Spain and elsewhere, lacked the window into the future available to those acquainted with the following three centuries, and so time and again, in every corner of Europe, he persisted in assuming that the ecumenical dream was no chimera but an attainable goal.

I believe the considerations outlined above to be most important in a general way, and they will guide and underline the aims and purpose of this book. I will not attempt here to find out in what manner Spanish political thinkers succeeded or failed in foretelling the political theories of the future. Neither will I seek to judge the value of their ideology in the light of doctrines in vogue two centuries later. Rather I will endeavor to understand what Spaniards, fully within the context of a fluid, flexible, and eclectic framework so characteristic of the European Renaissance, had to say about the timeless questions posed by political theory in every epoch and how they sought to solve the concrete problems proposed by the circumstances of their own age. The ideas of many notable figures will thus be surveyed and analysed. In particular I will often stress their preoccupation with the question of war.

War, its origin, practice, and consequences, is of exceptional importance here because it lies at the foundation of the political thinking of the Spanish school. But even putting the latter aside, it is manifest that the ideological milieu of the early sixteenth century invariably displays an almost morbid fascination with what Erasmus himself, in despair, called a 'disease of man's wit'. Under the circumstances, the inclusion in this book of a chapter devoted to the nature of the doctrine of the just war and its fate during the age under scrutiny is a thoroughly warranted one. One might ask, however, why not integrate the ideas on war of the thinkers studied directly into the context of their political thought. In the last analysis such organizational matters remain of course largely within the province of the author's caprice; but in this instance the extraordinary influence of Saint Augustine and Erasmus strongly suggested the wisdom of adopting a format allowing for a survey of Spanish thought on war against the background of Augustinian and Erasmian ideas.

One of the more telling criticisms of Spanish political theory found in treatises surveying European political thought in the sixteenth century is that the ideas of the School of Salamanca, the most distinguished component of the Spanish school, constitute nothing more than a belated manifestation of medieval Scholasticism. To be sure the magnitude of the debt owed by Vitoria and his followers to Saint Thomas cannot be denied. But it does not follow, as is often alleged, that this Scholastic foundation of a segment of Spanish political thought predestines its totality to failure on the grounds of acute obsolescence.

The sixteenth-century renovation of medieval Scholasticism was particularly strong in Spain where following the initiative of Salamanca the institutions of higher learning replaced Peter Lombard's *Sentences* with Saint Thomas' *Summa* as the universal classroom text.[1] The immediate result of this innovation was an endless stream of commentaries to the *Summa*, above all on questions 90–108 of the Prima secundae in which Aquinas expounds his doctrine of the law. In these lengthy, detailed, and numerous treatises – *De justitia et jure* and *De legibus* – which chronologically begin to appear in 1533–1534 and continue into the second half of the seventeenth century, the goal is to explain natural law as a system

---

[1] The change had already taken place at the University of Paris and had been pioneered by Peter Crockaert and Tommaso de Vio. Francisco de Vitoria, the innovator at Salamanca, had studied in Paris under Crockaert. At Alcalá (founded in 1508), however, Cardinal Cisneros created three separate chairs of theology corresponding to the three main contemporary currents: Thomism, Scotism, and Nominalism. For all this see L. Allevi, 'Francesco de Vitoria e il Rinascimento della scolastica nel secolo XVI', *RFN*, xix (1927), pp. 401–41; R. García Villoslada, *La Universidad de Paris durante los estudios de Francisco de Vitoria* (Rome, 1938); L. A. Getino, *El maestro Francisco de Vitoria y el renacimiento teológico del siglo XVI* (Madrid, 1941). V. Beltrán de Heredia has written extensively on the subject: *Las corrientes de espiritualidad entre los dominicos en el siglo XVI* (Salamanca, 1941), 'La Teología en nuestras universidades del Siglo de Oro', *AST*, xiv (1942), and *Cartulario de la Universidad de Salamanca. La Universidad en el Siglo de Oro*, ii (Salamanca, 1970). A. Guy, *Esquisse des progrès de la speculation philosophique a Salamanca au cours du XVIe. siècle* (Paris, 1943); V. Carro, 'Las controversias de Indias y las ideas teológico–jurídicas que las preparan y explican', *CT*, lxvii (1944), pp. 5–32, 'Los fundamentos teológico–jurídicos de las doctrinas de Vitoria', *CT*, lxxii (1947), pp. 95–122, *Las controversias teológico–jurídicas en el siglo XVI* (Salamanca, 1950), 'The Spanish theological–juridical Renaissance and the ideology of Bartolomé de las Casas', in *Bartolomé de las Casas in History* (De Kalb, Ill., 1971), ed. J. Friede and B. Keen, pp. 236–75.

of principles which directs, corrects, and serves as norm to human law.[2] The return, then, was not to the ailing Scholasticism of the fourteenth and fifteenth centuries, but to the vigorous Thomism of the thirteenth. What was adopted, moreover, was not in the manner of a slavish repetition of the master's teachings, but a methodology of proven soundness which might conceivably be applicable to the solution of the novel problems posed by the dawning age. Rigor, precision, simplicity, clarity, and elegance became the goals pursued by generations of jurists and theologians at Salamanca. If nothing else the nature of those goals should convince us that the Neoscholasticism pioneered by Salamanca did not exist in a cultural vacuum alien to or untouched by other intellectual currents.

Hence even if isolationism and traditional formalism had been sought by the early Neoscholastic masters, the very richness and complexity of Spanish intellectual life in the age of Erasmus would have impeded their triumph. To the native traditions, the early sixteenth century added Burgundian traits intensified by the arrival in the Peninsula of the Archduke Philip, his son Charles of Ghent, and their Flemish suits; the weight and authority of Italian humanism, influential in the Spanish kingdoms since the fifteenth century; and, above all, the formidable popularity enjoyed by Erasmus in Spain, particularly at the University of Alcalá, the center and academic bastion of Spanish Erasminism. It is only after the passing of the age of Erasmus and the coming of the age of Trent that dogmatism begins to permeate and hamper the flexibility of the orthodox purview.[3] Even then, however, when the waning of Alcalá's influence

[2] Cf. A. Folgado, 'Los tratados *De legibus* y *De iustitia et iure* en los autores españoles del siglo XVI y primera mitad del XVII', *CD*, CLXXII, 3(1959), pp. 275–302. These endeavors would result in the creation of a solid effort of jurisprudence based on an unprecedentedly clear formulation of natural law that would importantly influence the seventeenth century. According to Father Carro ('The Spanish theological–juridical Renaissance', pp. 251–2), Vitoria received two fundamental principles from Saint Thomas. First, 'the divine law, which proceeds from grace, does not annul human law, which proceeds from natural reason', and secondly, 'that which is natural, be it called law or right, faculty or power, is so consubstantial with the being that it remains immutable in every class of men and he cannot lose or acquire it through sin, whether he be Christian or pagan, black or white'. As we shall have occasion to point out, Sepúlveda quarrels with neither of those principles.

[3] On the Spanish Renaissance see A. F. G. Bell, *Luis de León* (Oxford, 1923), and *El Renacimiento en España* (Zaragoza, 1944); M. Bataillon, *Erasme et l'Espagne* (Paris, 1937), and the Spanish translation by A. Alatorre, *Erasmo y España* (2 vols., Mexico, 1966); M. Batllori's 'Lignes fondamentales de l'humanisme dans la Péninsule Ibérique', and R. Sugranyes de Franch's 'Les études humanistes en Espagne et au Portugal', are both contributions to the Congrés International des Études Humanistes, in *RLC*, xxx, 4(1956). J. A. Maravall has studied the subject extensively

left to its rival Salamanca the unchallenged mastery of the field, we must beware of identifying too readily the theological activities at Trent of Diego Laínez, Alfonso Salmerón, Melchor Cano (1509–1560), and Domingo de Soto (1495–1560), among others, with the political doctrines of Vitoria, Cano, Soto, and Suárez, or assuming that the latter merely mirrored the needs of religious controversy. Even into the seventeenth century the political thought of the School of Salamanca remained strongly conditioned by developments which had been so influential in shaping the teachings of its founder, Vitoria, and so closely bound with the cultural milieu and political circumstances of an earlier age.

All this suggests that we now turn to the study of the merits of an interpretation not infrequently proposed as the clue that explains the supposed dearth of significant political thinking in sixteenth-century Spain: the country's internal quiescence during this period.[4] This argument clearly implies that contrary to the case of, say, Erasmus, Machiavelli, or Bodin, no Spanish political thinker experienced the conditions of crisis which are so strongly conducive to the formulation of lasting and influential political doctrines. Thus Erasmus, European citizen by choice and the best and greatest embodiment of cosmopolitanism in modern European history, responds to the crisis which he believes Christendom is undergoing with a series of normative tracts. Machiavelli, driven by the collapse of the Italian state system after 1494, postulates the fundamentals of the doctrine of *raison d'État*. Bodin, *politique* and Frenchman, faces his country's crisis by formulating the legal characteristics of the power of the state and developing as a result the idea of sovereignty within the narrow confines of a national state. Now, it is clear that sixteenth-century Spain did not suffer the sort of crisis which in France and Italy contributed to the creation of influential political doctrines. It is incorrect,

in many of his works, especially *El Humanismo de las armas de Don Quijote* (Madrid, 1948), *Carlos V y el pensamiento político del Renacimiento* (Madrid, 1960), and *Antiguos y modernos. La idea del progreso en el desarrollo de una sociedad* (Madrid, 1966). On the influence of Italian humanism on Spanish historiography see the two studies by R. B. Tate: 'Italian humanism and Spanish historiography of the fifteenth century. A study of the Paralipomenon hispanae of Joan de Margarit, Cardinal Bishop of Gerona', *BJRL*, xxxiv, 1(1951), pp. 137–65, and 'Nebrija the historian', *BHS*, xxx, 3(1957), pp. 125–46. See also: A. Fontán, 'Introducción al humanismo español', *Atlántida*, iv, 22(1966), pp. 443–53; J. Cepeda Adán, 'El gran Tendilla, medieval y renacentista', *CuH*, 1(1967), pp. 169–87; and the pertinent sections of the New Cambridge Modern History, i, *The Renaissance*.

[4] G. R. Elton maintains that 'generally speaking, significant political thinking occurs only when there are significant political upheavals. Spain, as is not surprising in view of its pretty placid state, could show no writings of note.' In 'Constitutional development and political thought in western Europe', *NCMH*, ii, *The Reformation*, p. 459.

however, to conclude that Spain experienced no constitutional crisis whatever during the same period, and to explain on this basis her supposed
failure to contribute meaningfully to the political thought of the age.

At the beginning of the sixteenth century Castile was the one European
realm in which the foundations for a national state had been most soundly
laid – 'an early nationalism, a strong royal authority, a sense of community, and a respected and capable bureaucracy'.[5] This promising state
of affairs was soon disrupted beyond repair by the intrusion of a double
constitutional crisis. In less than a generation after the death of Isabel in
1504, Castile – as indeed the remaining realms of the union – found herself with a Holy Roman Emperor sitting on her throne and mistress of an
ever-growing assortment of overseas territories which did not fit into any
known political system. Torn between two versions of empire, Castile was
forced to depart from the straight road leading toward the modern state
and steer an ambiguous middle course.[6]

Awareness of these simple but important facts yields rewarding results.
It becomes clear that Spanish political thought in the sixteenth century is
not a continuous stream moving placidly and uneventfully along, but a
somewhat uneven road punctuated by some very visible markers. Even
within the relatively narrow boundaries of our period it is not difficult to
see how the events mentioned above influenced and shaped those markers.
Alonso de Castrillo, a Castilian writer in the early 1520s, reflects a
poignant sense of crisis and an almost morbid fear that the personality and
liberties of his country will be overwhelmed by the sheer weight of the
ecumenical whole to which it has reluctantly become appended. On the
other hand, barely a generation later Sepúlveda (also a Castilian), far
from harboring any misgivings concerning the preservation of his country's identity, writes as if Castile herself symbolized Spain and had become
the hub of empire as well. This transition from a state of baleful pessimism
to one of self-assured optimism, in reality nothing more than a reflection
in the realm of political thought of the swiftness with which Castile
surrendered to the beckoning charm of the imperial idea, is recognizable
as early as 1527 in Alfonso de Valdés. Its culmination takes place still
within the chronological boundaries of Spanish Erasmianism with Vitoria.
How completely this initial stage in Castile's constitutional trials had

[5] A. Domínguez Ortiz, *The Golden Age of Spain 1516–1659*, trans. J. Casey
(London, 1971), p. 6.
[6] J. A. Maravall, 'El descubrimiento de America en la historia del pensamiento
político', *REP* (1952), p. 236, and 'The origins of the modern state', *CHM*, VI, 4(1961),
pp. 789–808; also J. Vicens Vives, 'Estructura estatal en los siglos XVI y XVII',
Congrès International des Sciences Historiques, *Rapports*, IV (Stockholm, 1960),
pp. 1–23.

been surmounted by then is shown by Vitoria's concern, not with specific instances but with general principles of political philosophy as demanded by the second and more enduring aspect of the crisis, the discovery of America, as well as by a phenomenon of European proportions – the demise of the medieval empire and the emergence of the Renaissance state system.[7]

[7] Notable among works on Spanish political thought in English are B. Hamilton, *Political Thought in Sixteenth-Century Spain* (Oxford, 1963); and G. Lewy's excellent study, *Constitutionalism and Statecraft during the Golden Age of Spain: A Study of the Political Philosophy of Juan de Mariana* (Geneva, 1963). In French, P. Mesnard deals extensively with several Spanish political thinkers in his *L'Essor de la philosophie politique au XVIe. siècle* (Paris, 1952); R. Labrousse, *Essai sur la philosophie politique de l'ancienne Espagne: politique de raison, politique de la foi* (Paris, 1937). In Spanish, as might be expected, the literature is both immense and of uneven quality. Among periodicals, the following often carry articles on various aspects of Spanish political thought in the Golden Century: *Boletín de la Real Academia de la Historia, Estudios Americanos, Revista de Estudios Políticos, La Ciudad de Dios, La Ciencia Tomista, Anuario de la Asociación Francisco de Vitoria, Razón y Fe, Anuario de Historia del Derecho Español*. Among authors, probably the most distinguished is J. A. Maravall; particularly significant for our period is his *Carlos V* already mentioned. Also see E. Bullón y Fernández, *El concepto de soberanía en la escuela jurídica española del siglo XVI* (Madrid, 1935); C. Barcia Trelles, *Interpretación del hecho americano por la España universitaria del siglo XVI. La escuela internacionalista del siglo XVI* (Montevideo, 1949); L. Sánchez Agesta, *El concepto del Estado en el pensamiento español del siglo XVI* (Madrid, 1959), and his 'Ordine medievale e pensiero politico moderno', *Jus* (Università Cattolica del Sacro Cuore, Milano), vi, 1(1955), pp. 65–78, a brief analysis of Renaissance Spanish political thought; L. Pereña Vicente, 'La Universidad de Salamanca, forja del pensamiento político español en el siglo XVI', AS (Historia de la Universidad), 1, 2(1954); R. Fernández de Velasco, *La doctrina de la razón de Estado en los escritores españoles anteriores al siglo XIX* (Madrid, 1925); L. Rodriguez Aranda, 'El racionalismo en el pensamiento político español', *REP*, 119(1961), p. 117–46; P. de Vega (ed.), *Antología de escritores políticos del Siglo de Oro* (Madrid, 1966), with an introduction by E. Tierno Galván expressing an outlook toward Spanish political thought of the Golden Century different from mine; M. Moreyra Paz Soldán, 'Teorías políticas basadas en realidades concretas en el siglo XVI', *Revista Histórica* (Lima), xxx(1967), pp. 333–54.

PART I
MEDIEVAL CONSTITUTIONALISM, CHRISTIAN HUMANISM, AND NEOSCHOLASTICISM (1516–1539)

The opposition to empire: Alonso de Castrillo

The Habsburg succession

On November 26, 1504, Isabel of Castile died. For the next twenty years the Hispanic kingdoms in general and Castile in particular would live through severe internal storms which repeatedly threatened to tear asunder the delicate fabric of Spanish unity that the royal couple had wrought during more than thirty years of unceasing toil. At one moment it seemed as if Aragon and Castile would as of old go their own separate ways. At another it appeared that Castile might succeed in imposing upon her young sovereign the same kind of constitutional straitjacket which the Church in Council had once sought to force on the Pope.

The roots of Spain's twenty years of turmoil and the vicissitudes of her monarchy during the same period are sunk deep in the medieval soil; in those extraordinarily convoluted and vague principles which, more emotionally felt than rationally understood, often go under the name of medieval constitutionalism; the haphazard practices of a monarchical system which although strong on the surface could easily be brought to the point of crisis by the waning but still powerful forces to which the encroachments of central authority had brought lasting bitterness; and the uncertainties of the dynastic principle which through a succession of fateful demises brought the Trastámara inheritance into the hands of a foreign dynasty. If to these broad and remote antecedents we add the more immediate issues dominating Castilian and Burgundian politics between 1504 and 1516, the year of Ferdinand's death, the sordidness of the grim drama played out on the Castilian stage during the years preceding the revolt of her cities easily unfolds in all its stark nakedness. Castile's detestation of ambitious foreigners (an overwhelming theme present throughout the war of the *Comunidades*), that initial wariness toward her new sovereign (himself a foreigner) soon to be changed into outright antipathy and mistrust after Charles' refusal at the Cortes of

Valladolid (1518) to heed his subjects' demand that he curb the notorious
freedom of grasping aliens, her final outburst of wrath as a result of the
imperial election of 1519, were all inevitable sequels to the tragic farce
which for twelve years pitted Austrian Habsburg against Aragonese
Trastámara. It is hardly to be wondered under the circumstances that
during those years of crisis and turmoil Castilians should have longingly
looked back to the days of Isabel and Ferdinand as the golden age of good
rule; a fact which also explains how by the time of the *Comunero* outbreak the foundations had been laid for that political myth of great currency in later Spanish life which was to view the reign of the Catholic
Kings not only as the climax of good government respectful of the *leyes
destos Reinos* – namely, of the republic's constitutional order – but as the
embodiment of the national idea as well.

In the spring of 1506 the Archduke Philip and his wife, Isabel's
daughter Juana, arrived in Castile to claim the latter's inheritance. Aware
of her daughter's failing mental health and her son-in-law's notorious
incapacity Isabel had nevertheless failed to rely on her husband Ferdinand.
Upon her death the latter had, in obedience to his wife's testament, been
deprived of the perquisites and title of King of Castile. He was instead
confirmed in the ambiguous role of caretaker ruler during the absence of
his daughter (away in Flanders with her husband) defined by her mother's
will as *Reina propietaria de Castilla* (Queen proprietess of Castile). The
enmity that had characterized Philip's relations with his father-in-law
from faraway Flanders naturally increased with the arrival of the young
couple in Castile. Faced with the explicit provisions of his wife's testament and the opposition of Castile's most influential magnates, Ferdinand
surrendered the game and abandoning Castile returned to his Aragonese
dominions. In July 1506, the Cortes of Castile gathered at Valladolid to
recognize Juana as queen and Philip as her consort. The former Archduke's triumph, however, was short-lived, for he died toward the end of
September of that same year. A regency was immediately established
under the presidency of the Archbishop of Toledo, Jiménez de Cisneros.
After four years of internal disorder the Cortes recalled Ferdinand as
Castile's regent to rule in the name of his daughter Juana now hopelessly
insane. Ferdinand's administration was characterized by an endless
struggle against the factious higher nobility, a legacy which he would
bequeath intact after his death to the new regent Cisneros. The iron-
willed Cardinal, loathed as his government was by the Castilian magnates,
proved to be more than a match for his noble enemies. He ruled with
notorious intransigence during the remaining months of Charles'
minority until late in 1517 when, with Charles' arrival, ungracious dismissal and death visited Cisneros simultaneously.

With Charles' presence in the kingdom new winds of hope began to blow across the land. Perhaps now the uncertainties, disorders, and fears of the past thirteen years had finally come to an end. The optimism, however, lasted briefly. The new king was young, inexperienced, and unacquainted with his new subjects. Above all, he was dominated by his Flemish advisers, especially Guillaume de Croy, Sieur de Chièvres. The hated specter of foreign influence and greed, of which Castile had had a foretaste during the brief tenure of Philip I, again raised its head. By January 18, 1518, when the Cortes gathered at Valladolid to swear fealty to the new sovereign, Castilians were already protesting the iniquities committed by Charles' creatures. It was thus in a growing atmosphere of disaffection that the news of Maximilian's death and Charles' own election to the throne of the Holy Roman Empire arrived in Castile toward the beginning of 1519. Preparing his departure for Germany the new Emperor issued a summons for the Castilian Cortes to meet in Galicia and vote the needed funds for the trip. As the stormy meetings of the Santiago–La Coruña Cortes would prove, the indignation of the Castilian cities knew no bounds; not only had this alien king brought with him into the country a plague of insatiable locusts in the guise of counselors but now, after further financial exactions, he proposed to abandon his subjects in search of an imperial dignity to which Castilians were at this point supremely indifferent. The stage was set for what Seaver has called the Great Revolt in Castile.

The presumed incorporation of the Spanish realms into the complex fabric of the medieval Empire, then, elicited a swift and violent riposte on the part of Castile in the form of the *Comunero* rebellion, the implications of which are still only imperfectly understood but whose immediate origins have been described by Domínguez Ortiz in the following terms:

On hearing the news of his election as emperor he left to take ship at Corunna – but not before holding a Cortes which he cajoled and browbeat into giving him the money he needed for his journey and coronation. His Spanish subjects had now further cause for discontent: the monarch clearly would be absent for some time, while Spain would be incorporated into a supra-national structure in which its own separate interests would be lost to sight.[1]

[1] Domínguez Ortiz, *The Golden Age of Spain*, p. 48. On the subject of the *Comuneros*, see E. Benito, *Toledo en el siglo* xv (Madrid, 1961); P. Chaunu, *L'Espagne de Charles-Quint* (2 vols., Paris 1973); M. Danvila y Collado, *Historia crítica y documentada de las Comunidades de Castilla* (6 vols., Madrid, 1897); J. A. Maravall, *Las Comunidades de Castilla* (Madrid, 1963); R. Menéndez Pidal, 'Carlos V y las Comunidades vistas a nueva luz documental', in *El P. Las Casas y Vitoria* (Madrid, 1958); R. B. Merriman, *The Rise of the Spanish Empire in the Old World and the New* (4 vols., New York, 1918–34), iii; M. Quintanilla, 'El episodio de las Comunidades', *ES*, vi(1954); A. Salvá, *Burgos en las Comunidades de Castilla*

It also produced an abundant political literature sometimes eagerly sympathetic toward the new imperial dignity vested in the Spanish sovereign, often warily distrustful of its implications. Notable among the former is a jurist from Navarre, Miguel de Ulçurrum (or Ulzurrum), who in his *Catholicum opus imperiale regiminis mundi* (1525) strongly advocates in a most extreme traditional manner the imperial idea; and Pedro Mexía, whose *Historia Imperial y Cesárea* is more moderate but equally amenable to seeing Charles of Spain assume the responsibilities of imperial office. It is among those closest to the person of the Emperor, however, that we find a reformist zeal and moralist outlook intent on visualizing the Empire as both the image and the protector of the pure ideas of Christianity. Such is the position of Antonio de Guevara, the chronicler of the Emperor whose works enjoyed much popularity and wide circulation among the European learned public; and Charles' Latin secretary, Alfonso de Valdés, whose dialogues bring Erasmus' social and political teachings within a narrower framework of Spanish circumstances and idealize the figure of the imperial sovereign into a monarch capable of bringing about, without fear or bloodshed, a truly Christian universal monarchy.

Chronologically and thematically speaking, however, the Trinitarian friar Alonso de Castrillo antedates the works of the apologists for Empire. His *Tractado de República*, published in 1521 (the year that saw the defeat of the *Comuneros* at the battle of Villalar), personifies an approach to the Castilian constitutional crisis which is both alien to imperial ideology and influentially shaped by the ideas of medieval constitutionalism – a determined, if only implicit, rejection of the Carolinian *Weltanschauung*. This last is a specific point which must be clearly kept in mind as we explore the contents and meaning of Castrillo's ideology, for the period of the Catholic Kings which the author views nostalgically was anything but one of Castilian domestic retrenchment. Before the medieval imperial idea arrived in Spain snugly tucked away in Burgundian saddlebags, there had already been in existence a pure-bred Hispanic conception of imperial expansionism blending Castilian Atlantic interests in America, Aragon's Mediterranean policies, and the waning but by no means abandoned objectives of African expansion in the Mahgreb. Such an imperialism, believed to have been born and bred in purely Spanish conditions and nourished by age-old traditions and needs distinctly indigenous, was felt to offer no threat to the continued survival of those customs and institutions intuitively deemed by Castrillo, among others, to be quintessentially Castilian. By contrast and with no small justification as future events

(Burgos, 1895); H. L. Seaver, *The Great Revolt in Castile* (Boston, 1928); E. Tierno, 'De las Comunidades o la historia como proceso', *Boletín del Seminario de Derecho Político* (Universidad de Salamanca), May–October, 1957, n. 16–19.

would prove, the advent and imposition of an universal political conception grown from imperatives totally unrelated to Castile's own past was most unsettling to men like Castrillo. It is not, then, against imperialism *per se* that Castrillo thunders but against that version of empire out of which, he believed, nothing but unwelcome change would come to Castile.

Of gods and giants

In a short prologue addressed to Diego de Gayangos, Castrillo offers the reader a sketchy portrait of the causes of the revolt of the *Comunidades*. To begin with, he remarks, the responsibility for what happened in Castile rests by no means exclusively on the shoulders of the common people (*comunes*). A major share of the blame lies with 'those to whom change (*novedades*) is attractive and the most scandalous counsels invariably seem the healthiest'.[2] And who are these men? Castrillo is convinced that they are not native Castilians but foreigners, 'enemies of our republic and our people, for as such they provoke and incite others to burn houses and cause other forms of damage, not out of a zealous desire for justice but merely to quench their greedy thirst'.[3] The results are of course predictable.

Thus it is that land, possessions, home, children and wife are responsible for creating love for the republic. And there where the citizens lack those things they will also lack love. And those who want love are friends of *novedades*, and they, in turn, are those foes of peace whose natural inclinations are bent to cause the perdition of men and peoples. It is thus that the *conservación* of our human fellowship meets its undoing.[4]

Specifically who the malefactors are remains a moot question. From the general tenor of Castrillo's complaint, however, it is not unlikely that he sought to bring together under one single anathema the villains from both sides: those whose greed and exactions (and to them, I think, applies the epithet of 'foreigners') goaded the people to protest, and those who using the people's just wrath for their own purposes changed the entire complexion of the *Comunero* movement.

With the aid of that classical myth which depicted the war waged by the giants against Zeus, Castrillo metaphorically describes the course of the rebellion. The giants, fatherless and born of the earth, 'gathered themselves together in concert and maintaining that there was no reason for

---

[2] Alonso de Castrillo, *Tractado de república*, edition of the Instituto de Estudios Políticos (Madrid, 1958), pp. 7–8. Cited hereafter as *TR*.
[3] *Ibid.*
[4] *Ibid.*, p. 8.

the supremacy exercised by the heavens over the earth sought to storm the former, intending to precipitate Zeus from his throne and the minor gods from their houses'.[5] The giants, explains Castrillo, are synonymous with the 'common people in their lack of lineage and of distinguished ancestry'; their conspiracy against both the heavens (the king's 'exalted authority') and Zeus (the king, whose power is symbolized by the rays with which the god crushes the uprising) means the gathering of the *comunes* in revolt. The mountains that according to mythology the giants piled to reach the heavens represent the cities which the *comunes* brought together 'to offend the will of their king'. Finally, the minor gods are but the *caballeros*. None, however, Castrillo grants, can deny that at the beginning the common people demanded only justice. Alas, they soon sullied it with violence and 'it seems that those who require justice by breaking the reign of order and the *acatamiento* (reverence) with which justice must be demanded become unworthy of receiving the very justice which they seek'.[6]

These initial comments illustrate Castrillo's embittered alienation from those – the *Comuneros* – whose cause was just but who besmirched it with their excesses. Later on we shall meet the author's acerbic charges against the other side, those in power who make a travesty out of the art of ruling, 'among all the branches of knowledge the noblest and most enlightened, for it endeavors to sustain, succor, and defend our *conservación humana*'. In short, it is not altogether premature at this point to remark in passing that any suggestion of political favoritism will be very difficult to prove against Castrillo. For the moment, however, our interest is held only by the following question: how accurate are Castrillo's comments on and his appraisal of the *Comunero* movement? The answer is not easily arrived at, not because of any shortcomings in Castrillo's explanation – sketchy though that explanation is – but on account of the subject itself and the manner in which Spanish historiography has until recently either ignored it or debated it with partisan ferocity. Unquestionably, in terms of importance, historiographical shortcomings fall a far second to the complexities inherent to the nature of the *Comunero* movement. One difficulty, the absence of a single ideological position which could be said to embody the program of the rebellion, is of obvious significance. And so indeed it has been recognized by Maravall on whose work on the political ideas of the *Comuneros* I shall heavily rely in what follows. 'It would be absurd to demand as a pre-condition for recognizing the existence of a body of *comunero* thought unanimity in the ideas of all

[5] *Ibid.*, p. 9.
[6] *Ibid.*, p. 11. Castrillo is here espousing the moderate stand taken by Burgos' deputies to the Junta (see below).

groups and individuals who participated in the rebellion. There are, in fact, different currents present which often diverge among themselves and sometimes even contradict each other.'[7] Even a cursory study of the revolt, however, unequivocally uncovers the existence of one trend that probably explains Castrillo's condemnation of a movement which in its inception he obviously viewed with sympathy – its progressive radicalization.

The revolt of the Comunidades

On April 20, 1520, directly as a result of the lamentable course which events had taken during the charged meetings of the Cortes of Santiago–La Coruña, Toledo raised the standard of revolt against the royal administration and proclaimed a commune. On May 20, more than one month after the outbreak and despite the storm signs unmistakably conveyed by the unanimous surliness of his Castilian subjects, Charles I embarked for Flanders, Germany, and the Imperial crown – not, however, until after paying a visit to England and his aunt Catherine – leaving behind as regent his tutor Adrian of Utrecht. Nine short days after the king's departure the insurrection had spread to Segovia, Zamora, Madrid, Burgos, and Guadalajara. Following the example of Toledo, their citizens angrily and violently sought to square accounts with those among their deputies – *procuradores* – whom they suspected of having been too ready (whether through cowardice or greed did not matter to the enraged mobs) to capitulate to royal bullying at the recent Cortes in the matter of the *servicio* (a special appropriation which over and above the regular taxes could only be granted by the Cortes).

It would be a mistake, however, to assume that at this or any other time there was unanimity of views among the rebellious cities. The various programs put forward during the course of the rebellion by the *procuradores* members of the Santa Junta General del Reino, as the ruling body of the movement eventually came to be known, reveal disparate ideologies: Burgos, whose conventional moderation went little beyond the ordinary petition of grievances; Toledo, bolder and more radical as witnessed by the instructions drafted for its representatives; and the extremism of Valladolid's *enragés* weeks before Villalar. During the halcyon days of the Junta, however, the Toledo radicals were in control. Two important documents were drafted during this period: the manifesto of September 26, 1520; and the petition of October 20 of the same year. With the drafting of the petition the Junta fulfilled the task that had brought the *Comunero* movement into being. But this important document was by no means couched in the sort of language that one might

[7] Maravall, *Comunidades*, p. 17.

expect from suppliants. This is hardly surprising when one reflects that the petition was drafted by a body which little over a month before, in clear defiance of the royal authority already legally vested in the regent and his council, had organized a civil government centered around itself, had provided for its protection through a covenant of *alianza y hermandad jurada* binding on all cities, and had broadcast its achievements to the entire realm in the *Provisión en forma de manifiesto de la Junta a la Comunidad de Valladolid, a 26 de Septiembre de 1520.*[8]

The manifesto is swift and to the point. The incapacity of the Queen Mother Juana, Charles' absence, and the diabolical contumacy of the members of the Royal Council, have plunged the realm into chaos. In the bygone days of Ferdinand and Isabel the sovereigns had taken many excellent measures to insure their subjects' well-being. These admirable laws, however, now lie broken and scattered by evil rule – a state of affairs to which the cities themselves have been a part, for in their sloth and indifference they neglected to take those precautions which alone would have perpetuated the laws' beneficent reign. This tragic oversight the Junta intended to correct; and with a vengeance, for the revolutionary *procuradores* of Tordesillas (the seat of the Junta) now ringingly declared their intention to become the zealous guardians of the public weal. 'The cities, towns, and communes of this kingdom gather their strength and might in order to insure obedience to its laws and statutes (*fueros*). The kingdom assembles itself in the manner and style best fitted for guarding them.'[9] The revolutionary meaning is unequivocal. It is the *Reino*, representing not specific estates or classes but the entire commonwealth, and resting its strength on the power and influence of the cities which now becomes the protector of the public interest. The authority of the *Consejo Real* (Royal Council) is summarily made over to the Junta (the fiction that the *procuradores* are merely Juana's agents is of course maintained; it is useful because, among other things, it brands the queen's son an usurper)[10]

[8] Danvila, *Historia crítica y documentada*, pp. 82–5.
[9] *Ibid.*
[10] This was a very serious juridical point defended by the Salamanca doctor, Alonso de Zúñiga, who insisted that Charles had no right to take the title of king – as he had done in 1516 – while his mother was alive. In a letter dated November 13, Adrian informs his master that the Junta had made Zúñiga's claims its own. 'La junta envió a decir a la Reina Na. Sa. con el doctor de Salamanca que en mucho perjuico de Su Al. había usurpado V. Mat. nombre o título de Rey de Castilla.' (Danvila, *Historia crítica y documentada*, II, p. 481). The question served to bring forth the growing rift between radicals and moderates within the Junta. The former (Toledo) demanded that the Junta's decrees be drafted in the name of the queen without mentioning Charles. The latter (Burgos), on the other hand, refused to accept a resolution that would effectively have branded the king as an usurper. In this instance the forces of moderation carried the day and subsequent decrees bore

which now concentrates in its own hands all political power and prerogatives and therefore assumes the dual role of deliberative assembly and full-fledged governing body. This is indeed a *novedad*. Ultimate sovereignty is transferred to the community as a whole. No longer is the mystical presence of the body politic actualized in the person of the sovereign but rather in an assembly of the entire realm. The Santa Junta, then, becomes the embodiment of the idea of the commonwealth and its power as well; in the abnormal circumstances through which all agree Castile is passing, only the Junta *qua* representative of the *populus* has both the authority and the power to restore the broken reign of order and harmony.

It is against this monumental usurpation of the king's functions and privileges that Castrillo thunders when he likens the cities of Castile to the mountains heaped by the giants to reach Zeus and deprive him of his authority. It is one thing, he complains, to demand justice against the public trespassers; another to appropriate that supreme *potestas* that belongs to the sovereign alone. Castrillo is not unique. Identical feelings are to be found among the ranks of those rebels whose aims were more moderate than those of the Toledo radicals. And none among the voices of moderation was more consistent than Burgos'. In a letter addressed to Valladolid (at this time also a partisan of moderation) and dated September 27, 1520, Burgos voices serious misgivings about the course upon which the Junta has embarked. 'It is plain to us here that there is great novelty in the manner in which the Junta is approaching the business of government. Surely Your Lordship will agree that the Junta is going beyond the reasons for which it was summoned.'[11] It was our intention, laments Burgos, when we sent our deputies to join the Junta that the business at hand would be transacted by means of an embassy which would request of our sovereign good governance and his return to Castile. And this is precisely the substance of the next question which must be decided by the *procuradores*: should the Junta content itself with drafting a list of grievances, or should the deputies instead go ahead and both propose and execute the measures needed to restore peace to the realm? In other words, the Junta had in theory proclaimed itself to be both a consultative and an executive body of government; it was now imperative to decide whether to actualize that important claim.[12] Supplication or revolution, that was the question.

The protests of Burgos were of no avail; its misgivings succeeded only

the names of mother and son. On all this see J. Pérez, *La révolution des Comunidades de Castille* (Bordeaux, 1970).
[11] Danvila, *Historia crítica y documentada*, ii, pp. 88–91.
[12] Pérez, *La révolution des Comunidades*, p. 201.

in tempering the tone of the next – and the single most important – expression of the Junta's will. (By then, however, Burgos had defected to the royalist camp.) After much compromise and negotiation, on October 20, 1520, the *procuradores* carried to a conclusion the original task which had brought them together – the drafting of a petition of grievances. The *capítulos* of the petition were accompanied by a letter to Charles which was anything but conciliatory. It was instead 'a scathing and detailed indictment of royal rule in Spain'.[13] The king is respectfully but emphatically reminded that 'the laws of these your kingdoms' rest on 'natural reason'. These same laws obligate the subjects 'to prevent the king from doing whatever may imperil his soul, dishonor his subjects, or threaten the public weal' – precisely all the things that had come to pass in Castile, as the *procuradores* point out in a summary of what had transpired since the last Cortes. The king is moreover given notice that whatever the cities had done, they had 'done forced by what the laws of your kingdom prescribe'. Diplomatically, however, the Junta concedes that the '*mal gobierno*' to which Castile has fallen prey is the responsibility of evil and ambitious royal counselors who have transformed a rich land into a miserable desert.[14] Under the circumstances, the rebels conclude, the assembled realm must be vested with the power now misused by the scoundrels of the royal council.

The conclusion is clear. The *procuradores* demand that the authority heretofore arbitrarily deposited by the ruler in the hands of creatures capriciously selected be shared with those whom the laws of the realm – backed by natural law – recognize as responsible for guiding the monarch and protecting the republic's well-being. This constitutional yearning received its final touches in some of the *capítulos* included in the petition which follows the letter just mentioned. Their bulk consists of the usual odd combination of supplication and demand framing a long list of detailed and often seemingly puerile requests which one has come to expect from men reared in the tradition of the Cortes. A few, however, are explosive, as was realized by contemporaries like the royal chronicler

---

[13] Seaver, *The Great Revolt in Castile*, p. 165.

[14] The deputies are here using the well-known subterfuge of heaping on the shoulders of the king's advisers all the responsibility for the mismanagement of the realm's affairs. In his *Diálogo de Mercurio y Carón*, Alfonso de Valdés explodes the myth. 'Mas esta escusa [bad counsels] no es bastante, pues harta culpa tiene el príncipe que, conosciendo claramente ser un hombre malo, quiere tenerlo cabe sí, porque da causa que se piensa dél lo que se vee en su privado, pues es cosa muy averiguada que assí como un malo no admita en su compañía algún bueno, assí un bueno no devría admitir algún malo, y el que lo admite y conoscido lo sostiene, es causa que él también sea tenido por malo.' Edition of J. F. Montesinos (Madrid, 1971), pp. 50–60.

Pedro Mexía who interpreted them as 'blasphemy and notorious treason
...a perpetual Commune and destruction of the royal power'.[15] To begin
with, the *procuradores* demanded that on the king's absence a regent or
regents would be named 'from among the natives of Castile and León
with the Realms' concurrence and any other provisions demanded by the
law of the *partida*'.[16] The disastrous experience of the Santiago–La Coruña
Cortes had taught the Tordesillas deputies that one of their primary concerns must be to protect the future independence of the cities' *procuradores*.
The *capítulos*, therefore, contain various suggestions along those lines.
Representatives from the cities to the Cortes should include one member
from each local *estamento* or *estado* (state): church, *caballeros, comunidad*.
The various communities may endow their representatives with whatever
powers or instructions they see fit and 'the sovereign shall forever refrain
from interfering in any way or form with the granting or exercising of
the said powers'. Once assembled in Cortes the *procuradores* will be free
to 'confer and consult with each other as often as deemed necessary'.
Whoever receives, while *procurador*, gifts or favors (*mercedes*) from the
royal hands 'shall forfeit life and property'. The *procuradores* – the business at the Cortes concluded – shall promptly return to their respective
cities and once there, within a period of forty days, publicly and personally
account for their actions. Interesting as these provisions aimed at preserving the independence and honesty of the deputies are in themselves,
their startling significance becomes fully apparent only when understood
in the context of the extraordinary demand which closes this particular
capítulo.

Henceforth and in perpetuity, every three years, those towns and cities which
today in their own right may vote in Cortes shall elect their *procuradores* from
the three estates and convene them in assembly, even in the absence of the
monarch. The *procuradores* in congress shall see to it that the provisions of
these *capítulos* be complied with and discuss any matters and solve any problems relating to the office of and service to the Crown and the common weal of
these Realms.[17]

---

[15] Quoted in Seaver, *The Great Revolt in Castile*, p. 168.
[16] Alonso de Santa Cruz, *Crónica del Emperador Carlos V* (5 vols., Madrid,
1920–25), pp. 293–328.
[17] 'Item: que de aquí adelante perpetuamente, de tres en tres años, las ciudades y
villas que tienen voto en Cortes se puedan juntar y junten sus Procuradores que
sean elegidos de todos tres estados, como de suso está dicho en los Procuradores de
Cortes, y lo pueden hacer en ausencia de Sus Altezas y de los Reyes sus sucesores,
para que allí juntos vean y provean cómo se guarda lo contenido en estos Capítulos
y platiquen y provean en las otras cosas complideras al servicio de la Corona Real
y bien común de estos Reinos.' *Ibid.*, p. 303. William F. Church has observed that
in the theory of the French constitution elaborated between 1540 and 1600, 'the

The formulation of the Junta's constitutional aspirations was in this manner completed. Its heart and strength lay with the single crucial demand that deputies elected, paid, and controlled by the nineteen cities traditionally represented in the Cortes should in total independence convene periodically to watch over the Crown's behavior and, in effect, to rule the country. The pact, despite Tordesillas' protestations to the contrary, was not a pact of equals – as Charles and his supporters were quick to realize. For one thing, the sovereign was now explicitly prohibited from meddling in the affairs of the all-important assembly of the realm. For another, the *procuradores* in effect claimed the right to exercise control over the king's largesse; entire *capítulos* are thus devoted to the manner in which Charles and his successors shall grant favors (*mercedes*). But the matter does not stop there. In the lengthiest and most detailed of all the *capítulos* the Junta takes the extraordinary step of instructing the sovereign on all matters pertaining to the selection, functions, prerogatives, and limitations of the most important royal officials, particularly those who administered justice and those who represented the royal will and power in the cities: all members of the Royal Council; *oidores* or judges who sat on civil suits; *alcaldes* who judged on criminal affairs; *corregidores*, the single most important instrument in the royal bureaucracy used by the monarchs to bend the cities to their will; *veedores* or inspectors charged with the task of seeing to it that royal officials would perform their duties; *notarios*, whose duty was to draft and write chancellery acts. Perhaps the most significant request among the many with which the *procuradores* sought to hedge and limit the freedom of action of the royal creatures was aimed most explicitly at those officials who were part of the conciliar system, especially the Council of Justice: the Junta demanded that their tenure be limited and 'that they be *visitados* (investigated) every four years in the usual manner; and that those found guilty of misconduct in office be punished in accordance with the laws while those found innocent be rewarded by Your Highness'.[18] The *corregidores* were for obvious reasons even more stringently dealt with; the Tordesillas deputies proposed that 'no *corregidor* be henceforth appointed to a town or city unless it be at the request of the town or city itself; and that, moreover, once

state has been found to consist...of two primary portions: the social structure and the governmental authority. Each found its basis and limitations in the law of the land.' *Constitutional Thought in Sixteenth-Century France* (New York, 1969), p. 177. In their manifesto and in the *capítulo* now under scrutiny the *procuradores* show their revolutionary determination that in Castile the two shall henceforth be united in the Junta. The justification is by now familiar to us: a government in bankruptcy has defaulted on its obligations by breaking the law of the land (*leyes destos Reinos*).

[18] Santa Cruz, *Crónica del Emperador Carlos V*, p. 307.

appointed the *corregidor* shall remain in office for a period of one year, subject to prorogation once and only for the same length of time'.[19]

The melancholy fate of the proposals thus put forth by a motley array of merchants, *letrados*, artisans, *caballeros*, and bourgeois is well known.[20] They were dashed forever together with the armed strength of the *Comunidades* on the plain of Villalar, the twenty-third of April 1521. What course Spanish history might have taken if the cities of Castile had succeeded in imposing their will on their young monarch is a subject which clearly belongs in the realm of speculation. The consequences of the *Comunero*'s failure, on the other hand, is a valid subject for historical inquiry; neither, however, is the direct concern of this book. Having therefore briefly explored the fascinating events which brought into being a background so heavily weighing on Castrillo's consciousness we must now return to the central subject of this first chapter.

Nature and the origin of political authority

At this point it is of obvious interest to acquaint ourselves with the manner in which Castrillo views the figure of Zeus and the essence of his office – a subject inseparable from the complex and customary reflections concerning the nature of society, the state, and political authority. In olden days (presumably some form of golden age), begins Castrillo, men lived in widespread isolation throughout the earth.[21] Eventually, however, they abandoned their solitude and instead gathered in communities (*pueblos*). Indeed, Castrillo explains, men had no other choice, for God, wishing man to rule as sovereign over the beasts, endowed him with reason. It follows that men seek the company of their brethren and naturally form societies not merely in order to give aid and comfort to each other but because only among his peers will man find the opportunity to exercise the one gift which sets him apart from the beasts of creation.[22] Such is the theory

[19] *Ibid.*, p. 311.
[20] Maravall contends that the *Comunero* movement was the creation of the urban middle classes. By contrast, Pérez's studies have led him to conclude that there is no class homogeneity among the *Comuneros*. Instead, he argues, the revolution 'regroupe la bourgeoisie industrielle, là où elle existe (Ségovie), les artisans, boutiquiers, ouvriers, gagne-petit, *letrados*, enfin, capables de capter la malaise social et de le canaliser. En même temps, la révolution voit se dresser contre elle la bourgeoisie marchande et les nobles, deux catégories sociales aux intérêts complémentaires, associées aux bénéfices du marché de la laine; une partie de la paysannerie profite de l'occasion pour essayer d'échapper aux servitudes du régime seigneurial', p. 688. Pérez, on the other hand, shares Maravall's conclusions on the political side of the movement. 'Il s'agissait de mettre en place un gouvernment...de la bourgeoisie.' *Ibid.*
[21] *TR*, p. 66.　　　　[22] *Ibid.*, pp. 64–6.

which accounts for the appearance of the commonwealth. But in practice
how did the first *pueblo* come into being? Ironically enough the first two
pueblos (one for each of two epochs: before and after the Flood) were not
founded on the basis of reason and nature but by the malicious will of two
evil men, Cain and Nimrod (and also by the children of Noah).[23] And no
different is the origin of kingship. By nature all men were created free and
God never mentioned His intention to create man so that he could lord it
over other men.[24] The first man – Nimrod, king of Babylon – who imposed
his will over other men attained his goal through superior strength and
usurped the name of king.[25] Violence, aided and abetted by the people's
own reckless desire for change and innovation, imposed obedience and
servitude among men who are by nature free. Positive law then institution-
alized this obedience. In short, political authority does not rest upon
natural law; it is rather rooted in sin.

Clearly Castrillo (as Vives after him) recognizes that man was created
to live in the company of other men – a necessity commanded by God and
sanctioned by natural law. But neither the Trinitarian friar nor the
Christian humanist is willing to admit that this need for human companionship carries with it the concomitant of political authority. In other
words, naturally man is meant to be a social but not a political animal. In
De concordia et discordia in humano genere Vives is uncompromising:
politically constituted associations are mere palliatives needed, until the
coming of Christ, by man bound by his sinful nature. Castrillo is more
selective and his wrath is singlemindedly concentrated on the origins and
contemporary course of monarchy. But he is no monarcomach, either in
the figurative sense of the Junta or in the literal sense sponsored by the
Jesuit Mariana and others during the second half of the sixteenth century.
Change brought about the tyranny of political authority; further change
will surely fail to improve things. Only one rational course remains –
'once the world's innocence was corrupted no other way lay open but to
obey the monarch if greater evils were to be avoided. It is therefore
imperative for the sake of the common weal that the citizens render
obedience to the king.'[26]

Undoubtedly Castrillo, the enemy of the radicals among the *Comuneros*,
is no gratuitous friend of monarchy. His position is rather that of the

[23] *Ibid.*, p. 92.   [24] *Ibid.*, pp. 48-9.   [25] *Ibid.*, p. 45.

[26] *Ibid.*, pp. 59 *et passim*. Such cautious preliminaries, for example, are absent
from the work of the contemporary French political thinker, Claude de Seyssel. In
his *La monarchie de France* (1515) Seyssel, unquestioningly accepting the existence
of political authority, demonstrates, swiftly and to the point, that the rule of a
monarch is the best and that among contemporaries the French monarchy is the
'mieux réglée'.

pragmatist who, caught between the proverbial horns of the dilemma, opts for that alternative which offers, if not the best solution, at least the one which in practical terms promises to be the most workable. The *procuradores* of the Junta had endeavored to justify their claims to supreme political power in terms of that medieval constitutional theme which argued the origins of political authority to be the result of a free act by all the members of the community: the decision to vest the monarch with that *potestas* which hitherto had been equally distributed among the individual parts of the social whole. This power automatically reverted to its original owners should circumstances so require. Obviously the Junta felt that this was precisely the situation that had come to pass in Castile. The king had, without the kingdom's approval, accepted a foreign crown; a grievous decision indeed, for the *procuradores* keenly observed that since each state needs its own prince, for one man to rule two different and sovereign (*sin superior*) states was an absurdity. The king, moreover, had left the country and thus plunged it into a chaos where misrule and foreign greed reigned supreme. In consequence only one recourse remained if the commonwealth were to be spared further hardships: political power must be returned to its original fount, the people. In practice, of course, this meant the latter's representative, the Junta. In his own eclectic manner Castrillo aims to please no one and succeeds in partially offending all. With the radicals he agrees that the situation in Castile is melancholy indeed and with them he insists upon the need to restore the reign of justice. In addition he is in complete accord with the idea that a prince should confine his attention to the governance of one single state, thus denying the legitimacy of Charles' decision to accept the crown of the Empire. In all the other issues, however, Castrillo opposes the *Comunero* radicals, siding instead with the moderates (the local *politiques*, if one may be permitted such comparisons) from both sides who wished to preserve the privileges of the king's office and to cure Castile's ills.

On citizens and citizenship

It is for these reasons that Castrillo, emphasizing in the traditional manner the virtues indispensable to a vigorous commonwealth (prudence, concord, perseverance, and obedience), outlines a scheme which avoids the extremes of royal absolutism and revolutionary constitutionalism and returns to the balanced harmony of the medieval constitution by reinstating the classical elements of the latter in their appointed places. Castrillo begins with an explanation of the nature and purpose of the city. The '*ciudad*', he claims, 'is the noblest and highest of human assemblages.'[27] The bonds of friendly

[27] *TR*, p. 19.

intercourse and amicable conversation are nowhere stronger than within the confines of the city.[28] After mentioning that a kingdom is often composed of several cities – and pointedly avoiding any reference to the Empire – Castrillo gives the traditional Aristotelian definition of republic: 'Republic is a certain form of order or manner of living instituted and chosen by those who live in the same city.' At its head stands the king. We have already remarked on Castrillo's initial doubts concerning the legitimacy of political authority. Once these vacillations are overcome for the sake of coping with the stark realities of life, however, he is not to be budged from his stand in favor of obedience to the king, the most important in Castrillo's *quadrivium* of social virtues.[29] But obedience goes beyond mere political considerations: 'Thus I state that not only is the obeisance that subjects owe their king absolute and divine but, in addition, the same is true of the obedience owed by the slaves (or serfs) to their lords and by the latter to their superiors.'[30] The final result is a society severely organized along hierarchical lines where the underlying theme is obedience. This of course is nothing more than the reaction which always follows the experiences derived from the radicalization of an originally moderate movement. Those who sympathized with the original aims of the *Comunero* rebellion in its inception now turn against it in revulsion and become in the process more reactionary in their views than those who had opposed it from the start. And even this is but the beginning. Castrillo feels confident that he can identify the social element most responsible for the revolutionary turn taken by the *Comunero* protest. It is for this reason that he will deprive them of full access to the privileges of citizenship.

Just as was the case with the well-ordered city-states of antiquity, begins Castrillo, a modern republic is said to be properly constituted only if it rests squarely on the shoulders of the citizens. His concern with the nature and function of citizenship is therefore intense. This theme, incidentally, will practically disappear from Castilian political literature after him; in fact, not until we come to Sepúlveda and the waning of the Erasmian era will we encounter an emphasis on the citizen comparable to Castrillo's. Simple membership in the commonwealth is a necessary but not sufficient condition for citizenship. 'Only if a man shares in the power to participate in and judge on public affairs can he be said to be a citizen.'[31] Prudence,

28 *Ibid.*, pp. 20–21.
29 *Ibid.*, pp. 43, 59–60. Seyssel is of the same mind. 'Aussi, en tous les pays du monde y a telle distinction de peuple, et si est nécessaire selon raison naturelle et politique: tout ainsi qu'en un corps humain, faut qu'il y ait des membres inférieurs, servants aux plus dignes et supérieurs.' *La monarchie de France*, ed. J. Poujol (Paris, 1961), p. 124. Cited hereafter as *MF*.
30 *TR*, p. 62.
31 *Ibid.*, p. 25.

justice, meekness, honesty, equality, ability to command, and capacity for obedience are the distinguishing traits of true citizenship.[32] The next point to resolve is how to actualize these abstractions into the reality of contemporary society. To this end Castrillo envisions *toda república* as divided into three human groups: nobles (*caballeros*), merchants (*mercaderes*), and artisans (*oficiales*).[33] The virtues of citizenship are embodied in the first class. The nobles were created as defenders of the people out of whose bosom they emerged. As men multiplied so grew human deviltry; men were forced to choose from among themselves a more virtuous, just, and prudent man than the average to rule the community. 'Thus we speak of noble *qua* notable in virtue above that of the *comunes*.' So it came to pass that the commons made the nobles and the nobles made the kings.[34]

Castrillo defines the *mercaderes* to be those who labor under a spirit of greed, and *oficiales* those who toil with their hands.[35] Neither class can aspire to true citizenship, for the very nature of their occupations prevents them from possessing the excellence demanded of perfect citizens.[36] Castrillo deals harshly with the former.

Greed lies at the root of all evil. And since the covetous live alienated from virtue, it is inconceivable that those whose profession is to covet should be good citizens. For if a city be defined as a company of free men, how can we call citizen he who is the slave of his possessions? True, a city cannot exist without merchants and craftsmen anymore than it can survive without children. But just as the latter are not considered citizens the former are said to be *ciudadanos imperfectos* at best.[37]

The experience of the wealthy burghers of Burgos, who early in the revolt had given aid, comfort, and encouragement to the commons in their

[32] *Ibid.*, p. 25–8.
[33] *Ibid.*, p. 188. Seyssel considers French society to be divided along similar lines. 'Et en ces trois États, je ne comprends point celui de l'Église, dont je parlerai après; ains les prends ainsi que l'on fait en aucuns autres pays, à savoir: la Noblesse; le peuple moyen que l'on peut appeler le Peuple Gras; et le Peuple Menu.' *MF*, p. 121.
[34] *TR*, p. 190. Castrillo's emphasis on function contrasts with Seyssel's stress on lineage. See *MF*, pp. 122–3.
[35] *TR*, p. 198.
[36] *Ibid.*, p. 199.
[37] *Ibid.*, p. 200. The question of whether the members of the second and third *États* are full-fledged citizens is not explicitly discussed by Seyssel. However, the members of the *Peuple Gras* are especially fit to fill certain offices which Seyssel reserves for them (*Offices des Finances, Avocats, Procureurs, Greffiers*). As for the *Peuple Menu*, they are suited for 'menus Offices de Justice et de Finances, aussi de la Gendarmerie en quelque état inférieur de Gendarme; et de la Marchandise menue.' *MF*, bk. I, ch. XVI.

tumults, may well have been behind Castrillo's acrimonious attitude. He is not, however, unwilling to grant that indeed both *mercaderes* and *oficiales* desire and pursue the well-being of the commonwealth. What crucially differentiates them from their more fortunate peers of the noble class is the manner in which they endeavor to achieve the common aim. 'The nobles look after the republic's welfare through the sacrifice of their own interests in the altar of the common weal. The merchants identify the commonwealth's welfare with their own, while the *oficiales* seek the common good by, first and foremost, attending to their own needs.'[38]

Castrillo next shifts his ground to discourse on the two elements which exclude the middle class from the privileges of citizenship: wealth and greed. He believes that the evil of political authority resulted from the destruction of communal ownership which, in turn, was responsible for putting an end to the harmony of an egalitarian state of nature. Thus he explains the appearance of private property in much the same manner as he understands the origin of political power. In the beginning all things were held in common, but as a result of the same developments which brought about the servitude of man 'the world, against the natural order of things, was broken up among private persons'.[39] Today human law imposes a proprietary *status quo*, and he who endeavors to increase his share of goods violates justice and threatens the society of man with dissolution.[40] Such appears to be the context in which Castrillo formally defines 'greed'. On this basis the three social classes into which the commonwealth is divided now quite openly give way to their economic *alter ego*: the wealthy, the moderately well-to-do, and the poor. The close relationship binding the two divisions is explicitly stated. 'That perfection suitable for citizens cannot be found among the merchants, extreme as they are in their riches; nor is it to be seen among the *oficiales*, for their need is equally extreme; but among those who have average possessions, for they can live without forever yearning for more.'[41]

In short, then, 'the greater the number of these citizens of more moderate wealth a republic can boast the greater its happiness will be'.[42] It follows that when it comes to filling public offices neither the rich nor the poor must be appointed; the former, in particular, must be excluded,

[38] *TR*, p. 201.

[39] *Ibid.*, p. 224. Earlier (pp. 44–5) he had expressed himself in identical terms.

[40] *Ibid.*, p. 224. And the same result will be brought about if we try to turn the clock back. Just as Vives (and Erasmus) fears (see his *De communione rerum*) any attempt to restore communism, Castrillo warns that what is done is done and we must learn to live as best we can with private property. The alternative, as in the case of refusing obedience to political authority, is anarchy.

[41] *Ibid.*, p. 202.

[42] *Ibid.*, pp. 202–3.

for 'how can he who lives without justice give justice to the republic? If the rich man were also a just man he would not be wealthy.'[43] Castrillo's emphasis on economics is surprising although not totally unexpected. *Cubdicia* (greed) surfaces as the most dangerous threat posed to individuals, classes, institutions, the very fabric of the republic. Once again the connexion with the *Comunero* affair is patent. From the very beginning the rallying cry of the disaffected had been *libertad*; liberty initially understood purely in economic terms until its meaning, along with all else, was politicized. It was then a freedom from fiscal burdens which on this occasion was framed in very concrete terms: an end to the distribution among foreigners of public offices and benefices, no more selling of public posts, enforcement of the laws prohibiting the flight of coin from the realm. And the commons, eager also to shrug off the fiscal burden, readily joined their betters in the struggle. It was only afterward that once again it became clear what strange bedfellows *mercader* and *oficial* truly are. The defection of substantial portions of the wealthier elements among the bourgeoisie naturally followed. Castrillo's interpretation of the process is evident: legitimate complaints were transformed into revolutionary appeals by the greedy few who lured the destitute many. In both cases – those who, having, desired to keep and those who, lacking, yearned to acquire – avarice was at the root of all the calamities which agitated the Castile.

But what of the ruler himself? Castrillo views the mission of the ruler strictly in terms of justice, for 'in truth God's virtue is justice'.[44] Without justice the harmony given by human society would be shattered beyond repair and men would be compelled to live in fields and mountains like dumb beasts.[45] 'It is because of justice and that capacity for reason contained in justice that we are different from and better than animals.'[46] Greed, on the other hand, is a deadly threat to justice; and in his endless yearning to increase his share of goods, man violates justice and threatens society with dissolution. And it is precisely to avoid this disaster that the laws exist as the handmaidens of justice. It follows that he who as ruler of the republic applies the laws must combine in his own person all the characteristics that define the laws to be so; and the laws must be 'honest, just, agree both with nature and custom, necessary, profitable, and self-evident'.[47] Nothing, therefore, is more admirable in Castrillo's view than the ruler who increases the common welfare and sustains society in justice and peace.[48] The ruler must be free from the taint of greed; he must avoid purchasing with gifts the good will of the citizens; and he shall bestow offices and benefices purely on grounds of merit.[49]

[43] *Ibid.*, p. 212. [44] *Ibid.*, p. 222. [45] *Ibid.*, p. 223.
[46] *Ibid.*, [47] *Ibid.*, p. 225. [48] *Ibid.*, p. 215.
[49] *Ibid.*, pp. 215, 218, 219.

From what has been said so far one might conclude that Castrillo's prejudices toward the radical *procuradores* of the Junta have led him to adopt an unbalanced view of the roles played by the different groups composing Castilian society, and that he has placed the blame for the misfortunes of Castile entirely on the shoulders of the middle class. The first part of this verdict might stand if we are also willing to agree that the medieval constitution in effect discriminated against the third estate, for it is precisely on the basis of medieval constitutionalism that Castrillo consummates his scheme for the harmonious governance of the republic. As for the possibility that Castrillo decided to hold the bourgeoisie solely responsible for the calamities of Castile nothing could be farther from the truth. What Castrillo has just outlined is but a blueprint of what an ideally balanced commonwealth should be, precisely the sort of republic which had stood in Castile until the advent of troublous times. The state of affairs prevailing at present, he admits, is quite another matter. Castrillo accuses the nobility of betraying those ideals which brought them and their privileges into being. The noble knights are the natural defenders of the republic, but 'they forfeit their titles when they abandon the precepts of knighthood'.[50] Unhappily, this is precisely what has come to pass.[51] The noble class whose excellence and virtue in bygone days had made and unmade kings has through greed fallen prey to its creation. In other words, a class overwhelmingly functional in its origins has chosen to surrender its independence: the nobleman has become a courtier, an avaricious parasite. Castrillo's severity may owe a great deal to the behavior which the Castilian magnates had displayed in their mad scramble for favors and prebends during the brief reign of Philip I. Change, this time in the mores of the dominant class, has destroyed the virtues of those best equipped to wear the badge of citizenship. The consequences are far-reaching: the balance between royal power and the privileged class, the very keystone of medieval constitutionalism, has been ruined.

But what of the royal power? Has it been spared? Evidently not, for Castrillo, albeit more guardedly, hurls identical indictments at the kingly institution. True, the art of ruling is 'among all the branches of knowledge the noblest'. On the other hand, it must be owned that 'no dignity or office is so praiseworthy in itself that it will impart goodness to the holder'.[52] Castrillo concludes that political power has a corrupting influence on the manners and morals of mankind. And, he goes on, today's practice compounds the evil, for the 'longer power is deposited in the same hands the more virtue wanes and greed grows'.[53] To deposit the perpetual governance of the republic in a single man is accordingly to court disaster.

50 *Ibid.*, pp. 190–91.   51 *Ibid.*, pp. 196–7.
52 *Ibid.*, p. 165.   53 *Ibid.*

The longer a man remains in power the more grievous his depredations against the commonwealth will be; and his spoliations need not come to an end with his death, for their effects will linger on to haunt the republic long after the tyrant's demise.[54] Temporary rule, although by no means a panacea, Castrillo understands to be the better alternative. Neither the Greek commonwealths nor the Roman republic, he points out, knew peace until they decided to limit to one year the ruler's tenure. Only after the Romans opted for frequent changes in governors did the city become mistress of the world.[55] Perpetual political tenure, however, is but one of the twin nightmares which haunt the republic's peaceful slumber. Irresponsibility is the other and by no means less dangerous threat. 'It is absurd that even though we offer the ruler an obedience which nature does not force us to give, the ruler himself should not be compelled to answer for the misdeeds of his government...for, on the contrary, the higher the dignity the more detailed the account must be.'[56] In an extraordinary indictment of the dynastic system which in his own day, and with such dire results for Castile's future, surrendered the commonwealth's fate to the whims and caprice of heredity, Castrillo demands that the ruler be neither perpetual in his office nor irresponsible for his governance. It is bad and unnatural enough that man, free and equal to other men, should be forced to obey others of his kind. We court further catastrophe by allowing one man to govern forever, without compelling him to render account of deeds and misdeeds to his charges.

Conclusion

These are in broad strokes the ideas of a thinker who, addressing himself to important contemporary events, remains obviously unimpressed by the awesome nature of the office to which his sovereign has so recently been elevated. A thinker who admires the popular and democratic basis of the republics of antiquity, who deeply regrets the calcification experienced by the society of his own age, and who is dismayed by the manner in which political power is viewed by all as a divine gift and how this unnatural usurpation of man's pristine freedom is further corrupted by irresponsibly perpetual rulers. There is, moreover, no doubt that Castrillo interpreted the events which unfolded before his eyes as a crisis. Under the unswerving guidance of Isabel I, Castile had swiftly emerged from the

[54] *Ibid.*, p. 163.
[55] *Ibid.*, p. 167. Seyssel thinks precisely the opposite: 'ceux qui son allés par succession ont plus prospéré qui sont allés par élection, comme l'on peut voir de l'Empire Romain aux pris des autres'.
[56] *TR*, p. 168.

anarchy and chaos of Enrique IV's reign. Through a combination of charm and strength the Catholic Queen had brought internal peace and institutional stability to her realm. The future, therefore, must indeed have appeared bleak and unpromising to anyone living in Castile during the troubled years after her death. For everything seemed to point toward a return to the turbulent past, or worse, toward a future filled with an omnipotent form of monarchy unrestrained by any of the traditional checks. The dynastic uncertainty created by Juana's incapacity; the personality of her consort, a foreign prince surrounded by rapacious foreign courtiers, and the unseemly squabbles among the Castilian notables to win the favor of the new ruler; Philip's own struggles with his cunning father-in-law; the untimely death of the Archduke and the arrival of his son, Charles of Ghent, young, unknown, and raised in an alien milieu; the events which set upon Charles' head the added burden of the most prestigious crown in Christendom, even before he had had time to acquaint himself with his new subjects and thus in no small measure paving the way for the episode of the *Comunidades*: the oppressive influence of these developments, surely far from reassuring to those who considered stability to be the *summum bonum*, is clearly evident in Castrillo. And the fear of change characteristic of the medieval outlook must have been reinforced by the events of the times. In retrospect it is plain that Castrillo's fears were at least partially justified. The ideas of medieval constitutionalism – notably in Castile – faded and were never again to regain the vitality which Castrillo deemed so necessary. More-over, the crisis was satisfactorily surmounted – on the surface at least – shortly after Charles' accession to the Imperial throne and Castile enthusiastically embarked upon the strange task of becoming the nucleus of an empire which was neither completely medieval nor wholly modern. And thus Castrillo's little book remains an isolated monument in the realm of political thought celebrating the developments which led to what has been called the first modern revolution.

The evidence derived from the brief survey of Castrillo's thought which has occupied us in the pages of this chapter could hardly be said to argue in favor of any interpretation of Castrillo as a friend or admirer of those radicals among the *Comuneros* who strove with such enthusiasm to transfer political authority from the monarch to the commonwealth. It would be equally unreasonable, on the other hand, to include a man who so heatedly denies two of the most fundamental attributes (irresponsibility and dynastic succession) of Renaissance monarchy among the supporters of royal absolutism – a point of no small import if we bear in mind that the failure of the *Comunero* movement is a crucial crossroads in the constitutional history both of Castile and of Spain. A monarchy which had been universally understood as contractual now became largely absolute.[57] Within that framework of political ideas chronologically defined by the age of Erasmus, then, Castrillo shares a niche with those political thinkers – the advocates of constitutional monarchy – who for two generations spanning the first half of the sixteenth century are best represented among the jurists and humanists of France. The vitality of French constitutionalist thought is often explained by the country's keenly developed sense of national consciousness, unrivalled elsewhere. Maravall has convincingly shown that this also holds true for Castile for, although it would be difficult to argue in favor of a truly 'Spanish' national consciousness, the strength of Castile's sense of national identity is beyond question. This brings us roundly back once again to the *Comuneros*, for it is within the context of those ideologies voiced by the various radical and moderate groups that we discover, first, an impressive sense of community amounting almost to full national consciousness; and second, a widespread constitutional awareness no less strong for being largely intuitive. In short, the *Comunero* movement was a constitutional conflict in which all shades of moderation and extremism can be found. And Castrillo's rightful position within that conflict as an oracle of moderation need of course no longer be repeated. What differentiates the situation of Castile

---

[57] J. Russell Major has argued that 'the typical Renaissance monarchy...was.... constitutional, not absolute, in that there were laws, customs, and institutions which checked the authority of the ruler'. 'The Renaissance monarchy as seen by Erasmus, More, Seyssel, and Machiavelli', *Action and Conviction in Early Modern Europe*, ed. J. Siegel and T. Rabb (Princeton, 1969), p. 17. Few, I think, will dispute the general validity of this appraisal. And yet, as soon as we enter into the concrete complexities of a specific situation, the firmness of its contours begins to fade. We may think that the Renaissance monarchy was constitutional, but many among the *Comuneros* believed that in whatever awe of the laws and customs of Castile the monarchy may have stood before 1516, it surely had vanished by 1519. And their claim was backed by impressive proof: Charles had usurped the title of king in 1516 and again in 1518; he had silently acquiesced in the sack of the kingdom by the foreigners of his entourage; he had left the kingdom; he had sought another crown; he had exposed the laws of the realm to the mercies of evil men in a Royal Council chosen by himself, and had threatened the *libertades* of his Castilian subjects. A better description of the proverbial figure of the tyrant would have indeed been difficult to find. It was precisely to restore the balance of broken constitutionalism that the cities rose in defiance of their sovereign. And their defeat had certainly not contributed to the restoration of rule tempered by respect – lip service at best – for laws, customs, and local privileges. Or so we are told by Castrillo, whose melancholy is best attributed to his conviction that the monarchy had broken free of its traditional institutional restraints. In Claude de Seyssel, we are told by Russell Major, 'support may be found for this writer's interpretation of the Renaissance monarchy' (p. 25). Renaissance monarchy in France perhaps; certainly not in Castile.

from that of France at this time is precisely what makes the crisis of the *Comunidades* so significant an episode in the history of Spanish political theory and practice.

There had been in Castile, to be sure, men whose writings reveal their constitutionalist leanings and whose thought had given the *Comuneros* the doctrinal support needed to justify their conduct. But it was in the factious violence of rebellion that Castilian constitutionalism found its natural habitat. The constitutional theories of French political thought, on the other hand, evolved in the sedate atmosphere of an academic environment protected by two generations of comparative internal peace. Their ultimate fate, however, was to be not unlike that of their militant Castilian counterparts for they too would perish at the barricades during the course of the second half of the sixteenth century.[58] The result in both cases was identical: the unchallenged triumph of incipient monarchical absolutism.

If these brief comparative considerations are kept well in mind it is not difficult to explain the dearth of Spanish constitutional thinking throughout the Renaissance. In Castile, as in later sixteenth-century France, the best allies of the monarchy were the rebels themselves for through their excesses they forced the moderates to throw in their lot with the king. Libertarian constitutionalism might go to the head, but a strong king promised far greater protection for life and limb. After Castrillo, whose own constitutionalism was strongly tempered by the doubts aroused by the revolt, the monarchical order was unquestioningly accepted not only at the level of concrete reality, but at the doctrinal level as well. Spanish political thought henceforth either embraced the royal idea in an extreme imperial manner tempered only by the quasi-mysticism of Christian humanism (Valdés), or denied it only in its ecumenical side while implicitly accepting its other aspects (Vitoria). Only at a time when Erasmus' world was already on the wane is a questionable constitutionalism resurrected with Sepúlveda's own brand of imperialism. And this very constitutionalism, we shall have occasion to point out later, may go a long way toward explaining the mystery of why he was denied official permission to publish his *Democrates alter*.

[58] Those passions aroused in France by the Saint Bartholomew massacre which would in time be responsible for the *Réveille-Matin*, had been unleashed in Castile by the behavior of the Crown at the Cortes of Santiago–La Coruña and the destruction of Medina del Campo. And in their ultimate essence, the conclusions arrived at by the anonymous Huguenot and the radical *procuradores* were identical: the superiority of the people over the king.

2

Advocates for empire

Introduction

The activities of Antonio de Guevara, Alfonso de Valdés, and Juan Luis Vives encompass the first four decades of the sixteenth century – a period during which the dreams of ecumenical empire were given practical sustenance by the fortuitous concentration of so many different dominions into one single hand, only to have those hopes brutally dashed by Charles' failure to resist and turn the tide of events. The advent of Charles of Ghent to the throne of the Spanish kingdoms coincided with that brief period when it seemed that Christendom awaited the long-hoped-for cue that would launch a lasting era of harmonious concord. Thus it was that Erasmus, hopefully eyeing the youthful trio of kings apparently reared upon solid humanist foundations, felt that he was justified in foreseeing the dawn of a lasting golden age.

And it is precisely during the crucial period beginning with the crushing of the *Comunero* uprising and ending with the Emperor's departure for Italy that the treatises which will occupy us in the pages of this chapter were written. These are the years between 1522 – the *Comunidades* had been defeated by April of 1521, but it was not until October of the following year that the king proclaimed a general amnesty or *Perdón* which in reality was nothing more than a proscription list – and 1529 when Erasmianism became a way of life for so many Spanish intellectuals.[1] Bataillon has suggested the possibility of pinpointing even more clearly the date of Spanish Erasmianism: 'During the years from 1522 to 1525 all those local forces bent on religious and intellectual renovation begin to group themselves around the name of Erasmus; Spanish Erasmianism is born at that moment.'[2]

It was moreover during these crucial seven years that the Emperor, now residing continuously in Spain, became in fact as well as in name a Spanish

---

[1] Bataillon, *EE*, p. 232.   [2] *Ibid.*, p. 155.

king (marrying Isabel of Portugal in 1526, laying the foundations of his government, and basing his policies on Castile's manpower and financial support) and with the aid of his Castilian subjects, recalcitrant at first but progressively reconciled with their imperial master, attempted to carry out the program of what Maravall has called the first stage of his political thought: 'The struggle of a universal empire which cut off from its traditional roots and based instead in Spain endeavors with the latter's power to force peace upon the rulers of Christendom.'[3] Roughly spanning the years between the imperial coronation at Aachen (1519) and the Peace of Cambrai (1529) this initial period was presided over by the cosmo-politan and universalist ideals of Christian humanism which aimed at imposing over Europe the dream of the *universitas christiana* now under-stood as a viable political reality.

The ideological garment in which his advisers and admirers sought to clothe the young Emperor's first venture into the world of imperial politics notwithstanding, many Europeans took a dim view of the gigantic shadow now cast by the Habsburg stripling. The French in particular had good reason for feeling surrounded by the union of the Trastámara and Habs-burg inheritances.

This partially accounts for the continuous state of war which pitted Charles against two generations of French kings and their allies. That war was responsible for two events – the repudiation of the Treaty of Madrid and the sack of Rome – which in no small measure, according to Bataillon, encouraged those Spaniards spellbound by the Erasmian gospel to put forward a plan in which 'religious and political reasons are blended together into a complex mixture of Spanish hegemony, Christian unity, and general reform'.[4] Its essence can be discovered, on the one hand, in the hopes awakened in the hearts of the Erasmianists by the sack of Rome and, on the other, in the official version – probably written by Valdés himself – of the battle of Pavia.

It seems that miraculously God has given this victory to the Emperor so that he may not only defend Christendom and resist the Turk but once those civil wars (for no other name can be given to such discords among Christians) ended seek out Turks and Moors in their own lands. . .and in order that, as prophesied by many, under this most Christian prince the entire world may receive our holy Catholic faith and the words of our Redeemer be obeyed: 'Fiet unum ovile et unus pastor.'[5]

In a letter written to his friend Fevyn, Vives echoes Valdés' sentiments. 'It is said that a great number of enemies have allied themselves against

---

[3] Maravall, *Carlos V*, p. 123.   [4] *EE*, p. 226.
[5] Quoted in *EE*, p. 228.

Charles. But this is his destiny: to vanquish his enemies when in great number so that his triumph be all the more telling. In reality this is no more than God's will to show men how weak our forces are against His power.'[6] These words carry reverberations of the hopeful dream shared by the Emperor's unconditional supporters: Charles' victory over his enemies would be but the beginning of a golden age. We shall see later, however, that although it is an accurate appraisal of Valdés' yearnings this attitude is far from representative of Vives' own opinion.

We catch a further glimpse of the Erasmian program and the relentless manner in which its proponents at court sought to influence the Emperor in the expectancy with which Vives, in the preface to *De concordia et discordia in humano genere*, greets his sovereign's trip to Italy, and by the shift in imperial policy which Charles' decision to be crowned at Bologna portends – a shift which, meaning as it did a *rapprochement* with the Pope and the concomitant abandonment of the anti-Roman policies which had nourished hopes of reform, must have caused some consternation among Erasmus' followers at court. It is again Maravall who outlines the contents of this second phase in Charles' political development.

Current policies having failed to yield positive results, it became imperative to change direction, returning to the German–Italian tradition of Empire. Combining the weight which the imperial tradition still carried with the charismatic element added by a papal coronation would result in the strengthening of the Emperor's hand. Operating from such a solid base Charles would then reform the abuses within the Church thus cutting off the most important root of the Lutheran heresy, and making easier the latter's demise. With Italy pacified and Germany united peace for Christendom would become a reality.[7]

Such, at least, appear to be the guidelines suggested by the prospectus delivered by the Emperor himself in his address to the Royal Council (Madrid, 1528). The existence on the eve of the Emperor's coronation of a new imperial policy, then, seems to be incontestable. Where that policy comes from, however, is a different matter. Brandi detected the hand of the imperial Chancellor, Gattinara, and, more recently, Koenigsberger seems to share the same opinion. Menéndez Pidal, on the other hand, maintains that the Madrid speech was Guevara's work, a conclusion also accepted by Maravall.[8] Authorship aside, however, one thing remains clear: the new formulation of imperial designs outlined by the speech

---

[6] *Ibid.*

[7] Maravall, 'Las etapas...', p. 123.

[8] On this, see Maravall, *Carlos V;* R. Menéndez Pidal, *La idea imperial de Carlos V* (Madrid, 1955); P. Rassow, *Die Kaiser-Idee Karls V dargestellt an der Politik der Jahre 1528-40* (Berlin, 1932); F. Cereceda, 'El diálogo Menéndez Pidal–Brandi–Rassow sobre la idea imperial de Carlos V', *RF*, cxxxiv(1936), pp. 411–27.

parallels, at least in its ultimate objectives, the normative principles of that Messianic imperialism, mixture of political astuteness and naive faith in man's ultimate destiny, so distinctively a creation of the Erasmian imperialists during the twenties.

Alfonso de Valdés

Alfonso de Valdés was born in Cuenca, ca. 1490. Although we know little about his early years, it appears reasonably certain that he did not follow any consistent course of studies at the academic level. He had as friend and tutor the Italian humanist Pietro Martire d'Anghiera. In 1520 we find Valdés present at Charles' coronation in Aachen, and by 1522 official documents mention him as a member of the secretarial staff at court. In 1526 he became Latin secretary to Charles V. We do not know exactly when Erasmus and Valdés began their correspondence, although it is possible that their friendship dated from as early as 1525. The first letter of Erasmus to Valdés of which we have knowledge is dated March, 1527. What is certain is that from that date to his death in 1532, Valdés was in the thick of the battle raging between the Spanish admirers of Erasmus and his detractors.[9]

The works of Valdés which will arrest our attention here are the *Diálogo de las cosas ocurridas en Roma* (1527) written on the occasion of the Roman sack and purporting to be an account of the facts and events which led to that episode, and the *Diálogo de Mercurio y Carón* (1528–1529). With the contents and substance of the first we shall become acquainted in Chapter 5, for it is in the context of the war between Emperor and Pope that Valdés unveils his ideas on concord and discord. Here our interest will be largely monopolized by the second *diálogo*, a far more mature and carefully thought out work; it is out of the animated exchanges between Mercurio and Carón that Valdés' political views emerge.[10]

---

[9] For more details concerning the life and works of Valdés, see the following works: M. Bataillon, 'Alonso de Valdés, auteur du *Diálogo de Mercurio y Carón*', in *Homenaje ofrecido a Menéndez Pidal* (2 vols., Madrid, 1925), I, pp. 403–15, and 'Érasme et la chancellerie impériale', *BH*, xxiv(1924), pp. 27–34; E. Boehmer, *Bibliotheca Wiffeniana. Spanish Reformers of two Centuries from 1520* (3 vols., Strasbourg and London, 1874–1904); F. Caballero, *Alonso y Juan de Valdés* (Madrid, 1875); F. Eguiagaray, *Los intelectuales españoles bajo Carlos V* (Madrid, 1965); J. F. Montesinos, 'Algunas notas sobre el *Diálogo de Mercurio y Carón*', *Revista de Filología Española*, xvi(1929), pp. 225–66.

[10] The two *diálogos* were edited by J. P. Montesinos in 1928 and 1929 (Madrid), respectively. Unless otherwise indicated all subsequent references will be to those editions herafter cited as *COR* and *MC*. There are two editions of *COR* in English.

The entire thematic structure of *Mercurio y Carón* is woven about three basic elements in a manner reminiscent of Valdés' own threefold role as humanist, man of affairs and devoted servant of the Emperor, and advocate of religious reform. First, the state of confusion, disorder, and decay in which Christendom suffers and withers. The gravity of the situation is superbly portrayed in Mercurio's imaginary travels throughout the world, and the subject is periodically taken up again with formidable wit by the souls who representing the various orders of secular and religious society – bishops, cardinals, counselors, kings and their secretaries, priests and monks – are interviewed by the author as they demand passage in Carón's barque. Bishop and cardinal bear witness to the wretchedness of their spiritual governance; counselors and kings are held as examples of cowardice and tyranny; while secretaries stand accused of complicity in the crimes of their masters. It is against this background that Valdés unfolds his second theme: a narrative of political and diplomatic events framed to illustrate in what manner various and illustrious representatives of the secular order – France, England, Venice, the Papacy itself – conspired to thwart the peaceful schemes of the Emperor – the third component of Valdés' triad who occupies the center of the stage – and hold Christendom in chaotic thraldom.

In the second part of *Mercurio y Carón*, Valdés summarizes in a masterly way the political and spiritual tenets of evangelical humanism. Among all the wretched failures who call themselves rulers while disregarding the more elementary principles of the art of Christian governance, Charles alone emerges as an image of hope, the embodiment of personal honesty, religious sincerity, and political wisdom. And upon these imperial virtues Valdés founds his hope for the fulfillment of an evangelical program that will herald the dawn of a new era for mankind. Faithful to the programmatic pattern of Erasmus, whose *Institutio principis christiani* Valdés clearly takes as his model, the imperial secretary shuns all concern – a characteristic which he shares with Machiavelli – with the mandatory philosophical speculation about the origin and ultimate nature of political authority *de rigueur* among contemporary thinkers, a clear manifestation of that Erasmian temper so antagonistic to speculative subtleties. Thus Valdés does not ask (as will Castrillo, Vitoria, and, more surprisingly, Vives) whether political power is of natural law or a violation thereof. But abstract speculation is not the only major note absent from Valdés' concern. The more mundane and prosaic questions relative to such matters

The first appeared in London (1590). The second is that of J. E. Longhurst, *Alfonso de Valdés and the Sack of Rome* (Albuquerque, N. M., 1952). For a complete bibliography of the editions of Valdés' works see Boehmer, I, pp. 101 *et sqq.*

as institutions, the best form of government, the rights of subjects, or the role of the populace in the governmental structure of the commonwealth are equally passed over in silence. In other words, in Valdés we will search in vain for the philosophical thinker endeavoring to penetrate the arcana of politics or the practical man of affairs uniquely concerned with the outward mechanics of government. We find instead, as with Erasmus and More before him, the moralist seeking a cure for the ills of social injustice and the anarchy of political ineptitude.

The cause of those ills is quite plain to the humanist: man's neglect of Christ's teachings. The remedy, surely, is close at hand: a prince who retrieves those teachings from the pit of forgetfulness to which men have banished them will once again bring hope and peace to mankind. Accordingly the monarch, in the venerable tradition of mirrors for princes, becomes the unquestioned embodiment of the state's authority and his prerogatives the most complete doctrinal assertion of absolutism in the history of political thought. It is now upon the shoulders of one man that mankind's hopes rest – a most literal notion in the case of Valdés for whom there is no question that the epitome of the Christian prince is to be found in the person of his revered master, the Emperor. Undoubtedly the demands made on the man vested with such boundless power and trust by the humanist are enormous. And his hopes for survival under such burden will clearly lie with the strength to be drawn from his own Christian nature. Valdés, however, does not consider an upright Christian nature to be inherent in those born to the purple. On the contrary, just like Erasmus he believes that the prince must be a far better Christian than the average man, for the vices trivial in the latter become monstrous in the former. Only a relentless, uncompromising education – the very pillar of Valdesian and Erasmian political thinking – will prepare the ruler to bear the burdens of his office and station.

The pedagogical imperative, then, is part and parcel of Valdés' ideology, for he believes that the root of all the evils which devour Christendom is not man's flawed nature but his abysmal ignorance. How all-pervading man's ignorance really is and how appalling are its dreadful results, Valdés readily explains in the first part of *Mercurio y Carón*. Mercurio's worldwide travels yield a landscape of desolation in which the teachings, example, and commandments of Christ, are frenziedly trampled underfoot by a humanity seemingly gone berserk. Widespread and multiple as man's abominations are, however, they are not without hopeful exceptions. Here and there Mercurio has found pockets of virtue – men whose conversation and company, he informs Carón, is akin to the angels'. Persecuted as these men are for following Christ and believing in him, they never cease hoping; instead, they are 'forever praying to Jesus Christ that He banish from the world such blindness'.[11] This juxtaposition of opposites – evil and good, despair and hope, revulsion at man's depravity and trust in his perfectibility – is the dominant theme pursued throughout the dialogue by the author. It is of interest, therefore, to follow its evolution and how it finds its culmination in the person of the Christian ruler (the Emperor) who, pedagogue to all mankind, will break the fetters of ignorance with the twin weapons available to Christian man: reason and faith.

In this first half of the dialogue Mercurio is endeavoring to inform his friend Carón of the events which have transpired on the stage of European politics. Their conversation is periodically interrupted by the souls of the damned who on their way to hell demand transportation in Carón's boat. Generally speaking all the passing *animae* share one thing in common: painful surprise at finding themselves destined for the eternal fires. Particularly poignant is the puzzlement of those laymen who honestly thought that they had done everything needed to earn everlasting salvation. When Mercurio, for instance, remonstrates with the shade of the king's counselor that masses, alms, fastings, and pilgrimages are worse than useless in the eyes of God when purchased with ill-gotten wealth, the despairing soul cries out in anguish: 'What do I know about all that! Neither in confession nor during the sermons was anything said about that.'[12] Mercurio then proceeds to enlighten him explaining that all the outward trappings of religion (papal indulgences, '*candela del Papa Hadriano*', prayers, burial in Franciscan habiliment) avail nothing unless backed by good works which in turn are effective only if done through love of God. In wrath the hapless counselor demands to return to the world to punish the knavish clerics who thus cheated and deceived him.[13] The next wanderer, the soul of a man who in life had been a duke, further elaborates on this scheme of lay ignorance. 'I fervently desired salvation', explains the duke, 'but I was given to understand that by reciting the Count's prayer I would be protected from dying in mortal sin and from eternal damnation. As for purgatory, well, I had ten or twelve papal indulgences which protected me. In short, I thought that I had paradise in the bag.'[14] Further prodded by Mercurio the duke depicts how, feeling invulnerably protected by his armor of prayer and indulgence, he devoted all his waking hours to the good life and to enlarging his domains and possessions. In addition and 'so that I would be held in high esteem as a good Christian and upright man, I founded and built many monasteries and gave abundant alms to all friars'. But would it not have been better, he is asked, to have done your good works for God than to buy with them the world's sympathy?

[11] *MC*, p. 20.   [12] *Ibid.*, p. 40.
[13] *Ibid.*, pp. 40–43.   [14] *Ibid.*, p. 53.

'Yes', replies the duke, 'but I did not deem it essential since I felt that with my prayer and indulgences going to heaven was a certainty.'[15]

What comes to light from all this, then, is the monumental ignorance on matters of salvation and Christian good living afflicting the lay body of Christendom. By and large, however, malice is absent and only stupid bewilderment remains when the hapless *animae* are finally and irrevocably confronted with the magnitude of their blindness. And yet, great as the transgression of these men was, it pales in comparison with the guilt of those who willfully misled them into perdition. Not surprisingly, there-fore, in addition to the laymen's witlessness the shades of Valdés' ecclesias-tics are liberally endowed with a truly ecumenical cynicism tinged with slyness among the lower ranks (preachers, priests) and shot through with insufferable arrogance among the upper echelons of the Church's hier-archy. Just like his mentor Erasmus, Valdés in truth harbors no pity for the defilers of mankind.

The first among the breed to be introduced to the reader is a self-styled champion among preachers who had discovered an infallible method of filling the church to capacity: in public he feigned holiness, and upon mounting the pulpit he invariably couched the recriminatory tone of his sermons in such a manner that it would never touch those present. But why not tell the truth, asks Mercurio. With flawless logic the *predicador* points out that if those who flocked to his church were told the truth they might conceivably mend their ways and thus shame the cleric into better-ing his – a most unwelcome possibility in the preacher's view.[16] If to this brief sketch we add hypocritical sanctimoniousness and boundless conceit as further ingredients, we are left with a fine portrait of Valdés' unworthy priest – a man who without the slightest trepidation confesses to have been *de los christianos que se llaman perfectos*.[17] Bishop and cardinal differ only from this lowly 'perfect Christian' in the haughtiness of their demeanor. Asked by Carón about the nature of his office, the bishop proudly announces that 'to be a bishop is to dress in white rochet, to celebrate mass crowned with the mitre and with hand both gloved and ringed, to command the bishopric's clerics, to defend its income and spend the collected monies at will, to have many servants, and to distribute benefices'.[18] When Carón redefines the office along less prosaic and more spiritual lines the bishop is frankly bewildered. 'Never have I heard any-thing like that, or thought that being a bishop went beyond what I have just outlined.'[19] After further interrogation it transpires that the worthy bishop stands convicted, in addition to the crassest ignorance, of pride, simony, and lustfulness.

[15] *Ibid.*, pp. 53–4.   [16] *Ibid.*, pp. 27–8.   [17] *Ibid.*, p. 115.
[18] *Ibid.*, p. 61.   [19] *Ibid.*, p. 62.

The setting chosen by Valdés to expound his conception of the Christian prince has already been suggested: Europe once again plunged into a state of war shortly after the signing of the Treaty of Madrid by the rivalry of the two most powerful monarchs in Christendom. Evidently this represented a most useful stage for a man deeply involved in the realities of contemporary politics and driven by an ardent desire to point the way to a transformation of those realities. Mercurio, messenger of the gods and spokesman for the author, after much searching for his friend Carón finds him sitting atop a mountain and agonizing over his fate. Queried by Mercurio concerning his strange choice of residence so removed from the banks of the Stygian lake where he plies his trade, death's ferryman disconsolately explains his fears that the latest international developments may well promise a swift end to the war which so far has kept him happily busy; thus dreading unemployment Carón has left his newly purchased barque behind and taken quarters on a mountaintop in the hope of assaulting and waylaying the souls of the departed on their way to heaven. It further transpires that the incident responsible for Carón's despair centers around the knightly challenges which have passed between the king of France and the Emperor. The unhappy boatman shrewdly reasons that if the princely brawl takes place, as seemed likely for a time, Francis will be defeated, and once dead or prisoner the motive force behind all European turmoils will be removed. Against all odds, however, Carón still hopes and so, knowing Mercurio to have been an eyewitness to the events that may spell his unemployment, he anxiously asks his friend to unfold the tale of woe; perhaps, he ruminates, it is all a false alarm and murder and mayhem will happily once again prevail. As Mercurio reassures his friend that his fears are groundless because Francis has publicly refused to meet Charles in combat, the conversation is interrupted by the arrival of a soul in transit to heaven: the shade of good king Polidoro.

Polidoro was not always the ruler whose virtuous governance deserved for him eternal bliss. 'You must know', he confesses, 'that before being a prince I did not learn what it was to be a man.' This reversal of Christian humanism's most important priorities Polidoro blames on a faulty education which, far from emphasizing the duty to offer his subjects good rule, stressed instead ambition above else and fired his soul with an unquenchable thirst for conquest.[20] What Polidoro must have been like during the early years of his reign Valdés had outlined earlier when Mercurio and Carón interviewed the shade of the king of the Galatians. From the two friends' close questioning the figure of the proverbial tyrant slowly materializes: the republic exists for the king's profit and advantage –

20 *Ibid.*, p. 164.

leaving the administration of the realm in the hands of his counselors the king concentrates on aggrandizing his possessions through wars of conquest and on bullying his subjects into submission to his will; gambling, hunting, and women are the favorite royal pastimes; surrounded by good and evil men the king invariably favors the latter over the former because honest men endlessly remonstrate while scoundrels never nag; the laws are interpreted by the monarch as mere instruments to increase financial exactions; the king only keeps his word as long as it is both profitable and expedient to do so. Not unexpectedly in view of what we have learned of both duke and counselor, when it comes to matters of salvation the tyrant is no longer victimizer but victim. On the advice of his confessor who insisted that paradise awaited him, the king built temples and monasteries. He also prayed, although he had no idea of what he was saying. In short, for his salvation the tyrant trusted 'confessors, indulgences, papal pardons, and God's forgiveness'.[21]

It is clear that in Polidoro's case the one supreme tool which the Erasmian ideal believed available for the upbringing of the righteous ruler had been blunted early in the game. If, then, the king was to come to his senses before suffering the fate of his Galatian cousin recourse must be had to a *deus ex machina*. And this is precisely what Valdés proposes when he tells of the fateful night and mysterious servant who caused so great a commotion in the soul of the complacent monarch. 'Come to your senses, Polidoro...Do you not know that you are shepherd and not lord, and that you shall render account of these sheep to God, the lord of the flock?'[22] Polidoro's abysmal fear soon gives way to an understanding which forever erases ignorance; contritely, he vows to become a just ruler. What follows is a superb, if by no means new, statement of principles to be kept uppermost in the mind of the Christian prince. 'Henceforward, Lord, I pledge that I shall not be king for myself but for you; I shall no longer rule for my own benefit but for that of the people whose welfare you have entrusted to me.'[23] To be kept in mind at this point is a theme which now emerges and whose significance will occupy us in the pages of Chapter 5: the mystical bond which in the minds of Christian humanist thinkers kept peace and good governance irrevocably together. For the first measure taken by the rejuvenated monarch is to call to a halt the insensate warfare which heretofore had been the landmark of his reign. As Vives' writings (we shall see later) similarly urge, the meaning of Valdés' message is unmistakable: any attempt at political reform must be preceded and followed by peace. A ruler who is busy waging war can hardly devote any attention to the cares of his people.

Close upon the heels of conversion comes reform in the manner made

[21] *Ibid.*, pp. 90–99.   [22] *Ibid.*, p. 166.   [23] *Ibid.*, p. 168.

classical by Erasmus' *Institutio*. The king's inner council is ruthlessly purged 'of vicious, greedy, and ambitious men'. In their places worthy men are called in. And the king bluntly warns the newcomers that he will countenance no sycophants; evil counsels will be promptly rewarded with dismissal and banishment. Polidoro's next targets are the court parasites and hangers-on; they are promptly sacked. Those remaining in his entourage he compels to give to their children a practical education – himself, of course, setting the example ('I ordered my gentlemen to provide for their children's education in both the liberal and mechanical arts. . .and myself made provisions to insure that my sons and daughters would learn useful trades.').[24] After household and court the new king reforms the kingdom at large. Judges and ministers are forced to comply with drastically simplified guidelines in the administration of justice. New and sound criteria are adopted to aid the ruler in filling important ecclesiastical benefices – a most difficult task, complains Polidoro, 'for the inner virtues required of bishops can hardly be judged by external appearances'. The laws are reformed and lawyers closely watched. Administrative posts, high and low, 'I no longer filled bearing in mind favors, lineage, or personal services, but only the good of the republic'.[25] Frequent audiences to hear the complaints of the low against the high and periodic journeys throughout the length and breadth of the realm become the trademark of a new administration which prizes Christian behavior above all else and which easily forgives the small fry who have sinned through ignorance while punishing the mighty with Draconian rigor.

The dividends from Polidoro's new policies were not slow in coming: 'All those at court heartily endeavored to live like Christians and their example soon spread throughout my realms.' Valdés, then, views the king as the paradigmatic keystone which alone supports the entire structure of the Christian state. From the center, the throne, all good or evil emanates and contaminates the rest of the body politic. Ironically enough the rewards of good kingship are by no means limited to internal matters. The first concern of the converted king, we are told, was to stop his endless wars of conquest and aggression; but the expansion of his dominions went on unceasingly, for attracted by his good rule foreign peoples, lands, princes, and even infidels, eagerly sought to live under king Polidoro's governance.[26]

Valdés was of course perfectly aware that Polidoro's case, as he had pleaded it, was no more than a rare fluke, the child of a miracle, and that it would have been criminally naive to expect its regularly periodic repetition in the future. Dynastic succession, in many ways the nightmare of

[24] *Ibid.*, pp. 169–70.   [25] *Ibid.*, pp. 170–71.   [26] *Ibid.*, pp. 171–3.

contemporary political thought, demanded of Valdés something more
tangible than mysterious visitations in the dead of night. And the Spanish
humanist was not blind to the problem, as shown by Polidoro's deathbed comments. Noticing that his approaching departure is greeted with
consternation by his subjects, the king reminds them that he is going to a
better life and that his flock should be happy, not sad. 'They answered,'
Polidoro informs Mercurio and Carón, 'that they did not weep for me
but for themselves and the republic.'[27] The king sternly commands them
to shed their cares, for he leaves behind a son brought up in the principles
which Polidoro himself had discovered so late in life. It seems that
Polidoro had taken precautions to insure that the dangers of dynastic
succession would not jeopardize the well-being of his kingdom. These
precautions, the Christian upbringing of his son and successor, Valdés
recounts in what for all intents and purposes is a royal political testament,
an 'advice to his son' which his own master, Charles, would also leave
behind for the edification of his successor, Philip.

Polidoro's testament is not only interesting as a collection of maxims –
basically identical to those found in Erasmus' *Institutio* – designed to
guide and hedge the exercise of the awesome authority vested in the
prince, but significant as well in terms of another and more famous *vade
mecum* for rulers, Machiavelli's own *Il principe*. Both authors had been
professional diplomats thoroughly acquainted with the ruthless realities
of contemporary politics and were shrewd judges of their own times.
Both chose to write in the vernacular thereby endowing their thought
with the startling impact and immediacy denied Erasmus' *Institutio*; and
in both we read of that mood of despair so often encountered in Renaissance political thought.[28] The two secretaries share a common conviction
with equal firmness: man has willfully corrupted himself and contaminated
his own nature. They are equally at one on the need for drastic measures.
It is in the means to be applied and the ultimate goals to be reached that
their ways part, for whereas Machiavelli teaches how to cope with a
damnable reality without seeking to change it, Valdés, true child of the
Erasmian gospel, exhorts those who will listen to gather their strength in
a collective effort to modify that reality under the leadership of the
Emperor.

The prince must first learn to rule. 'If all men learn the trade which
yields their livelihood, why can you not learn to be a prince, the highest

---

[27] *Ibid.*, p. 175.
[28] M. Menéndez y Pelayo judged the prose of this dialogue to be the best written
during the reign of Charles V, with the sole exception of Boscán's translation of
Il cortigiano. See *Historia de los heterodoxos españoles* (2nd ed., 7 vols., Madrid,
1911–1932), IV, p. 203.

and most excellent of all professions? Should you be content with but bearing the name of king or prince without truly endeavoring to be one, that name you shall forfeit and be called instead a tyrant; for no true king is he who merely inherits the office without struggling at becoming one through his deeds. A king, and a free man, is he who rules and commands his own self first; a slave is he who has no control over that same self.' The people will faithfully reflect the character and behavior of the prince. The republic was not made for the king but the king for the republic, and many commonwealths have grown and flourished without a king but never a king without a commonwealth. The good prince will always strive to be loved rather than feared by his subjects, for fear has never maintained a lordship for long; he will always remain deaf to the opinions and un-couth counsels of the vulgar, drinking instead in the fountain of the philosopher's wisdom. 'Leave your realm if your kingship can only be defended at the expense of your subjects' sufferings, for, remember, your subjects are men, not beasts, and you be the shepherd of men and not the lord of sheep.'[29]

Very much in the tradition of that Erasmianism which he so uncon-ditionally represented at the imperial court, Valdés' political catechism amply transcends the narrow boundaries within which realists like Machiavelli willingly corralled their ideologies. The transformation of the ruler into the Christian prince and, through his example, the corresponding metamorphosis of his flock is to be understood literally as the total goal of Valdés' ecumenical reform. It is for this reason that in *Mercurio y Carón* we find much more than the normative juxtaposition of Polidoro 'before and after'; it is not the ruler alone who transmutes his own vices into virtues, but every representative component of society undergoes the same change: the worldly bishop becomes a true shepherd of souls, the cynical preacher is replaced by the exemplary messenger of Christ's gospel, the knavish counselor of princes gives way to the honest man, and the mun-dane friar yields to the saintly man. They are all pilloried and praised in turn. In this fashion an entire society, gradually but inexorably, is radical-ized into a true evangelical unity. And regarding the secretary's pragmatic radicalism there can be no doubt, a fact which perhaps accounts best for the absence from Valdés' thought of one element which is so characteristic of Spanish political ideology: the law.

The law, whether in its eternal, divine, natural, or human guise, in Vitoria's thought for example, is an ever-present theme because it is agreed that the laws – specifically, human or positive law – represent that invaluable mechanism whereby justice can be brought down from the

[29] *MC*, pp. 180–81.

realm of ideas and actualized to serve the needs of man's sociable nature. Hence the Dominican's insistence that an unjust law is a contradiction in terms. Moreover, Vitoria's position is that whatever changes may take place toward the improvement of man's social lot must be contained within the controlling and regulatory embrace of the laws. This conservative outlook is partly the result of the age's fear of violent change as harbinger of anarchy, partly a consequence of a lingering of that medieval awe which surrounded the idea of law. It is not difficult to imagine, then, how fatally constraining Vitoria's idea of change would be to a prince who, on Valdés' advice, attempts to break through the fetters of custom and tradition.

But Valdés' radicalization of reform has another important result. The political framework created by the School of Salamanca, we shall see when we come to Vitoria, demanded a sharp demarcation between the spheres of interest of the natural and supernatural orders; in effect, an apparent separation of Church and State. Such a separation is, at best, indefinite and vague in Valdés' scheme. True, at one time the secretary distinctly defines the difference between the functions of the Pope and those of the Emperor: It is the Emperor's duty to 'defend his subjects, maintain peace, dispense justice, reward the good, and punish the evil-doer'; while the Pope 'holds the authority to interpret Holy Scripture and to teach the Christian doctrine to the people'.[30] But it is soon confined to limbo. For, in truth, Valdés establishes no rigorous threshold between the secular role of the state and the spiritual mission of the Church. The violent denunciation of the Papacy which had been the central theme of the *Diálogo de las cosas ocurridas en Roma* is absent from Valdés' second dialogue. The author, however, leaves no doubt in the reader's mind that the ruler shall have a strong voice in the spiritual affairs of the kingdom; witness Polidoro's decision to remove unworthy bishops from office: 'As it was not within my power to punish them [worthless bishops] I suffered greatly at their hands until as a result of my endless importunities I was accorded a very broad papal prerogative which enabled me to deprive a faithless bishop of his see.'[31] Valdés thus drastically removes himself from the doctrine of the two swords and, indirectly but closely bound with his studied disdain for the law, tacitly decries the value of the Empire as a juridical concept. Fully within the Erasmian mainstream Valdés conceives the imperial idea as the convenient tool whose universal appeal will make more viable the adoption of a far less recognizable abstraction of equal ecumenical value: the *philosophia Christi*.

It would be most fitting to close this brief study of Valdés' conception of

30 *COR*, pp. 15–16.   31 *MC*, p. 170.

the Empire and the role of the Emperor with an excerpt from Dante's *Il convivio* (Trattato IV. 4) which superbly summarizes the Spaniard's own yearnings.

Il perchè, a queste guerre e alle loro cagioni torre via, conviene di necessità tutta la Terra, e quanto all'umana generazione a possedere è dato, esser Monarchia, cioè uno solo Principato e uno Principe avere, il quale, tutto possedendo e più desiderare non possedendo, li re tenga contenti nelli termini delli regni, sicchè pace intra loro sia, nella quale si posino le cittadi, e in questa posa le vicinanze s'amino, in questo amore le case prendano ogni loro bisogno, il quale preso, l'uomo viva felicemente; ch'è quello per che l'uomo è nato.

Juan Luis Vives and the concord–discord dialectic

Finally and more removed from a purely Spanish milieu than Valdés, we meet Juan Luis Vives who among Spaniards perhaps best personifies the broad and normative political universalism of Erasmus. Deeply as the problem of war partakes of the political theories of Spanish thinkers, nowhere – not even in Erasmus himself – could we hope to find a more accomplished marriage between concord–discord and politics than in Vives. And in this context a further word of explanation is very much in order, for my earlier decision to study the age's ideology on war in one self-contained chapter may appear in this instance to be somewhat questionable since it will force the sundering of his thought. All in all, however, I feel that the advantages derived from studying Spanish ideas on war against the traditional Augustinian background and the contemporary Erasmian framework by far outweigh the disadvantages. Ironically this is perhaps truest in Vives' case. Strictly speaking and in line with the general character of Christian humanist schemes, Vives' political thought rarely moves beyond a rudimentary and normative stage. In marked contrast, on the other hand, stands his preoccupation with war and peace; all of the latter's aspects are minutely and relentlessly scrutinized until in truth political theory becomes a mere tool for or adjunct to the endless search for peace. Even more emphatically than Erasmus, then, the Spaniard invariably links any item which may even remotely be identified as political with the concord–discord twins. Under the circumstances my goal in what follows will be limited to understanding the Emperor's role in the Vivian scheme of things, leaving further comments on Vives' political theory to Chapter 5.

Juan Luis Vives was born in Valencia in March, 1492. After the customary early training demanded of candidates for advanced studies he entered the recently founded University of Valencia. His sojourn at that institution was short and in 1509 we find him at the University of Paris where he remains for the next three years completing his formal education. In 1512 Vives leaves Paris for Bruges; two years later he briefly returns to the French capital and publishes his first work, *Christi Jesu triumphus*. We know little or nothing about the period between 1514 and 1517 but after three years of silence we meet the Valencian humanist again; this time in Louvain employed as preceptor to Gillaume de Croy, the young nephew of the Sieur de Chièvres, that redoubtable Flemish adviser of the future Charles V. The following year, 1518, Vives writes his *Fabula de homine* – 'the point from which any discussion of his philosophy of man must begin'.[32] Almost simultaneously, 1519, he begins his career as a professor at the University of Louvain where he meets its rector, the future Adrian VI, Antoine de Berges (to whom the *Fabula* is dedicated), Martin Dorp, Gracián de Alderete (the translator of Plutarch into Castilian), and above all, Erasmus.

The year 1522, marking the beginning both of Charles' seven-year Spanish sojourn and the persecution of the defeated *Comuneros*, finds Vives still in Flanders; he has completed and published his *Commentaries* on Saint Augustine's *City of God*. The work was received with open hostility by the theologians of Louvain, by this time a hotbed of anti-Erasmian sentiment. Almost simultaneously from faraway Castile arrived the news of Antonio de Nebrija's death; Vives was invited to occupy the late grammarian's chair at the University of Alcalá. We know nothing of the Valencian's answer except that he never went to Alcalá. Instead he chose to go to England and in 1523 (*De institutione feminae christianae*) he was teaching at Oxford.[33] Shortly afterward his new duties as Princess Mary's tutor forced him to abandon the university and join the royal court in London. The next five years Vives spent in England; his stay in the island, however, was not a wholly continuous one, for he often travelled to the Continent, especially to Bruges where in 1524 he was married to Margaret Valldaura. To this English quinquennium, among others, belong both the *Introductio ad sapientiam* (1524) and *De subventione pauperum* (1526). Henry's divorce and its concomitant results served to create an atmosphere which made Vives' further stay in England impossible. In 1528 he departed for Bruges and spent the remaining twelve years of his life in Flanders forevermore absorbed in problems and questions of an ethical nature. To this last period belong *De officio mariti* (1528), *De concordia et discordia in humano genere* (1529), *De*

---

[32] M. L. Colish, 'The mime of God, Vives on the nature of man', JHI, 23 (1962), pp. 3–20.
[33] For Vives' activities during his English period, see R. P. Adams, *The Better Part of Valor* (Seattle, 1962).

communione rerum (1535), and the *Linguae latinae exercitatio* (1538). He died on May 6, 1540.[34]

Vives lacks the passionate attachment to the imperial idea characteristic of Valdés; more cosmopolitan in outlook and tastes and free from the concrete obligations binding the imperial secretary as a man of affairs, the Valencian humanist certainly understands the role of the Emperor to be an important one; but, in the last analysis, not necessarily more essential or indispensable than that of other Christian princes. The one theme which without question holds pride of place in Vives' scheme is concord. And in the preface to *De concordia* he summarizes his program accordingly: 'No greater need has the world, nowadays tottering at the edge of final prostration, than for concord. Only concord will reinstate the fallen, retain what is now fleeing from us, and restore what has already been lost.'[35] The date of *De concordia* coincides almost exactly with that of *Mercurio y Carón*. Vives, then, was writing under the burden of events identical to those which had inspired Valdés' second dialogue; and to Charles V, central figure of those events, he dedicates the work. The preface, however, is more than a mere dedication to his sovereign. It is

[34] For further details on Vives' life and works, see: R. P. Adams, *The Better Part of Valor;* W. C. Atkinson, 'Luis Vives and poor relief', *The Dublin Review*, cxcvii (July–Sep., 1935); M. Bataillon, 'Autour de Luis Vives et d'Iñigo de Loyola', *BH*, xxx(1928), pp. 184–6, 'De nouveau sur J. L. Vives', *BH*, xxxii(1930), pp. 97–113, 'J. L. Vives, réformateur de la bienfaisance', *BHR*, xiv(1952); A. Bonilla y San Martín, *Luis Vives y la filosofía del Renacimiento* (Madrid, 1929); J. M. Castán Vázquez, 'La enseñanza del Derecho según Luis Vives', in *Homenaje a D. Nicolás Pérez Serrano*, I, pp. 62–81; J. Corts Grau, 'La doctrina social de Juan Luis Vives', *EHSE*, ii(1962), pp. 65–89; N. A. Daly, *The Educational Psychology of Juan Luis Vives* (Washington, 1924); G. Desdevises du Dezert, 'Luis Vives d'après un ouvrage récent', *RH*, xii(1905); R. García Villoslada, 'Luis Vives y Erasmo', *Humanidades*, 5(1953), pp. 159–77; L. A. Getino, 'Vitoria y Vives; sus relaciones personales y doctrinales', *AAFV*, ii(1931), pp. 277–309; J. B. Gomis, 'El Nuevo Mundo en Luis Vives', *VV*, i(1943), pp. 332–69; P. Graf, *Luis Vives como apologeta: Contribución al estudio de la apologética*, trans. J. M. Millas Vallicrosa (Madrid, 1943); J. A. Maravall, *Carlos V;* B. Monsegú, *Filosofía del humanismo de Juan Luis Vives* (Madrid, 1961), 'Los fundamentos filosóficos del humanismo de J. L. Vives', *VV*, xii, n. 47–48; E. Nys, 'Quatre utopistes du XVIe siècle', *Revue de Droit International*, xxi(1889); M. de la Pinta Llorente and J. M. de Palacio, *Procesos inquisitoriales contra la familia de Juan Luis Vives* (Madrid, 1964); M. Puigdollers Oliver, *La filosofía española de Luis Vives* (Madrid, 1940); L. Riber, 'Erasmo y Luis Vives', *BRAE*, 24(1945), pp. 193–224 and 26(1947), pp. 81–135; L. Thorndike, 'John Louis Vives', in *Essays...Dedicated to John Harvey Robinson* (New York, 1929), pp. 327–342; F. Watson, 'J. L. Vives and Saint Augustine's Civitas Dei', *The Church Quarterly Review*, lxxvi(April–July, 1913).
[35] J. L. Vives, *De concordia et discordia in humano genere*, in *Opera omnia* (8 vols., Valencia, 1784), v, p. 187. Cited hereafter as *CD*.

rather an encapsulated version of the theme which will fill the lengthy
pages of the *De concordia* itself. Europe, suggests Vives taking up again
a topic which he had discussed less extensively seven years before in a
letter to Adrian VI (*De Europa statu ac tumultibus*), is in the throes of
anarchy and Christendom lies helplessly on the threshold of irrevocable
partition. The princes wage endless secular war among themselves while
the proliferation of opinions and the disputes arising from it carry discord
into the very bosom of the faith. Clearly, the rulers must bring to an end
their own disputes and ordinary men should bridle their views. Above
and beyond these conditions, which must be met if a total catastrophe is to
be avoided, Vives stresses the imperious need for reform of the existing
spiritual structure. He wholeheartedly shares Valdés' confidence that
religious reform will remove the most important source of dissension; and
the way to reform can only be paved by the gathering of the Church in
Council.

It is when understood in this context – as we have seen also to be the
case with Valdés – that the role of the Emperor becomes exceptionally
important. Once again the prestigious imperial idea is used as the vehicle
to make possible the triumph of the *philosophia Christi*. Vives confesses
that he has followed closely Charles' career and that he is impressed by
what he has seen. Indeed, the young Emperor's accomplishments are of
such magnitude that the Christian humanist admits them to be not the
work of mere human nature but proof of God's aid and comfort. The task
ahead, however, is so fraught with difficulties and perils that the deeds of
the future must of necessity dwarf the successes of the past. The Emperor
will be like a second Hercules succoring Atlas. His ingenuity will be
taxed to the utmost; his heart and judgment will be endlessly put to the
test. He must rely on his own senses when possible; at other times he will
put his trust in faithful advisers or draw inspiration from those political
treatises so often consulted by princes. Above all, his will and intellect
must not be corrupted by adulation or weakened by partisanship or self-
interest.

This moving plea exhorting Charles to be the benefactor long-awaited
by mankind who will bring everlasting peace to the society of man does
not automatically raise the Empire to a position of political hegemony in
Vives' eyes, or exclude other rulers from sharing in the task. True, he
concedes, 'I have dedicated this work to you, in whose efficient hands and
powerful will lies so great a share of human concord and tranquillity...
But I do not write for you alone; I write for all, high and low, both princes
and men of all stations.'[36] For Vives, then, the imperial authority, albeit

<hr/>

[36] *Ibid.*, p. 192. In the past, Vives had addressed similar pleas to Adrian VI (see
above) and Henry VIII (the two letters of 1525).

of the first rank and certainly unobjectionable to him as a Spaniard, is never understood in the strict juristic manner characteristic of traditionalists like Ulzurrum; rather, it is no more than one among a handful of tools whose proper use should be conducive to bringing about the all-important goal: the peace of mankind.[37] To that end the entire strength of Christendom, from the highest to the lowest, must be mobilized. Peace and concord are not the concern of princes alone but the responsibility of every man who heeds the message of Christ. Only when this responsibility is understood and accepted by all will the cause of peace triumph. Under the circumstances it is easy to see that Vives' aim in *De concordia* goes beyond a mere appeal to the Emperor or the rulers of Christendom to lend their strength and influence to the cause of peace, and that he has more far-reaching aims in mind.

During a brief stay in Paris (1519) Vives delivered a lecture on the Ciceronian theme *Somnium Scipionis*. In it we read what appears to be an uncompromising approval of man's political organizations. 'There is to be found nowhere on earth a more agreeable or pleasing thing to our sovereign Lord God, who rules the roundness of the world, than those human commonwealths which bound by reason and law bear the common name of cities.'[38] More than a decade later a thoroughly disillusioned Vives intones a radically different chant. True, he concedes, man is a social animal. He was born for religion with God and society with other men; for that double purpose he was created, formed, and endowed.[39] It is a nature-ordained and compelling need felt by man that he shall be part of a single and universal society. But in his pride and rebelliousness man aspired to divinity and destroyed that society in which concord reigned, thereby unleashing discord upon the world. 'In the beginning Nature created among men that union which was later broken by malice.'[40] After the dissolution of the natural order, Vives continues, man attempted to replace it with various forms of imperfect union. The bonds of common citizenship linking those who live in the same city brought some men together; others gathered under the same religion; compacts, alliances, colleges, and other means of artificial association kept still other men united. What is important, however, is that the one natural and universal unity, which existed before man's sin, was destroyed, and no man-made union, not even the best and greatest of them all – the city – could begin to approach its perfection: the ties which bound some men together

---

[37] In the words of Maravall, 'Vives never formulates as the Empire's secular mission the idea of its political role being one aimed at directing or reforming society.' *Carlos V*, p. 284.

[38] *Opera*, v, p. 97.   [39] *CD*, p. 195.   [40] *Ibid.*, p. 388.

separated others and the result was to further increase the division of mankind.

The state, then, is not an institution decreed by nature; man is a social but not a political being. Returning to the same Augustinian position which Alonso de Castrillo had earlier made his own, Vives accepts the political order only as an outgrowth of sin, a result of 'differences imbedded in mankind by the guilt of old Adam'. This should be sufficient evidence to convince us that Vives cannot seriously countenance the possibility of bringing about a return to man's unclouded past through the agency of the state, imperfect child of man's despair – not even when its authority is that of the secular head of Christendom, the Emperor. Not now, Vives points out, because the state is no longer really needed. It lost its *raison d'être*, together with all other man-made institutions, once man learned the message of Christ – the 'new Adam'. All the uncertainty, confusion, and insecurity that brought the state into being have been ended by the appearance of Christ. Walls were torn down, fences destroyed, and the pristine unity of mankind was restored by the common bond of His teachings. Christ endeavored to make man accept once again this unity. And He saw that the easiest way to accomplish His task was through the love of man for his fellows. It is for this reason that He gave us but one commandment: to love one another.[41] Only man's persistent malice and his failure to see the error of his ways keeps him from returning to the flawless oneness of the Golden Age. And herein lies the true meaning of Christianity, for what else is a Christian but man returned to nature and his own birthright from which he was taken away by the devil?[42]

God, then, once again made it possible for man to return to his own true state. He has given fallen man the means, in the form of His Son's teachings, to recover the concord that yields a safe return to a pure and nature-ordained social order. Success, however, requires man's cooperation. Man shall first know himself and thereby indeed become a man. This knowledge will enable him to subdue the most iniquitous passion of them all: overbearing pride, the seed and fount of all discord. And through examination of self man will derive an additional blessing: the realization that his unaided will can control the passions but not destroy them. Only the infinite grace of God can accomplish this definitive feat. Fully aware of how much his weak nature needs God's aid, man is ready to ask of Christ the twin gifts for which he yearns: peace and universal society. And Christ gives willingly as long as what we request is truly peace, that is the tranquillity of spirit which will enable us to love our fellow men and to worship God with all our piety.[43]

[41] *Ibid.*, p. 389.   [42] *Ibid.*, p. 201.   [43] *Ibid.*, p. 337.

This is indeed quite a departure from Valdés' enthusiastic reliance on the powers of one man to return mankind to sanity. Not one man but every man is the Vivian recipe. As we shall shortly see there is no doubt in Vives' mind that rulers can accomplish much, not, however, as rulers in the Valdesian sense but strictly as pedagogues who will teach their peoples that only through the individual efforts of every human being will the ultimate *summum bonum*, concord, be brought about. What, then, we may ask, is the function of the state and the prince in this scheme of things so dangerously reminiscent of utopian anarchy? With the first part of the question I shall deal more extensively in the context of Vives' favorite concern: war and peace. And the ruler? In a letter dated in Bruges (October 8, 1525) and addressed to Henry VIII, Vives sketches with a steady hand the character, duties, and virtues which must adorn the good prince. First and foremost, we are told, it must be remembered that the ruler in the rough is like all other men, uncouth and uncultured. No prince is born great and learned. Just like any other ignorant mortal the king must be taught and chided, for upon no other pillars does wisdom rest; he needs someone to show him both his errors and how to amend them and thus gradually, through teaching and experience, polish and file away the rough edges of his character.[44] The need for education as the *malleus* of ignorance and wisdom's wet nurse Vives does not limit to the sovereign. Rather, the twin ideals of Erasmian pedagogy, *bonae litterae* and religion, are viewed as the indispensable companions of every adult citizen endeavoring to discover the correct nature of his civic duties. Thus reared in true appreciation of learning and profound in his respect for the writings of the faith, the Vivian citizen will disdain wealth, shun greed, and seek virtue as the only truly profitable gain. Sharing the educational imperative, however, is not the only link binding governor and governed together. It is on the contrary one manifestation of the total identification between the ruler and his commonwealth. For according to the Spanish Christian humanist the latter is but a reflection of the former.

All of the prince's passions are poured into the city he rules and transfused to his people...If the king is an evil man so are his subjects, and among the wicked there never is lasting concord...Thus we conclude that the first care of the prudent prince who wishes to preserve his kingdom for himself and his successors shall be to turn himself and his subjects into worthy men.[45]

Identical considerations compel Vives to suggest how the ruler will do well to reflect that in the governance of the commonwealth love is a far

[44] *Obras completas de Juan Luis Vives*, ed. and trans. L. Riber (2 vols., Madrid, 1948), II, p. 28.
[45] *Ibid.*, pp. 27–9.

more effective prop than fear. 'Nowhere can a weaker groundwork be found than that on which sits a monarchy buttressed by fear.'

Harsh governments are hard but not durable, for there being no stable tie linking prince and subjects the latter merely await a favourable opportunity to burst their shackles in violence. There is no form of coercion which will indefinitely keep an animal captive against his will; clearly the victim will have no other thought but to destroy that which stands as an obstacle to freedom.[46]

Vives' reason for this peremptory condemnation of grinding rule is soon made even more explicit: he shares with Castrillo the latter's deep fear of the unforeseeable possibilities implicit in change brought about by the unleashed instincts of the populace goaded beyond endurance by an oppressive prince. 'A king who cultivates virtue will rule a kingdom which cannot be seduced by *novedades*.'[47]

Conclusion

Drawing parallels and making comparisons is of course always a necessarily hazardous business, a shaky ground which the critic treads at his own and considerable risk. I do not think, however, that it is too far-fetched to point out in this instance that Valdés and Vives hold different views on the role and goals of princes in general and of the Emperor in particular – a fact which if not necessarily unexpected is nevertheless somewhat surprising in view of the philosophical affinities of both men and their unqualified reverence for a common master, Erasmus. In comparison with the detached universalism of Vives, Valdés' outlook clearly suffers from his excessive proximity to the events and the men who occupy his attention. But nowhere do the differences between the two humanists emerge more vividly than when they discourse on the obligations and duties of the ruler within the context of war. Thus Chapter 5 will show us Valdés proposing that the Emperor may be just the man capable of bringing into being – as the author himself admits – that most rare of all specimens, a just war. No such demigod do we find in Vives; on the contrary, the Vivian hero is the prince who spares his subjects any and all wars. Far from relying on the strength of one single man or group of men as Valdés does in his yearning to conjure up a millennium of peace, Vives forcibly enlists into his cause of total reform every member of the Christian commonwealth. The teachings of Christ and the dignity of man: Vives, program of social reform rests upon these twin foundations. His opposition to war, what we must expect the society of man to be like in practice, and the hopes for the transformation of society into something more in agree-

[46] *Ibid.*, pp. 28–9.   [47] *Ibid.*, p. 28.

ment with the Christian ideal, are all to be understood with reference to man's nature and the reforming impulse that it will receive once it follows the road pointed out by Christ. It is moreover evident that the process whereby man shall return to his rightful past necessitates the abandonment of all those makeshift institutions devised by him to survive in a hostile and imperfect world. The concord which universal unity requires (and promises) cannot be given by them, their compacts, and their agreements. Only man himself aided by his reason can begin the task. But above all it is the peace of Christ which raising reason to the realm of the spirit will make signatures, witnesses, oaths, and arms useless, for it eliminates the matter, the occasion, the causes of dissension.[48]

[48] *CD*, p. 332.

3

The discovery of America and the School of Salamanca: Francisco de Vitoria (I)

Introduction

Although it would be both artificial and misleading to attempt too strong a separation between the two phases of Spain's constitutional crisis, the fact remains that the discovery of America was directly responsible for the greater and possibly the more significant portion of her political literature in the age of Erasmus. No one who reads the account of the controversies over the nature and political fate of the Indians which rocked Spain's learned world during the first decades of the sixteenth century can possibly doubt that in the eyes of the Spanish publicists and of the government itself the questions under discussion were of the utmost gravity and import not only for Spain but, more significantly, for the whole political universe of man. To the discovery of America must be credited the appearance of a formidable propagandist for the cause of the Indians in the person of Bartolomé de las Casas,[1] and the erudite work of his determined opponent, Juan Ginés de Sepúlveda, exponent of a phase of Spanish humanism of Italian vintage and alien to the parallel current of Erasmian humanism. Above all, however, it was the New World and the political problems suggested by its incorporation into the Castilian Crown that bear the major responsibility for the emergence of a political philosophy best embodied in the writings of Francisco de Vitoria and his disciples and successors of the School of Salamanca.[2]

---

[1] On the political ideas of Las Casas, see L. Hanke, *Las teorías políticas de Bartolomé de las Casas* (Buenos Aires, 1935).

[2] The following are among the works which deal with one or more aspects of Vitoria's thought. Q. Albertini, *L'œuvre de Francisco de Vitoria et la doctrine canonique du Droit de la guerre* (Paris, 1903); L. Allevi, 'Francesco de Vitoria'; S. Alvarez Gandín, *Doctrinas políticas de Vitoria y Suárez* (Oviedo, 1950); C. Barcia Trelles, *Francisco de Vitoria, fundador del Derecho internacional moderno* (Valladolid, 1928); J. Baumel, *Les problèmes de la colonisation et de la guerre dans l'œuvre de Francisco de Vitoria* (Montpellier, 1936); V. Beltrán de Heredia, *Francisco*

The discovery of America faced contemporaries with a baffling problem: how to reconcile a society founded on premises alien to European experience with that familiar world whose social and political catechism depended so narrowly upon the moral and ethical truths of Christianity. The possibility of mere coexistence between the two cultures was contemplated, witness the case of Vitoria, and for this alternative the age was prepared by Europe's long experience with Islam. The realities of conquest and colonization, however, soon made this possibility obsolete, dictating instead that one society be absorbed into the other. But if this practical imperative was to be justified at all two basic conditions had to be met. On the one hand, at no time during the process of assimilation must the primary values of Christian conduct be violated; on the other, the Christ-centered worldview which owed its existence to those same values had to be, somehow, modified because the commonwealths to be absorbed were ignorant of them – a fact which goes a long way toward explaining the attention lavished by theologians and jurists on the propriety of converting the natives. And it is precisely in the dilemma thus presented to contemporaries that the disturbing novelty of the American challenge lay. To account for its unwelcome presence it became mandatory to effect some changes in the accepted Christocentric conception.

de Vitoria (Barcelona, 1939); H. Beuve-Méry, *La théorie des pouvoirs publics d'après Francisco de Vitoria* (Paris, 1928); V. Carro, *La 'Communitas orbis' y las rutas del Derecho internacional según Francisco de Vitoria* (Santander, 1962); 'Los fundamentos teológico–jurídicos de la doctrina de Vitoria', *CT*, LXXII(1947), pp. 95–122; G. Fraile, 'Francisco de Vitoria, norma y síntesis del Renacimiento ortodoxo de nuestro Siglo de Oro', *CT*, I(1934), pp. 15–26; E. Galán Gutiérrez, *La teoría del poder político según Francisco de Vitoria* (Madrid, 1944); L. A. Getino, *El maestro Fray Francisco de Vitoria* (Madrid, 1930); B. Hamilton, *Political Thought in Sixteenth-Century Spain* (Oxford, 1963); J. Larequi, 'Del "jus gentium" al Derecho internacional. Francisco de Vitoria y los teólogos españoles del siglo XVI', *RF* 83(1928), pp. 21–37; S. Lissarague, *La teoría del poder en Francisco de Vitoria* (Madrid, 1947); C. H. McKeena, *Vitoria and his Times* (Washington, 1932); I. G. Menéndez-Reigada, 'El sistema ético–jurídico de Vitoria sobre el Derecho de gentes', *CT*, XXXIX(1929), pp. 307–30; M. Mónica, *La gran controversia del siglo XVI acerca del dominio español en América* (Madrid 1952); E. Naszalyi, *El Estado según Francisco de Vitoria*, trans. I.G. Menéndez-Reigada (Madrid, 1948); L. Pereña Vicente, 'El concepto del Derecho de gentes en Francisco de Vitoria', *REDI*, v, 2(1952), pp. 603–28; D. L. Recasens Sitches, 'Las teorías políticas de Francisco de Vitoria', *AAFV*, II(1931), pp. 165–222; W. Shaetzel, 'La teoría de la guerra de Francisco de Vitoria y la moderna guerra de agresión', *Anales de la Universidad de Murcia*, XII 3-4 (1953–1954), pp. 407–24; J. B. Scott, *The Spanish Origin of International Law* (Washington, 1928), *The Discovery of America and its Influence on International Law* (Washington, 1929), *The Spanish Conception of International Law and of Sanctions* (Washington, 1934); A. Truyol Serra, *Los principios del Derecho público en Francisco de Vitoria* (Madrid, 1946); H. F. Wright, *Vitoria and the State* (Washington, 1932).

In other words, it became necessary to pass from a traditionally tested and thus satisfactory worldview centered around an exclusively Christian scheme of things in which reason and experience successfully harnessed the particular to the universal, into another which remained as yet formally undefined but which seemed more threat than reassurance. The source of this menace was unmistakably identified as change, the Nemesis of the medieval consciousness. Change which, for the moment at least, had to be equated with irrationality because, by the very uniqueness of the event to which it owed its existence, it remained a distinctly singular species free from any subordinate attachment to the accepted and comprehensive universal.

To the medieval mind – and I use the term here to denote no more than the Spanish doctors' dependence on premises strictly medieval in origin – the conclusion was patent: change in itself was not rational. Change was not a phenomenon intelligible in itself but an unwholesome disturbance of the order and harmony so dearly sought. Change was a dynamic intruder in a static world and it followed that if the latter was to be shielded from anarchy the singularity of the former must be subsumed under the universality of the laws which constituted, in a manner of speaking, the defense perimeter of the whole. The means, it was believed, were at hand and consisted of a technique (syllogism) and a referential repository of precedents (experience). In brief, it was evident that whether welcome or not change had come and the really important question now was: could it be controlled?

In my view this is the general context in which the political thought of the School of Salamanca must be understood and judged. And to argue that regardless of its newly found vigor Neoscholastic ideology was intrinsically incapable of producing the correct answer to the above question is merely to invite another query: how else could the problem of the discovery of America have been approached? It is a matter of record that neither Christian humanism nor the newborn realistic approach to political problems manifested much willingness or inclination to explore the possible impact of the New World on the social and political institutions of the Old. And so it was that with the single remarkable exception of Sepúlveda's attempt to apply those political principles developed by Italian civic humanism, only the traditional ideology proved willing or capable enough to attempt to understand and explain the significance of the most singularly novel event of the Renaissance. Moreover, it is clear that regardless of the weaknesses which may in fact have fatally handicapped the traditional approach to change, Vitoria does not seem to have felt in the least the weight of those shortcomings. On the contrary, when the discovery and conquest of America compelled learned opinion to formulate principles which would be common to both European and Indian and would thus serve as foundations for regulating their future relations, the Dominican searched for and found those principles in natural law – the *jus communicationis*. Difference of religion, the first and outwardly most important expression of change threatened by the discovery of America, was in this manner neatly circumvented by the application of a principle which sinks its roots not in revelation but in natural reason. 'Natural law was assumed to exist among all peoples, not merely among Christians; it was a natural system of ethics which neither depended on nor contradicted Christian revelation but could stand by itself.'[3] Thus within a tradition which itself had borrowed the concept of natural law from without its own boundaries, Vitoria finds and puts to use the common theme which regardless of difference of religion or even its absence binds men hitherto unaware of each other's existence, their own humanity.

But the introduction of the *jus communicationis* is only the beginning, the initial justification of the right of all men to freely establish contacts with one another. It was soon followed by a related principle conceptually broader and more far-reaching in its implications than its predecessor: the *jus gentium*. It is true that with Vitoria we do not reach immediately an unequivocal definition of the law of nations. What is clear is that in the Dominican theologian we identify a definite insistence on the rational origin of the *jus gentium*. It was left for his successors at Salamanca to further emphasize the dependence of the latter on the former. Soto, for instance, argues that 'both civil law and the law of nations are created by human reason'; and Suárez firmly postulates that 'the precepts of the law of nations have been introduced by man – either by the consent of the entire human community or its major part – of his own free will. It is therefore incorrect to argue that those precepts have been written into the hearts of men by the author of nature. They are part of man, not natural law.'[4]

The significance of the *jus gentium*, however, was not limited to its usefulness as the conceptual instrument capable of transforming the irrationality latent in the 'change' under discussion. On the contrary, in the view of the publicists of Salamanca it served equally well to tame the other crucial political development of the age, the emergence of the Renaissance state. The Spanish Neoscholastics were as aware as anyone else in Europe that the unity implicit in the abstract interpretation of the Holy Roman Empire was now more than ever a bygone ideal. In its stead they

---

[3] Hamilton, *Political Thought in Sixteenth-Century Spain*, p. 19.
[4] Francisco Suárez, *De legibus*, ed. and trans. J. R. Egillor Muniozguren (6 vols., Madrid, 1967), bk. II, ch. XVII, pt. 8. Unless otherwise indicated all future references will be to this edition.

observed a series of relatively compact political units sharing the territorial extension of the known globe. The element of novelty embodied in them, although not so drastic as that of America, promised a potential for change serious enough to threaten the stability supposedly guaranteed by the theoretical unity of yesterday. And this stability the Spanish school sought to preserve even in the context of the new *mise en scène* which grew to replace the medieval idea of empire. It is for this reason that the Salamanca doctors will not concern themselves with the theme closest to the heart of the age's political realists – namely, the desire to affirm, both *de facto* and *de jure,* that internal strength of the state which alone could improve its chances for survival in a milieu now openly recognized as hostile. The stability and harmony of the interrelated parts of that milieu, instead, was precisely the theme which overwhelmingly monopolized Vitoria's attention. It was clear to the Dominican, however, that the *jus gentium* could be no more than a normative tool designed to offer man an uncomplicated road toward harmony in a world characterized now by plurality rather than unity. And Vitoria was under no illusions concerning the persuasive power of exhortations based exclusively on reason. The evident unruliness of man would surely overwhelm the rational foundation of the law of nations, actualize the irrational potential of change, and result in a transition from harmony into anarchy, from cosmos into chaos. It was imperative to give a coercive property to the *jus gentium.* That task could be ideally fulfilled by the *jus belli* founded as its newly acquired partner and twin, the law of nations, on the unquestionable basis of reason made available through the treasurehouse of experience as the theory of the just war.

By virtue of his recognition of the pagan Indian polities as perfect states juristically on the same footing with their European counterparts, Vitoria transcended the reality familiar to all his contemporaries, and so influential in the development of modern political thought, of the passing of the old imperial idea and the emergence of a fragmented *respublica christiana.* As a result Vitoria's political world of man bears no trace of the parochialism of either ancients or moderns. It is neither bound by the spiritual frontiers which set the Latin Christendom of yesterday apart from the rest of the physical world nor confined within the progressively narrow national boundaries of the future. It is, on the contrary, a true universe of absolutely equal states whose extension is limited only by the size of the globe itself. It is clear that if such a conception, so different in scope from Machiavelli's or Bodin's, is to be a workable one – and concerning its feasibility the Spanish Neoscholastics harbored no doubts – various and formidable obstacles must be overcome. The story of Vitoria's political blueprint, accordingly, represents not only a remarkable example of

Spanish political thought in the early sixteenth century, but will also ideally serve both to test the resourcefulness of Neoscholasticism in dealing with what is unprecedented in this period and to illustrate some of the shortcomings which the age's deficient purview visited upon political philosophy, in Spain as elsewhere.

The fons et origo *of political power*

Vitoria was born in Burgos around the year 1492. By 1506 we find him in the Dominican monastery of San Pablo, still in his native city. It is at San Pablo that Vitoria begins the academic career which would take him to Paris where he became a student at the College of Saint Jacques. There, until 1512, he followed a course of philosophical studies which both served to lay the foundations of a humanist education and to prepare him for his subsequent theological pursuits. The next ten years the young Dominican spent under the tutelage of Peter Crockaert and other distinguished Parisian masters, and in 1522 he received his doctorate in theology. The following year finds him back in Spain teaching theology at the College of San Gregorio, in Valladolid, and five years later, 1526, he becomes Prima Professor of Theology at Salamanca. Perhaps the most notable incident to punctuate the rather uneventful remaining twenty years of Vitoria's life was his membership in the assembly of theologians which, in 1527, met in Valladolid to examine the orthodoxy of certain portions of Erasmus' writings. Not unexpectedly Vitoria, in common with his fellow Dominicans, condemned with 'firm moderation' (Bataillon's words) the questionable passages.[5]

---

[5] There are several modern editions – partial or complete but often accompanied by excellent introductions – of Vitoria's works. In Spanish: *Relecciones teológicas*, trans. J. Torrubiano Ripoll (3 vols., Madrid, 1917); *Comentarios a la Secunda secundae de Santo Tomás*, ed. V. Beltrán de Heredia (5 vols., Salamanca, 1932–1935); *Relecciones teológicas*, ed. and trans. L. A. Getino (3 vols., Madrid, 1933–1936); *Las relecciones De Indis y De jure belli*, ed. J. Malagó Barceló (Washington, 1963); *Relectio de Indis*, ed. L. Pereña Vicente (Madrid, 1967); *Obras. Relecciones teológicas*, ed. T. Urdánoz (Madrid, 1960). In French: *Leçons sur les Indiens et sur le Droit de la guerre*, ed. M. Barbier (Geneva, n. d.); *Les leçons de Francisco de Vitoria sur les problèmes de la colonisation et de la guerre*, ed. and trans. J. Baumel (Montpellier, 1936). In English: *De Indis et de iure belli relectiones*, ed. E. Nys, trans. J. P. Bate, in *The Classics of International Law*, gen. ed. J. Brown Scott (Washington, 1917), III; *Relectio Concerning Civil Power*, trans. G. L. Williams, in J. Brown Scott's *The Spanish Origin of International Law. Part I: Francisco de Vitoria and his Law of Nations* (Oxford and London, 1934), Appendix C. Unless otherwise indicated I will use Williams' (*DPC*), Nys' (*DI*) and (*LW*), and Getino's (*De potestate Ecclesiae prior; De potestate Ecclesiae posterior*, cited as *DPE* I and *DPE* II, respectively) editions. Williams and Nys translate as 'State' Vitoria's

A distinguished representative of Neoscholastic thought and devoted commentator of Saint Thomas, then, Vitoria well realized that even from a doctrinal point of view the idea of the medieval empire, the political side of Christendom's oneness, was well on its way to extinction. He sought therefore to devise the means whereby the unity of Christian Europe (an expanded unity, for it now included the lands of the west) would still be preserved under the new conditions promised by the dawning age. These conditions, both in Europe and America, shared one thing in common: the one inescapable companion of human society through the ages, war. No publicist endeavoring to understand – normatively or otherwise, from Machiavelli to Erasmus – the political realities of his own day could therefore ignore the one phenomenon which, integrated into man's social makeup, both lay at the basis of every contemporary conception of the state and touched man as an ethical being. And this applies singularly well to those thinkers (Las Casas, Sepúlveda, Vitoria) whose political beliefs were rooted in circumstances specifically born of war: the armed conquest of the Indian commonwealths in America. Thus the idea of war is an element of pivotal importance in the development of at least one significant aspect of Spanish political thinking in the age of Erasmus. In this as in other aspects of its political philosophy, Spanish thought fully belongs within the age's intellectual mainstream. Naturally enough, then, we must expect to encounter in every facet of Vitoria's political outlook that body of doctrine, the theory of the just war, which founded by Saint

civitas, communitas, and respublica. For reasons which the text will make evident, I have chosen to translate them as 'commonwealth' or 'republic' and indicate it with brackets.

From the point of view of Vitoria's contribution to political philosophy and international law, his relectiones occupy the center of the stage. A relectio was a special lecture delivered with particular solemnity and on an annual basis before the entire Faculty (often the whole university) on subjects which the author had more informally and briefly treated in the classroom during the current academic year. It is also to be noted that Vitoria's relectiones were never published by the author. They were offered to the public only after his death, on the initiative of his former students. According to Beltrán de Heredia the chronological order of the relectiones is as follows: De silentii obligatione, academic year 1526–1527, delivered on Christmas, 1527; De potestate civili, 1527–1528, Christmas, 1528; De homicidio, 1528–1529, June 11, 1530; De matrimonio, 1528–1530, January 25, 1531; De potestate Ecclesiae (I), 1530–1531, toward the end of 1532; De potestate Ecclesiae (II), 1531–1532, May or June, 1533; De potestate Papae et Consilii, 1532–1533, April–June, 1534; De augmento caritatis, 1533–1534, April 11, 1535; De eo ad quad tenetur veniens ad usum rationis, 1534–1535, around June of 1535; De simonia, 1535–1536, May–June, 1536; De temperantia, 1536–1537, sometime between 1537 and 1538; De Indis (I), 1537–1538, around January of 1538; De Indis (II), 1538–1539, June 18, 1539; De magia, 1539–1540, July 18, 1540; De magia posterior, 1540–1541, spring, 1543. The first edition of the relectiones appeared in 1557 (Lyons).

Augustine and further added to by a thousand years of Christian tradition sought to regulate the behavior of men among men and states among states.

According to Vitoria man forms societies partly to overcome his physical handicaps, partly to allow many of his talents to bloom and develop more fully.

To man alone, however, she [Mother Nature] granted reason and virtue, leaving him frail, weak, needy; drawing him forth from the wreck enfeebled, destitute, in want of everything...and scattering hardships throughout his life so that in truth, from the very moment of his birth he can only presage tears, weeping over his own frailty...Therefore, in order that proper provision might be made for these needs, it was necessary that men should not wander singly and in solitude, after the manner of wild beasts, but should dwell in a fellow-ship in which they might be of aid to one another...And truly the will, whose chief armaments are justice and friendship, would of necessity be entirely deformed and, so to speak, crippled, if it were separated from human society: justice, indeed, cannot be practised except by the multitude; and the same is true of friendship.[6]

In either case man is following and obeying the will of God who intended human beings to live together. The diversity of man's interests, as numer-ous and different as there are men, would break the community apart; and anarchy is undesirable and contrary to natural law. A form of authority highly concentrated and invested with coercive power is therefore essen-tial. The function of this authority is to preserve 'civil society...of all societies that which best provides for the needs of man'. And this is the ultimate cause which brings the civil power into being.[7] Man, then, seemingly emerges as both a social and a political animal.

This, in broad strokes, is the sequence of cause and effect that according to Vitoria created man's socio-political fellowships. It is important to notice, however, that Vitoria does not believe the social and political imperatives to have appeared simultaneously or that they owe their origin to identical compulsions. Intuitively obeying nature's mandates man sought the company of his fellows from the very beginning; in other words, man's sociability is explicitly commanded by the law of nature. On the other hand and in terms as uncompromising as Castrillo's, Vitoria insists that 'by natural law no man is king over other men; by natural law all men are born free'.[8] Vitoria in this manner presumably admits the existence of an historical interlude separating an age during which men lived as members of an universal society without ruler and enjoying their

[6] DPC, pp. LXXIV–LXXV.
[7] Ibid., p. LXXVI.
[8] Quoted in Naszalyi, El Estado según Francisco de Vitoria, p. 166.

good in common, from another when 'following the world's cataclysm, princes appeared; this is clearly seen in the case of Nimrod, son of Noah, and others. I nevertheless confess that material things continued to be held in common for about four hundred years more until men, by unanimous consent, decided to elect a prince who undertook to apportion mankind's riches.'[9] Close on the heels of private property followed the political partition of the world, and with it man entered the stage a political being.[10]

Finally, we read in *De potestate Ecclesiae prior* that even though in the state of innocence there was neither dominion nor coercive *potestas*, following the multiplication of the human race private property, princes, and governments had to come into being; otherwise disorder and confusion would have prevailed.[11] Strictly speaking, therefore, neither the social islands into which the universal society contrived by the law of nature was broken up, nor that *potestas* which alone can turn them into civil societies owe their origin to explicit instructions emanating from natural law. Rather, just as private property, they were created by historical circumstances. It would nevertheless seem that the 'unnatural' origin of this newly risen society of limited range does not unduly disturb Vitoria. For even more readily than Castrillo, he is willing to accept the hard facts of life and 'omit everything that happened before the flood'. In the process he sanctions two important facts: first, sovereign states are here to stay and thus whatever ecumenical scheme Vitoria may be aiming at will have to accommodate the autonomous nation state as well – a far cry from Vives' hopes; second, 'it is manifest that before the coming of Christ no one was vested with world-wide sway by divine law and that the Emperor cannot at present derive therefrom a title to arrogate to himself lordship over the whole earth'[12] – so much, then, for Valdés' dreams.

Having made up his mind concerning the legitimacy of political power Vitoria holds nothing back. 'All power. . .by which the secular [commonwealth] is governed, is not only just and legitimate, but is so surely ordained of God that not even by the consent of the whole world can it be destroyed or annulled.'[13] It is moreover evident that '[cities and republics] had not their fount and origin in the invention of man, but sprang, as it were, from Nature, who produced this method of protecting and preserving mortals. And under this head of the discussion it clearly follows that the same purpose and necessity underlie the existence of public powers.'[14]

It should not take an unusual amount of perspicacity to realize that with

[9] *Ibid.*, p. 167, footnote 8.   [10] *DI*, p. 132.
[11] *DPE I*, pp. 46–7.   [12] *DI*, p. 132.
[13] *DPC*, p. LXXII. See footnote 5 above for explanation of the use of 'commonwealth'.
[14] *DPC*, pp. LXXV–LXXVI.

the preceding words we have reached a serious impasse, for Vitoria has just laid down a foundation of natural law for the public power in striking contrast to and open contradiction with the ideas which I attributed to him earlier. Under the circumstances a further elaboration of this point is in order. First a word on the chronology of the sources: the passages in which Vitoria appears to stress the natural law origin of the civil power belong to the *De potestate civili*, a *relectio* delivered in 1528. The statements which I construe as disclosing a subtler relationship between natural law and political power (*potestas*), on the other hand, are found in the first *relectio* on the Indians (1539) and the master's lectures on the IIa–IIae of Aquinas' *Summa* (1534–1537). From the last of the two I have already quoted the pertinent selections. Even more telling, however, are those passages from *De Indis prior* where Vitoria discusses whether the Emperor is lord of the whole world. 'By natural law', he insists, 'mankind is free save for paternal and marital dominion. . .therefore no one by natural law has dominion over the whole world.' Above all, concludes Vitoria, 'Aristotle (*Politics*, bk. 1) says power is of two kinds, the one originates in the family, like that of the father over his sons and that of the husband over the wife, and this is of natural power; the other is civil for, although it may take its rise in nature and so may be said to be of natural law, as St Thomas say (*De regimine principum*, bk. 1, ch. 2), yet, man being a political animal, it is founded not on nature, but on law.'[15]

And herein lies the key to the problem, the span which bridges the gap between the two supposedly conflicting Vitorian viewpoints: civil power is of, but not founded on, natural law. It cannot be strictly said to be based on the law of nature because there was a period – a 'prehistory', as it were – when man did not live in civil societies. But neither is its existence contrary to natural law. When man began – the dawn of history – to set up civil societies, therefore, he was not acting in violation of nature's explicit commands. The determining factor, the *causa causans*, in the creation of circumscribed and politically organized (civil) societies, it follows, is man's will in the shape of human law (which may never contradict natural law). States are not created by natural law or under its compulsion but by the volitive act of man acting under the constraints of necessity, and nature can thus be said in this instance to remain neutral. From all this it is possible to put together the following pattern tracing the historical advent of Vitorian civil society. Before the Flood men lived in an universal society devoid of political instruments. After the catastrophe that destroyed most of mankind, and it would not appear too far-fetched to surmise that perhaps this is how Vitoria gives historical actuality to Adam's sin, human beings were compelled to live in civil societies. Why?

[15] *DI*, p. 131.

Because the unity of humankind's primitive fellowship having been broken (if we may paraphrase Vives), the new man could neither last for long in isolation nor exist among his peers without coercion. Hence the advent of civil society. But although man's condition and his needs changed after the Flood, natural law, emanating as it does from God's will, obviously remained the same. And if before the Flood natural law did not force men to live in civil societies it would contradict reason to propose that it did afterward. In short, it was neutral before and it stands neutral now; it neither sanctions civil societies nor prohibits them.

Both the bygone worldwide society which could survive without the aid of the state's coercive power and the newer territorial societies organized along civil lines are fit and sound human fellowships worthy of natural law, but only if understood within the relative context of human needs and their transitory nature. In his prehistory man's requirements were best fulfilled by a non-political society. Historical man, however, has other wants. And in the final analysis it is solely those wants embodied in human law which justify and are responsible for the advent of a form of human fellowship best characterized by the restraining tool designed to protect its survival: political power. But, we may well ask, if human law creates political power does it not follow that it is a human invention and that as such it can be abrogated by the unanimous consent of the members of the community? Obviously this question brings us back full circle to our starting point. Now, however, Vitoria's emphatic denial that the state can be done away by the united will of the ruled stands on surer ground. The state may have been brought about by human law, but it is not a human invention. The reason, the Dominican points out, is obvious. Human laws, it is true, are the answer to man's needs; the latter, nevertheless, are not the result of human caprice or fickleness. Nature is responsible for them and the state is therefore part of nature itself. In conclusion, it is beyond the power of man to menace in any way the existence of politically constituted society.

The function of the state and the end of civil society

So far we have examined in some detail Vitoria's views on the origin and legitimacy of political power. The next question to be dealt with suggests itself: what are the functions of the state? On the simplest and most obvious of those functions, the protection and preservation of society, we have already had occasion to comment: 'For if councils and assemblies of men are necessary to the security of mortals, it is also true that no society can continue to exist without some power to govern and provide for it; the use and the utility of the public power, and of the community, and of society are absolutely the same.'[16] The state (republic, *communitas perfecta*, civil society), then, is an entity brought into existence in order to protect and insure the well-being of man living in fellowship with his peers. To that end, Vitoria announces, the members of the community have for one thing willingly yielded to the *publica potestas* their right of self-defense, the inalienable privilege of every man. Henceforward the state undertakes to regulate hostilities among members of the same community by introducing an element of order into the affairs of man. The result is to bring about a radical change in the concept of war as waged within the boundaries of the commonwealth. Man is no longer pitted against man; it is the state against the evildoer. Issues are no longer decided by superior skill in the handling of weapons or by the improbable judgment of God but by the civil power dispensing justice through positive law. In this manner the state fulfills its obligation to provide a milieu propitious to peaceful coexistence within the community. But if the state is to accomplish this its appointed task it must be a self-sufficient entity autonomous and free from the interference of other similar entities. Hence the concept of sovereignty which defines the perfect community as that fully capable of meeting the demands and needs for which it was created.

At this point we observe the universe of man populated by a number of political devices created for the sole purpose of solving the problem of war – for what else, if not discord, threatens to destroy man's fellowship from within – at its most elementary level. But their creation, ironically enough, brings into being a variation of the very theme which they help to control. As Vitoria very carefully points out, the perfect community enjoys certain prerogatives which not even the unanimous consent of all the citizens can nullify. One of these prerogatives, the very keystone of the community's survival and continued existence, is the right of self-defense. 'The [commonwealth] may in no wise be deprived of this power to protect itself and to guard against injury from its own citizens or from aliens, a function which it should not fulfill if there were no public powers.'[17] But the Vitorian state cannot defend itself unless it is permitted to 'avenge a wrong and take measures against its enemies, for wrongdoers would become readier and bolder from wrongdoing if they could do wrong with impunity. It is imperative for the due ordering of human affairs that this authority be allowed to the States.' It follows that if the state is to carry to fruition the task begun with the creation of a milieu conducive to man's happiness it must supplement that early achievement with a second one: a protective barrier to safeguard that vulnerable milieu against all comers from without. In short, the state has the authority both to declare and wage war.[18] This in turn implies more than simple

---

[16] *DPC*, p. LXXVI.   [17] *Ibid.*, p. LXXXI.   [18] *LW*, pp. 168–9.

self-defense. As Vitoria clearly explains in the pages devoted to the subject (see Chapter 5 below) the state, in contrast to private individuals, cannot be constrained by the literal meaning of the word. Thus the classical phrase 'to avenge a wrong' is now said to contain implicitly all the conditions demanded by the doctrine of the just war. To avenge a wrong is to seek redress through arms if all else fails, to exact punishment and just compensation for the injury inflicted upon the innocent – in a word, to bring back the reign of justice.

The meaning of all this is obvious. We have now an all-embracing definition of war which covers everything from petty offenses inflicting injury upon the individual to conflicts among states. Evidently the emergence of the state has enthroned a new and broader meaning for the word 'war'. War, understood as the conflict among independent political units is therefore a direct result of the birth of the modern state. War creates the state and the state sanctions and institutionalizes war. It is around this inseparable dualism that all the ideas on war will revolve in the sixteenth century, directly or indirectly, and unless we remember this important fact our understanding of European political thinking during the period in question will remain incomplete. If in addition we bear in mind that the age witnessed the appearance of the sovereign territorial state and its concomitant, potential political anarchy, it is plain that the propositions just outlined together with their attendant corollaries represent the formal birth of international law. Doubtless this goes a long way toward explaining why the doctrines of Vitoria and his successors have so often been associated with the emergence of modern internationalism. The enthusiasm of twentieth-century internationalists, however, has obscured the importance of Vitoria's contribution to the political philosophy of his own day. In a similar but even broader vein, while students of international law have recognized the important role played by war in the development of the modern law of nations, historians of political thought – overemphasizing that side of Renaissance political ideas which hindsight tells us was the wave of the future – have badly overlooked the significance enjoyed by war in the schemes of the political theorists of the early modern period.

It would seem that in following the lead of Vitoria's reasoning we have been taken away from our original concern. We have not strayed far, however, for the protective duties of the political authority do serve as the basis for much of the Dominican's thinking. Still, we may ask ourselves, is protection the total *raison d'être* of the state? Insofar as the state embodies and actualizes that public secular power which 'is the faculty, authority, or right to govern the civil commonwealth', its goal and concern is the common weal: 'to order all its powers to the common good'.

It turns out, then, that we have discussed the function of the state but not the ultimate end to which the state is ordained. Or, to put it in a different manner, a politically organized fellowship exists under two distinct but complementary guises subsumed under one nature (which we shall shortly identify as the secular order). In its first guise, the state – and we may now establish a terminological convention by reserving this name to signify the coercive exercise of the public *potestas* – exists to subdue internal and external threats into impotence (the function of the state). In the second, the civil society, secure now under the protection of its restraining *alter ego*, struggles to reach that ultimate end: the common good.

It is plain that we have left ourselves with no choice but to ascertain the nature of that common good. In the threshold of the modern age the task is by no means an easy one; a crucial point which, we shall emphasize later, deprives the Vitorian scheme of much of its impact. Two avenues are open to Vitoria. On the one hand, there is the traditional alternative with its dogmatic insistence that everything on earth be to the ultimate and perfect felicity of mankind; on the other, the recently hatched pragmatic approach growing out of the immediate historical demands which discards all notions of the state being of necessity responsive to timeless ethical imperatives. In other words, is civil society's end to make man good or simply to make him secularly happy and secure? In his *El Estado según Francisco de Vitoria*, Father Naszalyi (whose ideas I will closely follow here) has framed the same question very aptly in the following terms: 'According to Francisco de Vitoria, is the end of the state a virtuous, moral, and perfect life for man, or rather peace and security in the city of man?'[19]

After poring over the author's commentaries to the Secunda secundae, Naszalyi, not surprisingly, confesses that it is not easy to decide conclusively where exactly Vitoria stands. In my view the reason lies in plain sight: the nature of civil society's end is inseparable from the most fundamental needs and the corresponding means to fulfill them which affecting and shaping man's very existence are responsible for creating civil society in the first place. Is it possible, for example, to be a good citizen without simultaneously being a good man? If we cannot hope to know the exact nature of the end, how can we hope to know the correct means to bring it about and so preserve intact the teleological roots of civil society – 'the need and reason for, the cause of, the means derive from the end'.[20] In what manner should we proceed to make sure that function and end will never come into conflict, that, for instance, war will never prevent civil society from pursuing its goal? To questions such as these answers untarnished by crippling qualifications will be forthcoming only if we are

[19] Naszalyi, p. 184.   [20] *DPE* I, p. 70.

willing either to make Machiavelli's dicta our own or to return to an uncompromising Augustinianism. Vitoria refuses to bend to either alternative. Instead, he searches for a middle way, a golden mean which he feels to be epitomized by the teleological aspects of Aristotle's thought.[21] We shall soon have occasion to observe with what degree of success his consistent efforts at formulating a golden mean solution for the more intractable aspects of the public *potestas* will meet. It would not be overstating the case, however, to point out at this time that even the flexibility of Neoscholasticism and its great capacity for compromise are of no avail in this instance.

The secular order and the ruler

Regardless of the difficulties involved in studying the origin, function, and end of civil society, one thing is clear: there is one power 'which directs earthly affairs and rules on worldly matters',[22] the *potestas civilis*. This secular or civil power holds its sway over the entire natural order. Its supreme embodiment is the king and to him Vitoria now turns.[23] The Dominican begins with a blast aimed at those who question the legitimacy of princely rule: 'There are certain persons, even some Christians, who not only deny that royal power is of God, but who even assert that all kings, rulers, and princes are tyrants and plunderers; so incensed are these persons against every form of domination and power, with the sole exception of democratic power.' An itemized list of the arguments presented by the enemies of monarchical government follows.[24] Vitoria answers the detractors of monarchy in the following manner: 'not only is...royal power, just and legitimate; but, in addition to this, the power of kings is derived from divine and natural law, not from the [commonwealth] itself, nor directly from men'. The necessary proof is immediately forthcoming.

Since the [commonwealth] possesses power over its own parts, and since this power cannot be exercised by the multitude (which could not conveniently make laws and issue edicts, settle disputes and punish transgressors), it has therefore been necessary that the administration of the [commonwealth] should be entrusted to the care of some person or persons (and it matters not whether this power is entrusted to one or to many); it has not been impossible, then, to transfer a power identical with the power of the [commonwealth].[25]

Having set on solid ground the rights of princes to head and rule their commonwealths – the republic creates the king – Vitoria moves on to

---

[21] *DPC* pp. LXXIII–LXXIV.   [22] *DPE* I, p. 9.   [23] *DPC*, p. LXXVII.
[24] *Ibid.*, pp. LXXVII–LXXVIII.   [25] *Ibid.*, p. LXXVIII.

consider in what manner the transfer of power from the whole community to the monarch has taken place. To start with, this transfer is a total one, for 'there are not two sorts of power – one, that of the king; the other, that of the community'.[26] In the past this question has been a source of vexatious misunderstanding because some authors have presumably discovered in Vitoria an early formulation of the social contract theory. Such a conclusion, I feel, oversimplifies the issue. For a social compact between ruler and ruled to have any binding meaning it is indispensable that the latter have something of their own to bargain with, in this case the capacity for self-government. But as a matter of fact Vitoria's scheme makes it clear that this capacity is not created out of nothing by a supreme and independent act of the community's unassisted will. It has rather been brought into existence by natural law operating indirectly through the instrument of necessity. The community's ability to rule itself, moreover, is as old as the emergence of historical society. Thus the same action that after the Flood brought men together into various and separate cells of human fellowship simultaneously transformed those cells into civil societies, namely, societies structured and ordered along political lines. In other words, 'The [commonwealth], then, possesses this power by divine DISPOSITION; but the material cause in which, by natural and divine law, power of this kind resides, is the [commonwealth] itself, which by its very nature is competent to govern and administer itself, and to order all its power for the common good.'[27]

Hence when the commonwealth, through a majority decision irrevocably binding upon all ('the act of the greater part is the act of the whole'), decides to set a king or some other magistrate over the *corpus politicum* it is merely transferring the capacity for self-government inherent in the commonwealth; that much depends directly on man's will, for nowhere is it decreed that human beings shall be ruled by one form of government to the exclusion of all others. Herein, incidentally, finds its justification Vitoria's belief that democracy, aristocracy, and monarchy are equally legitimate. And that is all, for the citizens may only pass on what has been given to them; they do not create, increase, decrease, or in any other way modify it. To do so would be beyond their competence and faculty inasmuch as it is the exclusive province and privilege of natural law. All this explains, among other things, Vitoria's dictum that there are not two sorts of power – one, the king's; the other, the community's. But it also invites the following question: precisely what is the nature of the 'power' which the community has deposited in the hands of the ruler?

Vitoria answers that it is not the civil power (*potestas*) *qua* the essential attribute or quality which alone is capable of creating a civil society that is

26 *Ibid.*, p. LXXX. 27 *Ibid.*, p. LXXVII.

transferred, but the authority (*authoritas*) to use for the common good the prerogatives intrinsic to the civil power; that is, the capacity to restrain through coercion. 'Even though the king is established by the commonwealth (for the commonwealth creates the king), the latter does not transfer to the king the civil power, but its own authority.'[28] To put it in another manner, having conventionally decided in earlier pages to reserve the word 'state' to describe that coercive side of the public power's personality which restrains both internally and externally, it now appears that we may conclude that the king is the state and the royal power the attendant license to use repression to bring malefactors to heel. It nothing else this conclusion should begin to reveal to us the pervasiveness which war enjoys in Vitoria's political thinking and how far the Dominican is from being persuaded by Vives' conviction that war is necessarily synonymous with irremediable discord. With war as an indispensable part of international relations we shall deal later. Now our attention is monopolized by the consequences which Vitoria's appraisal of the nature of the king's mandate entails for the individual commonwealth. What first of all comes to mind is the extent of the authority deposited by the commonwealth in the king. The question has been extensively studied by Naszalyi in the light of Vitoria's commentaries to the IIa–IIae.

Two instances are considered. According to the Dominican the commonwealth, on the one hand, may present the king with unconditional authority; on the other, the ruler's power may have been granted under certain restraining conditions which must be observed under penalty of forfeiture – tyranny. In neither case, however, is the sovereign's authority absolute (in the strictest sense of the word), for it always remains less all-inclusive and extensive than the commonwealth's own. The ruler, for example, may not alienate any portion of the national territory because the commonwealth is not his property. What has been transferred into royal hands, then, is not the state's *potestas* properly speaking, but its authority; the commonwealth does not invest the ruler with *dominium* over its parts but with the authority to act as its administrator. In other words, the prince is the nation's minister and caretaker; to rule means to fulfill the obligations implicit in the commonwealth's trust. And the Vitorian ruler is in the following sense no different from Valdés' own: both are an integral part of the community in that they discharge an *oficio* within it.

Still, once this limitation is recorded we are nevertheless left with the fact that the authority or administrative capacity given by the republic to its chosen leaders rests, in the case of a monarchy, fully upon the king's shoulders. 'Where there are already lawful princes in a State, all authority

28 *DPC* (Getino), II, p. 187.

is in their hands and without them nothing of a public nature can be done either in war or in peace.'[29] Since this authority implies the capacity to legislate for the common good it is clear that the king is the supreme legislator. Is the prince, then, above the law? In *De potestate civili* (n. 21) Vitoria discusses whether 'civil laws are binding upon legislators, and in particular, upon kings', and concludes that 'it is more probable that kings and legislators are bound by the law'. The proof is twofold.

First: that a legislator of this sort [above the laws] injures the State, and the other citizens if, being himself a part of the State, he does not bear a part of the burden...But since this obligation is indirect, we shall offer another proof. The laws which are made by kings have the same force...as if they were made by the whole State; but the laws made by the State are binding upon all; therefore, even those laws which are made by the king, are binding upon the king himself.

The Indian commonwealths of the New World and the perfect community

Vitoria's sanctioning of kingly supremacy in political matters is by no means confined to Christian commonwealths; it extends also to republics with different religious practices: 'it should not be a matter of any doubt that legitimate princes and potentates may exist among the heathen'.[30] With this impeccable opening gambit Vitoria, as early as 1528, prepared the ground for what would eventually be his contribution to the controversy over Spanish dominion in America. And it is not hard to see why, for if, as Vitoria intends to do, we want to insert the communities of the New World within the political universe of man we must first arrive at an unmistakable understanding of the conditions under which a group of men living together is said to constitute a perfect commonwealth.

In 1532 Vitoria delivers his *relectio De potestate Ecclesiae prior*. Expounding on the subject of the autonomous spheres of influence controlled by the secular and supernatural orders he finds occasion to write on the nature of the perfect commonwealth.

The temporal republic is a perfect and complete community: and if so it needs not be subject to any outside jurisdiction, for otherwise it would not be perfect. It follows that it can elect its own ruler since in temporal matters it is subject to no one.[31]

A community thus defined, according to Vitoria, imposes a decisive obligation on its ruler: 'A republic's ruler does not have the obligation to

[29] *LW*, p. 169. [30] *DPC*, p. lxxx.
[31] *DPE* II, p. 67.

preserve the well-being of another republic, regardless of how great the latter's importance may be, to the detriment of his own.'[32] In fact, the commonwealth's safety is so important that if unjustly jeopardized by another one it lies within its right to dismember the culprit.

The temporal republic (perfect and therefore self-sufficient) enjoys the privilege of keeping itself free from harm and to that end its power and authority may be used. For example: if the Spaniards are unable to avoid suffering constant injuries at the hands of the French, they may on their own authority and as if they were true owners, take the latter's cities, set up new princes and lords as rulers, and punish the malefactors.[33]

It is in the second *relectio* on the Indians (*De jure belli*), however, that Vitoria approaches the problem of defining – a difficult task, as he acknowledges – the perfect commonwealth most systematically.

What is a [republic], and who can properly be called a sovereign prince? I will briefly reply...by saying that a [republic] is properly called a perfect community. But the essence of the difficulty is in saying what a perfect community is. By way of solution be it noted that a thing is called perfect when it is a completed whole, for that is imperfect in which there is something wanting, and, on the other hand, that is perfect from which nothing is wanting. A perfect [republic] or community, therefore, is one which is complete in itself, that is, which is not a part of another community, but has its own laws and its own council and its own magistrates, such as is the Kingdom of Castile and Aragon and the Republic of Venice and others the like. For there is no obstacle to many principalities and perfect republics being under one prince.

Vitoria has seemingly not forgotten the distinction which he formerly made between the civil power's *potestas* residing in the commonwealth and nowhere else, and the *authoritas* vested in the king – which explains his remark that a perfect community is so only when it is not a part of another. Doubtless under the spell of the Spanish conciliar system – hence the word 'council' – the Dominican in this manner concludes that although the ruler is the most complete living embodiment of the community's self-sufficiency (sovereignty) he is nevertheless not quite its sum total. For example, two communities may share the same ruler and still enjoy totally unrelated sovereignties of their own. An independent ruler, therefore, is a necessary but not sufficient condition to make a commonwealth perfect. The community's power to declare and wage war, on the other hand, is a sufficient condition because it only materializes when the other indispensable conditions are met. True, that power is deposited in the king's hands; but not invariably, as shown by the following passage.

[32] *Ibid.*, p. 72.
[33] *Ibid.*, p. 79.

Here, however, a doubt may well arise whether, when a number of [republics] of this kind or a number of princes have one common lord or prince, they can make war of themselves and without the authorization of their superior lord. My answer is that they can do so undoubtedly, just as the kings who are subordinate to the Emperor can make war on one another without waiting for the Emperor's authorization, for (as has been said) a [republic] ought to be self-sufficient, and this it would not be, if it had not the faculty in question.[34]

If we pause to compare this statement with another which immediately preceded it, added confusion seems to result, for Vitoria stresses that 'the prince only holds his position by the election of the [republic]. Therefore he is its representative and wields its authority; aye, and where there are already lawful princes in a [republic], all authority is in their hands and without them nothing of a public nature can be done either in war or in peace.' The apparent predicament resolves itself satisfactorily, however, if we view Vitoria's position as one intent on setting the sovereignty of the nation-state on granitic foundations; an ironic twist, to be sure, that the father of modern internationalism should preface his universalist scheme by strengthening the one institution most potentially inimical to it. What Vitoria really seeks is to wipe off the board even the remnants of the old imperial idea – a preparatory move indispensable to the advent of his own ecumenical order. As will in due course become apparent, that order can only stand when the individual sovereignty of its parts (nation-states) is assured – a sovereignty defined in terms of the following: laws whereby the life of the community is ordered; a council administering its communal life; magistrates directing the activity and functions of the community toward its proper end;[35] a prince who knows no superior; and, above all, the warmongering faculty. In the end the following conclusion is inescapable: the faculty to declare and wage war, embedded even more firmly in the perfect commonwealth itself than in the prince, is the most fundamental (in that it implies all the others) of the necessary and sufficient conditions that go into the making of the republic. In previous pages, moreover, we identified this faculty with the need for self-defense, a capacity for the exercise of coercion which in turn we agreed to perceive as the civil power's function and called 'state'. In view of what has been said above, therefore, it is now justifiable to use, as far as Vitoria's scheme is concerned, 'state' in lieu of 'commonwealth' or 'republic' – an autarchic community, part of no other, whose protective shell created for self-defense encases an internal soft kernel organized as a perfect unit fully able to meet all the requirements indispensable to human fellowship, containing within itself all the means ordered to its end, and which exists

[34] *LW*, p. 169.
[35] Naszalyi, *El Estado según Francisco de Vitoria*, pp. 136–7.

as one among many identically endowed and ordered entities on a footing of absolute equality.

Vitoria is now prepared to answer the first question made mandatory by his decision to intervene in the discussions relating to Spanish colonial policy during the early part of the sixteenth century: are the Indian communities true commonwealths? In *De Indis recenter inventis. Relectio prior*, based on lectures delivered during the 1537–1538 academic year, the Spanish theologian explores the many doubts and subtleties surrounding this particular inquiry. Here are his programmatic intentions.

> The whole of this controversy and discussion was started on account of the aborigines of the New World, commonly called Indians, who came forty years ago into the power of the Spaniards, not having been previously known to our world. This present disputation about them will fall into three parts. In the first part we shall inquire by what right these Indian natives came under Spanish sway. In the second part, what rights the Spanish sovereigns obtained over them in civil and temporal matters. In the third part, what rights these sovereigns or the Church obtained over them in matters spiritual and touching religion, in the course of which an answer will be given to the question before us.[36]

Were there among the Indians, before the Spaniards' arrival, any who were the true princes and overlords of others? 'The people in question,' reflects Vitoria, 'were in peaceable possession of their goods, both publicly and privately. Therefore, unless the contrary is shown, they must be treated as owners and not be disturbed in their possession unless cause be shown.' And no other cause could be conceived unless that the Indians 'were sinners or were unbelievers or were witless or irrational'. The first two objections to the natives' exercise of true dominion the Dominican swiftly demolishes and buries under an avalanche of precedent and authority. 'Whether the Indians lacked ownership because of want of reason or unsoundness of mind' is a tougher nut to crack. Vitoria agrees that irrational creatures can have no dominion. 'But what about those suffering from unsoundness of mind? I mean a perpetual unsoundness whereby they neither have nor is there any hope that they will have the use of reason.' In this instance he wavers. 'Let our third proposition be: It seems that they can still have dominion, because they can suffer wrong; therefore they have a right, but whether they can have civil dominion is a question which I leave to the jurists.' Had Vitoria believed the Indians to be of unsound mind the matter would obviously have been terminated at this point. But in fact he does not at all consider the natives to be deprived of reason. A most significant concession, for the heated disputa-

[36] *DI*, p. 116.

tions which so often divided Vitoria's learned contemporaries centered precisely around this issue: the nature of the Indians and their questionable rationality.

> The Indian aborigines are not barred on this ground from the exercise of true dominion. This is proved from the fact that the true state of the case is that they are not of unsound mind, but have, according to their kind, the use of reason. This is clear, because there is certain method in their affairs, for they have polities which are orderly arranged and they have definite marriage and magistrates, overlords, laws, and workshops, and a system of exchange, all of which call for the use of reason...Now, the most conspicuous feature of man is reason, and power is useless which is not reducible to action.

Vitoria's conclusion is that in essence the Indian commonwealths stand on the same footing as any Christian state.

> The upshot of all the preceding is, then, that the aborigines undoubtedly had true dominion in both public and private matters, just like Christians, and that neither their princes nor private persons could be despoiled of their property on the ground of their not being true owners.[37]

Needless to say the Dominican's stand on this issue will substantially condition the orientation of his internationalism and give his ecumenical vision a coherence and grandeur conspicuously absent from the equally ambitious schemes of his Christian humanist contemporaries. On the other hand, this does not mean that Vitoria was unaware of, or indifferent to, the opinions of those who argued that the Indians seemed 'to be *servi a natura* because of their incapability of self-government'. As a matter of fact he attempts to answer those critics of the natives by expounding his own interpretation of that Aristotelian doctrine on which the critics themselves based their appraisal of and solution for the 'Indian question'. It is of interest to reproduce here Vitoria's entire explanation of Aristotle's intentions because we will extensively return to the subject in the context of Sepúlveda's supposed advocacy of slavery as the state best fitting the Indians' condition.

> Aristotle certainly did not mean to say that such as are not over-strong mentally are by nature subject to another's power and incapable of dominion alike over themselves and other things; for this is civil and legal slavery, wherein none are slaves by nature. Nor does the Philosopher mean that, if any by nature are of weak mind, it is permissible to seize their patrimony and enslave them and put them up for sale; but what he means is that by defect of their nature they need to be ruled and governed by others and that it is good for them to be subject to others, just as sons need to be subject to their parents until of full age, and a wife to her husband. And that this is the Philosopher's intent is clear from his

[37] *DI*, pp. 120–28.

corresponding remark that some are by nature masters, those, namely, who are of strong intelligence. Now, it is clear that he does not mean hereby that such persons can arrogate to themselves a sway over others in virtue of their superior wisdom, but that nature has given them capacity for rule and government. Accordingly, even if we admit that the aborigines in question are as inept and stupid as alleged, still dominion can not be denied to them, nor are they to be classed with the slaves of civil law. True, some right to reduce them to subjection can be saved on this reason and title.[38]

In sum, according to the Dominican the perfect state is not necessarily one whose members have knowledge of the true God. A state is a perfect community. In turn a perfect community 'is one which is complete in itself, that is, which is not part of another community but has its own laws and its own council and its own magistrates'. These are the necessary attributes characterizing a sovereign state, and thus the Vitorian state is not limited to Christendom; infidels, pagans, and heretics have the same potential as Christians to form perfect communities. The inadequacies of their spiritual position do not prejudice their rights to true dominion in things public or private. Christian law is not an essential prerequisite for the existence of a true commonwealth; only natural law is. And natural law can be known merely through the use of reason; perfection or lack thereof in a state is not a function of revelation but of reason. In the words of James Brown Scott:

The corner-stone of Victoria's [sic] system was equality of States, applicable not merely to the States of Christendom and of Europe but also to the barbarian principalities in the Western World of Columbus. The modern State is looked upon from within and from without. From within it is a thing of constitutional law; from without, of international law. From within it must be self-sufficient, in order to be a perfect State; from without it is but a member of the international community. These are precisely the elements to be found in Victoria's [sic] conception of the State.[39]

On the lawful and the illegitimate titles for the reduction of the Indians

In the presence of these imposing premises we cannot but ask, how does Vitoria propose to explain – let alone justify or sanction – Spanish intervention in America? To the end of clarifying this crucial issue are devoted the second and third sections of *De Indis*. 'It being premised, then, that the Indian aborigines are or were true owners, it remains to inquire by what title the Spaniards could have come into possession of them and of their country.' Following the rigorous pattern so characteristic of that systematic

[38] *Ibid.*, p. 128.
[39] Brown Scott, *The Spanish Origin*, p. 281.

technique which is the glory of Scholasticism at its best, the Spaniard lists first those 'titles [for the reduction of the Indians] which might be alleged, but which are not adequate or legitimate'. In the first place, since the Emperor is not and has never been lord of the whole world 'the Spaniards cannot justify...[t]heir seizure of the provinces in question' on the ground that their own king is the Emperor; identical argument applies to the claim that Pope could have given the kings of Spain sovereignty over the aborigines in question: 'the Pope is not civil or temporal lord of the whole world in the proper sense of the words "lordship" and "civil power"'. A third title, Vitoria continues, commonly proposed is one which accrues from the right of discovery – namely, that 'as the Spaniards were the first to discover and occupy the provinces in question, they are in lawful possession thereof, just as if they had discovered some lonely and hitherto uninhabited region'. Such pretext the Dominican dismisses with ill-concealed contempt: 'Not much, however, need be said about this third title of ours, because, as proved above, the barbarians were true owners, both from the public and from the private standpoint.'[40]

More serious, however, was the plea justifying Spanish occupation on the basis of the Indians' refusal to accept the faith of Christ; if nothing else its importance can be gauged by the fact that Vitoria sees fit to counter it by means of six propositions. First, 'before the barbarians heard anything about Christianity, they did not commit the sin of unbelief by not believing in Christ'. Second, 'the Indians in question are not bound, directly the Christian faith is announced to them, to believe it, in such a way that they commit mortal sin by not believing in it, merely because it has been declared and announced to them that Christianity is the true religion and that Christ is the Saviour and Redeemer of the world, without miracles or any other proof of persuasion'. Effective as the arguments thus forwarded in these two propositions may be in countering the Indians' absence of faith as a valid title for Spanish occupation, however, they should in no way be construed as proof of Vitoria's willingness to let the Indians escape the spiritual penalties incurred by arbitrarily rejecting the true faith. Propositions three and four are precisely aimed at clarifying this very point: 'If the Indians, after being asked and admonished to hear the peaceful preachers of religion, refused, they would not be excused of mortal sin', and 'if the Christian faith be put before the aborigines with demonstration, and this be accompanied by an upright life, well-ordered according to the law of nature (an argument which weighs much in confirmation of the truth), and this be done not once only and perfunctorily, but diligently and zealously, the aborigines are bound to receive the faith of Christ under penalty of mortal sin.' But, confesses the

[40] *DI*, pp. 129–39.

theologian in his fifth proposition, this may precisely be the essential ingredient absent from the manner in which the Indians have been introduced to the religion of the Spaniards. 'It is not sufficiently clear to me that the Christian faith has yet been so put before the aborigines and announced to them that they are bound to believe it or commit fresh sin.' And yet, even had the faith of Christ been presented to the Indians in a fashion beyond reproach it will not do to use the aborigines' refusal to abide by it as a reason to subjugate them. Such is the conclusion of Vitoria's sixth proposition. 'Although the Christian faith may have been announced to the Indians with adequate demonstration and they have refused to receive it, yet this is not a reason which justifies making war on them and depriving them of their property.'[41]

Granted, then, the barbarians' mere infidelity may not be a rightful cause for establishing Spanish rule over them. Indirectly, however, the sins which continue to plague their lives by this very refusal to embrace the faith of Christ are cause sufficient to justify Spanish dominion over them and their goods. This fifth title carried considerable weight among those thinkers – Sepúlveda, for example – who viewed the Indians' rational capacity with misgivings, an excellent reason, therefore, for us to examine it in some detail. Vitoria begins with a brief review of its supporters' general stand.

Another, and a fifth, title is seriously put forward, namely, the sins of these Indian aborigines. For it is alleged that, though their unbelief or their rejection of the Christian faith is not a good reason for making war on them, yet they may be attacked for other mortal sins which (so it is said) they have in numbers, and those very heinous. A distinction is here drawn with regard to mortal sins, it being asserted that there are some sins, which are not against the law of nature, but only against divine positive law, and for those the aborigines cannot be attacked in war, while there are other sins against nature, such as cannibalism, and promiscuous intercourse with mothers and sisters and with males, and for these they can be attacked in war and so compelled to desist therefrom. The principle in each case is that, in the case of sins which are against positive law, it cannot be clearly shown to the Indians that they are doing wrong, whereas in the case of the sins which are against the law of nature, it can be shown to them that they are offending God, and they may consequently be prevented from continuing to offend Him. Further they can be compelled to keep the law which they themselves profess. Now, this law is the law of nature. Therefore.[42]

The Dominican remains unmoved by the seeming persuasiveness of this reasoning. Instead he asserts that 'Christian princes cannot, even by the authorization of the Pope, restrain the Indians from sins against the

[41] *Ibid.*, pp. 140–44.   [42] *Ibid.*, pp. 145–6.

law of nature or punish them because of those sins.' Vitoria sustains his conclusion with proofs which, among other things, dramatically reveal the difficulties faced by contemporary thinkers when endeavoring to apply the abstract concepts of natural law to concrete instances. Thus he criticizes his opponents for justifying their advocacy of coercion 'either universally for sins against natural law [*contra legem naturae*], such as theft, fornication, and adultery, or particularly for sins against nature [*contra naturam*], such as those which Saint Thomas deals with (Secunda secundae, qu. 154, arts. 11, 12), the phrase 'sin against nature' [*peccatum contra naturam*] being employed not only of what is contrary to the law of nature, but also what is against the natural order [*contra ordinem naturalem*] and is called uncleanness [*immunditia*] in II *Corinthians*, ch. 12, according to the commentators, such as intercourse with boys and with animals, or intercourse of woman with woman, whereon see *Romans*, ch. 1'. This distinction between natural law and natural order will acquire even greater relevance when we examine (Chapter 7) the accusations levelled since the sixteenth century against Sepúlveda. Even in this instance it is put to good use by Vitoria.

Now, if they limit themselves [the defenders of the fifth title] to the second meaning [see above], they are open to the argument that homicide is just as grave a sin, and, therefore, it is clear that, if it is lawful in the case of the sins named, therefore it is lawful also in the case of homicide. Similarly, blasphemy is a sin as grave and so the same is clear; therefore. If, however, they are to be understood in the first sense, that is, as speaking of all sin against the law of nature [*contra legem naturae*], the argument against them is that the coercion in question is not lawful for fornication; therefore not for the other sins which are contrary to the law of nature...it is not every sin against the law of nature that can be clearly shown to be such, at any rate to every one.[43]

But it is in the context of the sixth title, the Indians' voluntary choice, that we see Vitoria at his best both as a shrewd judge of human nature and a pragmatist not unwilling to face up to the realities accompanying the Spaniards' appearance in the New World. 'For on the arrival of the Spaniards we find them declaring to the aborigines how the King of Spain has sent them for their good and admonishing them to receive and accept him as lord and king; and the aborigines replied that they were content to do so.' Vitoria approves of any such transference of dominion; in fact, he will later support the idea that a people have the right to change rulers – after all, what else could he possibly have meant when he reasoned that the ultimate source of political power lies with the commonwealth? But his approval is conditioned by the understanding that 'fear and

[43] *Ibid.*, p. 146.

ignorance, which vitiate every choice, ought to be absent'. Alas, this *sine qua non* of legitimacy Vitoria does not think was present in the case under consideration, 'for the Indians did not know what the Spaniards were seeking. Further, we find the Spaniards seeking it in armed array from an unwarlike and timid crowd.' In addition, the Dominican decides that even had these two conditions, absence of fear and ignorance, been rightly fulfilled it would still have been unlawful for the Indians to accept the Spanish king as their suzerain, for 'inasmuch as the aborigines, as said above, had real lords and princes, the populace could not procure new lords without other reasonable cause...[and] these lords themselves could not appoint a new prince without the assent of the populace'. In conclusion, 'seeing that in such cases of choice and acceptance as these there are not present all the requisite elements of a valid choice, the title under review is utterly inadequate and unlawful for seizing and retaining the provinces in question'. Faced with the seventh and last title – 'possession by a special grant of God' – Vitoria cannot repress a chuckle when dismissing it as nonsense with a shaft aimed at the self-righteous attitude of its proponents: 'would that, apart from the sin of unbelief, there might be no greater sins in morals among certain Christians than there are among those barbarians!'[44]

The doctrinal justification for depriving the various apologies for conquest listed above of their alleged legitimacy rests squarely on the basic assumption which decreed the existing Indian commonwealths to be on a footing identical with the nation-states of Christendom. Vitoria, however, does not fail to point out that such a privilege carries with it obligations whose violation will leave the Indians lawfully open to one form of intervention or another.[45] On the basis of acknowledging the Indian commonwealths as perfect Vitoria next goes on to examine the titles 'whereby the Indians might have come under the sway of the Spaniards'. On the grounds of natural society and human fellowship the Spaniards 'have a right to travel into the lands in question and to sojourn there, provided they do no harm to the natives, and the natives may not prevent them'. Violation of this human privilege spells out the first title enabling the Spaniards to subdue the malefactors. Implicit here is an uncompromising limitation of the rights enjoyed by the sovereign state: 'it was permissible

---

[44] *Ibid.*, p. 148.

[45] It is to be noted at this point that such intervention will invariably be accompanied by war. It cannot be otherwise, for Vitoria fully expects that the lawbreaker will oppose the just with weapons in hand. For this reason all the lawful titles for occupation listed below will be accompanied by recommendations on how to proceed forcibly against the lawless. I have omitted them here on the grounds that they will be best understood in the total context of Vitoria's analysis of the just war as reviewed in Chapter 5.

from the beginning of the world (when everything was in common) for anyone to set forth and travel wheresoever he would. Now this was not taken away by the division of property, for it was never the intention of peoples to destroy by that division the reciprocity and common user which prevailed among men, and indeed in the days of Noah it would have been inhumane to do so'.[46] What follows is a series of corollaries spelling out in detail the various nuances, from the rights of peaceful traders to the question of dual citizenship and the treatment of envoys, generally embodied in the idea that men have the privilege of and the obligation to engage in all possible forms of communication.

According to Vitoria the propagation of Christianity – 'Christians have a right to preach and declare the Gospel in barbarian lands' – is likely to bring into being several instances in which the Spaniards would be justified in subduing the Indians. To start with, 'if the Indians – whether it be their lords or the populace – prevent the Spaniards from freely preaching the Gospel, the Spaniards, after first reasoning with them in order to remove scandal, may preach it despite their unwillingness and devote themselves to the conversion of the people in question, and if need be they may then accept or even make war, until they succeed in obtaining facilities and safety for preaching the Gospel'. Victoria views this concrete case as one providing the Spaniards 'with another justification for seizing the lands and territory of the natives and for setting up new lords there and putting down the old lords'. Once the right to preach freely has been duly justified and protected it would not be too far-fetched to admit the possibility that some Indians may willingly embrace the faith. The existence of these new converts in the midst of the heathen masses could be precarious indeed. Vitoria seeks to provide for their safety by arguing that 'if any of the native converts to Christianity be subjected to force or fear by their princes in order to make them return to idolatry, this would justify the Spaniards, should other methods fail...in compelling the barbarians by force to stop such misconduct...and...at times in deposing rulers'.[47]

This is a clear example of intervention on behalf of the right of a minority. But what happens when precisely the opposite comes to pass, namely, when as a result of an unusually successful preaching campaign 'a large part of the Indians were converted to Christianity'? Under these circumstances Vitoria does not hesitate to arm the head of the Church with dangerous quasi-temporal weapons: 'the Pope might for a reasonable cause, either with or without a request from them [the converted Indians], give them a Christian sovereign and depose their other unbelieving rulers. The proof hereof is in the fact that, if this were expedient in order to

[46] *DI*, p. 151.　　　　　　　　　[47] *Ibid.*, pp. 157–8.

preserve Christianity because of fear that under unbelieving rulers converts would apostatize, that is, would lapse from the faith, or that their rulers would seize the opportunity to harass them, the Pope can change rulers in the interests of the faith.'[48] The proposal sounds reasonable and harmless enough in the present situation; when placed in the context of precedent – the medieval papal–imperial struggle, for instance – and of the relations between Vitoria's own secular and transcendental orders to be reviewed in the following chapter, it acquires ominous overtones indeed.

Another possible title is founded either on the tyranny of those who bear rule among the aborigines of America or on the tyrannical laws which work wrong to innocent folk there, such as that which allows the sacrifice of innocent people or the killing in other ways of uncondemned people for cannibalistic purposes...And it is immaterial that all the Indians assent to rules and sacrifices of this kind and do not wish the Spaniards to champion them, for herein they are not of such legal independence as to be able to consign themselves or their children to death.

It is to be noted that Vitoria is not here condoning intervention for the sake of punishing sins against natural law, but in line with his stand on the subject as reported above for the sake of sheltering the innocent. Innocence, incidentally, is now defined by Vitoria in terms which transcend the individual's own choice; a conclusion doubtless reminiscent of and founded on Christianity's injunctions against all forms of self-immolation. Voluntary choice, rejected before by Vitoria, is now accepted, albeit in more refined form, as a legitimate sixth title: 'If the Indians, aware alike of the prudent administration and the humanity of the Spaniards, were of their own notion, both rulers and ruled, to accept the King of Spain as their sovereign. This could be done and would be a lawful title, by the law natural too, seeing that a State can appoint any one it will to be its lord, and therefore the consent of all is not necessary, but the consent of the majority suffices.'[49]

The eighth and final title – the seventh is straightforward enough: the defense and aid of 'allies and friends' – is exceedingly interesting because it goes to the heart of Sepúlveda's own justification for Spanish rule in the Indies, and also because Vitoria, heretofore so assertive and sure of his ground, now hesitates and wavers.

There is another title which can indeed not be asserted, but brought up for discussion, and some think it a lawful one. I dare not affirm it at all, nor do I entirely condemn it. It is this: Although the aborigines in question are (as has been said above) not wholly unintelligent, yet they are little short of that condition, and so are unfit to found or administer a lawful State up to the

---

[48] *Ibid.*, pp. 158–9.   [49] *Ibid.*, pp. 159–60.

standard required by human and civil claims. Accordingly they have no proper laws nor magistrates, and are not even capable of controlling their family affairs; they are without any literature or arts, not only the liberal arts, but the mechanical arts also; they have no careful agriculture and no artisans; and they lack many other conveniences, yea necessaries, of human life. It might, therefore, be maintained that in their own interests the sovereigns of Spain might undertake the administration of their country, providing them with prefects and governors for their towns, and might even give them new lords, so long as this was clearly for their benefit. I say there would be some force in this contention; for if they were all wanting in intelligence, there is no doubt that this would not only be a permissible, but also a highly proper, course to take.[50]

There is no doubt that the Dominican's doubting has brought us roundly back to the old irreducible proposition linchpin for the entire controversy over the New World: the rationality of its inhabitants. This subject, which will be more fully taken up again in future pages within the context of Sepúlveda's ideology, is one whose importance in shaping Spanish Renaissance political thought can hardly be overestimated. And not merely because of its direct and immediate impact on the issue of the American question – by no means a negligible one, for, as just reported above, it was capable of perplexing Vitoria – but, above all, because it embodies a group of ideas inseparable from the political philosophy of thinkers like Vitoria and Sepúlveda: the doctrine of the just war, natural law, the *jus gentium*, civil and natural slavery. Not unexpectedly, then, these concepts will play an overwhelming role in the remaining chapters of this monograph. All too often Vitoria and Sepúlveda, particularly the latter, neglect to offer the kind of detailed explanation that the modern reader finds most helpful in relation to such things as the law of nations and the differences between civil and natural slavery. It would not be idle or without purpose, under the circumstances, to briefly concentrate our attention at this time on a man who not only deals concretely with such matters as our authors sometimes neglect to treat in depth, but whose unquestionable authority is amply justified by his reputation as the foremost Spanish jurist of the sixteenth century.

A brief excursus: Diego de Covarrubias

Just as Vitoria, from his chair of Prima, was responsible for the creative impetus which dominated Salamanca's Neoscholasticism until well into the seventeenth century, Diego de Covarrubias y Leyva is the figure reigning supreme over the Salmantine jurists. The 'Spanish Bartolus' was

[50] *Ibid.*, p. 161.

born in Toledo, in 1512, the son and grandson of architects. Strictly speaking, then, he belongs to the generation immediately following that of Vives, Alfonso de Castro, Vitoria, and Sepúlveda, the men whose accomplishments are synonymous with the reign of Charles V. As such he is the contemporary of luminaries best included in the age of Philip II: Melchor Cano, Fray Luis de León (1527–1591), Luis de Molina (1536–1600), Benito Arias Montano (1527–1598), Fadrique Furió Ceriol (1527–1592). His inclusion in a study broadly concentrating on publicists of the first generation, those who may properly be called Renaissance thinkers, is justified in terms similar to those which explain the presence of Furió Ceriol – his uniqueness – for Covarrubias is the age's most influential Spanish legal mind.

At the age of ten or eleven the future legist marched off to Salamanca already equipped with a knowledge of Latin and Greek. There he began his studies under Arias Barbosa and Hernán Núñez, both eminent classicists. In 1527 Covarrubias enrolled in the Faculties of Canon and Civil Law. In addition he seems to have devoted some attention to theology, attending the lectures of both Vitoria and Soto. Seventeen years after his arrival in Salamanca, Covarrubias was awarded the doctorate, presumably in both Laws; the following year he became Professor of Canon Law at the same institution. One event occurred in 1548 which brought the jurist into direct touch with America. By royal command he became part of the commission convened at Salamanca to study the advisability of granting permission for the publication of the *Democrates alter*; shortly before that he had lectured on the Indian question. In general Covarrubias seems to have shared the commission's mood: while praising Sepúlveda's learning and scholarship he found the humanist's presumed stand on Aristotle inadmissible. It was also at this time that Covarrubias' expertise in canon law made him the obvious candidate to represent the Emperor at the Council. After his return from Trent he was appointed to various posts by Philip II; in 1572, five years before his death, he became President of the Consejo de Castilla.[51]

[51] For these and other details of Covarrubias' life, see L. Pereña Vicente, *Misión de España en América 1540–1560*, and 'Diego de Covarrubias y Leyva, maestro de Salamanca', *REDC*, xi, 31(1956), pp. 191–9. See also Nicolás Antonio, *Bibliotheca hispana nova*, i; M. Hernández Vegas, *Ciudad Rodrigo. La catedral y la ciudad* (Salamanca, 1935), ii; F. Schaffstein, *La ciencia europea del Derecho penal en la época del humanismo* (Madrid, 1957); F. Marcos Rodríguez, 'Don Diego de Covarrubias y la universidad de Salamanca', *Salmanticensis*, vi, 1(1959), pp. 37–85; A. Marín López, 'El concepto del Derecho de gentes en Diego de Covarrubias y Leyva', *REDI*, ii(1954), n. 2–3, pp. 505 *et sqq.* According to Pereña Vicente, Covarrubias began to publish his works in 1545. And in 1554 his *In regulam peccatum* (cite l hereafter as *Peccatum*) appeared in print, a *relectio* which includes

One of the subjects discussed by Covarrubias in his *Practicarum quaestionum liber* is the manner in which all power and jurisdiction associated with the Castilian commonwealth resides in the king. In the course of the discussion the jurist speaks of the origin and legitimacy of political authority. He begins by unquestionably admitting man's sociability. In addition he points out that if civil society is to be of any service at all to mankind it must be headed by a ruler. This ruler only the commonwealth itself has the privilege to name, for God did not – immediately – give any society either king or prince.[52] In conclusion, the republic, created by God through the agency of natural law, may and ought to transfer its *potestas civilis* to those who with the title of king, prince, or magistrate, will care for the safety and well-being of the commonwealth.[53] In what manner is this transfer of power to take place? Covarrubias believes that in practice such a goal may be attained in either of two ways. On the one hand, the community may effect the exchange by universal suffrage. Such practice being somewhat cumbersome, however, it is advisable to simplify matters in the following manner: only the most notable among the community's members shall exercise the privilege of suffrage and their decision will be binding upon the entire commonwealth. This, in view of Covarrubias' conviction that of the three traditional regimes the royal is the most desirable, is of course nothing more than elective monarchy. On the other hand, he willingly concedes, it is possible to arrive at the same result through the hereditary principle.[54] The republic's capacity to create the ruler notwithstanding, Covarrubias emphasizes that its authority is not a human invention; it is ordained of God through natural law.[55]

None of this, to be sure, is revolutionary or even new. But we must bear in mind that Covarrubias' central purpose is not to discourse at length on abstract political theory; but to arrive, after a cursory examination of the theoretical background, at conclusions of practical legal value

most of the topics to be studied here. His lectures on the Indians were never published separately. Instead, the general concepts developed in them were included in Chapters 9–11 of *In regulum peccatum,* devoid now of their historical context. The text of the original lectures has been published by Pereña Vicente in *Misión.* The works of Covarrubias may be consulted in several different editions; among them those of Salamanca (1572, 1577), Frankfurt, Antwerp, Lyons (1661), Geneva (1762). The references to *Peccatum* will be from the Salamanca (1558) edition of the *relectio* (*Regulae peccatum, de reguli Iuris lib.6 Relectio*); the references to *Practicarum quaestionum liber* (cited hereafter as PQL) are from the edition, among other selections from Covarrubias' works, by M. Fraga Iribarne in *Textos jurídico-políticos,* trans. A. Río Seco (Madrid, 1957).

[52] *PQL,* pp. 248–51.   [55] *Ibid.,* p. 273.
[54] *Ibid.,* pp. 262–70.   [53] *Ibid.,* p. 252.

in this concrete instance connected with the particular issue of royal authority as exercised in Castile – a subject which of course lies beyond the scope of this book. What is of great interest to us, however, is what Covarrubias has to say on war and natural law. To the former problem in general we will shortly give considerable time and space. But since no jurists are represented in the forthcoming discussion there is perhaps no better place or time than here and now to give Covarrubias a hearing on the subject. The reasons are not solely altruistic; on the contrary, they are essentially practical, for the legist discusses the all-important questions of natural law and the *jus gentium* in a context – human liberty and servitude – framed against the problem of war.

With characteristic sobriety Covarrubias – in *In regulam peccatum* – opens the discussion with a statement of purpose: he will confine himself to exploring those circumstances under which a war is said to be just. To begin with, the most necessary condition that a war must fulfill if it is to be just is that it be declared by a sovereign prince.[56] Granting that the war is declared by the rightful authority, it also demands that the causes be just. And self-defense is an irrefutably just cause, as is the attempt to prevent the commonwealth from falling into the hands of a tyrant or to preserve the republic's territorial integrity and that of its people. Covarrubias holds that this twofold just cause is identical to what Saint Thomas, Cajetan, and Johann Eck – Luther's opponent at Leipzig – call the avenging of an injury. Of course, the supreme authority confirming the truth of this conclusion is none other than Saint Augustine. A third cause of undoubted justice comes into being when the subjects contumaciously refuse to obey the authority of their lawful sovereign; a fourth, reducible to the first, arises when it becomes necessary to have recourse to arms in order to recover property unjustly and violently taken. A fifth cause for commencing a war concerns the right of passage; in other words, it is licit to war upon him who denies us peaceful traveling privileges through his domains.[57]

At this point Covarrubias' study of the just war question leads him to consider the Emperor's lordship of the whole world. The point is couched in terms reminiscent of his early *relectio* on the Indians: 'We must not overlook whether the Emperor has the right to declare war on the heathen because...they refuse him obedience, or because the heathen worship idols, or because of their crimes against natural law and the persecution of the Christian religion.'[58] The jurist's answer is as uncompromising as Vitoria's. 'The Emperor...is not lord of the world, neither in what concerns jurisdiction nor in what pertains to *dominium*.'[59] It follows that

[56] *Peccatum*, pt. II, ch. 9, n. I.   [57] *Ibid.*, pt. II, ch. 9, n. 1–5.
[58] *Ibid.*, pt. II, ch. 9, n. 5.   [59] *Ibid.*, pt. II, ch. 9, n. 5.

the Emperor may not declare war against non-Christians merely because the latter refuse him submission and obedience.[60] Moreover, it is illicit to declare war against them on the basis of infidelity only.[61] Still, the jurist concedes, there are also instances when it is just to declare war against the unbelievers: first, when they occupy lands which in ages past were part of a Christian ruler's jurisdiction, a clear reference to Islam; second, if they attack and persecute Christians; third, when they refuse obedience to the authority of their prince; fourth, if they impede the free preaching of the Gospel.[62] In short, 'Christian princes may, in justice, declare against the infidels a war either of defense or vindication; but they may not wage a punitive war on those among the heathen upon whom they have no jurisdiction.'[63]

Now Covarrubias touches upon a theme which both Vitoria and Sepúlveda view as of primary importance: 'If mere infidelity is not a just cause for war one may rightfully ask if such a war may be justified by the fact that the infidels commit many crimes against nature and the natural appetites.'[64] Those who answer the question in the affirmative, continues the author, argue that such a war is a vindicative one, for it seeks to avenge the offense offered God by such abominable crimes. On the basis of the authority of 'Saint Thomas and his followers', however, Covarrubias concludes that such argumentation is insufficient to justify the war. True, those who refuse to worship the one true God sin grievously against natural law; still, such contravention does not justify the Christian prince in waging war against the sinners. On the related crime of idolatry the Salmantine doctor has some interesting opinions significant in the context of similar considerations by both Vitoria and Sepúlveda. He begins by asking rhetorically: 'What shall we say of idolatry? Is it cause enough to declare war against the unbelievers?' It is often argued, he answers, that such a war is just by divine authority as written in Deuteronomy. But, he counters, any one who carefully meditates on this point will soon realize that God's command to the children of Israel to destroy the idolaters and to deprive them of their goods and territories is a special case, one which rulers cannot imitate for their jurisdiction is clearly limited to their own subjects. Moreover, the idolatry practiced by the peoples of the Old Testament is one which carried with it the slaughtering of innocent victims and the immolation of children to the idols. For this reason it was imperative to succor the innocent; and on such ground a just war could be declared by the secular authority, even without the incentive of divine commands.[65]

[60] *Ibid.*, pt. II, ch. 9, n. 9.
[61] *Ibid.*, pt. II, ch. 10, n. 1.
[62] *Ibid.*, pt. II, ch. 10, n. 3.
[63] *Ibid.*
[64] *Ibid.*, pt. II, ch. 10, n. 4.
[65] *Ibid.*, pt. II, ch. 10, n. 4–6.

In conclusion, a war against idolaters cannot be said to be just if it is merely waged to avenge an offense committed against God. It may justly be waged, however, if, on the one hand, the idolaters oppose the preaching of the Gospel or in any other fashion encumber the Christian faith, for then the war becomes a defensive one. On the other hand, the war is justifiable in order to protect the life of the innocent – provided, of course, that the idolaters in question belong to the category described in Deuteronomy.[66] But this, Vitoria and Sepúlveda agree, is precisely the condition prevailing at least among some aborigines of the New World.

Covarrubias brings to a close this portion of *Peccatum* with the following words: 'We have briefly commented on the justice of war in order to understand better how those things which are captured in war either become the legitimate possession of the victor or must, in conscience, be restored to the vanquished.'[67] Precisely the sort of argument (the 'things' in question are the soldiers who have been taken prisoner) which justifies us – in our effort to ascertain Covarrubias' opinion on natural law, international law, and civil and natural slavery – in presenting the jurist's ideas on war at this early stage. In the eleventh chapter of *Peccatum* (Part II) the following question is implicitly posed: if the captives made in a just war justly become the victor's property and if, on the other hand, men are naturally free, how can these apparent opposites be reconciled? What is the essence of natural law and the *jus inter gentes*, and in what manner do they resolve the difficulties created by the sanctioning of certain forms of slavery?

Needless to say, nothing is of greater significance to all this than a sound and clear definition of natural law.

In my opinion *jus naturalis* is that which God taught all the animals of Creation – both rational and irrational. It manifests itself in men through their natural light; in the brutes it is apprehended through instinct. Therefore, both what is known by animals endowed with reason through natural light and what is apprehended by the brutes through instinct alone is known as *jus naturalis*. It follows that the principles discerned by man by means of his natural lights and the consequences which necessarily derive from those principles and are privy only to rational beings may be called *jus gentium*, in order to differentiate it from the *just naturalis* which nature has decreed shall rule men and the brutes simultaneously.[68]

In other words, the law of nations applies only to man; natural law governs all creatures. Both, however, are truly of *jus naturalis*. And this, continues Covarrubias, is precisely what Saint Thomas means when he separates the

66 *Ibid.*, pt. II, ch. 10, n. 5.   67 *Ibid.*, pt. II, ch. 10, n. 6.
68 *Ibid.*, pt. II, ch. 11, n. 4.

jus gentium – which is restricted to men; is apprehended by *ratio naturalis*; and is confirmed as natural, not absolutely but *secundum quid*, that is, insofar as it is useful and convenient to the human *conventus* – from the *jus naturalis* common to all animals and said to be natural in an absolute manner and of itself as, for example, the union of male and female, the education of their offspring, and other similar instances. It is clear, continues the author, that both men and the brutes devoid of reason often act similarly. The difference lies in that the former carry out these actions compelled by the *jus naturalis* taken *formaliter* (that is, insofar as the compulsion derives from reason), whereas in the latter the *jus naturalis* acts *materialiter* only (*'id est quod ad actus etiam brutis commune est'*). It follows that natural law, taken absolutely, can be understood either formally or materially. Formally, natural law is a repository of first principles; determining what is absolutely just in itself as defined by reason only and not concerned with whether it is convenient or useful to anything beyond itself. To this category belong such axioms as 'we must rule ourselves by reason', 'we must do evil unto no one'; and all others which embody that which is just in its absolute essence without reference to the benefits which may accrue from them. On the basis of these premises derived from Saint Thomas, Covarrubias agrees with the Dominican doctor that the *jus naturalis* is different from the *jus gentium* in that the latter does not derive from absolute natural reason but from natural law aimed at the utility and convenience of something else. And this is why jurists sometimes consider the law of nations to be identical with natural law while at other times they judge it to be different. To what has been said, Covarrubias concludes, 'I add with pleasure what I have read in the treatise *De justitia et jure* of Domingo de Soto (bk. 1, q. 1, art. 3), namely, that those principles which can be deduced from the absolute nature of things are of natural law; on the other hand, those which do not emanate from the absolute nature of things but, rather, may be deduced when those things are considered in relation to the circumstances surrounding them and are ordered to certain ends, are said to belong to the *jus gentium*.'[69]

Having established the difference between the law of nature and the law of nations Covarrubias returns to his central preoccupation: the *jus belli*. Pursuing his inquiry into the nature of slavery resulting from defeat in war the jurist asks whether there is some manner of servitude which may in truth be said to be of natural law and decreed by nature. His answer is simple and to the point: 'as Aristotle points out, it is beyond question that some men are *naturae servi*. Nature itself has decreed that the less wise and perfect are destined to be ruled by better endowed men.

[69] *Ibid.*

God Himself created humankind in such a manner that some are superior to others in *scientia et virtus*.' The authorities cited, in addition to Aristotle, are Plato, Cicero, Saint Ambrose, Saint Augustine, Turrecremata, and Domingo de Soto, among others.[70]

Covarrubias emphatically points out that the servitude thus defined has nothing to do with war. On the contrary, 'the servitude which we have said to be instituted by nature has nothing to do with violence and coercion. It is rather born out of the honor and reverence owed the old by the young, the noble by the lowborn, the father by the children, the husband by the wife; it also results from the fact that it is useful for the less able that he be subjected to the more talented.' Consequently, the jurist proceeds, this natural servitude, which seems to have prevailed even during the world's period of innocence, has nothing to do with that herile condition which was later established by the *jus gentium* and which seeks, not the well-being of the subject, but only the benefit of the ruler.[71] The latter condition is in truth slavery, derives from the *jus gentium*, and comes about as a result of the law of war whereby the captive becomes subject – against natural liberty – to another's *dominium*. Covarrubias agrees with, among others, Justinian's opinion that all men are born naturally free. But this is strictly true only if understood in the context of that age when men lived solely under the compulsion of natural law. As human malice grew it became necessary to safeguard the well-being of the commonwealth against those who would destroy it by waging unjust wars. And to punish these malefactors civil slavery came into being; slavery sanctioned by human and international law permitting war captives to become slaves. And even though slavery is contrary to nature – man's natural freedom – both Aristotle and Saint Augustine teach that it has been made mandatory, through the unanimous consent of all peoples, by man's malice and to punish those who would wage unjust wars against their neighbors.[72] In conclusion, Covarrubias rejects the notion that slavery is of natural law. Since the latter creates men free it only sanctions man's subordination to man in political terms and on intellectual grounds, or in consideration to age and family hierarchy.

In view of what shall transpire in forthcoming chapters it is highly pertinent that we close our brief study of Covarrubias with some relevant comments relating to Sepúlveda. To begin with, the presence of Soto among the authorities relied upon by Covarrubias is of considerable significance; for in his *De justitia et jure* (bk. IV, q. 2, art. 2) Soto admits the naturalness of that subjection which binds the less wise to the more intelligent.

[70] *Ibid.*, pt. II, ch. II, n. 5.   [71] *Ibid.*
[72] *Ibid.*, pt. II, ch. II, n. 2–4.

Aristotle. . .rightly identified two kinds of *servitus*: one natural and another legal. Natural servitude is that exerted by men of greater talent over those of lesser intellect. For, in the same manner as the soul has the advantage over the body, there are within the human race men better endowed than others. And for this very reason nature, in its wisdom, gave some men the wit to command and others the strength to serve.

Equally important is Covarrubias' own agreement with Aristotle on the same question. And both scholars had been members of the Salmantine commission which had judged against Sepúlveda on the matter of the second *Democrates* – a treatise largely woven around Aristotle's idea of natural servitude understood in a manner not substantially different from Covarrubias' and Soto's interpretation. Moreover, Soto – although not Covarrubias – also sat at the Valladolid *junta* of theologians (four) and jurists (six) which presided over the Las Casas–Sepúlveda disputation. The final report of the jurists – which included representatives from three Councils: Castile, Military Orders, and Inquisition – unanimously favored Sepúlveda, a fact not without significance for often during the American controversy jurists and theologians are found ranged in opposing sides of the issue. Uncertainty clouds the theologians' individual reports. Soto may have refrained from drafting his; Arévalo (the only non-Dominican among them) favored Sepúlveda; and it may have been Bartolomé Carranza who sided with Las Casas. The case of the remaining theologian, Melchor Cano, presents some singularities. He left Valladolid bound for Trent before presenting his own conclusions. But without question he would have been opposed to Sepúlveda, for he had earlier gone on record against him. Moreover, Cano, although in general terms agreeing with Covarrubias and Soto on the twofold nature of servitude, rejects his colleagues' conclusions on the question of political *dominium*. First, *servus* is he who is subjected to his lord in such a way that he has no power of his own. Second, we also call *servus* the man who is the ruler's subject; for instance, the citizens are the prince's *servi* in the second sense, and so are the children their father's *servi*.[73] So far Cano's stand in no way differs from Covarrubias'. But the theologian goes on to deny that any man can be *servus* (in the second manner) to any other man – the one exception, of course, being the children and the wife within the family. The reason is simple: no man has been created lord by nature; at best he has been invested with political authority by other men. He is willing to concede, nevertheless, that the wisest should be elected to rule. A suggestion that must be understood precisely as such: merely an exhortation to follow the

[73] Melchor Cano, *De dominio Indiorum*, q. 1, n. 12; in Pereña Vicente, *Misión de España en América*. Cited hereafter as *Dominio*.

most prudent course. And it is precisely in this exhortative, as opposed to comminatory, spirit, argues Cano, that Saint Thomas' reflections on the subject must be interpreted.[74] Finally, Cano emphasizes, 'a sovereign cannot conquer the barbarians for the latter's benefit'.[75]

[74] *Ibid.*, q. 1, n. 13.
[75] *Ibid.*, q. 1, n. 15.

4

Francisco de Vitoria (II)

The international order: sovereignty vs. jus gentium

Despite the perplexing timidity revealed by his sudden vacillations – all the more unexpected on account of the assertiveness previously displayed – Vitoria's decision to endow the Indian republics with all the attributes defining the perfect commonwealth still stands; and it automatically postulates over and above the secular order exemplified by the state an additional entity: the international order. As a consequence two forces are brought into endless confrontation. One is the *respublica* or *civitas*, a perfect community which tends toward total independence; the other is mankind, constituting *aliquo modo* a universal *respublica* which antedates the partition of the globe. Correspondingly, there come into existence several forms of *jus* aiming at as many individual well-beings and whose overlapping prerogatives must be harmoniously reconciled one way or another, for such is the price exacted by the universal good.

The unfolding pattern is interesting in the extreme, its apparent circularity notwithstanding. In the beginning there existed a universal society. It was, in a sense, destroyed; and in its stead the nation-state, protected by the formidable defenses which sovereignty gives it, emerged as the consummate embodiment of the natural order. No sooner, however, has the order of the state in this fashion been raised to a position of unquestionable supremacy in the realm of earthly affairs than Vitoria with seeming perversity affirms its subordination to a still more telling form of fellowship – the international order – tracing the ancestry of its ideals to the universal society of man's prehistory. Regardless, therefore, of how powerful the internal bonds which give reality to the territorial state's autarchy may be, their vigor cannot hope to match the strength of the shackles which somehow fetter together all the orb's perfect communities into a *totum* seeking to reproduce the completeness of primeval society. An ideal, surely, which in its essentials in no way differs from Vives' claim

98 Francisco de Vitoria (II)

that the coming of Christ has made possible a return to the ecumenical unity of yesterday. In short,

the international community...in the Victorian [sic] system, possesses the inherent right to impose its will – in the form of law applicable to the individual State – and to punish its violation, not because of a treaty, of a pact or a covenant, but because of an international need. For just as the State is not a 'perfect' State if it be not self-sufficient so would the international community be imperfect if it were not self-sufficient in a superior and universal sense and if it could not impose its collective judgment, in the form of the law of nations, upon humanity...and upon the States as members of the international community.[1]

The question suggested by all this is obvious: what can keep the myriad components of the whole from bursting apart in chaotic anarchy? The answer, so Vitoria would have it, is equally self-evident: the *jus gentium*.

The subject of the *jus inter gentes*, which more than any other single item in Vitoria's scheme defines his political doctrine, is most extensively treated in the Dominican's study of question 57 (*De justitia*), article 3 (*De jure gentium et naturali*), of Aquinas' IIa–IIae.[2] Vitoria begins by asking 'whether the law of nations may be distinguished from the natural law'. The answer comes in the shape of two propositions.

The first proposition is: That which is, in the first way, equal and absolutely just, is called natural law; that is, it is of natural right. The second proposition: That which is equal and just in the second way, as it were a certain disposition of things with relation to a third just thing, is *jus gentium*. And so that which is not in itself just, but is derived from human statute firmly established in reason, is called *jus gentium*, so that, on its own account it does not imply equity, but on account of something else, as in the matter of war, and other things. Whence it appears that the *jus gentium* may be distinguished from the *jus naturale*.[3]

It would seem, then, that the *jus gentium* is the product of necessity. In other words, the law of nations bears to natural law as the creation of civil society does to man's pristine and universal fellowship. If this analogy holds, the *jus gentium* should be defined not as of natural law but as of human law. And this is precisely Vitoria's conclusion. In opposition to the jurists the theologian judges 'the natural law [to be] an absolute good, and not a relative good: but the *jus gentium* is only relatively good...the *jus gentium* has no equity of itself, from its own nature, but was established

---

[1] J. Brown Scott, *The Spanish Origin*, p. 283.
[2] Cited hereafter as *DJG*. Unless otherwise indicated all references will be to the translation of F. C. Macken, in J. Brown Scott's *The Spanish Origin*, Appendix E.
[3] *DJG*, p. cxi.

as inviolable from agreement among men. And so I answer the principal doubt with this conclusion: That *jus gentium* ought to be placed more under positive law than under natural law.'[4]

In a very real sense this admission opens a Pandora's box, for if the *jus gentium* is merely of positive law we may properly ask whether men are morally bound to obey it. To begin with, Vitoria explains, 'concerning human written law, there is no doubt but that to act contrary to it is a sin, because those laws, as we have said many times, are binding in the court of conscience'. But, after all, the *jus gentium* remains an unwritten law. True, he concedes, 'but we say of the *jus gentium* that a certain kind of the *jus gentium* is from the common consensus of all peoples and nations'. In addition, 'the *jus gentium* so closely approaches to the natural law that the natural law cannot be preserved without this *jus gentium*'. It follows that 'it is always illicit to violate the *jus gentium*, because it is contrary to the common consensus'.[5] This argument is couched in even more forceful terms in *De potestate civili*.

International law has not only the force of a pact and agreement among men, but also the force of law; for the world as a whole, being in a way one single State, has the power to create laws that are just and fitting for all persons, as are the rules of international law. Consequently, it is clear that they who violate these international rules, whether in peace or in war, commit a mortal sin.[6]

But since the *jus gentium* is admittedly not of natural law, is it true that the latter cannot be observed unless the former be obeyed? Vitoria answers that the law of nations is 'not wholly necessary, but nearly necessary' to the conservation of natural law. Since the rational imperative is in this manner confessed to be missing, Vitoria resorts to expediency: if there were no *jus gentium* natural law would survive only with great difficulty: 'Indeed the world could go on, if possessions should be held in common as is the case among the religious; however, it would be with great difficulty for men would be likely to rush into discords and wars.'[7]

This appeal to expediency is a discordant note in a scheme which true to the scholarly tradition nourishing it is otherwise so solidly founded on reason. Undaunted Vitoria proceeds next to ascertain whether international law, anchored not on natural but on positive law, can be abrogated. He denies this possibility 'because, when once anything is established from a virtual consensus of the whole world, and admitted it, it is necessary that the whole world should likewise agree as to its abrogation; but that, however, is impossible, because it is impossible that the consensus of the whole

---

[4] *Ibid.*, p. cxii.
[6] *DPC*, p. xc.

[5] *Ibid.*, pp. cxii–cxiii.
[7] *DJG*, p. cxiii.

world could be obtained for the abrogation of the law of nations'.[8] So far, then, Vitoria has set down on secure foundations both the validity and authority of the *jus gentium*. It is in the nature of things, however, that recognition of a given authority's legitimacy and its prerogatives should be but the first step. In other words, a *vis directiva* is a necessary but not sufficient condition for the fulfillment of those ends for which the authority was created. A *vis coactiva* is indispensable. What, then, is the law of nation's coercive organ? Hamilton maintains that Vitoria 'makes no attempt here to solve the problem of coercion'.[9] And Menéndez-Reigada does not stray too far from this conclusion when he notes: 'The subject of the supranational authority is the collective reason of the whole world, but the organ capable of authoritatively formulating international law does not yet exist.'[10] Morally sanctioned, for its ethical obligation is beyond doubt, the *jus gentium*, so the argument goes, lacks 'clout'. In my opinion this point of view does not quite correspond to the facts, for Vitoria does in fact endow the law of nations with a coercive organ – the just war. Its shortcomings lie elsewhere, in the direction of who – the prince waging a just war – is the executor of that coercive *potestas*, a subject which can be taken up most prifitably in the context of the next chapter.

The order of grace

It would not, I hazard to say, be too far off the mark to insist that Vitoria's scheme as offered so far suggests a structure of secular jurisdictions whose hierarchical distribution brings to mind the shape of a pyramid. At the broadest level lies the individual, not meant to live alone and therefore possessing no defined jurisdiction; next, the family, governed by the will of the father; further up we meet those imperfect communities whose juridical existence is doubtful since they are ruled by the authorities of the perfect communities to which they belong; next comes the state with all its privileges and prerogatives. Finally, at the very apex, lies the all-embracing authority of the whole society of man. One important segment of the Vitorian system, however, is missing – the supernatural or transcendental order, one which I have so far omitted because its far-reaching implications can be properly gauged only against the background of Vitoria's full secular blueprint.

In *De potestate Ecclesiae prior* Vitoria categorically asserts the existence of two *potestates* indispensable to the preservation of justice; one to manage worldly affairs and rule earthly life, and another to govern

8 *Ibid.*
9 Hamilton, *Political Thought in Sixteenth-Century Spain*, p. 105.
10 Menéndez-Reigada, 'El sistema ético–jurídico de Vitoria', p. 320.

spiritual matters and order the spiritual life of man.[11] The reason for the presence of these two levels of authority is evident, for if the well-being to which man must be directed and the evil from which he must be separated pertained only to social life one *potestas* would suffice. As it is, the life of the faithful is aimed not only at the civil end but, more energetically and principally, at his eternal salvation; two powers are therefore needed. But, Vitoria asks, are these two *potestates* of equal right? In what sense may they, if at all, be said to be different? The Dominican answers that the difference between the two lies in their origin. Whereas the civil power is of natural law there is far more to the spiritual *potestas* than the law of nature. The former accrues from the republic because it serves to achieve her natural end; but even though natural law springs from the divine will its province does not extend beyond the confines of nature and neither, therefore, does that of the civil power. The limit thus set for the secular *potestas*, on the other hand, does not bind the spiritual, for the latter, now resting with the Church, is both mediately and immediately of divine positive law and as such its authority goes well beyond the power not only of the particular state but that of the whole world as well.[12] Vitoria, then, brings his answer to a conclusion with a teleological note which bodes ill for the future of his scheme: not only are the two powers in question different, they are also unequal in relation to one another: 'Everything that has a goal must be considered in relation to that goal; therefore, the end of the spiritual power (and so the power itself) is superior to that of the temporal authority in the same measure as the perfect well-being and felicity of man exceed the human and earthly happiness.'[13]

It is also unquestionable, however, that the temporal republic is a perfect republic. As such it need not be subordinate to anything external to itself, for otherwise it would no longer be complete.[14] Under the circumstances the civil power can in no way be dependent on the spiritual power. And yet, is the civil power truly and unconditionally autonomous? Is there no hierarchy of order between the temporal authority and the spiritual *potestas*? This is the question asked since the thirteenth century by all those publicists who, while rejecting the solution of Marsilius of Padua, had nevertheless attempted to emancipate the civil authority from the supervision of ecclesiastical power. Vitoria himself concludes that even as the civil *potestas* is complete, perfect, and has its own immediate end, it is also in some way *ordinata ad potestatem spiritualem*. The proof is that human happiness being imperfect, it has to be ordained (*ordinatur*) to some higher end – that perfect beatitude which is the supernatural happiness;

[11] *DPE* I, p. 9.   [12] *Ibid.*, pp. 40, 42.
[13] *Ibid.*, p. 61.   [14] *Ibid.*, p. 67.

the two *potestates*, then, cannot possibly be understood as one would two entirely different republics, as for instance, France and England.[15]

The subordination of one power to the other is further demonstrated by the following fundamental condition: if the civil government caused any harm to the spiritual administration, even if through actions useful and proper to the civil power, the king would have to change them. The validity of this axiom is confirmed by the fact that the Church is one body; and it does not become two because there is a civil and a spiritual republic. In a body everything is united and interwoven: the offices, the ends, the authorities; and since in no way could we say that spiritual things are because of the material ones we must conclude that, on the contrary, the latter depend on the former.[16] Again, cautions Vitoria, two things must be remembered. The first one relates to the relation between secular authority and the Pope. Doubtless the latter is the embodiment of the spiritual *potestas* and in this sense the former is subject to his authority. But this under no circumstances must be taken to imply that civil authority is in any way subordinate or subject to the Pope's temporal power.[17] Secondly, the unequal nature of the two orders does not arise as a result of any imperfection on the part of the civil *potestas*; within its own province the latter is perfect. It cannot be said that the civil power is in bondage to the spiritual in the same way that the authority of a governor depends on the royal authority or *eo modo quo ars, sive facultas inferior dependet a superiori*. The power of the former is neither independent nor perfect whereas the authority of the secular order is in itself and by virtue of its very essence independent, absolute, and perfect. The most conclusive proof, Vitoria claims, lies with the fact that even if there were no spiritual power or eternal life there would still be a civil power.[18]

Let us now attempt to schematize what we have so far learned of the structure of Vitoria's scheme and how its shape is molded by the further refinement which the author's interpretation of the two orders' independence inevitably introduces. To start with, the scaffold supporting the Vitorian universe is a harmonious system composed of various autonomous orders whose true independence can only be understood in terms of the ends they serve and for which they come into being in the first place. The first of these orders, the sovereign commonwealth or state, is of natural law, independent of any other order, and *ordinatur* to an end which is also independent of the end associated with any different order. The end of the state is valid and objective everywhere in the world; it cannot therefore be called specifically Christian because its basis being the

[15] *Ibid.*, pp. 72–3.   [16] *Ibid.*, p. 118.
[17] *Ibid.*, p. 72.   [18] *Ibid.*, p. 71.

very nature of the perfect community it is as valid for Christian as for pagan states. The whole Vitorian idea of the state rests on this foundation:[19] what touches upon matters pertaining to worldly affairs is the province of the state, and within that province the ends of the state are purely secular and unchallenged by any other order.

The same thing applies to the authority of the *jus gentium* within the scope of man's secular *totus orbis*. This much the secular and international orders have in common. But there are in the world matters which transcend both the law of nature and its close associate, the *jus gentium*. Man's salvation is an example – indeed, the most ultimate and telling of all. To care for this need of man exists a third and superior order, the transcendental, decreed by divine positive law. The worldly life of man, then, develops against a framework given by the balanced and harmonious coexistence of the order of the state and the order of the world community. The total life of man, however, thrives against a still more complete background which supplements the secular framework by adding to it the third, or supernatural, *ordo*. The implications of all this, if we may anticipate the conclusion derived from the analysis which follows immediately below, are crucial because although the Vitorian state is a purely secular institution in both ends and means it does not possess a morality, an ethical self originating and justifying itself along secular lines. Although the end of the state is secular the ethic ruling over it and conditioning the nature of the means does not belong to the province of the state; it lies within the purview of the order of grace. Obviously the Vitorian commonwealth can never become a Machiavellian state; rather, the state as conceived by the Dominican rises implicitly as an alternative to Machiavelli's. But the price to be paid for this solution is high indeed because justice remains the very foundation of the Vitorian state. And not only is justice the ultimate goal of a well-ordered republic, it is both inseparable from the Christian ethic and the heart of that tool, war, which alone yields the means of restoring the broken reign of harmony within the international community.

At this point it will not be altogether inappropriate to bring this section to a close with a remark born out of what has been said in the last paragraph above: the supernatural order which hitherto we had studied only in its relations to the temporal domain now extends its pervasive influence, with justice as the instrument, into the international order as well. Let us see how.

[19] Naszalyi, *El Estado según Francisco de Vitoria*, pp. 127, 128.

Vitoria on justice

I maintained earlier that the only means whereby Vitoria could bring Europe and America together was by, first and foremost, defining beyond question the nature of the secular order. We have seen how his efforts in this direction necessarily created a second, or international, *ordo* together with the concomitant need to untangle their conflicting jurisdictions. This already strained situation was further complicated by the appearance of a third order whose interests, although non-secular in nature, seriously affect the spheres of interest of the other two. In my view it is precisely in the search for that balance among the three competing jurisdictions of these orders, without which he could not possibly hope to attain the primary goal he seeks, that the shortcomings of Vitoria's scheme can be most profitably identified. This balance (and I will raise what follows to the category of postulate), demands the successful definition of a set of interlocking concepts – civil law, nature, *jus gentium*, war, sovereignty, justice – whose given attributes enable the jurisdiction of the three orders to complement one another without however in any way interfering with each other's prerogatives. To reach that end with any degree of permanence, the author must first manage to resolve the antinomy between a tradition which ever since Saint Augustine's time wove justice, man, war, and the state into one seamless whole, and those contemporary realities which often rebelled against one or more of its components. Of the latter none is of greater import or more universally influential than justice, that very keystone of Vitoria's political construct to which we must now turn our attention.

It has often, and rightly, been pointed out that medieval theology owes Saint Augustine an immense debt. But it must at the same time be confessed that his doctrines did not remain totally unchanged during the Middle Ages; on the contrary, medieval thinkers often modified, consciously or unconsciously, the Augustinian scheme. A case in point of importance to us is the idea of justice. One of the fundamental premises of Augustine's thought demands that the goal of the political order be the achievement and preservation of peace. Peace is essential because it is the precondition for the existence of justice and only in the latter's presence can we say that it is possible to have a true state. In other words, for the Bishop of Hippo justice and justice alone is the bond which can unite men as a true *populus* in a real *respublica*.

But what is justice? Ideally justice consists in rendering unto each his due, in not withholding from man anything that rightfully belongs to man. Alas, no earthly state, be it pagan or Christian, incorporates that ideal definition. At best what we may hope to find in earthly society is but a poor image of the justice, the boundless felicity which truly exists only in the heavenly city. A measure of harmony, concord, and temporary peace among the members of the commonwealth: these are the highest things to which man, in view of his wretched nature, may aspire while living in the earthly city. They constitute and define that faulty justice which shall prevail in the city of the flesh.[20] It is with this concept of justice in mind that we must approach Augustine's definition of a commonwealth.

But if we discard this definition [Scipio's: 'an assemblage associated by a common acknowledgment of law, and by a community of interests'] of a people, and, assuming another, say that a people is an assemblage of reasonable beings bound together by a common agreement as to the objects of their love, then, in order to discover the character of any people, we have only to observe what they love. Yet whatever it loves, if only it is an assemblage of reasonable beings and not of beasts, and is bound together by an agreement as to the objects of love, it is reasonably called a people; and it will be a superior people in proportion as it is bound together by higher interests, inferior as it is bound together by lower. According to this definition of ours, the Roman people is a people, and its weal is without doubt a commonwealth or republic.[21]

The phrase 'and it will be a superior people in proportion as it is bound together by higher interests, inferior in proportion as it is bound together by lower', will be of exceptional interest to us later when we discuss Sepúlveda's views on the American Indians; in fact, much of what follows will bear importantly on the basic concepts of the humanist's political program. For the moment, however, our concern lies solely with the manner in which Vitoria follows the path suggested in Saint Augustine's statement.

We have seen how Vitoria postulates the autonomy of the secular order and the existence of an international community of nations based not upon religious persuasion but on reason. At first sight, then, it would appear that, in line with Saint Augustine's thoroughly amoral definition of republic, he is willing to follow his own argument to its logical conclusion and to countenance a state of affairs divorced from the traditional Christian position which sought to create a moral framework against which the structure of the state could function both ethically and efficiently. A position, in other words, which does not necessarily, and this is the important

[20] On this, see H. Deane's interesting analysis of Augustine's ideas on the state and justice in *The Social and Political Ideas of Saint Augustine* (New York, 1963), ch. iii and iv; and especially his comments (pp. 122–3) on *The City of God*, bk. xix, ch. 24; also R. Martin, 'Augustine's two cities', *JHI*, 33(1972), pp. 195–216.
[21] Saint Augustine, *The City of God*, bk. xix, ch. 24.

point, reflect that upheld by the Bishop of Hippo. How extensively the intervening millennium had elaborated upon the Augustinian idea of justice is proven by the reception accorded Machiavelli in the sixteenth century. The nature of the Vitorian premises, then, seems to portend the appearance of a state rising above ethical considerations and striving to be judged solely in terms of the success or failure with which it meets the dictates of necessity. This ethical autonomy of the state would in turn, again from the point of view of the post-Augustinian Christian ethico-political tradition to which Vitoria belongs, give rise to two moral structures: one for the political power and another for the individual; a public and a private morality conceived not as the interlocking parts of an ecumenical scheme but totally independent from one another. Nothing, however, could be further removed from Vitoria's mind than that the good prince of Christian tradition should give way to the pragmatic ruler of the Renaissance. The universality of the Christian ethic is neither denied nor compromised by the Spanish theologian; on the contrary, it is re-affirmed. In order to understand how this is accomplished it will be necessary to review some of Vitoria's ideas on law and justice as they appear in his writings.

Closely following Saint Thomas the theologians of the Spanish school attributed five meanings to the word *jus*: first, 'that which is just', in the sense of that which is owed someone, the object of justice; second, the 'law', the reason and rule of that which is just; third, 'jurisprudence', the science or art of that which is just; fourth, the 'place' or 'tribunal' where it is applied; fifth, the 'sentence' dictating that which is just. Most frequently, however, they gave the word *jus* a twofold meaning: *jus* as synonymous for *justum*, and *jus* as implying *lex*, a norm or rule for that which is just. The general opinion of these theologians, moreover, was that *jus* in its principal and genuine meaning indicated that which is just and owed to someone. However, it is common to find more than one meaning in certain words. Such, the theologians claimed, was the case with *jus* in its meaning as *lex*. Strictly speaking, therefore, *lex* is not *jus* but the reason for and the cause of that which is just. *Jus* properly and primarily means that which is just, correct, right – a faculty contained in the things themselves. *Lex*, on the other hand, is the norm, rule, authoritative standard prescribing that which is just.[22]

22 For all this see A. Folgado, '*Los tratados De legibus*'. In his edition of *The Political Ideas of Saint Thomas Aquinas* (New York, 1960), D. Bigongiari remarks on Aquinas' use of *ius* (p. 212) in the following manner: 'This word has given rise to confusion. Like *droit*, *Recht*, *diritto*, etc., *ius* has two aspects: viz., that of a regulative *norm*, and that of a *faculty* to a claim. Today the first is called "objective", and the latter "subjective" *ius*. In English we have two different words for these two

So far as the specific case of Vitoria is concerned the word justice is to be understood in two different ways. Lecturing on question 57 of Aquinas' IIa–IIae, the Dominican argues that broadly speaking justice is taken to imply any and all forms of virtue. On the other hand, he also admits that justice may have a more restricted and particular meaning: that of restitution, of giving unto others what is rightfully theirs. This second, more restricted and narrow, meaning Vitoria seems to prefer and uses (although, as we shall see, the first is never far from his mind).[23] Thus for him the essence of justice lies in giving to each what is owed him.[24] This 'particular' definition of justice does not attempt to regulate or deal with man's ethical life. Its task is far more prosaic and utilitarian; justice controls man's actions in his relations with other men.

The preceding differentiation between justice's two basic meanings is important in that, for one thing, it helps to understand the difference between 'right' and 'law'. Having thoroughly explored the question Naszalyi concludes that although Vitoria uses right and law interchangeably as words there is implicit in his thought an important distinction between the two. To the dissimilitude between the particular and the general meaning of justice corresponds a parallel differentiation between the meaning of natural right and natural law. In other words, natural right is to natural law as the particular is to the general meaning of justice. Just as Vitoria makes his a particular, restricted concept of justice which is embraced by a more general meaning of the same word, he considers that there is also a natural right contained in a broader normative concept, natural law. On the basis of this conceptual agreement Vitoria points out that *jus* (right) does not derive from *justitia* (the will to give each his 'right'); on the contrary, it is its object. *Jus*, moreover, is the same as *justum*; and since law is the cause of that which is just (*justum*) it necessarily follows that *jus* is not the same as law,[25] although the law is the *ratio juris*. In practical terms this means that a man's or a community's right is the faculty or power possessed by somebody or something in accordance with the law. To usurp or in any way impair that right constitutes an injury. It is of interest, therefore, to be able to tell whether and when something is of natural right. With this purpose in mind Vitoria outlines three propositions. First, whatever is sanctioned by all through their natural lights as just and whose opposite is considered by reason to

aspects: *ius* as *norm* is "law"; as a *faculty* it is "right". Confusion arises when the subjective term "right" is used to translate *ius*, *droit*, *Recht*, in the objective sense of "law". St Thomas seldom uses *ius* in its subjective sense.'

23 Beltrán de Heredia, *IIa–IIae*, III, q. 57, a. 1. n. 5, pp. 3–4.

24 *Ibid.*, n. 4, pp. 2–3.

25 Quoted in Naszalyi, *El Estado según Francisco de Vitoria*, p. 76.

be unjust is deemed to be of natural right. Second, all that which is deduced and inferred rightly from the principles themselves is of natural right. Third, that which is probably of natural right in such a manner that there is no observable possibility to the contrary is of natural right.[26] By the terms of these propositions, then, natural right implies a relationship which, creating a bond between two given entities (man and man), is by and of itself just. But there is more, for Vitoria also insists that there are relationships (community and community, or man and community) which although not necessarily just of and by themselves become so because they are imperative to the preservation of harmony among men. Natural right in this second manner is properly called *jus gentium*, another reason why the law of nations is not the same as natural law.

From all this we must conclude, first, that Vitoria confines the concept of right within the secular and international orders' spheres of influence; it has nothing to do with the order of grace. Second, since right is the object of justice it follows that the process whereby the fulfillment of someone's (man's) or something's (the community's) right is accomplished is justice. This concrete brand of justice, therefore, must be the 'particular justice' spoken of above; a species strictly circumscribed to regulating man's (or the community's) worldly dealings with other men (or communities) and thus in principle indifferent to his (or its) ethical or moral life (the concern and province of justice taken in the first, general, sense). What are the implications of this definition of justice? The strict boundaries within which Vitoria restricts the meaning of justice and natural right appear, on the surface at least, to define very clearly his conception of civil society and its end. 'Nay, it seems to be of natural right [*jus naturalis* is used here to indicate natural right] also seeing that otherwise society could not hold together unless there was somewhere a power and authority to deter wrongdoers and prevent them from injuring the good and innocent.'[27] The end of civil society (the state), according to these premises, is to insure the well-being of the citizens, not to watch over their spiritual felicity.

A critique of the Vitorian system

It is only proper, I feel, that we should introduce this section devoted to a critique of the Vitorian system with some of the questions inescapably proposed by the material surveyed in the pages, especially the last ones, of the present chapter. Does what we have said about Vitoria's justice in the second – particular – way in fact necessarily lead to a conception of the

[26] *IIa–IIae*, III, q. 57, a. 2, n. 4, pp. 8–9.
[27] *LW*, p. 172. See also *DCD*, bk. XIX.

state tailored along the lines of Augustine's amoral republic or Machia-velli's *raison d'État*? In other words, have we endowed the Vitorian state with an ethic all its own? Does the just war understood as the means of redressing individual or community injuries lose under the circumstances its universally normative character to become instead a mere coercive adjunct to a *jus gentium* now postulated as identical with a narrowly conceived definition of justice? And what happens to a *totus orbis* founded on the law of nations when the latter avowedly owes its existence only to a subtle nuance in the definition of 'right'? How are we to understand Vitoria's frequent references to the 'just ruler' who wages a just war to restore the broken harmony of the international order? Finally, how are we, from the vantage point forced upon us by a restricted understanding of justice, to make sure that this war (about the true dimensions of whose justice we now entertain legitimate doubts) will never interfere with the prosecution of society's end (about which we still know very little).

Let us begin the attempt to deal with these questions by first returning to the example of the virtuous man and the knave. A strict interpretation of Vitoria's justice in the particular sense implies that a virtuous and saintly citizen, a just man by the standards of justice understood in the general sense, who violates the compacts of man (and thus becomes unjust in the eyes of particular justice) is subject to punishment by the state. Conversely, a sinful man – a lawbreaker, if judged by general justice – who behaves in accordance with justice (particular) may not have his conduct censured or punished by the state.[28] Now, I have often reiterated in the past that for Vitoria the end is essential in that it embodies the reason for being of the means; and not only in the case of the state, for all processes, human and natural alike, are directed toward the realization of certain normal wholes. For this ultimate accomplishment have the apparatus of society, state, *totus orbis*, and their accompanying parapher-nalia in the last analysis been created. In a sense this handiwork is not without a certain touch of deviousness, for in appearance its aims are exclusively pointed inward whereas in truth although the task of the state is not immediately to create a virtuous man, mediately it has no other. The formidable autarchy in ends and means with which the state has been endowed is really nothing more than yet another link in the chain of means which ultimately find their unique justification in the upbringing of a virtuous man worthy of everlasting life. It follows from all this that Vitoria has no choice but to deny that the saintly man who by reason of his virtue embodies all possible definitions of justice can conceivably violate the compacts of the secular order (its human laws); or that a sinful man, a

---

[28] Naszalyi, *El Estado según Francisco de Vitoria*, p. 186.

man who willfully breaks his covenant with God, could possibly be a good citizen.

In conclusion, that form of justice which finds its ethos within the boundaries of the worldly orders must be subsumed under the aegis of a larger whole – justice in the general sense – in the same manner as the secular and international orders, the rightful province of particular justice, are *in ordinem* the order of grace, general justice's domain. Only on the basis of this interpretation is a full appreciation of Vitoria's double accomplishment possible. First, it provides a strong justification for the existence of the state as an institution untrammelled by considerations irrelevant to its function, without falling into that Machiavellian fallacy which shields the civil power so thoroughly from all outside interference as to turn it, paradoxically, into an usurper of functions – such as judging on the ethical contents of means and ends – which the age's opinion unanimously acknowledged to be beyond the state's ken. In this, however, neither Vitoria nor the school of which he was the founder is unique or exceptionally original. Much weightier is the Spaniard's second contribution: the creation of a rational *totus orbis* broader than Christendom and solidly anchored in a secularly oriented definition of justice which the Machiavellian scheme of things could not possibly accommodate and thus automatically rejected. Partially, then, Vitoria has succeeded in assimilating some of Machiavelli's advantages while dodging at the same time the more serious shortcomings of the Florentine secretary's political doctrine. Partially, however, is here a key word, for so much bounty exacts a heavy toll. And the price is that all the roads paved by Vitoria irrevocably lead to an ultimate conception of justice which is both the cause and the effect of the Christian ethic.

The anomalies and contradictions inherent in the tradition inspiring Vitoria's plan, and so the plan itself, become apparent when we reflect that the latter's central theme is not the state itself but the unstable dialectic growing out of the formulation of two secular orders, the state and the worldwide community of commonwealths, endowed with conflicting jurisdictions. Unlike Machiavelli, Vitoria does not attempt to arrive at the necessary principles which will enable the state to survive in a hostile world. Neither does he yearn for a return to the warless and utopian golden age of the Christian humanists. Rather, through the use of reason and the application of Christian doctrine Vitoria endeavors to turn war, the permanent state of conflict resulting from the endless dialectic between the two secular orders, into an instrument of justice. Reason he applies when he defines the state. The principles of Christian doctrine he already finds embodied in the doctrine of the just war. The just war, the truest means of giving reality to the ideal of Christian justice, is the one thing

capable of preserving the international order – that gathering of autonomous cells which owe their origin to nothing but reason and necessity –
from anarchy. And in a very real sense here lies the core of Vitoria's
attempt to harmonize the secular imperatives of his own age with the
transcendental postulates of his intellectual heritage. But now as in the
past this does not lead to a pact of equals. The perfection of the material
world remains with Vitoria but a reflection of the true perfection of the
supernatural realm. Society, the state, morality, war, justice, all stand not
on their own secular foundations but as parts of an indivisible whole
having their deepest roots in the ultimate dictates of revealed truth. In a
truly secular state we wage war to insure that secular justice is restored:
justice, the state, war, are all inseparably bound together. But in a
Christian state we have far more: we have the state, justice, and war
inextricably chained together to and by a higher bond – Christian morality.
In short, with Vitoria we find no attempt at truly separating the two
realms but a remarkably refined effort at articulate integration.

The contradictions involved in such an attempt are broadly speaking
the same that bedeviled western thought from the thirteenth to the
eighteenth centuries. In the case of Vitoria and in view of the task he has
undertaken these contradictions are nowhere more glaring than in his
struggles to insert the Indian states into a universe which despite surface
appearances is still postulated in its fundamentals as thoroughly Christian.
How can the idea of an international community of autonomous states
kept together in harmony by a coercive instrument founded upon revealed
truth be reconciled with the premise that a heathen commonwealth knowing not the true God can be a *bona fide* state and thereby gain entrance to
that community? Is it really possible, given Vitoria's premises about the
origin, nature, and functions of the just war, to maintain that the Indian
communities stand at the same level as the Christian states? The answer is
obviously no and the conclusion is inescapable: the communities of the
New World cannot be incorporated into a scheme based upon traditional
values. But even if the main stumbling block, the Indian states, is written
off and we are left with a political universe inhabited purely by Christian
states, does Vitoria's blueprint insure the preservation of even a semblance
of order in that universe? Again the answer is no and for two reasons.

First, Vitoria maintains, as he must, that the temporal power is in some
way *in ordinem* the spiritual power. Once again the theme that doomed
the universality of Vitoria's plan threatens to ruin even its remnants. It is
difficult to suppress the feeling that we have once again been drawn back
to the old nightmare of the two swords. True, Vitoria emphatically denies
the Pope's authority in secular affairs and emancipates the civil authority
from the supervision of ecclesiastical power. But as the protracted Church–

State controversy had demonstrated until the days of Marsilius of Padua it is not possible to take away with the left hand what has been granted by the right. The end result is to create an atmosphere of uncertainty from which, should the opportunity arise (and the New World had all the makings of one), convincing arguments could be drawn to support doctrinally the secular ambitions of a militant Papacy. It is inconceivable that such a contingency could ever be countenanced, regardless of how doctrinally vague, by a ruler of the Renaissance.

Secondly, the temper of the age demanded far more than a mere doctrinal structure to ward off the international anarchy foreseen by Vitoria himself. And it is precisely this substance that Vitoria's plan lacks. When seen *in toto* the secular side of his scheme proposes a hierarchy of jurisdictions already likened to that of a pyramid: the individual followed by the family, the state, and the all-embracing authority of the whole society of man. Vitoria strenuously struggles to define the nature of this authority and where it is embodied. The reason is a simple one: the stability and coherence of his entire design depend upon the extent of his success. Having rejected the authority of Pope and Emperor while at the same time retaining the ecumenical idea that at one time or another they sought to represent, Vitoria has no alternative but to provide two things: first, some form of *potestas* endowed with almost unlimited jurisdiction over the states (in fact, with the same type of jurisdiction over the members of the international community that the latter have over their own citizens); second, a mechanism of coercion which fulfilling the same tasks as the laws perform within the frontiers of the individual republics shall be capable of enforcing the will of that authority. The former is the *jus gentium*, the latter the just war. And the most obvious and immediate consequence of both constraints is to limit the autonomy of the state.

The claims to sovereignty presented by Vitoria in behalf of the parts (the states) notwithstanding, it is clear that the authority of the whole (the international community) must be superior. Inevitably, contradictions arise between Vitoria's definition of sovereignty and the attributions vested on the *jus gentium* – first of all because Vitoria has no clear idea of what the *jus gentium* really is. At one point it seems to be designed to emphasize that the recognition of the state's independence does not grant the latter the power to disregard the interests of the *totum* for the sake of satisfying its own; in other words, it is a primitive attempt at arresting the incipient malady of *raison d'État*. On the other hand, the *jus gentium* is also conceived as a universal declaration of rights aimed at reminding men of their membership in the worldwide brotherhood of mankind and vaguely conceived to protect man from the state. This last becomes evident when Vitoria, again in the context of the American problem, studies the Spanish right to intervene in the internal affairs of otherwise autonomous states to protect the innocent. To the absence of a really clear-cut postulation of the nature and breadth of the *jus gentium* we must further add that in practice the dialectic between the state and the international order, between national sovereignty and *jus gentium*, must be resolved by war. But the just war, Vitoria tells us, may only be waged by a sovereign prince (see Chapter 5). The disturbing result is that when the immanent authority of the law of nations materializes, it blends with the sovereign authority of a ruler who is suddenly exalted to the role of international judge. As a consequence two forms of sovereignty of vastly different value emerge: the overpowering sovereignty of the prince waging a just war, and the questionable sovereignty of his victim.

In addition to having failed to reach the two basic goals which it was designed to attain Vitoria's plan stands condemned on the grounds of being a thoroughly abstract scheme. While its principles are solidly grounded and developed, the structure of those institutions capable of giving it both meaning and reality is totally forgotten. (In his *Constitutionalism Ancient and Modern*, Professor C. H. McIlwain levelled a similar charge against medieval constitutionalism.) Vitoria clothes the eternal motif of war in juridical trappings of an impressive ethical quality. But the workings of his scheme are vitally weakened by its dependence upon the good will of the participants and the triumph of justice through purely deterministic means. Should either of these conditions fail to be present the verbal framework of necessity crumbles into dust. On both counts the responsibility for the failure of Vitoria's construct lies with the incapacity of the worldview on which it is founded to account satisfactorily for some of the imperatives peculiar to the reality of a given age.

Conclusion

In the last few pages – in apparent contradiction to my earlier claims – I have seemingly denied both the originality and soundness of the political ideology of Francisco de Vitoria, one of the most distinguished exponents of Spanish political thought in the age of Erasmus. The truth of that assertion notwithstanding the fact remains that the contribution of the School of Salamanca to the history of political thought is a remarkable one in three areas: natural law, the law of nations and the individual rights of man, and the outlook which insisted, in contrast with the growing territorial parochialism which was to dominate Western political thinking, in viewing the society of man not as limited by artificial and impermanent national boundaries but as an indivisible one coterminous with the eternal physical frontiers of the inhabited globe itself. It must be remembered, and this is the crucial point, that the destructive criticism just outlined above is the product of an historical insight normal to us but clearly unavailable to an eclectic and transitional age best characterized by an all-pervading but often undetected dialectic between ancient and modern. The failure of Vitoria's plan to fully attain the complex goals it aimed at, then, should in no way be understood as proving the perspicacity of those thinkers who, seemingly having recognized the irrevocable passing of all forms of political universalism, opted in their writings for the means of strengthening the state to assure its survival in a political milieu which they chose to accept as inevitably anarchical. Such foresight is recognizable only in retrospect and it was not at all self-evident to contemporaries, Spaniards or otherwise.

In my view the lesson to be derived from the study of Vitoria's political ideas is a twofold one. On the one hand, if we stand within the context of the age itself we are forced to admit that political universalism was not an obsolete remnant of the past surviving in Spain alone but a vigorous political philosophy fitting certain contemporary realities and perfectly accredited among important segments of European political opinion. On the other hand, if we choose to profit from four centuries of political insight we must conclude that not only the thought of Vitoria and the Spanish school but the entire contribution to political philosophy of the age of Erasmus – Christian humanist evangelicalism and Machiavellian empiricism – stands either accused of lack of originality or suspect of ideological insufficiency.

Erasmus is a case in point. The Dutch humanist, like so many other publicists of the day, believed that man is a political and social animal. Because man by nature's very design has been brought into the world destitute and unprotected[29] he needs the society and fellowship of other men 'that they, joining their strength and power together, should repel the violence of wild beasts and robbers'.[30] The Erasmian state implicitly results from man's sociability; it is a rather simple institution whose function is to insure the well-being of the people and whose authority is embodied in the prince.[31] The simplicity of Erasmus' political scheme lies

[29] D. Erasmus, *Erasmus Against War*, ed. J. W. Mackail (Boston, 1907), p. 6; cited hereafter as *DBI*. This edition is a reprint of the first English translation (1533–1534) of *Dulce bellum inexpertis*. This anti-war treatise is an enlarged version of a letter written by Erasmus to the Bishop of Saint Bertin in 1514, and published as a part of the 1515 edition of the *Adages*.

[30] D. Erasmus, *The Complaint of Peace* (New York, 1948), p. 11; cited hereafter as *QP*. First published by Froeben at Basel in 1517, the *Querela pacis* was promptly translated into the major European languages. The English translation used here is that of Thomas Paynell (1559), modernized by J. W. Hirten.

[31] D. Erasmus, *The Education of a Christian Prince*, ed. and trans. L. K. Born

precisely in that the idea of the state is not carried beyond this primitive stage. The origin and purpose of the state having been broadly determined it is not the latter as an abstract entity but the prince, the incarnation of its power, who becomes the subject of Erasmus' preoccupation. The Erasmian prince, the man who has been entrusted by God with the welfare of his fellows, is the true Christian prince; he who having embraced Christ with his most intimate affections expresses his love for Him by his pious deeds.³² To his own ethical superiority and Christian piety the good ruler must add constant surrender to the dictates of reason and willingness to heed the advice of others.³³ Such a man does not need the artificial constraints of custom, parliamentary bodies, or written constitutions because his powers of self-examination and his understanding of the true meaning of Christ's teachings will unerringly point the way toward the well-being of his flock.³⁴

Against this rather flimsy political structure – one of the more serious shortcomings of Christian humanist political thought – the problem of war looms high indeed. And as with the Neoscholastic Vitoria, human discord plays a pivotal role in the political thinking of the Christian humanist Erasmus. As I shall more conclusively demonstrate in Chapter 5 when the latter explores the practical implications of his acceptance of the political order, Erasmus is also compelled to accept a series of premises which are integral parts of the traditional theory of the just war. Thus in the context of the problem of war, so important a factor in the age's formulation of political schemes, there is no fundamental difference between Neoscholasticism and Christian humanism. To be sure, the form, the methodology, and secondary objectives are different. Whereas for Erasmus war must be done away with, for Vitoria its transformation into an instrument of justice is desirable. But in both writers the underlying assumption binding and conditioning their schemes is the same: the Christian ethic is valid everywhere, for man as well as for the state.

The age, however, was suggesting with ever increasing imperiousness the idea, old in practice but never doctrinally admitted until Machiavelli, that there exist two forms of ethical conduct: one for man and another, different, for the state. This suggests that perhaps the Florentine's approach to the problem of war, inseparable from his view of the state, succeeded where Neoscholasticism and Christian humanism failed. But if abstraction is the cardinal sin of the traditional approach, Machiavelli, by

(New York, 1968), p. 159; cited hereafter as *IPC*. The *Institutio principis christiani* was first published in 1516 by J. Froeben. Also in *Opera omnia*, ed. J. Clericus (10 vols., Leiden, 1703–1706), II.
³² *IPC* (*Opera*), p. 567D.   ³³ *IPC* (Born), p. 189.
³⁴ *IPC* (*Opera*), p. 574E.

reason of his very astuteness as an observer, suffers from an equally damaging malady – parochialism. As a result he disregards some of the age's traditional imperatives. More specifically, he neglects to observe that although the traditional Christian outlook failed to satisfy all the conditions indispensable to the new age's temper it still remained an operator influential enough to bar the success of a doctrinal justification of society, the state, and war in purely secular terms.

Clearly, then, neither the abstractions of Neoscholasticism, nor the shallow concreteness of political empiricism, nor the idealism of the Christian humanists sufficed in isolation to explain a phenomenon – war – which by reason of its universality touched upon all aspects of the life of the Renaissance, abstract and doctrinal as well as real and pragmatic. Doctrinal schemes founded upon past conceptions of man and his relation to the world are sufficient to account for the ancient imperatives still strong in this age of transition but inadequate to explain the new ones. Conversely, explanations based purely on the observation of immediate needs provide only a very partial answer. The shortcomings of both these approaches to the problem of war and the state are fundamentally influenced by the central theme mentioned above: the ethics of man and of the state. As we have seen, the Neoscholastic approach favored the indivisible universality of a Christian morality applicable equally well to man and the state and deposited in the hands of the universal Church. The problem, then, reduces itself to the following: in view of the insufficiency of the old and the new tools to account for the problem of war–state in an age whose shape is the result of the joint efforts of old and new, how to replace the main stumbling block, namely, the visible moral authority of Christianity, with a worldview capable of accommodating comfortably the imperatives that in a given age condition the life of man.

The conflicting nature of these imperatives in the early sixteenth century and the inadequacy of the conceptual tools available did not permit the growth of such an alternative. Magic, supported and nourished in its beginnings by some aspects of humanism, attempted to provide the age with a purview from whose limitless frontiers man could view the existential problems inherent to life in society with the confidence that only full certainty about his own nature and the world surrounding him could give. But the Renaissance Magus was found wanting; and it was modern science, the refined daughter of Scholasticism and empiricism, which provided the necessary answers in the seventeenth century.[35] It is from

[35] Renaissance magic bears importantly on the universal purview of the age of Erasmus. For this and the development of early modern science see the following works: C. Agrippa, *Of the Vanitie and Uncertaintie of Artes and Sciences*, trans. J. Stanford (London, 1575); G. della Porta, *Natural Magick* (London, 1659); N.

the perspective afforded by this triumph that we can best understand the inadequacies and shortcomings – in Spain as elsewhere – of the intellectual tradition of the early sixteenth century when called upon to cope with a subject so complex and all-embracing as man and his relation to the world which surrounds him. In the early sixteenth century the fully developed organismic conception of the universe coexisted with an embryonic view which maintained that it was possible to separate man from nature and to integrate the two again into a resulting whole very different from the *totum* of tradition. The full expression, the climax, of this new way of envisioning nature is to be found in the great systems of the seventeenth century; and it is characterized by a new relationship between experience and thought, between the world of the senses and the realm of abstraction. Man, the repository of the secondary qualities, those qualities which are in truth devoid of existence and are no more than mere appearances, becomes separated from the surrounding world of nature which embodies the primary qualities. This separation, first fully suggested by Galileo,

Copernicus, *De revolutionibus*, Preface and Book I, trans. J. F. Dobson; G. Galilei, *Opere* (1890), *Dialogues of the Two Chief Systems of the World*, trans. S. Drake (U. of California, 1953), *Dialogues Concerning Two New Sciences*, trans. H. Crew and A. de Salvio (New York, 1952); G. Pico della Mirandola, *Conclusiones* (1535). Among secondary works, see: R. M. Blake *et al.*, *Theories of Scientific Method;* E. A. Burtt, *The Metaphysical Foundations of Modern Physical Science* (New York, 1960); E. Cassirer, *The Individual and the Cosmos in Renaissance Philosophy*, trans. M. Demandi (London, 1963); R. Collingwood, The *Idea of Nature* (Oxford, 1945); A. C. Crombie, *Robert Grosseteste and the Origins of Experimental Science* (Oxford, 1953), *Medieval and Early Modern Science* (2 vols., New York, 1959), II, and *Augustine to Galileo* (London, 1952); E. J. Dijksterhuis, *The Mechanization of the World Picture*, trans. C. Dikshoorn (Oxford, 1961); P. Duhem, *Le système du monde* (Paris, 1954); A. J. Festugière, *La révélation d'Hermes Trismégiste* (4 vols., Paris, 1950–1954), also his edition of the *Corpus Hermeticum* (4 vols., Paris, 1945 and 1954); E. Garin, *Medioevo et Rinascimento* (Bari, 1961), and *La cultura del Rinascimento italiano* (Florence, 1961); E. Grant, 'Late medieval thought, Copernicus, and the scientific revolution', *JHI*, XXIII(1962), pp. 197–220; A. R. Hall, *The Scientific Revolution 1500–1800* (Boston, 1960); M. Boas, *The Scientific Renaissance* (New York, 1962); H. Haydin, *The Counter-Renaissance* (New York, 1960); A. Koyré, *Ètudes Galiléennes* (Paris, 1939), and *Mystiques, spirituels, alchemistes* (Paris); T. Kuhn, *The Copernican Revolution* (New York, n.d.); E. A. Moody, 'Empiricism and metaphysics in medieval philosophy', *The Philosophical Review*, LXVII(1957), pp. 145–63; C. G. Nauert, *Agrippa and the Crisis of Renaissance Thought* (Urbana, Ill., 1965); H. R. Randall, 'The development of the scientific method in the school of Padua', JHI, I(1940); E. Rosen, *Three Copernican Treatises* (New York, 1939); L. Thorndike, *History of Magic and Experimental Science* (6 vols., New York, 1923–1941); D. P. Walker, *Spiritual and Demonic Magic from Ficino to Campanella* (London, 1958), and 'Orpheus the theologian and the Renaissance Platonists', *JWI*, XVI(1953), pp. 100–120; F. Yates, *Giordano Bruno and the Hermetic Tradition* (Chicago, 1964).

creates a new concept of truth. Coexisting with the traditional concept of ultimate and indubitable truth – revelation – there is now an equally lofty truth derived from the primary qualities through the medium of mathematics, the truth of nature.

The Galilean separation of man from nature had created the reverse problem: to discover some form of linkage which while preserving the special character of each would make them genuine and intelligible parts of the same whole. Newton's law of gravitation offered the eighteenth century the necessary connection.[36]

The harmony attained by the eighteenth century after the process of separation and reintegration was carried through is precisely what the great syntheses of the thirteenth century had sought. Clearly, the harmony pursued by the latter could not be the result of a pact of equals for, regardless of the efforts of Saint Thomas and Vitoria, revelation had to take the upper hand in the end. The great systems of Scholasticism repeatedly attempted to reconcile reason with revelation and to harmonize the two. But there could be no thought of separating man from nature even temporarily because it was inconceivable to separate man from God.

It is clear that quite different conclusions will be drawn from the study of man's existential problems such as war and his membership in political commonwealths according to whether we observe them from within the scheme of tradition or this newer framework. The nature of the traditional worldview demanded that man and all his deeds be smoothly integrated into an harmonic *totum* of which God was the First and Final Cause and where God made His presence felt through, partially, man's reason and, overwhelmingly, revelation. In this framework war is not only the secular concern of the state, but touches upon those elements said to belong properly in the supernatural plane: morals, ethics, religion. If the problem of war and the state is understood from the second viewpoint it becomes a purely secular question the answer to which can be sought without the imperative need to refer to transcendental agencies. The significant conclusion to all this is that in the early sixteenth century important developments began, and only began, to take shape which pointed in the direction of the need for considering the problem inherent in man's nature as a social and political being in terms less all-embracing than tradition could

---

[36] 'The correlation between nature and human knowledge has now been established once and for all and the bond between them is henceforth inseparable. Both members of the correlation are quite independent, but by virtue of their independence they are, nevertheless, in complete harmony. Nature in man, as it were, meets nature in the cosmos half way and finds its own essence there.' E. Cassirer, *The Philosophy of the Enlightenment*, trans. F. C. A. Koelln, and J. Pettegrove (Princeton, 1951), p. 44.

possibly offer. Had the age had at its disposal the marvelous intellectual foundation, a foundation purely of the mind unaided and unhindered by the determinism of spiritual imperatives, which was the heritage of the generations following the triumph of the mechanization of nature, the remarkable plasticity of the conditions generally prevailing in the early sixteenth century would have enabled its thinkers to give more valid answers to the problem of war–state. A crucial by-product of their solutions would then have been a greater capacity for molding the growth of European socio-political institutions along patterns better fitted for controlling the processes responsible for war. This was certainly the goal of Francisco de Vitoria.

Given the circumstances examined in the pages of this and the preceding chapters, is it accurate to dismiss the political ideas of the Spanish school in the first half of the sixteenth century as either inconsequential or obsolete? I think not. With the exception of Machiavelli's cold pragmatism all currents and themes prevalent in the European political thought of the day were well represented in Spain, and their shortcomings, if indeed shortcomings they be, are certainly not peculiar to the Spanish product alone. Above all, we encounter among Spanish publicists a profound concern with the problem of war. Under the circumstances the need for a close examination of the doctrine of the just war needs no further apology. Nevertheless, before fully turning our attention to Saint Augustine's ideas on the subject and the contribution of the early sixteenth century, certain introductory remarks are very much in order and will serve to preface the contents of the next chapter.

5

The age of Erasmus on war and peace

Introduction

The age of Erasmus struggled in countless schemes to articulate the means of restoring society to the order and tranquillity which, it was believed in some quarters, had prevailed in some remote age. And nowhere is this anxiety more poignantly expressed than among those Christian humanists who 'strove to describe, as a model for their age, the outlines of a radically improved social order'. How melancholy the plight of European society was in their eyes is exemplified by Vives' *De concordia*: 'No greater need has the world, nowadays tottering at the edge of final prostration, than for concord. Only concord will reinstate the fallen, retain what is now fleeing from us, and restore what has already been lost.' The Vivian 'world', however, is but Christendom, the product of a novel intellectual tradition which preserved 'many traditional features of the medieval schools in Renaissance attire'. For one thing, the common characteristic of the Christian humanist social blueprints is the relative parochialism which confines them to the well-known experience of Western Europe, the familiar needs of a social order based upon the acceptance of Christian values, and their failure to understand the political significance of the emerging nation-state. Incomplete as those schemes may have been before 1492, they had become totally inadequate after the discovery of new territories and peoples across the ocean. This shortcoming of Christian ideology is a serious one, as we shall fully learn in later chapters when, in contrast, Sepúlveda's eclectic attempt at constructing a universal society is examined. At this point we are specifically concerned with the lessons to be drawn, as far as political theory is concerned, from the ideas on war to be surveyed in this chapter.

Undoubtedly, the anarchy of the fifteenth century and the intermittent state of warfare which plagued the early part of the sixteenth influenced the attitude of the age of Erasmus toward the problem of war. The search for a means to end discord altogether was the concern of some scholars, the desire to discover a way of controlling and regulating it the pre-occupation of others. But high above Christian humanist, Neoscholastic, and Protestant invariably loomed the haunting specter of the age-old theory of the just war. The answer to the queries posed by human discord may appear on the surface to be different and even conflicting. Upon close examination it is not difficult to conclude that barring extreme positions the differences are basically small. In all cases the admitted assumption, explicit or implicit, is that the state and war go irrevocably together. Moreover, all the publicists surveyed accept that war is not an isolated phenomenon to be studied apart from other aspects of man's existence. On the contrary, discord is frankly viewed as part of an integrated whole embracing all sides of man both on this earth and in his afterlife. War both lay at the basis of every contemporary conception of the state – if one goes so does the other, if either stays both must remain – and touched man as an ethical being.

To my mind, the cardinal reasons for the unanimous belief in the dependence of the state on the concord–discord dialectic are two in number and closely related. The first is to be sought in the currency of the Augustinian invention which maintained that the state was created to restrain man's anarchical nature and in turn forced into being the doctrine of the just war. The Neoscholastics of the Spanish school universally rose to the demands implicit in these assumptions and concluded that war cannot be separated from peace any more than the latter can be isolated from justice, the *raison d'être* of the political order. The meaning of all this is not hard to discover. To begin with, it suggests that political thinking at this time used as its starting point a double assumption: man's flawed nature and his enmity toward man. And to this rule even Machiavelli is no exception. To the political theorists of the time, as we have already had occasion to note when studying Vitoria's political thought, war is both the discord between two men and the holocausts among nations. No difference of principle is involved between the two. And it is for this reason that our publicists, to a man, are so anxious to discover the consequences of Christ's appearance in the midst of mankind. If war had been perceived by the age as an impersonal contingency merely incidental to the coexistence of impersonal entities (states) then Christ's role would have been irrelevant to the discussion. Instead, no single author failed to emphasize the appalling human quality of war in both its guises. Vives, Erasmus, Vitoria, Menno Simons, all agree: war is the responsibility of every man. And this carries over into the state. Thus Erasmus writes as if, for the purposes of war, the prince were the state; and, albeit with different results, an identical assumption underlies Machiavelli's political doctrine. Vitoria broadens the principle even further, for the Dominican is concerned not only with the fate of individual men – the innocent – within the state but also with that of single states within the international community. Because war remains such a personal experience, then, the dilemma of Christ's message, so unequivocally aimed at individual man, must be resolved.

In this manner we arrive at the second cause mentioned above; one which is indeed overwhelming in its significance and the heart of this chapter on war. As one reflects on the beliefs held by our authors, it is not difficult to conclude that they are all groping for a satisfactory answer to the same elusive question: what is the precise nature of the change brought by the coming of Christ into human relations? Christian humanist, Neoscholastic, Anabaptist, they will one and all, in their search for conclusive explanations to the riddle, be invariably compelled to juxtapose both Covenants and assign them unequal value. Those who accept the reality of Christ's peace must then claim that His teachings have made obsolete the Mosaic injunctions. The advocates of the theory of the just war, on the other hand, will in effect acknowledge the continued supremacy of the Old Testament; although of necessity simultaneously attempting to preserve an outward balance between the two sources of the faith through the argument that Christ's teachings possess exhortative value and remain the key to a contemplative life, while the commands of the Law retain their comminatory character. The upshot of all this is of eminent importance. A debate born out of a deceptively simple inquiry (to find a remedy for man's turbulent nature shall) irrevocably condition the manner in which both schools will understand the nature and role of political authority.

Construed in these terms Christian humanist political thought reduces itself to an attempt to extend into the realm of praxis the message of the *philosophia Christi*. The obvious limitations of such a view are responsible for Erasmus' difficulties and his ultimate surrender to the traditional position. Neoscholastic political thinking, by contrast, is firmly rooted in the assumption that the validity of the Old Covenant – in reality, as these publicists readily admit, nothing more than the Hebrew version of natural law – is eternal, and that for the purposes of political affairs (human relations might conceivably be a better phrase, or what Sepúlveda calls the active life) the coming of Christ made no difference whatsoever. This last conclusion, if misconstrued, could be heady wine indeed. Principally because it may suggest to the unwary a fraternal bond binding the Spanish school and Machiavelli together. Although I have already pointed out that any such conclusion would be misleading, it may be well worth repeating that common axioms do not necessarily imply identical corollaries. Regardless of what Machiavelli's political doctrines may be, the position of the Spanish doctors is clear. After granting Christ's teachings advisory value at best and admitting the universality of Mosaic law, the Spaniards logically proceeded to identify the latter with classical notions of natural law conveniently placed at their disposal by the new learning. The result is a matter of record: starting with that concern for the problem of war so deeply felt among all sectors of the European intelligentsia, the School of Salamanca succeeded in elaborating a political ideology exactingly dependent on natural law principles which simultaneously served to modernize, by secularizing it, the law of nature. Thus was the way paved for the transformation of natural law into the scientific form of political theory so admired by the seventeenth and eighteenth centuries.

Saint Augustine

Saint Augustine offered the early Church a system of reference against which to weigh and solve the problems and riddles suggested by the need to harmonize the city of God with that of man, everlasting life with temporal existence. And among them none are of greater import than the ends of the state and the nature of war.

What is war? War, Saint Augustine asserts, is the terrible scourge of humanity inherent in the very existence of the earthly city.[1] It is character-

---

[1] Saint Augustine, *The City of God*, trans. M. Dods, in *A Select Library of the Nicene and Post-Nicene Fathers of the Christian Church*, ed. P. Schaff (14 vols., Buffalo, 1887, and New York, 1907), bk. xv, ch. 4, p. 286; cited hereafter as *DCD*. All subsequent references to the works of Saint Augustine, unless otherwise indicated, are to this edition. On early Christian ideas about war see the following: R. H. Bainton, 'The early church and war', *HTR*, 39(1946), pp. 189–211; C. J. Cadoux, *The Early Christian Attitude Toward War* (London, 1919); W. E. Caldwell, *Hellenic Conceptions of Peace* (New York, 1919); A. Fitzgerald, *Peace and War in Antiquity* (London, 1931); J. Fontaine, 'Christians and military service in the early church', *Concilium*, 7(1965), pp. 107–19; S. Gero, 'Miles gloriosus: the Christian and military service according to Tertullian', *CH* (1970); E. A. Ryan 'The rejection of military service by the early Christians', *Theological Studies*, 13(1952), pp. 1–29. Among the more useful works to be found on the subject of war from Saint Augustine to the end of the Middle Ages, we have: D. Beaufort, *La guerre comme instrument de secours et de punition* (The Hague, 1933); Y. de la Brière, 'La conception de la paix et de la guerre chez Saint Augustin', *Revue de Philosophie*, Nouvelle Sèrie, 1(1930), pp. 557–72; also by the same author: 'Les étapes de la tradition théologique concernant le Droit de juste guerre', *RGDIP* (1937), *La conception du Droit international chez les théologiens catholiques* (Paris, 1929), *Le Droit de juste guerre* (Paris, 1938); P. Brock, *The Political and Social Doctrines of the Unity of the Czech Brethren* (The Hague, 1957); M. Chossat, *La guerre et la paix d'après le Droit naturel chrètien* (Paris, 1918); H. Deane, *The Social and Political Ideas of Saint Augustine* (New York, 1963); L. Delboz, 'La notion éthique de la guerre', *RGDIP*, xxiv(1953), pp. 16–39; J. Eppstein, *The Catholic Tradition of the Law of Nations* (London, 1935); J. Hale, 'War and public opinion in the fifteenth and sixteenth

istic of the imperfect felicity to be secured in the earthly city that life in it shall be a mixed blessing and war and strife its inseparable companions. The interaction of war and peace is a natural state of affairs in the city of man; and the peace sought by man in order to enjoy his earthly goods 'is purchased by toilsome wars'.[2] The earthly city, within the limitations imposed by the fact that it is an imperfect form of association, endeavors to attain the highest degree of well-being possible. This well-being consists in the enjoyment of earthly goods in peace, and this peace it only knows how to achieve through war. Only in the heavenly city are 'eternal victory and peace never-ending' possible. This is not to say, however, that all wars are waged with the laudable purpose of achieving peace. On the contrary, war appears in the city of the flesh under various guises. It is often counselled by the 'vice of restless ambition' and the 'lust for sovereignty'. The result of an enterprise undertaken under such conditions is to bring untold calamities to the human race. Such were the majority of the wars waged in antiquity. Thus, the life-span of the Roman empire was an endless chain of wars, foreign and domestic.[3] These 'impious wars waged for the insane pomp of human glory' Saint Augustine consistently condemns throughout the *City of God*, although at the same time he admits that they were in truth nothing more than the natural outcome of a state of affairs which saw man living in ignorance of the true religion.[4] There are wars, however, which can be said to be both lawful and legitimate, for war is one of those things which while illicit under other conditions becomes rightful and just under God's command or that of established authority.[5]

It would be misleading to conclude from all this that Saint Augustine is insensitive to the horrors of discord. On the contrary, he is deeply moved

centuries', *Past and Present*, 22(1962), pp. 18–35; M. H. Keen, *The Laws of War in the Late Middle Ages* (London, 1965); C. L. Lange, *Historie de l'internationalisme* (2 vols., New York, 1919); P. Monceaux, *L'Église et le Droit de guerre* (Paris, 1920), and his 'Saint Augustin et la guerre'; E. Nys, *Le Droit de la guerre et les précurseurs de Grotius* (Brussels, 1882), *Les origines du Droit international* (Brussels, Paris, 1894), *Le Droit des gens et les anciens jurisconsultes espagnols* (The Hague, 1914); R. Regout, *La doctrine de la guerre juste de Saint Augustin à nos jours* (Paris, 1935); L. Rolland, *Les fondateurs du Droit international* (Paris, 1904); L. Sturzo, 'La communauté internationale et le Droit de la guerre', *CNJ*, 18(1931); J. D. Tooke, *The Just War in Aquinas and Grotius* (London, 1965); A. Vanderpol, *La doctrine scolastique du Droit de guerre* (Paris, 1919); C. van Vollenhoven, *The Law of Peace*, trans. W. Carter (London, 1934); R. S. Hartigan, 'Saint Augustine on war and killing: the problem of the innocent', *JHI*, 27(1966), pp. 195–204.

[2] *DCD*, xv 4, p. 286.   [3] *Ibid.*, xix 7, p. 405.
[4] *Ibid.*, iii 30, p. 61.
[5] Monceaux, 'Saint Augustin et la guerre', p. 15. Saint Augustine, *Reply to Faustus the Manichaean*, xxii 73, p. 300, cited hereafter as *CFM*.

by the disasters brought about by war regardless of the justice of its cause.[6] But, argues the Bishop of Hippo, the real evil of war lies not in the death of those who do battle, for men are destined to die sooner or later; nor is it to be found in the material havoc wrought by war, deplorable and horrible as the destruction and misery always are. What is truly wicked is the depraved intention and corrupt spirit of those who often wage war, the 'love of violence, revengeful cruelty, fierce and implacable enmity, wild resistance, and the lust for power...' And it is precisely to punish these evils that good men should lawfully undertake wars.[7] What really counts in establishing the difference between an illicit and a legitimate war, therefore, is the cause and ends which are served, and the authority that sanctions the war. In brief, Saint Augustine distinguishes three kinds of war in the earthly city: illegitimate wars provoked by evil passions, ambition, and love of violence; righteous wars undertaken at the command of God; and just wars waged for just reasons, aimed at a just end, and sanctioned by the lawful authority. Of the last two the former is of no interest to us because of its indubitable sanctity. It is with the last one, the just war, that we shall be concerned.

Are Christians permitted to wage war? Saint Augustine flatly rejects the pacifism and anti-militarism of many of the Early Church Fathers. He will instead never miss an opportunity to affirm that the military profession is in no way incompatible with the Christian faith, finding abundant evidence to support his views in both Covenants. Thus in the Old Testament he discovers that God has made some exceptions to His 'own law, that men shall not be put to death'.[8] But it was in the New Testament that the pacifists of the Early Church and the Manichaeans of Augustine's own time sought and found the most damaging evidence indicting war and supporting their own position.[9] Saint Augustine is of a different mind. The most emphatic injunctions against violence that we might come upon in the New Testament, he explains, are not to be understood as condemnations of war. Thus when Christ admonished Peter to 'put thy sword into its sheath; for he that taketh the sword shall perish by the sword', it was because Peter had used the sword without the consent of authority. 'To take the sword is to use weapons against a man's life, without the sanction of constituted authority. The Lord indeed had told His disciples to carry

[6] *DCD*, XIX 7, p. 405.   [7] *CFM*, XXII 74, p. 301.
[8] *DCD*, I 21, p. 15.
[9] The subject of violence is considered in the following passages of the New Testament. Matthew *5*:1–12, 21–23, 38–48, *6*:9–15, *8*:5–13, *18*:21–22, *26*:51–54; Luke *1*:76–79, *2*:13–14, *3*:12–14, *6*:31, *10*:29–37, *14*:31–32, *22*:35–38, *23*:33–34; John *2*:14–17, *13*:34–35, *14*:27, *15*:4–12, *17*:11, 20–23, *20*:19–21; Romans *14*:17–19; I Corinthians *13*:1–13; Ephesians *4*:1–16, *6*:14–15; Philippians *4*:7–9; I John *3*:17–18, *4*:7–11, 18–21.

a sword, but He did not tell them to use it.'[10] It is often argued, Saint Augustine continues, that when Christ said 'I say unto you, that ye resist no evil' he banned the use of violence. This conclusion is not valid because when Christ admonished us to resist no evil His purpose was only to banish from us the desire to take pleasure in revenge; in other words, what He requires of us with His words is not a bodily action but an inward disposition. On the strength of the evidence, then, it is incorrect to say that God could not enjoin warfare because of the words of Christ. Or, to put in another manner, the injunctions of the Old Testament are not invalidated by utterances found in the New.[11] The meaning of John the Baptist's exhortation to the soldiers who came to receive baptism is explained with equal ease. When John admonished the soldiers to be content with their pay, Saint Augustine argues, he did not imply that they should cease serving as soldiers. Since the law of Christ forbids the faithful neither to carry the sword nor to use it on occasion, Christians should not think that it is impossible for any one to please God while engaged in military service.[12]

Needless to say any war in which a Christian is unquestionably permitted to participate becomes automatically a just war. In *Quaestiones in Heptateuchum* Saint Augustine defines the just war in the following terms: 'The just wars, after the common definition, are those which avenge the injuries, when a people or a state neglect to punish the wrongs committed by its citizens or to return those things unjustly taken. Without any doubt that war commanded by God is also just.'[13] A just cause and a legitimate authority: such are two of the basic ingredients that enter into the composition of the just war.[14] Its goal and purpose is the third and missing essential element. Both the need for a legitimate authority to declare war and the objectives of the just war are in conformity with the demands of natural law, 'for the natural order which seeks the peace of mankind ordains that the monarch should have the power of undertaking war if he thinks it advisable, and that the soldiers should perform their military duties in behalf of the peace and safety of the community'.[15]

What, then, is the goal of the just war? Its objective is twofold. First, it

---

[10] *CFM*, xxii 70, p. 299.

[11] Saint Augustine, *The Letters of Saint Augustine*, Ep. xlvii (Saint Augustine to Publicola) 3–4, p. 293; Ep. cxxxviii 12–14, pp. 484–5. Cited hereafter as *Letters*. See also, *CFM* 76, p. 301.

[12] Monceaux, 'Saint Augustin et la guerre', p. 14. Also, *Letters*, Ep. clxxxix (Saint Augustine to Boniface) 4, p. 553; Ep. cxxxviii (Saint Augustine to Marcellinus) 15, p. 486; *CFM*, xxii 76, p. 301.

[13] Cited in Deane, *The Social and Political Ideas of Saint Augustine*.

[14] *CFM*, xxii 75, p. 301.

[15] *Ibid.*

seeks to punish evil. When force is required to inflict the punishment, right conduct demands that good men wage war in obedience to God or some lawful authority.[16] This punitive facet is nothing more than the extension into the world of states of the internal mechanism whereby justice is administered in a well-ordered community. It is imperative, however, that in both cases violence be kept to a minimum. Granted that wicked men who are a threat to their fellows must not be accorded the freedom to perpetrate further crimes; it is moreover the duty of every Christian to punish the evildoer for the latter's own benefit and eternal salvation. But justice should be satisfied without having recourse to such extremes as maiming and killing.[17] Peace, understood as the *tranquillitas ordinis*, is the second and overriding concern of the just war. Order, in turn, is the distribution that allots things equal and unequal, each to its own place.[18] Peace is truly the fundamental aim and end of war frequently embodying the punishing of evil as well, for the evils punished by a just war are those very same ills that banish peace from the earthly city thus preventing men from fully enjoying their worldly goods.[19]

But again let no one be mistaken, for even a just war is 'an evil and horrible thing'. Even he who wages a just war will, if he remembers that he is a man, lament his onerous duty.[20] Peace, on the other hand, is a thing universally desired. It follows that war may only be waged to obtain peace, 'for every man seeks peace by waging war, but no man seeks war by making peace'.[21] This desire for peace is so widespread that it is found even among the wicked. There is of course a difference between the peace desired by the righteous and that sought by the wicked: whereas the former endeavors to establish the rule of God and thus bring about His peace, the latter strives to impose his own tyrannical government and to make an unjust peace prevail. Nevertheless, man cannot 'help loving peace of one kind or another'.[22] It is moreover plain that men who are able to distinguish what is right from what is wrong will have no difficulty in concluding that the peace of unjust men is no true peace at all.[23] The corollary is evident: an unjust peace not being preferable to a just war, the former must not be allowed to prevail thus making mandatory the existence of the latter.

The importance of justice in Saint Augustine's thought is common knowledge. Its influence in shaping his ideas on war can hardly be

---

[16] *Ibid.*
[17] *Letters*, Ep. cxxxiii (Saint Augustine to Marcellinus) 1, p. 470; Ep. cxxxviii 13, p. 485.
[18] *DCD*, xix 13, p. 409.
[19] *Letters*, Ep. clxxxix 6, p. 554.
[20] *DCD*, xix 7, p. 405.
[21] *Ibid.*, xix 12, p. 407.
[22] *Ibid.*, xix 12, p. 408.
[23] *Ibid.*

exaggerated. War must be waged in a just manner, with a just end in mind, must be born out of a just cause, and declared by a just authority. In this sense the Bishop of Hippo introduces into the Christian sphere the notion of equity as it had been developed by pagan moralists such as Plato and the Roman Stoics. The difference is that Saint Augustine applies the ethical tradition to man rather than the citizen. As a result the allegiance to the state, of paramount importance among pagans, is overruled by an unquestioned subservience to God.[24] And herein lies the weakness that Saint Augustine's successors passed on to the sixteenth century. For given the power and personality of God it is inconceivable that whoever has faith in Him will seek elsewhere the practical assurance that the just cause will indeed triumph.[25]

Under the circumstances, how is one to construe the defeat of the just? Saint Augustine answers that this painful result by no means exhausts the resources of the divine will to eventually restore the harmony of order and the triumph of justice.[26] What it all means is that the catastrophes which are such an integral part of the city of man are visited even upon the just. The difference between the disaster which overtakes the wicked and the calamities that afflict the righteous is that in the former case a merited punishment is meted out to the guilty whereas in the latter his misfortune is a sign of redemption. For no matter how just the just be, they also have faults to expiate. Righteous men must see in this Providential punishment the opportunity to apply themselves diligently to further and more strenuous efforts aimed at the moral and spiritual improvement of society.[27] In conclusion, God may sometimes decide to award victory to wicked men. Regardless of whom the laurels of victory go to, however, it is all a part of the will and design of God who humbles the vanquished for the sake of either removing or punishing their sins.

A corollary necessarily to be inferred from Saint Augustine's proposition concerning the justice of some wars is that under certain circumstances it is lawful for Christians to kill. When explaining the meaning of the commandment 'Thou shalt not kill' the Bishop of Hippo had distinguished two cases in which it is permissible to put another man to death without breaking the Old Testament's injunctions. Under any other conditions 'whoever kills a man, either himself or another, is implicated in the guilt of murder'.[28] The first case applies to self-defense,[29] although

---

[24] See Deane, *The Social and Political Ideas of Saint Augustine*, ch. III.
[25] Monceaux, 'Saint Augustin et la guerre', pp. 22–3.
[26] H.-X. Arquilière, *L'Augustinisme politique* (Paris, 1955), p. 569.
[27] *DCD*, I 1, p. 2; V 23, p. 104.   [28] *Ibid.*, I 2, p. 15.
[29] Saint Augustine, *The Free Choice of the Will*, trans. R. P. Russell (Washington, 1967), p. 81. Cited hereafter as *DLA*.

it is to be noted that Saint Augustine has some serious reservations on that score, as witnessed by his statements in a letter to Publicola and certain passages in *De libero arbitrio*.[30] The second case applies to soldiers or public functionaries acting in defense of others or their city. Indeed, a soldier who fails to do his duty is guilty of treason to the state.[31] In this manner Saint Augustine also sanctions defensive war as lawful. 'One can, therefore, without passion, obey a law enacted for the protection of its citizens when it commands that an enemy force be met with the same kind of force. The same may be said of all public servants who are subject to the ruling powers according to the existing law and established order.'[32] But what happens when the soldiers are convinced that the war they are ordered to wage is an unjust war? In matters of personal self-defense Saint Augustine grants the individual a great deal of latitude, for he may refuse if he so chooses to defend his goods, virtue, or life against the violence of other men. This choice the Bishop of Hippo denies the soldiers. Instead, he demands obedience of them regardless of the circumstances.[33]

Saint Augustine bequeathed his medieval successors a complex of ideas of extraordinary and lasting influence, a basic fabric on which the Middle Ages embroidered extensively and profoundly: theologians, canonists, lawyers, mystics, heretics – from Isidore of Seville to Aquinas, from Raymond Lull to Wyclif and Peter Chelchitzky. All at one time or another dealt with the subject of man, the state, and war from premises proposed by the Bishop of Hippo. This is not to say that all his conclusions were uncritically accepted. Chelchitzky's genuine pacifism, for example, is a clear rejection of Augustine's doctrine on war.[34] But within the more orthodox stream of medieval thought Saint Augustine remained largely unchallenged. In the words of Regout, 'Saint Augustine laid the foundations which made possible all subsequent building. Within his doctrine are enclosed the three conditions essential to the undertaking of war and invariably invoked throughout the history of the theory of the just war: the authority of the prince, a just cause, and right intention.'[35] A judgment, we shall see, also largely applicable to the sixteenth century.

An important characteristic of Saint Augustine's writings is that they are works of exhortation and controversy designed to answer questions posed by the conditions of his own age. These, of course, were not the same as those prevailing in the early sixteenth century. But the sense of

[30] *Letters*, Ep. xlvii 5, p. 293; *DLA*, pp. 81, 82.
[31] *DCD*, 1 26, p. 17; *Letters*, Ep. xlvii 5, p. 293.
[32] DLA, p. 82. [33] *CFM*, xxii 75, p. 301.
[34] See Brock, *The Political and Social Doctrines of the Unity of the Czech Brethren*.
[35] Regout, *La doctrine de la guerre juste de Saint Augustin*. p. 44.

crisis was common to both periods and its effects identical in that it caused a reappraisal of the fundamental tenets which guided man both as a Christian and a socio-political being. Thus, an essential ingredient in the sixteenth-century sense of crisis was the question of war, one which acquired phenomenal significance precisely because of the continued currency of that Augustinian scheme whereby man, the state, and war were all securely woven into one single theme. Our next task, therefore, will be to see how the age of Erasmus received Saint Augustine's postulates on war and to appraise its own contribution. Special emphasis will be placed on Erasmus himself. The choice needs no justification, for nowhere can we hope to find a better or more accomplished formulation of the Renaissance's concern with the problem of war than in the writings of this most distinguished and influential Christian humanist.

Erasmian pacifism and the Neoscholastic doctrine of the just war

Erasmus' diatribes against violence and the profound contempt he felt for its practitioners have often been judged to be proof of his pacifism. If, however, we understand pacifism to be a posture toward war comparable to that of Tertullian, Chelchitzky, or some of the sixteenth-century Anabaptists, then Erasmus was not a pacifist. In addition to elaborating on this point, I shall attempt to show that barring extreme positions such as Machiavelli's any departure from strict pacifism inevitably leads to an acceptance of those principles espoused by the theory of the just war.

Among contemporary Neoscholastics the problem of war was intimately bound to a complex conception of the state. Such is not the case with Erasmus for whom war literally remains a 'disease of man's wit'. In this sense Erasmus never takes the momentous step marking the appearance of the modern state: the transition from war conceived as hostility between two individuals to war understood as the exclusive prerogative of the state. War continues to be associated in his mind with individual man. Of course, in the reality of the day when in practice war was waged by states its individualism could not be maintained without concessions. And herein lies the great usefulness of the prince. By incorporating the idea of the state so completely with him, Erasmus dispenses with the need for taking into account difficult abstractions while at the same time acknowledging the inevitable: the existence of the state.

Although based on far more elaborate doctrinal premises, the advocates of the theory of the just war held the authority of the prince in a similarly high esteem. This concordance of views between Erasmus and Neoscholasticism is not without significance, for as we shall soon see the prince's role as the unchallenged arbiter of war and peace is central to both. It is therefore of interest to record Vitoria's unqualified support of the prince's authority to wage war.

Second proposition: Every State has authority to declare and to make war... Third proposition: A prince has the same authority in this respect as the State has. This is the opinion of Saint Augustine (*Contra Faustum*): 'The natural order, best adapted to secure the peace of mankind, requires that the authority to make war and the advisability of it should be in the hands of the sovereign prince.' Reason supports this, for the prince only holds his position by the election of the State. Therefore he is its representative and wields its authority; aye, and where there are already lawful princes in a State, all authority is in their hands and without them nothing of a public nature can be done either in war or in peace.[36]

Having deposited his faith and trust in the prince Erasmus is obviously in a position to remove war from the face of the earth with one stroke. Society cannot exist unless the more virulent forms of discord are banished; indeed, he argues, the troubles plaguing today's society stem from the fact that discord is rampant.[37] Discord is contrary to reason and ethics, both of which decree the need for society; discord is a violation of the law of nature and the law of God. In either case the transgressor is man. It is therefore up to individual man to stop discord. And in the case of that form of discord known as war the individual in question is none other than the prince, a rational and ethical being – rational because he is a man and ethical because he is a Christian. Such is broadly the nature of the Erasmian pattern which weaves society, the state, and war into a single unit containing the principles of the Christian humanist tradition in their fullest expression. And those principles rest on a foundation identical to that which supports the premises of Neoscholasticism: rational and ethical man.

What, then, is the difference between the viewpoints represented most typically and effectively among the Neoscholastics of the age by the School of Salamanca and the ideas of Erasmus? At this point we are already in a position to suggest that the most significant difference is a methodological one: abstraction as opposed to empiricism. Whereas orthodox opinion attempts to meet the demands of praxis by means of a thoroughly abstract framework, Erasmus' constant concern is to purge society of evils which he has empirically identified. But contrary to what this estimate may suggest at first sight, it is in the end the Spanish internationalists who disclose the more comprehensive grasp of contemporary reality and of its possibilities. Erasmus' early treatises on war, on the other hand, are

[36] *LW*, pp. 168–9.
[37] The subject is repeatedly considered in both *DBI* and *QP*.

plentifully supplied with grandiloquent rejections of violence which are little more than a collection of moralizing maxims.[38]

Although Erasmus never systematizes his two categories of man – rational man and Christian man – into a scheme capable of suggesting a twofold interpretation of war – one for war waged by, among, or against Christians and another as practiced by Christians – it is clear that they play no small part in shaping his views on war. In those propagandistic tracts (*Dulce bellum inexpertis*, *Querela pacis*) in which Erasmus castigates with such wrath man's warlike nature, he seems to envision the latter as a being living under two constraints: the commands of nature and the injunctions of Christian doctrine. The Erasmian man, then, is a Christian living in the midst of Christian society. At best this is a limited view of his own age; but it serves his purpose well, for it provides an uncomplicated point of view from which to damn an intolerable reality: Christian man slaughtering Christian man, and Christian king waging merciless war against Christian king. But Christ, Erasmus argues, taught us nothing but peace.[39] And what the master taught with His example the disciples continued to practice. Of what else but love, peace, charity, and meekness speak John, Peter, Paul?[40] Let those who claim that the 'law of nature commands, it is approved by the laws, and allowed by custom, that we ought to put off violence with violence'[41] remember that the law of Christ 'that is of more effect than all these things, commanded us...[that] we should do well to them that do ill to us'.[42]

With these arguments Erasmus answers the age-old question: are Christians permitted to wage war? As it might be expected this is a question carefully explored by the representatives of Neoscholasticism. Following in Saint Augustine's footsteps the Spanish school rejects Tertullian's denial that Christians may take up arms. Vitoria is swift and to the point: 'Passing over outside opinions, however, let my answer to the question be given in the single proposition: Christians may serve in war and make war.'[43] Nevertheless, pointing out that in the New Testament several injunctions are found which seemingly forbid even self-defense, Vitoria concedes that it is not enough to dismiss them with the argument that they are not matters of precept but merely of counsel. It is therefore not enough to think that Christians are permitted to wage war; convincing proof is essential. And this proof Vitoria offers in eight propositions. Three of them admit what the age for the most part accepted: to apply violence in self-defense is permissible. Suárez concurs: 'Defensive war is not only waged by public magistrates but also by private persons: for it is

[38] *DBI* (Mackail), p. 24.
[40] *Ibid.*, p. 960AB.
[42] *Ibid.*

[39] *DBI* (*Opera*), p. 959E.
[41] *DBI* (Mackail), p. 46.
[43] *LW*, p. 166.

always lawful to repel force by force...The reason is that the right of
self-defense is a natural and necessary one.'⁴⁴ And this right not even
Erasmus questions seriously. But it is with the last four Vitorian axioms
that we are most directly concerned, for in them Vitoria argues that
offensive wars are also allowed to Christians.

A fifth proof with regard to an offensive war is that even a defensive war
could not be waged satisfactorily, were no vengeance taken on enemies who
have done or tried to do a wrong. For they would only be emboldened to
make a second attack, if the fear of retribution did not keep them from wrongdoing. A sixth proof is that...the end and aim of war is the peace and security
of the State. But there can be no security...unless enemies are made to desist
from wrong by fear of war, for the situation with regard to war would be
glaringly unfair, if all that a State could do when enemies attack it unjustly was
to ward off the attack and if they could not follow this up by further steps. A
seventh proof comes from the end and aim and good of the whole world. For
there would be no condition of happiness for the world, nay, its condition
would be one of utter misery, if oppressors and robbers and plunderers could
with impunity commit their crimes and oppress the good and innocent, and
these latter could not in turn retaliate on them. My eighth and last proof is one
which in morals carries the utmost weight, namely, the authority and example
of good and holy men. Such men have not only defended their country and
their own property in defensive wars, but have also in offensive wars sought
reparation for wrongs done or attempted by their enemies.⁴⁵

Throughout its long history the theory of the just war had one fundamental purpose as its main goal: to examine all the avenues whereby war
could be controlled and turned into an ethical means of justly settling
disputes. Under the circumstances it would have been unrealistic to limit
the analysis to acts of strict self-defense. The apparatus of the doctrine of
the just war, instead, was designed to sanction offensive war – a form of
violence which emerges when some time has elapsed between the infliction
of the injury and the attempt at redress by the injured party. The line of
reasoning which at bottom sought to justify (conditionally, of course) the
waging of an offensive war thus claimed that only the fear of war will
keep malefactors in line. This fear, if it is to accomplish its purpose, need
imply not only the possibility of failure should the attacked be successful
in defending themselves, but also the threat of retaliation to be visited
upon the heads of those who unjustly engage in acts of violence. To carry
out such a program in practice was a task recognized as beset with
difficulties. For instance, Catejan, Aquinas' commentator and the man
most responsible for the revitalization of Scholasticism, acknowledges the

⁴⁴ Quoted in Eppstein, *The Catholic Tradition*, p. 108.
⁴⁵ *LW*, p. 167.

pitfalls and dangers inherent in the transition from an act of simple self-defense to one of premeditated violence. 'It is not here a question of justifying a defensive war, for according to natural law a people has the right to defend itself when unjustly attacked. The difficulty comes when one wishes to justify a war initiated by oneself.'[46] But neither Cajetan nor his followers were deterred by the risks.

Vitoria's – and Cajetan's – institutionalization of discord Erasmus rejects out of hand and will relentlessly attack it in all his anti-militarist writings, although he will later implicitly accept it. Nature, law, customs, we have seen him argue, are said to sanction war; but the Gospel most emphatically does not. And the word and example of Christ are for the Christian humanist the ultimate authorities. The roots of the Erasmian normative approach to the problem of war (and politics) are then to be found in the New Testament. Undoubtedly this should be a rather familiar conclusion by now. The importance of the role played by the Gospel in the debate on war, however, justifies both its reiteration and an additional observation; namely, that stress on the teachings of the New Testament did not preclude other authors from admitting that under certain conditions war may become inevitable and even desirable. One such author was Josse Clichtove, Christian humanist and one of the leading luminaries of the powerful Parisian faculty of theology.

Erasmus' unquestioning allegiance to the New Testament is also in sharp contrast with the approach best exemplified by the Spanish school. Spanish political thought from Vitoria to Suárez traditionally relied on the twin foundations of reason (natural law) and faith, understood to be embodied in the teachings of the Old Covenant and the New, respectively. Vitoria himself, in the third of the proofs mentioned above, claims that the waging of war by Christians is 'also allowable by the law of nature, as appears from the case of Abraham...and also the written law...But the Gospel forbids nothing which is allowed by natural law...Therefore, what was lawful under natural law and in the written law is no less lawful than under the Gospel law.'[47] The law of nature, ascertainable through reason and therefore the very pillar of man's *vita activa*, is available to all men. And Christians are particularly fortunate because in the Old Testament they have a sure guide to the principles of natural law. The teachings of the New Testament are thus reduced by inference to the status of counsels to be literally obeyed only by those who seek the sublime rewards of the *vita contemplativa*. And war, so much a part of man's life

[46] Cajetan, *Commentaria in IIam IIae Summae Theologicae St. Thomae Aquino* (1517), in the Editio Leonina of Saint Thomas' works (Rome, 1895), III, q. 40, a.1, s.II.

[47] *LW*, p. 166.

in society, cannot be properly understood in terms other than those founded on the law of nature. If we reflect, then, that the Spanish jurists of the sixteenth century are among the most competent students of natural law and that Spanish political thinkers founded their internationalist theories on natural law bases, it is no wonder that they should have similarly been the keenest and most articulate exponents of the doctrine of the just war.

On grounds (the teachings of Christ) inherently different from those pressed into service by orthodox opinion, Erasmus has denied that Christians may wage war. His chagrin is therefore understandable when he sees that despite the clear admonitions commanding Christians to love one another discord and strife are forever and everywhere rampant. And for what causes do men shed the blood of other men? Men die because of the 'little childish anger of another man'; a real or an imagined slight; an insignificant article omitted from some overlong treaty; a miscarried wedding; a 'merry scoff freely spoken'.[48] More serious and equally frequent is the tyrannical ambition of some princes whose passions, bridled in peace by vigorous laws and strong counselors, find freedom and fulfillment in discord.[49]

These telling arguments are never far from the consciousness of the proponents of the theory of the just war; and their whole ideology is devoted to answering them. Difference of religion, extension of empire, a prince's ambition, warns Vitoria, do not justify a war. 'There is a single and only just cause for commencing a war, namely, a wrong received.'[50] And even then the provocation may not justify warlike violence, for 'not every kind and degree of wrong can suffice for commencing a war'.[51] Draconian measures, then, have no place in Vitoria's scheme; instead, the punishment must be commensurate with the crime. At the other end of the Salmantine tradition the Jesuit Suárez upholds the same idea: '[War] must be properly conducted and a sense of proportion kept at the beginning, during hostilities and after the victory...The reason for this general conclusion is that, while a war is not *per se* evil, yet, because it may bring many misfortunes, it is one of those undertakings which are often ill done, and therefore it needs a good many conditions to make it just.'[52] A just war, it follows, must not and cannot be undertaken lightly. Only four reasons will be listed by Vitoria as fully justifying the waging of a war: firstly, in defense of ourselves and what belongs to us; secondly,

---

[48] *DBI* (Mackail), p. 14; *QP*, p. 30.
[49] *DBI* (Mackail), p. 58. See also Erasmus, *Scarabaeus aquilam quaerit*, in *The Adages of Erasmus*, trans. Margaret M. Phillips (Cambridge, 1964), pp. 273–83.
[50] *LW*, p. 170.
[51] *Ibid.*, p. 171.
[52] Quoted in Hamilton, *Political Thought in Sixteenth-Century Spain*, p. 142.

to recover things taken from us; thirdly, to avenge a wrong suffered by us; fourthly, to secure peace and security'.[53]

But, continues Erasmus as if intent on giving orthodoxy no respite, even in the rare instances when a war may be said to have been undertaken with right intention and to punish a grievous injury the result is the same, for the evils of discord far outstrip its blessings. There is no war regardless of the justice of the reasons which caused it and with how much moderation it is begun and prosecuted that will not carry in its wake an immense amount of crimes and calamities; and these evils are always most grievously shared by the innocent and harmless folk who never deserved to be visited with such a plague.[54] Under the circumstances it is better to let one transgressor go unpunished than to subject thousands to the horrors of war.[55]

Tradition did not neglect this important theme. Indeed, a good part of the argumentation proposed by Saint Augustine's followers has to do with the ways and means of preserving the innocent from the hardships of war. Thus Vitoria remarks that 'the deliberate slaughter of the innocent is never lawful in itself...wrong is not done by an innocent person. Therefore war may not be employed against him...[since] it is not lawful within a State to punish the innocent for the wrongdoing of the guilty. Therefore this is not lawful among enemies.'[56] As we shall shortly have occasion to observe, concern with the welfare of the innocent is so deeply ingrained in Vitoria that he argues that a prince may lawfully go to war against another sovereign ruler to protect the latter's subjects from further depredations at the hands of the tyrant. On the other hand, even the innocent are expendable given circumstances of enough gravity. The reason is simple: on the authority of Saint Augustine whatever is necessary to bring about the goal of war – the securing of just peace – is also lawful.[57]

Second proposition: Sometimes it is right, in virtue of collateral circumstances, to slay the innocent even knowingly, as when a fortress or a city is stormed in a just war, although it is known that there are a number of innocent people in it and although cannon and other engines of war cannot be discharged or fire applied to buildings without destroying innocent together with guilty. The proof is that war could not otherwise be waged against even the guilty and the justice of belligerents would be balked...Great attention, however, must be paid to...the obligation to see that greater evils do not arise out of the war

---

[53] *LW*, p. 182.

[54] Erasmus, Letter to Charles V (Basel, January 13, 1522), in *Obras escogidas de Erasmo*, trans. L. Riber (Madrid, 1964), p. 1238. Cited hereafter as *Obras*.

[55] *DBI* (*Opera*), p. 965A.

[56] *LW*, p. 178.   [57] *DI*, p. 155.

than the war would avert. For if little effect upon the ultimate issue of the war is to be expected from the storming of a fortress or fortified town wherein are many innocent folk. it would not be right, for the purpose of assailing a few guilty, to slay the many innocent.[58]

Thus it will not do, as suggested by Erasmus above, to grant impunity to the evildoer for the sake of the innocent's welfare. The result, argue the Spanish doctors unanimously, would be to further encourage the rapacity of the lawless and so plunge humanity into further chaos.

With these formidable conclusions Erasmus was thoroughly familiar. He remains, however, completely unimpressed choosing instead to ask the following rhetorical question: in view of the senselessness of war as we have depicted it why should a good prince even contemplate the possibility of undertaking wars? It is often said that it is only proper and fitting for a prince to fight for his rights. But who, after all, cannot find rightful titles to clothe his lust for power in respectable garments? And even assuming that the prince is indeed an honest man there is no guarantee that his rights are beyond questioning. Given the changes and alterations that the affairs of man undergo with the passage of time, who can want a title? At one time or another cities and countries have changed hands and those who today occupy this land yesterday belonged elsewhere. In short, no right or title claimed by man is beyond reproach.[59] An interesting and important semantic game is involved here. Erasmus was as well aware as any of his contemporaries that the phrase 'the rights of princes' meant nothing less than the inviolable rights and privileges of the entire community whose political nature found embodiment in the ruler. But the humanist elects to ignore this meaning emphasizing instead a more literal one. There is method in this, however, for Erasmus is at this point whole-heartedly interested in stressing the quality of contemporary reality; and undoubtedly in that praxis the European ruler was most often unable to distinguish between his own caprice, family or dynastic ambitions, and the true interests of his subjects. Erasmus' point, then, is well taken: how can a war be said to be waged to vindicate the rights of the whole when the prince is unable to distinguish between his own ambitions and the privileges of the commonwealth? Under the circumstances, concludes the Christian humanist, the truly wise man and gentle prince will ask himself the following question: is the goal I seek so important, the vindication of my rights so sacred that 'it will recompense the exceedingly great harm and loss to my people'?[60] Clearly the Erasmian prince has but one alternative. He must not concern himself with what he may gain by maintaining what he believes to be his rights but only with the threat posed by war

---

[58] *LW*, p. 179.   [59] *DBI (Opera)*, p. 965B.   [60] *DBI* (Mackail), p. 51.

to what he already possesses. If he weighs the blessings of peace against the ills of war he will reach but one conclusion: an unjust peace is far better than a just war.[61] And even if after all these considerations Christian men still cannot rise above the banality of material possessions and must insist on what they believe to be the sanctity of their rights, why go to war when it is so easy to submit disputes to the wise arbitration of upright men? Venerable abbots, wise and learned bishops, experienced noblemen of great age – any of these men could be called in to settle the petty quarrels of princes with justice and discretion.[62]

The position of tradition on this point is unequivocal: under no circumstances can an unjust peace be preferable to a just war. Vitoria and his followers are adamant. And the strength of their stand lies once again with the authority of the Bishop of Hippo. Saint Augustine had formulated a concept of peace which brooking no compromise was to serve for centuries as a most unimpeachable canon.

The peace of the body then consists in the duly proportioned arrangement of its parts. The peace of the irrational soul is the harmonious repose of the appetites, and that of the rational soul the harmony of knowledge and action. The peace of body and soul is the well-ordered and harmonious life and health of the living creature. Peace between man and God is the well-ordered obedience of faith to eternal law. Peace between man and man is well-ordered concord. Domestic peace is the well-ordered concord between those of the family who rule and those who obey. Civil peace is a similar concord among the citizens... The peace of all things is the tranquillity of order. Order is the distribution which allots things equal and unequal, each to its own place.[63]

The well-ordered concord which is the peace between man and man cannot exist in the earthly city, we have seen, for long without war. 'He, then, who prefers what is right to what is wrong, and what is well-ordered to what is perverted, sees that the peace of unjust men is not worthy to be called peace in comparison with the peace of the just.'[64] And it is in the very nature of the earthly city that just men shall be forced to wage war to obtain peace.

We have already had occasion to remark how the Spanish theologians insisted that the alternative to a just war is chaos and anarchy. There are, however, some important nuances involved in their position that should be clearly noticed and understood. To begin with, Vitoria remains deaf to anything but the more rigorously abstract meaning of the phrase 'the rights of princes'; not that he refuses to account for the presence of tyrants who willfully pervert that meaning. Rather, he simply endeavors to

[61] *DBI (Opera)*, p. 966B.　　　　[62] *Ibid.*, p. 966C.
[63] *DCD* xix 13, p. 409.　　　　[64] *Ibid.*, xix 12, p. 408.

transcend the impermanent quality of bad rulers by stressing an abstraction which is both permanent and ideal. The prince, then, goes to war to protect the inalienable rights of his charges. To do otherwise would be to betray the trust which alone justifies the existence of political authority. And this is why the Dominican theologian cannot accept Erasmus' dictum. Should the prince refrain from waging a just war and prefer instead an unjust peace, he would violate the trust placed in him by his flock – and natural law. But is this true in every instance? Vitoria concludes that it is incorrect to assume that a just war, merely by being just, will invariably attain the goal sought after, a just peace. And precisely because there are circumstances under which even a just war will not bring about an equitable peace, Vitoria concludes, the righteous prince must be extremely cautious when he studies the necessity – the strength of the injury inflicted on 'his' rights – of waging a just war. It is for this reason that the Spanish Neoscholastics were all for settling disputes by arbitration.[65]

Should arbitration fail to bring about an amicable solution recourse must be had to war. Even then, however, Vitoria claims that it is up to the prince to see to it that 'greater evils do not arise out of the war than the war would avert'.[66] A war, no matter how just, must not be undertaken if it promises to yield more ill than good. 'No war is just the conduct of which is manifestly more harmful to the State than it is good and advantageous; and this is true regardless of other claims or reasons advanced to make of it a just war.' Once it has been ascertained that the war, if waged, will not be the proverbial remedy causing the death of the patient, the next step is for the ruler to make unquestionably certain that his cause is indeed just. And this certainty cannot be given by the prince's opinion alone.

On this point let my first proposition be: This belief is not always enough. As for proof I rely, first, on the fact that in some matters of less moment it is not enough either for a prince or for private persons to believe that they are acting justly. This is notorious, for their error may be vincible and deliberate, and the opinion of the individual is not enough to render an act good, but it must come up to the standard of a wise man's judgment, as appears from [Aristotle's] *Ethics*, bk. 2. Also the result would otherwise be that very many wars would be just on both sides, for although it is not a common occurrence for princes to wage war in bad faith, they nearly always think theirs is a just cause. In this way all belligerents would be innocent and it would not be lawful to kill them.[67]

[65] Quoted in Hamilton, *Political Thought in Sixteenth-Century Spain*, p. 146.
[66] *LW*, p. 179.
[67] *Ibid.*, p. 173.

Regardless of his personal honesty, then, a ruler is not fit to decide unilaterally on such weighty matters, for 'the possibility of a mistake on his part is not unlikely and such a mistake would bring great evil and ruin to multitudes. Therefore war ought not to be made on the sole judgment of the king nor indeed on the judgment of the few, but on that of many, and they be wise and upright men.'[68] Herein, therefore, lies one standard which may aid in the search for certainty: the judgment of wise men. The implication is clear. The prince himself must be both a good and prudent man advised and surrounded by good and wise men who shall partake of the duties and responsibilities of the government – an idea endlessly stressed by Erasmus himself throughout the pages of the *Education*. The difference, already mentioned above, is that the Erasmian prince and his counselors will use the Gospel as the sole source of their inspiration; whereas the Vitorian ruler and his aides will seek advice on secular matters in natural law. In addition, Vitoria is keenly interested in avoiding that deplorable state of affairs in which a war is apparently just on both sides. Since this can only take place through ignorance, the best solution is to subject the matter to the careful scrutiny of the wise. But there is another reason behind the theologian's insistence that no doubts be harbored concerning the justice of a ruler's cause. One of the most important premises supporting Vitoria's scheme is the power to dispense justice vested in the prince who wages a just war. 'A prince who is carrying on a just war is as it were his own judge in matters touching the war.'[69] The reasons are obvious.

If a State can [punish] its own citizens, society at large no doubt can do it to all wicked and dangerous folk, and this can only be through the instrumentality of princes. It is therefore certain that princes can punish enemies who have done a wrong to their State and that after a war has been duly and justly undertaken the enemy are just as much within the jurisdiction of the prince who undertakes it as if he were their proper judge.[70]

Once the authority of the prince to wage a just war has been accepted he becomes the sole judge competent to resolve the issues involved. Vitoria sees the warring just prince as the repository, both *de facto* and *de jure*, of that subtle authority associated with the total community of man, the *jus gentium*. It is therefore necessary, argues the Dominican, to eliminate all possible ambiguities concerning the justice of a ruler's cause. And so the prince's new role is both a privilege and a burden, for he must forego all vindictiveness and behave with the impartiality of a common judge. Should he do less he would become a lawless man. The prince who takes excessive measures against his foe automatically forfeits the justice of his cause, for the avenging of a wrong and the punishment of the guilty must always be tempered by the notion of justice. A just war, then, is a perishable commodity and a war begun justly may lose its justice through the wrongful actions of the prince. The judge must not brutalize the convict, for even though the latter be guilty the former is a Christian ruler and not a ruthless conqueror. To sum up: war must not be declared unless the ruler is certain of the justice of his cause; war cannot be waged if it pledges to produce more harm than good; a sovereign waging a just war must proceed with equanimity. Doubtless these are important restraints which circumscribe the manner in and the circumstances under which even just wars may be waged. Most significant of all, however, is Vitoria's emphatic belief that the ultimate and truest test of the righteousness of a war is whether it will bring good to the whole: 'Since one nation is a part of the whole world, and since the Christian province is a part of the whole Christian State, if any war should be advantageous to one province or nation but injurious to the whole or to Christendom, it is my belief that, for this very reason, that war is unjust.'[71]

Erasmus' fascination with the potential for virtue encompassed by the office and person of the Christian prince is not one bit less intense than Vitoria's. In his propagandistic treatises he seeks to shock his readers by showing the absurdity of war. The purpose of the *Education* is not entirely dissimilar, although now he aims his message at one man. But this one man, given the humanist's reliance on the ruler as the only available mechanism for change, is of crucial importance. Unquestionably, the very nature of a treatise trying to acquaint a man who must deal in the reality of affairs of state with the rational and ethical principles which must govern his conduct demands a shift in emphasis: from an emotional to a profound and dispassionate analysis of the possibilities open to the one man possessing the power to declare or stay war.[72] That this essential shift is kept to a minimum is a measure of Erasmus' limitations as a political thinker. He once again counsels that at no time must a prince be more careful than when he weighs the possibility of going to war;[73] it is a foregone conclusion that the good Christian will shrink from war and instead endeavor to find other alternatives.[74]

These ideas have not only been offered already by Erasmus himself but have of themselves no intrinsic novelty, for they were thoroughly familiar to the traditional school of the just war. Still, the *Education* admits in this context two very significant points. First, Erasmus concedes the existence of circumstances which may leave the prince no alternative but to have recourse to arms. Second, the prince does have rights and these must not

[71] *DPC*, LXXXII.
[73] *IPC* (Born), p. 249.
[72] *DBI* (*Opera*), p. 966C.
[74] *Ibid.*, p. 252.

be violated. All this suggests two important questions. What are the circumstances under which the prince must resort to war? What are these princely rights? These questions are not only fundamental to the theory of the just war, but they are also an integral part of any discussion of the nature of man viewed as a social and political being, and crucial to the understanding of the state in its relations with other states and with its own subjects. But Erasmus, although writing about man, society, and the state, does not attempt to answer them. Instead he urges the ruler who insists on defending his rights with weapons in hand to ask himself the following question: 'Shall I, one person, be the cause of so many calamities?'[75]

As might well be expected this is a question by no means neglected by Vitoria; indeed, his interest yields the three canons of the ethics of war, a blueprint which while based on Saint Augustine would nonetheless do honor to Erasmus at his most normative.

First canon: Assuming that a prince has the authority to make war, he should first of all not go seeking occasions and causes of war, but should, if possible, live in peace with all men, as St Paul enjoins on us (Romans, ch. 12). Moreover, he should reflect that others are his neighbors, whom we are bound to love as ourselves, and that we all have one common Lord, before whose tribunal we shall have to render our account. For it is the extreme of savagery to seek for and rejoice in grounds for killing and destroying men whom God has created and for whom Christ died. But only under compulsion and reluctantly should he come to the necessity of war. Second canon: When war for a just cause has broken out, it must not be waged so as to ruin the people against whom it is directed, but only so as to obtain one's rights and the defense of one's country and in order that from that war peace and security may in time result. Third canon: When victory has been won and the war is over, the victory should be utilized with moderation and Christian humility, and the victor ought to deem that he is sitting as judge between two States, the one which has been wronged and the one which has done wrong, so that it will be as judge and not as accuser that he will deliver the judgment whereby the injured State can obtain satisfaction, and this, so far as possible should involve the offending State in the least degree of calamity and misfortune, the offending individuals being chastised within lawful limits; and an especial reason for this is that in general among Christians all the fault is to be laid at the door of their princes, for subjects when fighting for their princes act in good faith and it is thoroughly unjust, in the words of the poet, that 'for every folly their kings commit the punishment should fall upon the Greeks'.[76]

The balance of Erasmus' ideas on war as they appear in various treatises dating from the early years of the century constitute, on the surface, a clear rejection of the tenets indispensable to the theory of the just war. Christians

[75] *Ibid.*, pp. 253–4.   [76] *LW*, p. 187.

may not wage war, for the teachings of Christ are emphatic rejections of violence binding upon His followers. The rights of princes are in the best of cases questionable, and in the worst a web of fabricated lies woven to justify the evil passions of rulers. A war waged to protect the innocent is a myth because the innocent are the very ones upon whose shoulders the scourge of war is laid most heavily. A just war may perchance exist, but it is highly doubtful. Evildoers, criminals, murderers, are never punished in war; indeed, far from it, they are the very ones who under the name of soldiers wreak havoc upon the human race.

Are we to conclude, then, that Erasmus and the advocates of the just war are separated by an unbridgeable chasm? I think not, and for two reasons. In the first place, we have seen that the Neoscholastic position is far from dogmatic. All the dangers which Erasmus identifies as besetting the theory of the just war are considered and accounted for by Vitoria in a manner which by the middle of the century had turned the traditional position toward war into a very flexible fabric. The real difference between Erasmus and Vitoria seems to be that the balance of the former's ideas advocated in the treatises here surveyed stresses Erasmus' belief that it is impossible to translate the concept of the just war into reality, a belief that lends credence to the conclusion that Erasmus is a pacifist. And this brings us to the second of the reasons promised above. Erasmus' fascination with the nature of war remained unabated until the end of his life. And in his later years, with the illusions of his halcyon days shattered, a less uncompromising position toward war emerges from his writings. If this later stand is understood in the context of the breadth and plasticity of Vitoria's own it is not difficult to admit that a *rapprochement* between these two representative thinkers is indeed possible.

The question of Erasmus' change of attitude toward war in later writings has been treated in detail elsewhere.[77] I shall limit myself here to summarizing those findings. Christians may wage war. Christians may wage war against Christians. War, if it is to be war and not *latrocinium*, must be waged with *recta intentio* and no thought for self-aggrandizement. War must always be the last remedy to be resorted to only when mediation and the utmost forebearance have utterly failed. War must be conducted

---

Erasmus' change of heart may have been influenced by the official attitude of the powerful Parisian Faculty of Theology toward 'pacifist' ideas. In May of 1526, Noel Beda, the Faculty's Syndic, published his *Annotationes*, a scathing attack on Lefèvre d'Étaples' opinions on war and peace. While Beda's wrath was aimed primarily at Lefèvre, Erasmus also came in for a share, and in June of the same year the theologians censured and formally condemned a French translation of the *Querela pacis*. See W. F. Bense, 'Paris theologians on war and peace, 1521–1529', *CH*, xli, 2(1972), pp. 168–85. On Erasmus' later thoughts concerning war, see my article, 'Erasmus on the just war', *JHI*, xxxiv (1973), pp. 209–25.

in such a way as to be bloodless, short-lived, and not injurious to the innocent. It must only be waged for the public well-being, the safety of the republic, and the aid of one's friends in distress. These conclusions bring Erasmus into the fold of those thinkers who accept that war may under certain circumstances be just. That this should be so in the case of Erasmus takes us again to the argument proposed at the beginning concerning the danger besetting the age's pacifism. No one could doubt Erasmus' genuine hatred of war. But neither can it be denied that his fear of internal dissension and revolution is equally overwhelming.[78] And this is precisely the tangled web trapping would-be pacifists. For, as Erasmus confesses, to accept the lawfulness of the magistrate's sword necessarily implies acceptance of the prince's; and from there on there is no stopping.

Vives on concord and discord

Although undoubtedly the most prominent representative of his school Erasmus is by no means the only Christian humanist concerned with the phenomenon of war. What, then, is the position of the more influential among his correligionists and disciples – Vives, More, Rabelais, Alfonso de Valdés – on this question? To a man they seem to have advocated not only ideas paralleling those of Erasmus but to have shared with him as well the same ambivalence toward the traditional doctrine of the just war.

Of all the scholars mentioned above it was perhaps Juan Luis Vives who came closest to the master's (in some ways even surpassing his) passionate opposition to war. In his *De concordia et discordia in humano genere* the Spanish humanist's thought is primarily guided by the following considerations: the natural oneness of human society and discord's role in both destroying that unity and preventing its return; man's responsibility for his own wretched fate, his hope for the return of universal society, and the obstacles lying in the path of this desire; the impermanent character and relative value of man-made institutions and the threat posed by war to the stability of the most important of them all, the state. Vives will endlessly argue that concord is the only cure for the world's ills and it is man himself, not the state or a prince, who will bring true and everlasting peace to the world.

As Vives sees it, therefore, discord is both the formidable obstacle in the path toward final and everlasting reform and the witness which testifies since time immemorial to man's stubborn refusal to mend his ways. Those same traits unique to mankind which make possible the existence of society lead to concord among men. Concord brought humanity together;

[78] Erasmus, Letter to Martin Bucer (1527), in J. Huizinga, *Erasmus and the Age of the Reformation* (New York, 1957), pp. 343 *et sqq.*

it founded, aggrandized, and preserves cities; it introduced those arts beneficial to life, the well-being of tranquillity, the cultivation of the spirit; it made men great in wisdom, erudition, virtue.[79] Discord on the other hand embodies all those factors which isolate man from other men. It filled men with fears and terrors, made them suspicious of their peers everywhere. Discord – breaking the bonds of peace – dispersed the human community, destroyed cities, brought hunger and plague. Discord is responsible for laziness and immorality and finds its staunchest defenders among the licentious soldiery.[80] But, what took man away from the right course precipitating him instead into his present state of despair? Why, in other words, is mankind forever waging war against itself? Vives answers that man's ambition is to blame. Man lost his humanity because he refused to be content and satisfied with it. He ambitioned the divinity of God and in his mad attempt to scale forbidden heights he plunged himself into the bottomless abyss of discord.[81] Vives nevertheless claims that this desire of man to emulate God is not evil or wrong in itself; what is wicked and reprehensible is the means by which he chose to fulfill his ambition. Had man chosen a different road to elevate himself who knows to what pinnacle of wisdom he might have soared. Instead, falling prey to the devil's adulation man rose to such dizzy heights of arrogance that the ensuing fall was indeed grievous.[82] Despite man's sin, however, the road is still open because God in His infinite mercy sought to redress what man had willfully corrupted; to that end His own Son was sent to earth. Thus man's true plight lies no longer in the magnitude of the disaster that overtook him in his presumption. Rather, man's worst enemy is his inability to forget, to erase the evil memory of his great failure. And this is why he lives the present as a slave of the past wickedly blaming nature for the discord which agitates his daily life. The desire to rise above his peers, the passion for authority and power, the thirst for influence, honors, fame, the sin of pride – these are the causes of his endless plight.[83] And these causes will disappear when man in alliance with God shall do away with 'all those makeshift institutions devised by him to survive in a hostile world'.[84]

This last idea does not appear to disturb Vives unduly although it is alarmingly reminiscent of the many apocalyptic solutions to society's ills enjoying wide currency during the age. The reason is implicitly given by

---

[79] *CD*, p. 321.   [80] *Ibid*.

[81] For Saint Augustine's ideas on the subject see *The Social and Political Ideas of Saint Augustine*, p. 17.

[82] *CD*, in *Obras completas de Juan Luis Vives*, ed. and trans. L. Riber (2 vols., Madrid, 1948), II, p. 87.

[83] *CD (Obras), passim*.   [84] See above, p. 89.

Vives himself. He does not contemplate the advent of reform in any sudden and cataclysmic manner; on the contrary, it will shortly become clear that he does not welcome revolutionary upheavals as the means to bring about the millennium. Instead Vives conceives the eventual disappearance of those institutions devised by man for self-protection as a slow and gradual process resulting directly from man's growing awareness, aided and abetted by education, of his dual nature as a rational being and a child of Christ. Vives, then, is by no means a revolutionary. His political philosophy, based on a somewhat surprisingly tacit acceptance of the state, is simplistic in outlook and limited in goals: the state, a human and imperfect institution, will at best provide a comparative haven where man can partially fulfill his social yearnings. For that limited purpose, Vives implicitly concedes, man's compacts may be enough. In this manner the role of the state, despite the author's rhetorical pleading with princes to bring about international harmony, is confined to the preservation of a just social order within its own frontiers. And no one is better prepared to carry out the task successfully than the true Christian prince. Although Vives' political thought is evidently incomplete and sketchy his acceptance of the state as a desirable, if only temporarily, institution creates very serious problems for the internal logic of his system. The substance and import of these difficulties emerge only directly out of Vives' attempt to answer the arguments of those who maintained that under certain conditions the waging of war is justified. For instance, to the argument that the recovery of property unjustly taken away from its rightful owner is a sound reason for declaring and waging a just war Vives replies that this appeal for the restoration of stolen property is more often than not used simply to disguise greed. True, he admits, private possessions are in accordance with natural law;[85] but avarice and greed invariably lie at the root of all wars. 'Our insides are hardened by the desire to possess; it turns us into merciless savages and expels from us all feelings of humanity and meekness.'[86] How, then, knowing that all violence and discord originate in this evil desire to forever increase our possessions can we justify a war aimed at satisfying this yearning for property? 'An excellent reason it is, indeed! To enrich a scoundrel unworthy of the air he breathes you do not hesitate to deprive so many good men of their patrimony, their children, their lives!'[87]

In line with his inclination to examine empirically what the Scholastic tradition tended to confine to the realm of the abstract, Vives explains what happens in effect when the orthodox concept of just revenge is put into practical terms. A hasty word, an unintended slight, a trivial insult

[85] For a full exposition of Vives' ideas on property see *DCR*.
[86] *CD (Opera)*, p. 219.   [87] *Ibid.*, pp. 218–19.

are magnified by man's overbearing pride into deadly affronts to his honor and only revenge accompanied by the abundant shedding of blood can mitigate them. But, after all, what is honor? 'Honor is nothing more than a certain homage paid by those who judge virtue with the right criterion.'[88] Fools, on the other hand, believe that honor is something to be forever soothed and praised and pay little regard to the source of adulation. This lack of discrimination makes them easy prey to the real or imagined slights of the unworthy. And herein lies a foolish but prevalent cause for discord for, Vives observes pessimistically, it is the fool's definition of honor which predominates in the affairs of man. Moreover, the relations among states are often conditioned and swayed by the touchy vanity of those fools who being rude and therefore dominated by judgments born out of passion and not out of the calm contemplation of truth furiously embrace the foolish definition of honor and precipitate wars to revenge a real or imagined slight. Such is the origin, Vives maintains, of the Franco-Spanish rivalry which began with Charles VIII's invasion of Italy.[89] However, he proceeds, let us assume that the injury inflicted upon us is not only real but grievous as well. What shall we do in that case? If we seek to revenge ourselves we should first know what vengeance is: 'Two are the kinds of vengeance: one is bestial, the other diabolical. Neither is human.'[90] It follows that those who demand vengeance equate themselves with beasts or become accomplices of the devil, for none other is the origin of discord. Vengeance is born of vengeance in a cycle that never ends, forever yielding misery and banishing concord from the society of man. What do we pretend to achieve with vengeance? Retribution? But the injury is inflicted by the spirit, the will of he who wrongs; and the spirit is the one thing which man cannot touch with either knowledge or revenge. On the other hand the injury does not exist if there was no desire to wrong. In conclusion, it is far more fitting for man to forgive than to pursue the bitter satisfaction of revenge: 'Is vengeance comparable with the sweet fruit, the ineffable pleasure of forgiveness and reconciliation? Vengeance is a base satisfaction and a bestial appetite...who had ever reason to repent of having shown clemency?'[91] Orthodox opinion from Saint Augustine to Vitoria had viewed vengeance as a means of punishing the guilty and forcing him into the path of righteousness or at least of harmlessness. With Vives vengeance becomes at best a ridiculous manifestation of man's folly, at worst an exercise in man's surrender to his bestial instincts. The best way to concord is not vengeance but charity. Concord would be re-established and consolidated far more rapidly if both contenders, yielding their respective pretensions on the altar of charity

88 *Ibid.*, p. 282.   89 *Ibid.*, p. 283.
90 *Ibid.*, p. 233.   91 *Ibid.*, pp. 326–7.

and benevolence, would: he who injured repent and he who was injured forgive. This is the shortest path to the concord taught us by the Son of God.[92]

But the strongest argument presented by the defenders of the doctrine of the just war was that under certain conditions the safety of the state, and therefore that of society, can only be preserved by waging war against the wicked enemy who seeks the destruction of the commonwealth. Is this really true, asks Vives? Does war, no matter how just and saintly, indeed preserve the state and man from harm? To begin with, he replies, discord necessarily endangers the very position and dignity of the ruler who is the embodiment of the state's majesty. The king who is waging war neither controls his kingdom nor is able to aid the laws and succor equity; quite on the contrary, against his own will he finds himself forced to endure all sorts of affronts to justice and the laws because he cannot punish the evildoer. 'Do we call this government? Is this political power? Is it not rather a dungeon full of vermin and darkness?'[93] And the pillars on which the edifice of a well-ordered society rests soon begin to crumble. With the neglect of justice, which all recognize to be the nexus of human solidarity, liberty perishes. And liberty is what makes a man look at his fellows as men, not beasts.[94] In that well-ordered society where concord reigns unchallenged the laws give security and protection to the righteous while confining the wicked with bonds of fear. Discord changes all that. Banishing justice and destroying the laws, discord protects the evil and punishes the good.[95] And there is more. War not only subverts justice and liberty in the commonwealth but, by turning the king into a tyrant, precipitates internal dissensions and civil strife. The expenses of war will force even the righteous sovereign to load his subjects with financial exactions that will surely squeeze the poor people dry.[96] The citizens will inevitably be alienated by such tyrannical behavior and whereas in peace the ruler was the object of affection in war he becomes the target of hatred. This will surely doom any commonwealth, for no empire preserves its security without the people's benevolence.[97]

According to Vives, then, a prince who is busy fighting a war will neglect the management of his own realm and thus open the door to all forms of internecine struggles. Far from protecting the people of the commonwealth, war will expose them to the brutality and avariciousness of the soldiery, the bestial instrument of man's insanity. And far from insuring the safety of the state and the society which the latter embodies, war brings into their midst its own natural camp followers: rebellion and

92 *Ibid.*, pp. 231–2.
93 *CD (Opera)*, p. 281.
94 *Ibid.*, p. 314.
95 *Ibid.*
96 *Ibid.*, p. 281.
97 *Ibid.*, p. 282.

internal anarchy. Such are the results of war waged without; a conclusion of great significance indeed. A brief recapitulation of Vives' premises will show us why. Man is a social animal naturally destined to live among his peers. The outward manifestation of man's sin, war, soon broke the ecumenical character of society. Forced to salvage what he could, man, in his new and wretched life, devised the state to protect the fragmentary pieces of his formerly monolithic society. Eventually, with the coming of Christ, man's universal society became once again a possibility. This potential, however, will not be actualized unless man comes to his senses – to which goal is devoted Vives' entire normative ideology. Until that happens man must protect the state at all costs, for it remains his only hope for the preservation of the various social islands in which man's nature finds relative fulfillment. And the enemy today as in the bygone epoch of society's oneness is discord; specifically war among states. Thus the same war which the Neoscholastics understood would preserve the state, Vives argues, threatens to sink the various rafts affording protection to man; while guided by reason and Christ he seeks to reach the promised land: the Golden Age of social unity. In a sense, then, for Vives the integrity of the *respublica Christiana* is not beyond hope of recovery.

This should further our understanding of Vives' attitude toward the Anabaptists. His prejudices against them (the *De communione rerum* was written in 1535, five years before his death) were exclusively shaped by the wretched example of the Münsterites. For Vives as for his contemporaries the Anabaptists were not an evangelical movement espousing principles not entirely unlike his own but a fanatical fifth column single-mindedly devoted to the subversion of internal peace, men whose activities, if unchecked, sorely threatened the stability of those holds to which men precariously clung while awaiting the return of the millennium. These reprobates, we are reminded, would force mankind into an unnatural pattern of life based upon the community of material things. Their aims are not unlike those of Spartacus who unleashed the wars of the slaves, Catilina who conspired against the fatherland, or those pirates whose greed is the scourge of land and sea.[98] A war waged against such evil-doers, it follows, is not the reprehensible activity against which Vives inveighs, for 'force alone can domesticate force'.[99] In fact it is not war at all but a 'police action'. 'Those among you who behave in such a reprehensible fashion force princes and magistrates into the path of cruelty. Should they behave differently they would fail in that duty imposed upon them by God – the defense of their peoples.'[100] Vives, however, is not blind to

[98] Juan Luis Vives, *De communione rerum*, in *Obras*, I, pp. 1414–15. Cited hereafter as *DCR*.
[99] *Ibid.*, p. 1414.   [100] *Ibid.*

the fact that among the lunatic fringe which he so unequivocally disowns and banishes from the community of man there are those who have been deluded. Toward them the Christian humanist recommends clemency. As for the leaders, those whom he brands as 'shameless, villainous, cretinous knaves who manipulate the gullible for their own greed or other unmentionable purposes', Vives harbors no mercy. 'They must be abandoned to the civil power; their fate must be sealed by "he who not without cause wields the sword". For, if he brandishes it without passion against thieves, adulterers, and cheaters, why should he not unsheathe it, equally without passion, against this stenchful pit source of all evil?'[101]

Even after this brief excursion into Vives' thought on war and state it is difficult to discover conclusively whether the Christian humanist was aware of the possible conflict of interest arising out of his simultaneous acceptance of the state – albeit as an ephemeral institution doomed to an eventual demise – and his rejection of war. The reason for this uncertainty, it seems, is that Vives, in contrast to Erasmus, never felt compelled by circumstances to temper his indictment of war among Christians or understood the need to view war in less broad and all-embracing terms. His study of the Anabaptist case might have put him on the right track, but he forestalls the inevitable by a timely definition of the Münster episode and all other future such movements as a problem of dimensions strictly internal to the state. Had Vives, however, squarely faced in this instance what he has implicitly accepted throughout his lengthy indictment of discord, namely, that war, whether between two men or two republics, still remains war, the sophistries invoked to support a distinction between internal strife and international anarchy would have been superfluous. As it is we can in truth only grasp at straws and suggest that it may be argued, as it may with far stronger cause in the case of Menno Simons, that Vives' admission of the magistrates' right to wield the sword is to all intents and purposes a fateful concession exhibiting all the dangerous characteristics of a Trojan horse.

Christian humanism and conditional bellicism: Valdés, Rabelais, and More

Whereas Vives' dubious surrender to the pragmatic logic of the theory of the just war is both reluctant and involuntary, such is decidedly not the case with his compatriot Valdés, with the scathing chronicler of the Picrocholine War (Book I of *Gargantua and Pantagruel*) François Rabelais, or with the Oxford reformer and creator of an utopian society Thomas More. The imperial secretary, with the practical spirit of a man

[101] *Ibid.*, pp. 1415–16.

of affairs which we have already had occasion to observe, stands alone as having applied to a concrete contemporary event – the papal–imperial struggle climaxed by the sack of Rome (1527) and followed by a war of pamphlets to which in defense of his master he contributed the *Diálogo de las cosas ocurridas en Roma* – that ideology of which he was the standard bearer at the court of Charles V.

In typically Erasmian fashion, Valdés unquestionably accepts that Christ stood for peace. 'Obviously the Author of peace considers nothing more abominable than war.'[102] Those who search the evangelical doctrine shall find nothing but peace, concord, unity, love, and charity,[103] for Christ gave us peace when he was born and peace when he died.[104] And not only is war contrary to Christian doctrine but it goes flatly against the intentions of nature as well. 'Nature equipped all animals with the means for defense and attack. Man was the only creature not so provided. In the image of God he comes from heaven, where complete harmony prevails. God did not mean for man to wage war. He wanted as much harmony among men as there is among angels.'[105] What Christ taught and nature ordained is surely binding on man. It is the duty of princes, then, to see to it that peace shall reign in the world: 'With your neighbors, O prince, endeavor always to be at peace and in amity.'[106] Describing Grangousier's reaction to the news that Picrochole has treacherously invaded his lands, Rabelais gives us a view of war and Christianity not unlike that of Valdés.

The day of conquering kingdoms to your Christian neighbor's loss is long since past. To imitate the ancient Herculeses, Alexanders, Hannibals, Scipios, Caesars and that ilk is contrary to the profession of the Gospel. Does not Christ enjoin us each to preserve, rule, keep and administer his own lands and possessions? Does He not forbid us to make hostile invasion upon others? Is it not true that what the Saracens and Barbarians once called prowess, we term wickedness and brigandry? Pricochole had done better to stay within his frontiers, governing his land like a true king, than to intrude on mine and plunder it. For, by wise rule, he would have enlarged his boundaries; by robbing me, he will meet his destruction.[107]

And More in no uncertain terms informs his readers how much his matchless Utopians despise violence: 'War, as an activity fit only for beasts and yet practiced by no kind of beast so constantly as by man, they regard with utter loathing. Against the usage of almost all nations they

---

[102] *COR* (Longhurst), p. 26.
[103] *COR*, p. 23.   [104] *Ibid.*
[105] *COR* (Longhurst), p. 29.   [106] *MC*, p. 183.
[107] François Rabelais, *Gargantua and Pantagruel*, trans. J. Le Clerq (Modern Library, New York, n.d.), bk. 1, ch. 46, p. 131. Cited hereafter as *GP*.

count nothing so inglorious as glory sought in war.'[108] But even if deaf to the appeal of Christ and the commands of nature, asks Valdés, what man can remain unmoved as he witnesses what a fearful plague war, even the justest of wars, really is?[109]

In Book II of the *Diálogo de Mercurio y Carón* Valdés discourses on the qualities that must adorn the good prince. We are told by the soul of the just prince appearing before Mercurio and Carón how the ruler must forever remind himself that he is the shepherd of his people and that for their sake he must forego all lust for conquest. And as the dead soul spins its tale, the reader is reminded of the manner in which Vives refuted those who argued that war may be often fought to insure the safety of the state. 'All my senses and faculties were absorbed in war and none could I spare for the most important of all my tasks, the good governance of my subjects.'[110] This and similar passages are particularly interesting because Valdés is not a pacifist. On the contrary, the possibility that a prince may be forced to wage war is frankly admitted and sanctioned. Thus the same soul who advises peace points out that a ruler shall not hesitate to wage war if the well-being of his subjects is at stake. The strength of this familiar argument will be even more evident when we come to survey Valdés' reflections on the papal–imperial bickering which led to the sack of Rome. All the same, in *Mercurio y Carón* Valdés, now removed from the hectic bitterness of 1527, establishes what for all practical purposes is a mystical bond between war and politics.

Do you think that your kingdom has profited from your rule? You took it rich and prosperous, and now you leave it poor and destroyed. Is this the glory and renown sought by good princes? Is it just that for the sake of adding one or two provinces more to your jurisdiction so many lands be destroyed? What are you doing? What do you search for? What is that which so obstinately you search for is not eternal infamy in this world and everlasting torments in the other?

The same idea is masterly sketched by Rabelais who unhesitatingly admits the legitimacy of a defensive war. A case in point: Grangousier, perplexed by Picrochole's unprovoked attack, swiftly recovers and vows to do his duty. 'I must seize lance and mace with trembling hands to succor and protect my unhappy people.'[111] Grangousier's resolve is even more forcefully expressed in a letter written to his son, Gargantua, urging him to come to his sire's aid: 'Accordingly, my dear son...haste not only to the defense of your father...but also to that of your people, whom reason orders you to protect and preserve.'[112] Valdés is of the same mind.

108 Thomas More, *Utopia*, ed. E. Sturz (New Haven, London, 1968), p. 118.
109 *COR* (Longhurst), p. 33.   110 *MC*, pp. 164–65.
111 *GP*, I, pp. 28, 90.   112 *Ibid.*, I, pp. 29, 91–2.

For both writers, in effect, whether a prince shall fight entirely depends on whether peace or war is the better way for the welfare of his flock.[113] Just as in the case of the theorists of the just war what is really damnable in the eyes of both humanists is those wars waged for the self-interest and ambition of the ruler. And what Erasmus concedes only grudgingly, both Rabelais and Valdés freely grant: wars waged in self-defense are acceptable. More is no exception. 'Their [Utopians'] one and only object in war is to secure that which, had it been obtained beforehand, would have prevented the declaration of war.'[114] The Utopians' hatred of war does not prevent them from being quite ready for it. 'Men and women alike assiduously exercise themselves in military training on fixed days lest they should be unfit for war when the need requires.'[115] They are willing to go to war 'to protect their own territory' and 'if any king takes up arms against them and prepares to invade their territory, they at once meet him in great strength beyond their borders'.[116] But whereas Rabelais and Valdés examine only the instance of self-defense as a justifiable cause for war, the English humanist goes farther afield into ground clearly staked out by the theorists of tradition. More's Utopians are not only ready to fight in defense of the commonwealth's safety, but they are also more than willing to break a lance for their friends and the innocent in general.[117] The Utopians become particularly incensed by attacks against their nationals and friends—a page eminently lifted by More from the book of the theory of the just war.[118]

To be sure, the wars and the characters narrated by More and Rabelais are imaginary. But the events described by Valdés are both very real and very similar, or at least the secretary's version of them is, to the adventures of Grangousier and Picrochole. And it is upon foundations identical to those listed in Grangousier's letter to Gargantua that the Emperor's servant sets the central subject of the *Diálogo de las cosas ocurridas en Roma*: the war between Charles V and Clement VII. Valdés' purpose is stated in the opening paragraphs.

First, I'll show you why the Emperor is not to blame for what happened in Rome. Second, I'll show you that it was God's judgment which brought about the punishment of that city. God realized that the Christian religion was being disgraced by the incredible wickedness practiced so widely there. He intended that Christendom should wake up and clean house so that we could live again like the Christians we're so proud to be.[119]

Having explained his goal Valdés proceeds to set the stage for his extended

---

[113] *MC*, p. 183.   [114] *Utopia*, p. 120.   [115] *Ibid.*, p. 118.
[116] *Ibid.*, pp. 118, 129.   [117] *Ibid.*, p. 118.   [118] *Ibid.*, p. 119, 120.
[119] *COR* (Longhurst), p. 25.

argumentation in favor of the Emperor's innocence. 'My feeling is that the Emperor's duty is to defend his subjects, to keep them at peace, and to dispense justice by rewarding the good and punishing the wicked.'[120] The role of the Pope is equally well-defined.

My understanding is that the papal office was established so that the Pope might explain Holy Scripture and teach Christian doctrines to the world...His constant endeavor would be to see that peace and harmony reign among Christians. And finally, as the supreme pontiff on earth he would provide a living example of the holiness of Jesus Christ, our Redeemer.[121]

Far from this, however, the Pope insisted on provoking war. It is the perfect instance of a just war: unjustly begun by Clement it must be accepted by Charles.

While the Emperor was doing his duty by defending his subjects, the Pope was neglecting *his* duty by waging war against him. It was the Pope who destroyed the peace and started a new war in Christendom. Under the circumstances one cannot blame the Emperor for the ensuing evils, since he was only doing his duty by defending his subjects. The Pope, on the other hand, is hardly blameless. His duty was to maintain peace; instead, he stirred up a war among Christians.[122]

Should the culprit, in accordance with the doctrine of the just war, be punished for his unjust behavior after the conclusion of the war and the triumph of justice? In view of the exalted and even holy character of this particular felon Valdés perforce treads carefully. To begin with, our secretary argues that the Emperor never ordered his troops to enter Rome and '*prender el Papa*'.[123] But even if he had he would have been justified.[124]

Charles' cause, then, was unimpeachable. For the sake of Christian harmony, however, he was willing to foresake his just rights. But at this crucial juncture God intervened decisively.

120 *Ibid.*
121 *Ibid.*, pp. 25–6.
122 *Ibid.*, p. 26. In a scathing letter violently denunciatory of Valdés' position and his version of the events climaxed by the sack of Rome, the Papal nuncio, Baldassare Castiglione, argues that far from provoking war the Pope 'never intended to mistreat the Emperor, but thought only of repressing the unheard-of acts of insolence and extortion being committed by the Emperor's troops in Church lands'. The responsibility for the war and the failure of peace does not rest with the Pope, but with 'those who had few possessions and who, in their greed, wanted to acquire money by any means at all and consequently showed no regard for the Emperor's honor, committing the greatest enormities in his name'. Castiglione to Valdés, in Longhurst, Appendix, pp. 112–13.
123 *COR*, p. 44.
124 *COR* (Longhurst), pp. 42–3.

As a matter of fact, when the Emperor received the terms of the truce he immediately approved them, despite the unjust conditions. This he did without regard to his honor and reputation...By his actions, the Emperor showed how much he wanted the Pope's friendship, since he was even willing to accept an unjust agreement rather than seek just vengeance...But by the will of God, who had decided to punish His ministers, the agreement was so long delayed in arriving here, and its ratification so late in being returned there, that before it arrived the events of Rome had already occurred.[125]

Erasmus and Saint Augustine are superbly blended in this passage. Following the master's exhortations, Valdés portrays Charles as willing to accept an unjust peace rather than wage a just war. But the eternal *deus ex machina* thwarted his good will and used the imperial army as the Bishop of Hippo had told his readers that He had used the Gothic barbarians. The Emperor and his general, Hugo de Moncada, according to Valdés, were therefore nothing more than the tools of God's wrath, just as the king of the Goths had been but His instrument over a thousand years before.[126]

Perhaps one of the most fascinating aspects of the theory of the just war is the manner in which its basic axioms provide innumerable ways of skinning the proverbial cat. And the episode just referred to is a case in point. Doubtless remembering his Saint Augustine as dutifully as Valdés, Castiglione, in the aforementioned letter to the imperial secretary (see footnote 122), gives another version of God's intentions: 'We come much closer to the truth and to a Christian concept of it if we say that God allowed such a serious and harsh persecution of His Church in order that the Pope, cardinals, prelates, and all those who have suffered so patiently, might merit an award in heaven, rather than be punished for their so-called vices.'[127]

So far, little has been said here on the Protestant contribution to the question of war. It would be fitting, then, to conclude this section with a few comments on the subject. The conservative spokesmen of the Protestant Reformation are on the whole singularly arid when it comes to their contribution to the study of the problem of war. Luther, Calvin, Beza, Zwingli, all accept without much questioning the presence of discord among men and often justify it on most traditional grounds. In this connection it is significant to note that their political views are equally conservative and their political philosophy rarely goes beyond an affirmation of the divine character of political authority and the obedience, at least in political matters, owed the ruler by his subjects. When we move to the radical wing of Protestantism, however, the situation changes drastically, at least as far as the question of war is concerned. For the first

[125] *Ibid.*, p. 45. [126] *Ibid.*, p. 57. [127] *Ibid.*, p. 110.

time since Chelchitzky we witness the strong and sustained return of Biblical pacifism. On this occasion, moreover, the doctrines of Scriptural anti-militarism were not limited to any one particular area but spread instead over the length and breadth of Western Europe, and were thought to offer a deadly threat to the political and social stability of Christendom. And it is when we study the ideas of Anabaptist publicists and the reaction they elicited from conservative religious quarters that we once again become aware of how close the nexus between war and the state really was in sixteenth-century European thought.

In the midst of the truly bloody character of the sixteenth and seventeenth centuries, both in war and in religious persecution, the consistent and continued non-resistance of peaceful Anabaptism is remarkable with its complete rejection of war and personal violence, and its insistence upon religious liberty. About the clarity and absolutism of the Anabaptist position there can be no question...With minor exceptions such as Balthasar Humaier (d. 1528) and the short-lived revolutionary Münsterites (1534 ff.) and Batenburgers, the entire movement from Courtrai to Königsberg and from Bern to Budapest, whether Swiss, German, Flemish, Austrian, or Moravian, openly and vigorously broke with the universally accepted war system, or with 'the sword' as they called it.[128]

With these words Harold S. Bender has described the position of the radical wing of the Reformation on the question of whether or not Christians should partake of war. And among the many leaders of the movement who stated their opposition to discord Menno Simons stands out as the learned and articulate spokesman of the influential Anabaptist movement in the Netherlands.

Menno strenuously labored to dissociate the body of Anabaptism from the turgid reputation it had acquired in the eyes of European public opinion as a result of the Münster episode, and to convince rulers that his brethren were a threat neither to their authority nor to the stability of the European social fabric. Inevitably, in pursuit of this objective, he is forced into concessions which do not harmonize with the Anabaptist rejection of the world. On the one hand, the true magistrate must be a Christian and his right to wield the sword is recognized. On the other, those in the community who by the example of their lives have the highest claims to being called Christians find themselves excluded from the magistracy by the very nature of those claims. Thus the same men who according to Menno do not withhold their allegiance from the political power 'are prepared to forsake country, goods, life, and all for the sake of peace'. The implications of such a declaration of principle could hardly have

[128] H. S. Bender, 'The pacifism of sixteenth-century Anabaptists', *The Mennonite Quarterly Review*, 30(1956), n. 1, 6.

escaped Menno's magistrate: on the issue of war and peace (as on the question of infant baptism and the swearing of oaths) the Anabaptist would unhesitatingly jettison Caesar in favor of God. In other words, in times of peace the brethren refuse to shoulder the responsibilities implied in the magistracy and essential to the continued existence of the commonwealth; in times of strife, by denying it their aid and comfort, their pacifism *à outrance* necessarily dooms the stability and integrity of the state. As a case in point let us see how Menno's premises affect the most complete political framework surveyed so far in the pages of this book – Vitoria's.[129]

The Vitorian state is instituted for the well-being of all the members of the commonwealth and as such it must coexist in harmony with other orders endowed with privileges and functions of their own. The Anabaptist, insofar as their ideology is here represented by Menno Simons, affect the jurisdiction of two of the orders comprising the Vitorian system: Church and state. Outwardly the brethren pose no threat to the stability of Vitoria's political order. They pay their taxes and respect and accept the authority of the magistrates. They cannot be accused of behaving unjustly, for nothing could be farther removed from their minds and hearts. And Vitoria would be the last man to disagree with Menno's recommendations concerning the ruler's duty to protect the helpless, govern for the benefit of the common people, and rule with Scriptural fairness. But it is also here that the problem lies. For Vitoria, man is a social and political animal, and his life is bound to that of the community as a whole. The harmony of the Vitorian system hinges on this point: if the happiness of man is not integrated into the happiness of the community the whole system mandated by God collapses. But Menno's man, strictly speaking, is neither a social nor a political animal. In their rejection of the world his regenerated want to have as little to do as possible with the tainted affairs of this earth; at best they are passive spectators. And coupled with this rejection of sociability there is a tendency toward individualism which dictates the very premises that have led Menno to react passively to the secular society of man in the first place: obedience to the word of God as revealed in Scripture, an obedience which is necessarily founded on the individual's examination and interpretation of the latter. Inevitably, Menno's passive individualism stabs at the established orders

---

[129] Menno Simons, *The Complete Works of Menno Simons*, ed. J. C. Wenger, trans. L. Verduin (Scottdale, Penn., 1956). Menno's ideas on war and the state are found in the following works: *The Blasphemy of John of Leiden, Reply to False Accusations, The True Christian Faith, Brief and Clear Confession, Foundation of Christian Doctrine, The New Birth,* and *Epistle to Micron;* and the following pages of the *Complete Works:* 43–8, 94, 193, 214, 347, 423–4, 549–56.

with two horns: one invades the province of the supernatural by denying
the exclusive right of its embodiment, the Church, to interpret Scripture –
indeed, it does more, for it destroys the Church and sets in its stead a
Conventicle. The other thrusts at the secular order with the individualistic
conclusions derived from the former. And again the best possible illustra-
tion is given by the question of war. The refusal of the righteous to wage
war is not overly important on the surface. Within the Vitorian system
there is ample room for those who refuse to heed the call to arms on the
grounds that they are convinced of the injustice of a particular war. What
is crucially significant, however, is Menno's dogmatic assertion that there
is no such thing as a just war because Scriptural law flatly forbids
Christians to wage war. It may be argued that this is in no way different
from Erasmus' early strictures against violence. But whereas the Christian
humanist eventually admitted the possible justice of some wars, the Anabaptists lived and died by their pacifist creed. And this fact alone makes
Menno's apparent acceptance of two irreconcilables, the Christian character of the magistrate and his right to wield the sword, all the more difficult
to accept. In truth, then, Menno's stand in practice threatens the existence
of the Church and contradicts its teachings. His refusal to partake of the
common task of self-preservation threatens the established order of society
because it denies the state the right of self-defense. In the eyes of conservative opinion on both sides of the religious controversy Menno stands
accused of heresy and sinning against natural law.

Conclusion

What conclusions can we draw from this brief scrutiny of noted Christian
humanist apologists for peace? In reality none that have not already been
suggested. Still, I think it worthwhile to state once again how much these
writers abhor violence. Men of good will and fine sensibilities, they stand
helpless before a fact of life which although simple enough to observe
appears to defy all understanding of its true nature. They all exhort,
entreat, beg contemporaries to come to their senses. But to a man, the
more they search for ways and means to end the evil the greater their
helplessness grows until, willingly or reluctantly, completely or partially,
they must admit the seeming wisdom of Saint Augustine's ruthless
realism.

Throughout the preceding pages I have repeatedly sought to stress the
existence of a nexus of cause and effect binding war to political theory;
this in my view is the paradigm ruling the study of political thought in
the age of Erasmus. Influenced by tradition and pressed by the demands
of praxis, the Spanish school understood that the harmony deemed essen-

tial by Saint Augustine could only be achieved in terms of a balance between the two political orders, national and international, which rule man's life. Man's nature being what it is, however, we must not expect this balance (peace) to be permanent. Peace is not a static concept but a dynamic one which, like the Augustinian good, periodically fades. War cannot be permanently banned any more than evil can. And just as the latter can only be overcome by the individual effort of man, war will only be tamed by the state. The Augustinian premise concerning man's nature was equally respected by Christian humanism. No matter how profound their confidence in man's perfectibility, Christian humanism could not but admit that man had sinned against God.[130] From the start it accepted tradition's one great assumption, man's depravity. And from this concession it would never recover. To be sure, the writings of Erasmus and Vives are full of an intuitive awareness that society may be responsible for man's perversity. But doubt still lingers. Haunted by their acceptance of man's past fault, Christian humanists are doomed to admit in the end what tradition had recognized from the beginning: the only hope for peace lies with the state. Their political theories, just as those of Neo-scholasticism, are inseparable from their understanding of war and irrevocably shaped by it.

And such is also the case with out next subject, Sepúlveda. Neither Christian humanist in the Erasmian or Vivian tradition nor fully of the Neoscholastic persuasion, Sepúlveda shares in the age's conviction that war and political authority go hand in hand. He will thus find in the principles of the just war that cement capable of keeping two antithetical elements together: a universal society whose formulation had been made mandatory in the eyes of Spanish intellectuals by the discovery of the New World; and a concept of the state based both on dynastic and territorial principles, as demanded by Europe's political fragmentation – the twin characteristics, incidentally, of the growing Spanish empire. In this context it is important to mention Sepúlveda's unique case among the thinkers

---

[130] It is of interest in this context to mention J. R. Hale's appraisal of the crucial doubt which tormented sixteenth-century explanations of discord. 'All the same, the irritant that nagged many writers toward generalization was doubt about who did determine the predisposition of the human organism at birth. "Man's debased nature"; "natural disposition, or habit converted into nature"; "the natural disposition of men": such phrases haunt the inquiry into conflict. No matter how much information turned up, the origin of the tendency toward good or bad, peaceableness or violence, remained a void. On one side lay the already socialized human being. On the other lay – original sin? Hereditary degradation from a Golden Age? Was violence determined or conditioned?, and if the latter, who invented it?' J. R. Hale, 'Sixteenth-century explanations of war and violence', *Past and Present*, May 1971, p. 16.

surveyed here. Educated in Italy, Sepúlveda was heir to the veneration in which classical learning was held in humanist circles. On the other hand, he was far from scornful of Scholastic learning. Faithful to Aristotle, he remained a devout Christian profoundly attached to the formulae of tradition and impartially finding inspiration in the Philosopher, Saint Augustine, or Saint Thomas, as the occasion demanded. The hybrid flavor of his thinking explains the hostility of some theologians who saw him as an unrestrained worshipper of antiquity, or the animosity shown by some humanists (Julián Páez de Castro, in a letter to Zurita, wrote: 'In what concerns doctor Sepúlveda I do not know what to say save that I think of him as man *non sana capitis*, who neither in his letters nor in his dialogue knows what he is talking about for lack of *principios*'), particularly those belonging to the imperial coterie, who viewed him as a theologian defender of the despised Scholastic traditionalism.

PART II
THE WANING OF ERASMIANISM
(1539-1559)

6

Humanist foundations for a universal society: Juan Ginés de Sepúlveda (I)

Life and times

Juan Ginés de Sepúlveda's long life extended over the first three reigns which followed Spain's dynastic unification. He was born ca. 1490 of respectable but humble parents in the small town of Pozoblanco, near Córdoba. Very little is known of his early life and it is to be conjectured that he received his elementary education in the nearby city of Córdoba. We know, however, that in 1510 he was admitted to the recently founded University of Alcalá where for three years he studied philosophy under Sancho de Miranda. At the end of this first academic apprenticeship, Sepúlveda left Alcalá to study theology at the Colegio de San Antonio de Sigüenza where he remained until 1515. On the 14th of February of the same year, the young scholar received from the hands of Cisneros a letter of introduction to the authorities of the Spanish College (Colegio de San Clemente, founded in 1364 by the great Cardinal Gil de Albornoz) at Bologna where he was to spend the next eight years in the ordinary course of theological studies required for the doctorate. We know from Sepúlveda's own testimony that by early 1523 he was doctor of theology and arts.

It is precisely during these years at Bologna that Sepúlveda became not only a competent theologian and an accomplished humanist, but a protégé of some of the great patrons of humanism in Italy as well. Cardinal Giuliano de Medici (the future Clement VII), Alberto Pio (Prince of Carpi), Ercole Gonzaga, the general of the Dominicans Cardinal Cajetan, Aldus Manutius (whom he met at the house of the Prince of Carpi), Pope Adrian VI are among his friends and protectors. The duties of friendship and the demands of his own scholarly research explain his repeated absences from Bologna after 1519, a date which marks the beginning of his association with the Medici family. From this period as a student at Bologna also date his earlier works: *Errata Petrii Alcyonii in interpretatione Aristotelis* (lost); the *Historia Aegidiana* (Bologna, 1521), a biography of Cardinal Albornoz; and the translation of two Aristotelian works – *Parvi naturales* (Bologna, 1522), dedicated to Cardinal Giuliano de Medici and Alberto Pio, and *De ortu et interitu* (Bologna, 1523) dedicated to Adrian VI.

In 1523 Sepúlveda abandoned San Clemente forever. In August of the same year, a short two months after his name had been taken off the student rolls of the college, he published in Rome his second extant original work, the *Dialogus de appetenda gloria* or *Gonsalus*, dedicated to his Spanish patrons the Dukes of Sessa, a powerful family of Córdoba. From 1523 to 1526 the humanist divided his time between visits to Carpi and the pontifical court in Rome where he had found employment as official translator and commentator of Aristotle. It is in this capacity that he publishes *De mundo ad Alexandrum* (Bologna, 1523), dedicated to Ercole Gonzaga; a translation of the *Commentaries* of Alexander of Afrodisias to Aristotle's *Metaphysics* (Rome, 1527), dedicated to Clement VII; the *Meteorum libri IV* (Paris, 1532); the *Politica* (Paris, 1548); and in 1526 the *De fato et libero arbitrio* against Luther. The following year the sack of Rome by the mutinous imperial soldiery found him still in the Eternal City and forced him, in the company of the Prince of Carpi, to seek asylum in the Castle Sant'Angelo. Shortly afterward the Spanish humanist departed for the south of Italy, entering the service of Cardinal Cajetan whose *Commentary* on the New Testament required the cooperation of Sepúlveda's expert knowledge of Greek. Back once again in Rome he joined the household of the Cardinal of Santa Cruz, Francisco de Quiñones, an aristocratic prelate who had been sent to Rome by Charles V to effect a *rapprochement* between Emperor and Pope. Sepúlveda, then, was with the papal court when on August 12, 1529, Charles disembarked in Genoa on his way to Bologna to be crowned by Clement VII. Among those sent by the Pope to receive the Emperor was Cardinal Quiñones and with him Sepúlveda (and Erasmus' implacable persecutor and archenemy, Diego López Zúñiga).

Included in Charles' splendid entourage was a host of Spanish devotees of the new learning, worshipful of Erasmus whose *philosophia Christi*, we have seen, they endeavored to complement with an imperial Messianism which they believed would surely bring about the Erasmian ideal of the Golden Age. But in Bologna, a center of Aristotelian renaissance, the Spanish enthusiasts encountered a milieu very different from their own. Italy possessed its own humanist tradition, and Erasmus was to Italians little more than another distinguished member of the humanist brotherhood; his indictment (*Ciceronianus*) of Italian humanism had not caused undue furor in the Peninsula. And much to their surprise the Spanish humanists found their compatriot Sepúlveda to be a Roman humanist to his fingertips. Praised by the master in the *Ciceronianus* as a young author of promise, Sepúlveda did not appear to have been unduly overwhelmed by the honor. In fact, it is not unlikely that he may have shown his admiration for Erasmus to be somewhat less than lukewarm. The reason is clear. Between 1525 and his death in 1531 not long after his arrival in France, Alberto Pio had been involved in a controversy with Erasmus which had progressively grown in bitterness. On January 7, 1529, the Prince of Carpi published a scathing attack accusing the Dutch humanist, among other things, of having aided and abetted the Lutheran revolt. Erasmus promptly answered with a *responsio* of his own resolutely denying Alberto Pio's charges. The latter's reply was posthumously published in Paris (March, 1531), a fact which did not deter Erasmus, in turn, from composing a violent rebuttal of his critic's arguments. And it was precisely to defend his dead patron and friend that Sepúlveda entered the lists with his *Antapologia pro Alberto Pio* (Rome and Paris, 1532) refuting, in a firm but courteous tone, Erasmus' own charges and reiterating Carpi's position (the former's conciliatory answer led to further friendly exchanges between the two humanists which continued until his death). Shortly afterward Alfonso de Valdés, whom Sepúlveda had met in 1529, reproved him for his attack on Erasmus. Sepúlveda's answer (dated 1533) explains that he bears the Dutch humanist no ill will but that, on the other hand, he cannot partake of Valdès' unconditional admiration for the master.[1] In its later stages the Erasmus–Sepúlveda correspondence shifted ground from its original controversial aspects to a more sedate exchange of opinions concerning mainly the Greek language. In 1529,

---

[1] Liber II, Epistola VI, in *Opera* (4 vols., Madrid, 1780), III. In this reply to Valdés' reproaches, Sepúlveda in turn laments the secretary's excessive veneration for Erasmus. 'You are so preoccupied with Erasmus, so protective of his glory, that you give the impression of being more Erasmian than Erasmus.' He – Sepúlveda – has written the *Antapologia* 'to defend Alberto Pio's cause. In it is reflected the attitude of a friend who counsels, not that of an enemy who injures...I did not write the book in search of vainglory; I am not so foolish or incompetent that I need to resort to foul play to become famous. Moreover, I do not count myself among those who believe that a polemic with Erasmus suffices to make his opponent's reputation. And that is precisely what you believe because you see Erasmus as divine and you read his writings as if they were oracles. You should know that I have lived for many years in a country nursery of sages and orators. It is their fame which I would like to equal. And take note, for many among them see Erasmus in a different light and do not praise him so lavishly as you do – a view, incidentally, largely shared by our own people. Do not, therefore, think – as I believe you do – that I, although far from despising Erasmus, stand open-mouthed before him to the extent of believing that a polemic will turn me into a famous man.'

however, Sepúlveda's mind may not have been favorably disposed toward Erasmus or shared the fervorous admiration of the latter's Spanish disciples.

The Spanish humanist, always as a member of Quiñones' household, followed the imperial suite on its way from Genoa to Bologna and composed in Charles' honor a brief tract exhorting the Emperor to wage war against the Turks, the *Cohortatio ad Carolum bellum suscipiat in turcas* (Bologna, 1529). After the Emperor's departure Sepúlveda returned to Rome and his duties at the papal court. Not long afterward, however, we find him away from Rome and once more in Bologna whence Clement VII had journeyed to meet the returning Emperor, December 1531. It was during this sojourn in Bologna that the *Democrates primus* (published years later, in 1535) was conceived – the direct result, it seems, of numerous and lengthy conversations with members of Charles' suite.[2] In September, 1534, Sepúlveda's protector since 1519, Clement VII, died; and two years later (April 1536) Charles, fresh from the triumphs of his Tunisian campaign, entered Rome and took Sepúlveda into his service as imperial chronicler. The year 1536, then, marks the end of the Italian phase of Sepúlveda's life.

His return to Spain was characterized from the start by a sharp division of his time between the fulfillment of his duties at court during the summer months, and retirement to his lands of Pozoblanco in the winter when he devoted his attention to scholarship on the one hand and the relentless accumulation of wealth on the other.[3] In 1542 Charles V appointed the humanist to the post of preceptor to Prince Philip whose education had been placed under the supervision of Juan Martínez Siliceo, a reputable scholar trained at Paris, professor of philosophy at Salamanca, and Archbishop of Toledo. During the same year we find Sepúlveda in Monzón with the Emperor and the prince. Philip shortly afterward departed for Aragón to seek official recognition by the Aragonese Cortes as heir to the throne. It was during this journey that, at a dinner in Barcelona, Sepúlveda met in convivial companionship with the Constable of Castile and other high dignitaries of Philip's entourage. The subject of the conversation, politics and the best form of government, served as the

---

[2] Curiously enough, the existence of the first *Democrates* is due to an incipient pacifist movement of protest among the students of the Spanish College. See A. Losada, *Fray Bartolomé de las Casas* (Madrid, 1970), p. 249.

[3] See the long list of ecclesiastical benefices in A. Losada, *Juan Ginés de Sepúlveda a través de su Epistolario y nuevos documentos* (Madrid, 1949), pp. 154–6. This, of course, was in addition to the salaries and other perquisites he received as a member of the court's bureaucracy.

central core for Sepúlveda's *De regno*, published in Lérida in 1571.[4]
Sepúlveda died two years later in November, 1573.[5]
The year 1545 marks the beginning of a period of intense frustration
for Sepúlveda. For the next lustrum or so he became embroiled in controversy with Fray Bartolomé de las Casas, the formidable defender of the
Indians, over the nature and fate of the natives of the New World. The
story of that bitter imbroglio has been repeatedly told elsewhere and so it
need not be examined here.[6] It is of interest to mention, however, the
three works which were part of Sepúlveda's dispute with Las Casas; the
Democrates alter (a sequel to the *Democrates* of 1535), the *Apologia pro
libro de justis belli causis* (Rome, 1550), and the *Proposiciones*. Sepúlveda's failure to secure permission for the publication of the first sparked
the controversy, for the humanist blamed Las Casas for his difficulties.
We shall presently deal at length with this important treatise. Sepúlveda
wrote the *Apologia* to explain the position taken in the *Democrates alter*
and to refute the slanderous accusations with which its contents had been
clouded. In view of what will be discussed later it is important to mention
briefly what the author says in his defense. It was Sepúlveda's presumed
advocacy of unconditional war against the Indians which had raised eye-
brows both at Alcalá and Salamanca and had led those institutions to
recommend against the publication of the *Democrates alter*. The author
acknowledges this to be the heart of the issue: 'The question, you say, is
whether it is licit to wage war against the Indians, depriving them of their
political authority, possessions, and temporal goods – and even kill them,
should they offer resistance – so that, once despoiled and subjected, they
will more easily be converted by the missionaries.' Sepúlveda heatedly
protests against this interpretation of his words.

To present my doctrine in those terms is offensive and shows the ill will of
those from whom your arguments were taken...they lie when they state that

[4] One concrete reference to this episode is found in Sepúlveda's correspondence, in
a letter addressed to Manrique de Lara, Duke of Nájera, who was among those
present at the banquet. See Liber IV, Epistola XIV, in *Opera*, III.
[5] For this brief sketch of Sepúlveda's life I have relied mainly on Losada's *Juan
Ginés de Sepúlveda* cited above. See also T. Andrés Marcos, *Los imperialismos de
Juan Ginés de Sepúlveda en su Democrates alter* (Madrid, 1947); A. F. G. Bell,
Juan Ginés de Sepúlveda (Oxford, 1925); J. Beneyto Pérez, *Ginés de Sepúlveda,
humanista y soldado* (Madrid, 1944); Nicolás Antonio, *Bibliotheca hispana nova*. On
the exchange with Erasmus see M. P. Gilmore, 'Erasmus and Alberto Pio, Prince of
Carpi', in *Action and Conviction in Early Modern Europe*, ed. J. Siegel and T. Rabb
(Princeton, 1969).
[6] See, among other works, Losada's *Fray Bartolomé de las Casas*, and Friede's and
Keen's *Bartolomé de las Casas in History*. Most recently, the work by L. Hanke,
All Mankind is One (De Kalb, Ill., 1975), describes the controversy in detail; it also
includes an extensive bibliography relating to the subject.

I undertake to protect the injustices and impious robberies...To make my position clear I must repeat that I do not argue in favor of despoiling the barbarians or reducing them to slavery (*servitus*). I advocate, instead, that they be subjected *Christianorum imperio* to prevent them from impeding the propagation of the faith, persecuting preachers, and insulting God with their idols and other things; and this for the benefit of the barbarians themselves. In this manner, then, should the question under discussion be posed.[7]

Finally, the *Proposiciones* was Sepúlveda's version of what had transpired at the meeting of theologians (Valladolid, 1550–1551) gathered to settle the controversy between himself and Las Casas. After briefly recounting the vicissitudes of the whole affair, Sepúlveda proceeds to defend his personal integrity, presumably impugned by Las Casas. In a lengthy passage the humanist emphatically denies that in the *Democrates alter* he advocated slavery for the American Indians. At this point its contents are of passing significance; but in the context of Chapter 7 its categorical statements, and the fact that they are written in the vernacular, have an importance difficult to over-estimate. Even at this early stage, then, it is worth quoting the passage in its entirety.

What I affirm and have written is, in sum, that the conquest of the Indies – to subdue those barbarians, extirpate their idolatry, force them to observe natural law even against their will, and after subjecting them to preach the Gospel to them with Christian meekness and without force – is both just and holy. Once subdued the Indians must not be killed or turned into slaves (*hacer esclavos*) or deprived of their goods (*haciendas*), but let them be subjects (*vasallos*) of the king of Castile and pay their tribute (*tributo*) in the manner determined and commanded by our kings through the instructions (*instrucciones*) given to their deputies (*Capitanes generales*). And whatever is done in violation of the aforesaid is reprehensible and sinful, and those guilty shall answer to God. That which is taken by force and outside the law of war (*derecho de guerra*) is robbery and restitution must follow. Our question lies in whether or not all this is true. The Bishop of Chiapa – who has read this a thousand times in my writings – persists, instead of endeavoring to refute my arguments, in telling of the cruelties and plunderings committed by the soldiers (and also those of which they are innocent) and in accusing me of encouraging such conduct. He well knows – as do all who have read my book, of wide circulation throughout Christendom – that those evils cause in me greater revulsion that they provoke in him, and that in my book I condemn them with all the necessary harshness. Even though such was never the heart of the question under discussion, for the cruelties, injuries, plunderings, and sins of which the soldiers are most assuredly guilty in all wars in no sense detract from the justice of a given war – if the war is just to begin with...In short, everything which he attributes to me

---

[7] *Apologia pro libro de justis belli causis*, in *Opera*, IV, pp. 329–31.

is false, as is well-known by those who have read my book – and he knows that better than anybody.[8]

Stoic oneness, Aristotelian pluralism, and Saint Augustine's doctrine of the just war

Early interest in the social and political implications of the discovery of America appears not to have been very widespread among most Europeans.[9] For obvious reasons Spain was the one exception, and it is among Spanish publicists that we first discover an active interest in broadening the scope of the *respublica Christiana* to include groups of men hitherto ignorant of the Christian religion. The important point, then, is that the meeting of European and Amerindian called for a reappraisal of conventional views of society. It demanded, on the one hand, that political philosophy return to the Stoic idea of universal society and, on the other, that the emerging nation-state be justified on the basis of a modified Aristotelian foundation. The return to Stoic ideals – imperative for an age both fond of seeking inspiration in classical standards and destitute of a worldview of its own capable of serving as adequate canon – could not, however, be accomplished in a merely rhetorical vein or in the normative manner prescribed by Christian humanist thought; rather, it had to be carried out with a sense of potential unknown since Roman days.

The European milieu of the early sixteenth century offers a panorama not unlike that of the ancient world after the death of Aristotle; the link between Stoicism and certain aspects of Spanish political thought in the age of Erasmus, therefore, is no mere coincidence. For over a millennium the triumph of Christianity had simplified matters, enabling western political thinkers to speak for the most part of the world as coterminous with Christendom. With the opening of the sixteenth century that simplicity vanished. And just as the Stoic school grew as a result of the emergence of that Hellenistic world which had shattered the restrictive insularity of the Greek city-state, bringing about the *cosmopolis* in place of the *polis*, so the discovery of America was responsible for broadening the social and political horizons of western Christendom.

It must not be forgotten, however, that the success and permanence of

---

[8] *Proposiciones temerarias, escandalosas y heréticas que notó el doctor Sepúlveda en el libro de la conquista de Indias*, in A. M. Fabié, *Vida y escritos de don Fray Bartolomé de las Casas* (2 vols., Madrid, 1879), II, Appendix 25, pp. 336–51. The two volumes are numbers LXX and LXXI of the *Colección de documentos inéditos para la historia de España;* cited hereafter as *Proposiciones*.

[9] On the question of the impact of the New World on the Old see J. H. Elliott, *The Old World and the New 1494–1650* (Cambridge, 1970).

Stoicism in the ancient world owed much to the skill with which the philosophers of the Middle Stoa adapted the early Stoic ideals to the demands of praxis and the eclecticism prevalent in the Hellenistic world after ca. 150 B.C. Zeno, the founder of the Stoic school, had divided 'men into two classes, those who live according to divine reason and those who do not'.[10] In ethical terms this meant 'that there can be no degrees in virtue and no middle point between virtue and vice';[11] certainly an unpalatable doctrine at a time when 'men in earnest about good right living felt the need of practical precepts, of rules for the daily conduct of life'.[12] Forced by circumstances, then, the later Stoics (especially Panaetius, an admirer of Plato and Aristotle) attempted to close the 'chasm which the older Stoicism had left between the world-state, composed of wise men, and ordinary communities, composed mostly of fools'.[13] As a result of the eclecticism of Panaetius – 'a return to the ethical and political writings of Plato and Aristotle'[14] – and his followers (the composite philosophy of Cicero is the best example), the 'daring moral theories ...of the founders of Stoicism tend to disappear from sight, and are replaced by shrewd good sense and worldly wisdom: in short by the doctrine of "making the best of both worlds"...and it was from this standpoint that Stoicism so rapidly won its way with the Roman nobility of the last century of the Republic'.[15] In the later Stoics we note an almost total concentration on practical ethics, a compromise which resulted in a fitting adaptation of philosophical abstraction to the realities of the worldwide society created by Roman power. And it is again Panaetius who carries the day, denying the antithesis between the ideal community of wise men and ordinary social relationships.[16]

But the demands of worldly wisdom exacted one further concession from Panaetius' disciples, this time in the realm of politics. Clearly, although the all-embracing breadth of the Roman empire was an excellent practical example of the Stoic *cosmopolis* its long history of conquest and domination had to be explained and justified. It became therefore necessary to admit that some men are rulers while others must be ruled – a reassertion, in modified form, of the political principles of the Aristotelian city-state. Such, Athenaeus tells us, was the opinion of Posidonius (first

---

[10] M. E. Reesor, *The Political Theory of the Old and Middle Stoa* (New York, 1951), p. 10.
[11] R. D. Hicks, *Stoic and Epicurean* (New York, 1910), p. 87.
[12] *Ibid.*, p. 362.
[13] G. H. Sabine and S. B. Smith's edition of Cicero's *De republica* (Columbus, 1910), p. 10.
[14] *Ibid.*, p. 29. See also Cicero's *De finibus* 4. 28.
[15] E. V. Arnold, *Roman Stoicism* (New York, 1958), p. 303.
[16] Cicero, *De legibus*, 1. 10. 28–31.

century B.C.).[17] We find substantially the same argument in Cicero's *De republica* (bk. I, ch. 34).

The age of Erasmus groped toward a goal in no essential sense dissimilar from that of the Stoa: one universal society ruled by one universal law (natural law in one case, the law of Christ in the other). Roman universality had forced Stoicism to adapt itself to a compelling praxis. Conversely, the Erasmian, Vivian, and Valdesian ship had foundered on a different rock: the emerging nation-state which exploded the myth of the imperial idea and deprived their normative, humanitarian, and worldwide society of its protective cocoon. With the halcyon days of Spanish Erasmianism rapidly on the wane, the task of reconciling the universal society contemplated by the Utopian humanists and demanded by a world in physical expansion with the territorial state which had brought back a pluralism reminiscent of Aristotle's time fell upon the shoulders of two pragmatists: Vitoria and Sepúlveda.

Vitoria we have already met. In my view a proper understanding of Sepúlveda's scheme must start with the recognition that his plan is rigorously conditioned by a political Aristotelianism willing to be subsumed upon occasion to the needs of Stoic ideology. And vice versa, for Sepúlveda believes in the universality of society but not necessarily in that of political structures; indeed, he seems to be completely oblivious to the idea of the Holy Roman Empire. Thus, because he accepts the existence of autonomous states Sepúlveda's 'Stoicism' will be consciously modified by Aristotelian and civic humanist influences – the two familiar traditions closest to the new political phenomenon of the Renaissance sovereign state. In addition to accepting the political division of mankind Sepúlveda supports and strengthens it by means of an instrument of Augustinian vintage: the doctrine of the just war. To all appearances this should imply a weakening of the Stoic idea of man's ecumenical brotherhood. In reality it does not, for Sepúlveda takes extreme care in reinforcing what he has seemingly just jeopardized by emphasizing, first, that each man has his appointed place in the hierarchy of a worldwide society; and second, that man's brotherhood is actualized when, regardless of political divisions, everyone fulfills his moral duties.

A cautious balance between Stoicism and Aristotelianism is what Sepúlveda in effect strives to achieve when he attempts to expand the notions of society current at the time in order to make room for the newly discovered human groups, and devise a just and stable hierarchy capable of offering all men the good life. In terms of the unprecedented experience afforded by the discovery of America the significance of this goal is difficult to overestimate. We are not here witnessing merely an attempt to

---

[17] Reesor, *The Political Theory of the Old and Middle Stoa*, p. 54.

devise another more or less clever political scheme, but a substantial effort aimed at formulating a society whose universalism transcends the relative parochialism of the Christian purview and can only be matched by the ambitious breadth of Stoic ideology. Sepúlveda, moreover, believed that it was possible to avoid the political catholicism seemingly concomitant to a universal society and to preserve intact, with the aid of the theory of the just war, the political particularism which characterized both Aristotle's political doctrine and the praxis of Sepúlveda's own age. And this, together with his success in carrying out his proposed task in terms far more secular than were possible to those theologians of the School of Salamanca who wrote extensively on the subject of America, gives the true measure of Sepúlveda's contribution.

But, we may ask, on precisely what foundations shall this society rest? Summarizing what has been suggested above it rests, first, on a mixture of humanism and traditionalism; a blending of those Stoic and Aristotelian ideas which Italian civic humanism had enshrined as commonplaces in the consciousness of Renaissance Europe, with the iron-clad authority of Saint Augustine's doctrine of the just war. In addition, Sepúlveda relies on a model of man which although conventionally orthodox in its outlines in effect goes beyond the customary Christian framework by reason of the universalizing consequences of its dependence on natural law and reason. It is the partial goal of this and the following chapter to explain, on the one hand, how Sepúlveda, on the basis of a methodology founded on this modified model of man, judges what he understands to be the institutions and mores ruling civil life in the Indian commonwealths; and to inquire, on the other, on the status assigned by the humanist to the American natives within the universal society of man.

Vita activa *and* vita contemplativa

It has been rightly pointed out that one of the questions most earnestly discussed by all scholars down to the age of Erasmus touched upon the comparative value of the active and contemplative forms of living, and the difficulties attendant to any attempt at bringing both into accordance. And in this also the classical tradition had anticipated and guided subsequent thinking. The Early Stoics, for instance, did not suggest that the wise man should not take part in political affairs, and Zeno himself is reputed to have advocated participation in public affairs as a duty founded on human nature. On the other hand, they do not seem to have emphasized it too strongly. In later Stoicism the emphasis on the active life is more marked. Panaetius, although failing to evaluate the respective merits of the active and contemplative life, argued, according to Cicero, that:

Nature likewise through the power of reason associates man with man in the common bonds of speech and life...She also prompts men to meet in companies, to form public assemblies and to take part in them themselves; and she further dictates, as a consequence of this, the efforts on man's part to provide a store of things that minister to his comforts and wants – and not for himself alone, but for his wife and children and the others whom he holds dear and for whom he ought to provide; and this responsibility also stimulates his courage and makes it stronger for the active duties of life.[18]

It was Cicero himself, however, who most fully compared the merits of activity and contemplation. He deemed the former superior, and concluded that the form of activity offering man the best opportunity to live in accordance with nature and reason is a career of public service – the highest good to which man could aspire.

In this pagan tradition – and, of course, those of Augustinian Christianity and civic humanism which followed it – Sepúlveda often reflects on the excellence of the two ways of life open to man. Taking after the compromises of the Stoics, Sepúlveda, in an age of geographical expansion, was forced to find general canons which in social and political questions would apply to Christians and non-Christians alike. One important result was to be the progressive secularization of wisdom which would, in theory at any rate, pave the road toward some form of political participation in the affairs of the commonwealth by those non-Christian elements now a part of the Christian *civitas*. Closely related to this theme what explicitly holds our interest at this point is the fact that Sepúlveda finds in the traditional dialectic of contemplation and activity the first clue in his search for the status of the Indians within the society of man. Fully aware of the absurdity implied in judging Indian mores and institutions within a purely Christian context, Sepúlveda comes upon an immediate alternative in the Ciceronian emphasis on a life of civic activity. And among his political treatises it is in the *Democrates primus* that we meet the most extensive concern with the various concepts with which we shall be concerned in this section: the active and contemplative forms of living, wisdom, the moral and intellectual virtues, prudence, justice.

Remarking on the nature of the goals pursued in this dialogue the author explains how, on his return to Bologna, he was surprised to find a number of young Spanish aristocrats students at his old *alma mater* and devoted to the *bonae litterae*. Sepúlveda's pleasure, however, was marred by the presence of 'certain scruples in religious matters' among his young friends; these reservations, it transpires, centered around an 'expressed fear that a valiant soldier may not simultaneously discharge the duties of his profession and comply with the precepts of the Christian religion'.

[18] *De officiis*, 1. 4. 12. The Loeb edition.

This, in effect, is the central context in which the Spanish humanist's discussion of the merits of the active and contemplative *vitae* will be elaborated. A specific case of marvelous potential, for it provided a fitting framework for that concrete activity which had most vexatiously taxed the ingenuity of countless Christian thinkers through the centuries and around which Sepúlveda's own quarrel with Las Casas would revolve: war. The central nature of this theme is reiterated at the beginning of the *Democrates primus* itself when Democrates ('a Greek, protagonist of this disputation' who acts as the author's mouthpiece) mentions the 'noble young Spaniards' who 'maintained that the soldier's profession is not compatible with the precepts of Christian philosophy'. Of identical persuasion is the mind of Leopoldus, 'a German a trifle Lutheran in his inclinations', who with Alphonsus ('an old Spanish soldier') closes the dialogue's cast. The book's argument, then, pivots around a double ideological linchpin: Leopoldus' premises embodying his conviction that soldiers cannot be soldiers and remain Christians – in essence, that some aspects of the *vita activa* are prohibited to the faithful – and Democrates' magisterial attempt to convince his friend of his error.

Broadly speaking, Sepúlveda rarely understands contemplation in the classical, pagan sense of withdrawal from the cares of the world into devotion to the pleasures of learning. Rather, he associates contemplation with a Christian pursuit of transcendental wisdom. The old Augustinian position which held the superiority of Christian over worldly wisdom is adopted by Sepúlveda. But if a man's spiritual *negotium* has come in Sepúlveda's mind to take possession of *contemplatio* it is no less true that the earthly concerns of the Christian have also been staked out as a realm unto itself, an *ordo naturae*, a form of wisdom called *vita activa*. Never is this separation better recorded, and we may well remember Vitoria's own struggles to preserve the autonomy of his own two orders, than when Sepúlveda decides to devote the *Democrates'* first part to enquiring whether 'one can be both a courageous soldier and a good Christian'. He goes swiftly to the point.

Since there are two kinds of virtue...one 'intellectual' and the other 'moral', the Aristotelians maintain that in order to live well and to be happy it is enough to practice either kind. Now, those who occupy themselves with the search for truth and the contemplation of excellent things are considered to be the happiest. But Aristotle concretely limits himself to that happiness which can be found by mortal man and not that called 'eternal life' by the theologians and which consists in the clear and manifest contemplation of God.[19]

[19] Juan Ginés de Sepúlveda, *Democrates, sive de convenientia disciplinae militaris cum christiana religione dialogus*, in *Opera*, IV, 238–9. Cited hereafter as *DP*. See also A. Losada's translation, *Democrates primus* (Madrid, 1963).

It is true, concedes Sepúlveda, that Aristotle mentions that kind of perfect felicity which derives solely from the knowledge of the true God ('beatitude'); but the Philosopher understood it to be beyond the grasp of mortal men and to belong only in the province of the immortal gods. The limitations placed on the pagan Aristotle, however, no longer apply after the coming of Christ and 'just as the great philosophers praise above all others the life of those wise men who imitate, within the boundaries of what is humanly possible, that of God, so we must understand that Christians have two ways of life open to them, both honorable and conforming to the mandates of the faith but one endowed with greater excellence than the other'.[20]

Evidently feeling that a careful elaboration of this point is necessary, Sepúlveda launches into a detailed comparison of the two *vitae*. He calls the New Covenant to his aid and reflects on the story of Martha and Mary (Luke 10. 38). Paraphrasing and elaborating upon Christ's words, Sepúlveda praises the life of those who imitating Mary 'occupy themselves with the knowledge of truth and the contemplation of divine things' as being the more perfect.[21] In the same passage the Spanish humanist, determined to get his point across in all its clarity, insists that Christ did not seek to minimize the importance of those 'who place their virtue at the service of human needs'. The important thing, he concludes, is that men are under the obligation to embrace the practice of the moral virtues (activity) or the intellectual virtues (contemplation) – a judgment which clearly proves Sepúlveda's determination to identify contemplation with a wisdom (the knowledge of things divine) of exclusively Christian vintage.

But associating intellectual virtue with religious contemplation may have placed him at a distinct disadvantage, for such a drastic step carries with it a suggestion that Christians have no source of inspiration and counsel of their own to guide their progress along the path of moral virtue and are consequently forced to rely on the teachings of the pagans for counsel in matters of *negotium*. To account for this potential difficulty Sepúlveda, who never for a moment loses sight of the fact that the main question under consideration is whether a Christian may carry out certain civil duties (such as killing in war) seemingly contrary to the tenets of his faith, takes a momentous step: he divides Scripture into two parts, assigning separate and specific roles to each.

Since none of these two forms of living is prohibited to Christians both Christ in the Gospel and the Apostles in their Epistles gave us precepts relative to both. Some are necessary and sufficient to live well and in conformity with the Christian religion, to wit, the Commandments of the Decalogue to which

[20] *DP*, p. 239.   [21] *Ibid.*, pp. 239–240.

all natural laws refer and which are the essence of civil life; others are profitably applied to a more perfect life toward the practice of which Christ and the Apostles exhort us.[22]

One brief and final remark in the context of the passage just cited may well be brought forward now in token of further and more detailed scrutiny in pages to come. The moral virtues which Erasmus and others had succeeded, during the early part of the century, in identifying with a wisdom synonymous with ethics, Sepúlveda forces to stand on a solid Scriptural basis. Good and faithful humanist though he is, Sepúlveda is a better Christian, and although his notion of the active life will unfold in the shade of Aristotle's teachings he seems to warn us that pagan wisdom is helpful but not essential; for the faith alone contains the needed precepts for a good active life as well. To this extremely important commitment Sepúlveda significantly adds the idea that natural laws are in some fashion tied both to the Law and the moral virtues, a notion by no means confined to the *Democrates primus* as we shall have occasion to observe when studying its sequel. *In toto* the contents of this passage holds a promise of great relevance to our forthcoming study of Sepúlveda's view of the Indians.

Activity and the moral virtues

The first journey of their disputation concluded, Democrates and his friends begin the second day of conversation with a subject which, although contextually similar to the one just discussed, is also narrower in scope and subtly shifts the entire argument from the contemplative to the active life. Alphonsus, the soldier, is uncertainty's spokesman in this instance. He confesses the essence of his doubting: courage and honor, virtues so necessary to military life, may not accord with that behavior prescribed for a Christian by his faith. The basic theme, of course, remains the same: activity vs. contemplation. But with a twist, for the tone now shifts from contemplation to activity: 'It is necessary that we speak of those virtues which, in the judgment of wise men, principally shape the glory of the knight or soldier.'[23] The virtues in question are fortitude and magnanimity, 'said by the philosophers to belong to the moral group'. The problem at hand, then, reduces itself to the following: may some moral virtues be prohibited to Christians? Through his mouthpiece Democrates, Sepúlveda argues that all the virtues are so inextricably entwined that to deny one means to deny all, 'and from this we may easily deduce that if courage and magnanimity were denied to Christians so would all the other

[22] *Ibid.*, p. 241.   [23] *Ibid.*, p. 253.

virtues'.[24] Needless to say, Leopoldus disagrees. 'If a Christian, in order to obey the commands of his faith, fails to do what is demanded of him by fortitude and magnanimity by no means can we say that he is lacking in other virtues.'[25] It turns out, however, that Leopoldus' appraisal is based on an interpretation of Christian doctrine not shared by Sepúlveda nor free from Lutheran taint.

A Christian honors and practices the virtues not only for the sake of their intrinsic honesty and his own need to obey the mandates of *recta ratio* but, far more, in order to obey God's commands – weightier and of greater authority as they are – and because a Christian is under compulsion to direct all his works toward God as the highest and ultimate end.[26]

Democrates immediately voices his outraged protest against an idea which, if unchecked, clearly opens the way for a return to the ataraxy, contempt for learning and *ratio*, and monopolistic hoarding of wisdom inherent in early Christianity – one which he attributes to his friend's flirtations with Lutheranism. 'How', he asks, 'can you think that only Christian doctrine is capable of correctly pointing the virtues to their ultimate goal?'[27] As far as those Christian teachings which deal with manners and mores are concerned, concludes the Greek scholar, they are little or no different from Peripatetic doctrine.[28] 'Do you not see', he badgers Leopoldus, 'how agreeable Aristotelianism and Christian doctrine are to each other in what touches upon mores and customs?'[29] No doubt Sepúlveda felt the danger to be both clear and present: the revolt against an established Church which had finally come around to finding a niche within its doctrinal bosom for the active wisdom of the ancients was resurrecting all the animosities between *fides* and *ratio*. Evidently the Spanish humanist interpreted in this manner Luther's emphasis on the worthlessness of good works. Leopoldus eventually surrenders to Democrates' persuasive power and concedes that the intrinsic reason which compels men to follow and honor the virtues lies in that decorousness so indispensable to their name and nature.[30] Democrates loses no time in taking advantage of Leopoldus' admission and reasserting on this basis his argument that the Christian who rejects fortitude and magnanimity will equally exclude the other virtues. Thoroughly irritated by the ruthless manner in which his friend takes advantage of any opening, regardless of how cautiously qualified, to thrust his point relentlessly home, Leopoldus accuses him of 'endeavoring to rectify the precepts of the Christian religion with the canons of Aristotle'.[31] Democrates, of course,

[24] *Ibid.*, p. 256. [25] *Ibid.*, p. 257. [26] *Ibid.*
[27] *Ibid.* [28] *Ibid.* [29] *Ibid.*, p. 258.
[30] *Ibid.*, p. 259. [31] *Ibid.*, p. 260.

denies the charge and refusing to sanction a return to the restrictive Augustinian definition of *sapientia* dismisses the accusation as the invention of the 'teachers of the Lutheran heresy'. Thereby going on record against the Reformation's attempt to substitute the Thomist conception of wisdom with Augustine's, he reasons instead that Aristotle's 'maxims, in the judgment of almost all learned men, resemble less the doctrine of philosophers than natural law and the decrees of *recta ratio*'.[32] When we speak of mores and seek to understand what nature contains and what it rejects, none does it better than Aristotle. Under the circumstances, Democrates explains, 'when I rest on Aristotle you, Leopoldus, must understand that I am adducing natural law, of which he was a great interpreter'.[33] In conclusion, 'let it be understood that Christians are no different from the Peripatetics when both discourse on those virtues and vices judged through natural reason, for both conclude it to be an error to depart from nature and *recta ratio*'.[34]

Sepúlveda's ultimate aim appears clear throughout. Strictly speaking *contemplatio* has become religious contemplation. In this manner postulated as most aptly the province of Christianity, *contemplatio* is explicitly raised (as the realm of supernatural knowledge) to a plane of unconditional, if theoretical, superiority. The dividends are not slow in coming, for having in effect relegated contemplation to a Christian limbo, Sepúlveda – in a manner not unlike Guicciardini's disposal of *fortuna*'s unpredictable influence in history, to mention but one instance – is ready to deal with activity, the orb of the moral virtues. In principle at least it is plain that the Spanish humanist has succeeded in outlining a scheme unquestionably superior to Vitoria's uncertain and indecisive juggling with the secular and transcendental orders. And from this point onward, it emerges from his protracted sparring with Leopoldus; Sepúlveda prepares to concentrate on those aspects of man's life – manners, customs, mores – that can be best understood through *recta ratio*. It is the bailiwick of reason to which both man and Christian man may gain entrance, for their respective keys – Aristotle and the Law – fit the lock equally well. The Old Covenant, Aristotle, *recta ratio*, and natural law are the necessary and sufficient instruments used to advantage in comprehending, appreciating, and following a life of activity. Missing as yet, however, is a closer scrutiny of the heart of the *vita activa*: the moral virtues.

To begin with, at the outset of the second journey we are informed by Leopoldus that the moral virtues – Sepúlveda counts justice, prudence, fortitude, magnanimity, and liberality among them – are not strictly given by nature. Neither are they exclusively yielded by man's will. Rather, our

[32] *Ibid.*, p. 262.   [33] *Ibid.*, p. 264.   [34] *Ibid.*, p. 265.

crypto-Lutheran concludes, 'they are born out of the habit of right doing'.[35] Moreover, the moral virtues require that theory and practice, intention and action, blend in harmony, for he who for the sake of philosophy's teachings and *recta ratio* loves virtue must simultaneously conceive the firm purpose of never ceasing to do what is right. Precisely for this reason it is said that such a man, as long as he partakes of the virtues through his free will only, shares in them but imperfectly, for he does not hold them fully in ownership.[36] In other words, it is not enough to know the right path or to desire to follow it; a firm and unalterable commitment must be made to practice that which reason tells us is the right conduct.

The somewhat impatient remarks of Alphonsus, however, soon force the conversation into more concrete channels and the discussion once again returns to the twin subjects of fortitude and magnanimity. But not for long, for Leopoldus' comment concerning his fear that a soldier's virtues – and, by extension, all the others – may depend on nature's capricious endowment, gives Sepúlveda the needed pretext for a return to the general theme of the moral virtues. Democrates identifies two distinct groups among them: one comprising those moral virtues which fall under the category of 'natural' – the other those said to be *rationis*.[37] It is the first group which monopolizes the Greek scholar's attention:

Natural virtue is a certain natural inclination, independent of reason, which moves us to do certain things (works) – deeds, for example, of fortitude and liberality. Such inclination is inborn with us and gradually grows and develops unless actively arrested by its opposite. We may best appreciate this in young children, for some manifest a tendency toward virtue while others lean toward vice; these natural habits proper to children cannot be the object of either praise or censure because they are involuntary inasmuch as they are deprived of reason's guiding light.[38]

When natural virtue, however, is wedded to another, that which is most properly called virtue and is invariably escorted by *recta ratio*, the virtuous habit is most easily engendered and its roots sunk deepest. The offspring, concludes Sepúlveda, is that most perfect virtue which creates great men worthy of the highest praise. Man's natural condition, then, is akin to the land which even though naturally fertile must be plowed and cultivated if it is to yield the right fruits. Of course, when the fields are naturally unproductive and sterile great diligence and endless toil are needed for meager returns. The best results, it follows, accrue when, in man as in the land, nature and reason harmoniously concur.[39]

At this point Sepúlveda injects into his discussion of the moral virtues

35 *Ibid.*   36 *Ibid.*   37 *Ibid.*, p. 281.
38 *Ibid.*   39 *Ibid.*, pp. 281–2.

two concepts inseparable from them: *justitia* and *prudentia*. The concept of justice and its meaning had been briefly surveyed earlier when Democrates, seeking to temper the enthusiasm of Alphonsus' definition of justice as the universal cocoon enfolding all forms and manners of virtue, proceeded to identify two categories of justice: 'one properly defined as the constant and perpetual exercise of the will in the direction of giving to each his own; the other, known as legitimate and taken in a very ample sense, we accept as synonymous with virtue'.[40] The significant result of this twofold definition of justice is that it leads Sepúlveda to conclude that justice of the second kind is identical with virtue understood in a 'universal sense', on the grounds that 'whoever engages in the practice of virtuous work must automatically circumscribe his actions within justice's boundaries'.[41] Now, however, Sepúlveda briefly mentions justice in connection with his definition of the will as a reasonable appetite: 'Aristotle called justice that virtue whereby he who possesses it does and wants just things.'[42] Much greater significance is given to *prudentia* in the passages now under discussion. Sepúlveda categorically maintains that the proposed ideal balance between nature and reason, the optimum yield which is the true virtue, is attained through prudence 'without which no moral virtue can exist and whose presence announces that of the other virtues'.[43] Prudence, then, is 'defined as a habit, made true through reason and aiming at accomplishing those things which are good for man'.[44] Sepúlveda shrewdly concludes that it is no doubt possible to misuse virtue in its raw, natural state; but when reason in the guise of prudence enters the stage the diamond formerly in the rough is now polished beyond improvement making it impossible for this newly created true virtue to be corrupted or to be put to bad use.

The role in this fashion attributed to prudence leads Sepúlveda one step further. No single human act, he points out quoting Aristotle, exists that is not common to both body and soul. The moral virtues, therefore, cannot be properly understood as originating in only one aspect of man; they are part of the entire human composite. The proof proposed by the author in support of this striking conclusion is by no means easy to isolate unambiguously but it is part of a general scheme which to all appearances unfolds in the following manner. Reason (*intellectus, mens*), according to the Spanish humanist, is nourished by the intellectual virtues and its nature best defined in terms, first, of a *pars contemplativa* devoted to the contemplation of truth and, second, an active side at the service of the *vita activa*.[45] *Recta ratio* in the first sense has as its function the apprehension of truth;

40 *Ibid.*, p. 276.   41 *Ibid.*   42 *Ibid.*, p. 283.
43 *Ibid.*, p. 257. See also *De regno*, p. 102.
44 *DP*, p. 282.   45 *De regno*, p. 115.

appropriately enough, it is part and parcel of that portion of the human soul which is endowed with reason. There is, however, a second side to the *anima* which is devoid of reason although it can be subjected to reason's control. And to this realm, Sepúlveda suggests, belong both *recta ratio qua ratio activa* and the appetites. When reason, having grasped truth through contemplation, seeks control over the appetite (*appetitus*) it abandons its contemplative function donning instead the mien of activity. As such, reason now transforms the appetite into a 'rational appetite' or *voluntas*.

So far Sepúlveda has in a few strokes conceived and elaborated a landscape occupied, on the one hand, by that truth whose apprehension through *contemplatio* creates an awareness of the good which causes in turn the advent of the moral virtues in potential form and, on the other, by a tamed appetite (will) yearning to actualize that potential. The canvas is, as yet, unfinished. A third intervention of *recta ratio*, this time in the guise of prudence (the epitome of 'active reason'), is needed to fully realize the promise implicit in a will desirous to do what contemplative reason has identified as good. And only when this final stage is reached, concludes Sepúlveda, can we say the moral virtues to be deserving of the name: 'Without reason and the understanding which only prudence can perfect the moral virtues can neither be brought into being nor, even after their creation, put into practice, for it is one thing to be virtuous and another to act virtuously.'[46] The overwhelming role played by reason in this complex scenario needs little comment. The will is a 'reasonable' appetite. When deprived of *recta ratio* the will, defective, reverts to the category of mere appetite from which prudence is absent and therefore unable to operate courageously or moderately or justly. 'It is for this reason that the active life is attributed to that side of reason protected by prudence. *Recta ratio* is like the architect in human life and rules the civil life.'[47]

Sepúlveda further remarks that the body itself contributes to the moral virtues, a fact which heredity amply bears out. In heredity, he continues, we found our commonly shared hope that those born of virtuous parents, regardless of their social status, will in turn also be inclined to virtue, for it is so willed by nature that the children shall be akin to the parents.[48] Nature, it is clear, not infrequently offers a predisposition to virtue. But, on the other hand, nature neither gives virtue completely nor does it absolutely take it away from anyone, provided that the use of reason remains, 'for no one is born so irremediably vicious that he can completely destroy both reason and what the theologians call free will'.[49] Admitted the importance of genetics, it nevertheless pales in comparison with the significance of

[46] *DP*, pp. 282–3.   [47] *Ibid*., p. 283.
[48] *Ibid*.   [49] *Ibid*., p. 284.

education. 'Nothing is so efficacious to remedy natural vice as a sound education. There is, then, a great difference between raising children servilely, as is the case among the poor, and educating them liberally as happens with the offspring of the rich and the noble.'[50]

This last remark, closing the second journey of the dialogue, most convincingly introduces us to the subject of wealth as the central topic monopolizing the three friends' attention during the third and last journey of their conversation. It is again Leopoldus who opens the floor to the ensuing argumentation: first, wealth and magnanimity (as defined by Democrates) are incompatible; second, the riches accumulated by the Church are in large measure responsible for its moral decrepitude. On the basis of such evidence Leopoldus concludes that wealth is responsible for the corruption of mores and customs. Democrates retorts that wealth is not an infallible guide to wickedness; nor is poverty a sure sign of blessedness – not all rich men are evil anymore than all poor men are good. It is true, he grants, that both Saint Paul and the Apostles preferred poverty to opulence. But the choice was made in the same spirit that led them to prefer chastity above marriage: as a token of the perfect life which they elected to lead. In what pertains to matters of the civil life, however, wealth is often a useful instrument capable of contributing to the consummation of virtue; in other words, it enables intention to become action through good works. The *vita officiosa,* the goal and aim which is the moral virtues' *raison d'être,* hence cannot exist without prosperity's aid. And there is more, for the benevolent influence of affluence extends to the life of those who choose to devote themselves to the search for intellectual truth (contemplation understood here in a strictly pre-Christian sense): the scholar in his study. Deprived of the means of subsistence the philosopher's spirit necessarily shrinks from the search for truth to concentrate upon the pursuit of those things indispensable to the preservation of life and health.[51]

Leopoldus willingly concedes the strength of Democrates' case for wealth; but he remains unconvinced. After all, he claims, it may be true that wealth enables the virtuous man to practice his righteous inclinations, but the fact remains that the crucial ingredient which turns virtue into true virtue is not the actual performance of the good work itself but the inclination and will to do so.[52] In short, if someone living in poverty conceives the idea and manifests the will to apply the riches which he does not in reality possess to the performance of good works that man can be fully considered to be a virtuous man; in other words, righteous disposition is everything, consummation of that inclination little or nothing. Needless to say, Democrates emphatically disagrees with this view. Granted, he

[50] *Ibid.*   [51] *Ibid.,* pp. 296–300.   [52] *Ibid.,* p. 300.

has already admitted, that the will to do something must be present beforehand. But there is more, for it is proper of the will both to desire to do something and to command man's other powers to actualize that appetite. This is nothing more than a part of that universal pattern whereby the end of each thing lies within its function; for instance, the end of the horse is to run. In the concrete case of man his end and function is to wish to do (good) and to act upon his intention (good works). It is beyond doubt that the latter is more perfect than the former.[53]

Sepúlveda goes still further. We have already mentioned how the end of each and every act or thing is whatever the thing or act itself aims at. Furthermore, the truth or falsity of a given proposition, the subject matter of the *intellectus*, lies in the mind. This same mind or reason (contemplative) which apprehends both truth and its antithesis and therefore creates general referential categories against which the good or evil of a particular deed must be judged also tames (active) the appetite into will. The qualitative nature of a given act/thing, therefore, is not given by the will. The latter merely desires the concrete advent of the former, and in this sense and this sense alone can the act/thing be said to be the object matter of the will, whose desirability has been ascertained by reference to existing standards previously devised by the contemplative reason. 'And from this it clearly follows that works possess a greater excellence than the will.'[54] Man, Democrates continues, is not 'a marble statue' but a body complemented by a soul endowed with reason; the soul conceives a deed or act which then must be given outward shape by the body. Perfection, then, lies 'in the voluntary deed emerging from reason'. *Virtutum ratio* is understood to lie with man's free will, but perfection consists in the willfully executed good work.[55] When a good work, voluntarily conceived, cannot be carried to fruition it is said to be imperfectly conceived – a conclusion which retains its validity regardless of the reasons for failure, even if the adduced reason is poverty. As with Leonardo Bruni, Sepúlveda's virtue is the gift or quality of consummating a desirable course of action.

Democrates' lengthy discourse on virtue in the end carries the day: the three friends agree that the gifts deemed indispensable for a soldier, *fortitudo et magnitudo animi*, are indispensable to the network of virtues said to be a Christian's standard equipment. The importance of those gifts is proven by Sepúlveda's extended probing into the meaning of fortitude, magnanimity, and glory for a soldier. We are not here directly concerned with that question, but Sepúlveda's discussion of the subject is indirectly relevant to us because it serves to illustrate one of the more striking facets

[53] *Ibid.*, pp. 304–305.   [54] *Ibid.*, p. 305.
[55] *Ibid.*, p. 307. See also *Democrates alter*, p. 50.

of Spanish political thought in the sixteenth century and beyond: the painful awareness that man, in his endless search for the fitting golden mean, is forever compelled to walk a tightrope of virtue precariously stretched over an abyss of vice.[56] From this burden Spanish political thought in the Renaissance could not free itself, hence its high ethical content. Christ, wisdom, justice, reason, prudence, and unquestioned faith in man's perfectibility are its allies; man's weak nature and the pressures of praxis are its foes. The most pressing task of the Spanish tradition, then, was to provide a satisfactory solution to the historical dialectic which pitted man as an individual shaped by the teachings of Christ (or natural law's) and man as a member of the group, a social being victim to the formidable demands of reality – a view of history, incidentally, in no significant way different from that of Vico's *Scienza Nuova*. From this admittedly frustrating labor the Spanish tradition, to a man, refused to be waylaid, a fact that explains both their rejection of Machiavellian solutions and the ultimate 'weakness' – judged so only if we fail to grasp the supremely onerous quality of the job – of their schemes.

The fundamental line of Sepúlveda's reasoning, that contemplative wisdom is intrinsically better but active wisdom often more necessary, places him alongside the tradition of civic humanism with Bruni, Palmieri, Manetti, and Alberti. Understood in the context of an age which saw western Europe seething with the excitement and expectancy produced by Luther's revolt, the importance of this idea must not be dismissed lightly. In his study of the secularization of wisdom from Petrarch to Charron, E. F. Rice concluded that 'the gradual process by which wisdom was transformed from intellectual *eruditio* to a moral virtue, from theoretical knowledge to probity in action',[57] best exemplifies the changes in the meaning of *sapientia*. In a very real sense this is precisely the process illustrated in the dialogue between Democrates and Leopoldus. The former is the advocate of the 'modern' emphasis on a natural wisdom, an *ars vivendi* to be identified later, in a specifically socio-political context, as the root and branch of *bene vivere*. The latter defends a clearly Augustinian position and, significantly, earns the author's rebuke for his crypto-Lutheranism. If, as Democrates will imply time and again with an earnestness bordering on anguish, we concede that in fact there exist certain duties essential to civic life which cannot in good conscience be undertaken by a Christian, we are reducing to naught that frail doctrinal structure which through the centuries western thought had reared to house in harmony the inheritance of the pagan world and the faith of

---

[56] *DP*, pp. 226–313.
[57] E. F. Rice, Jr., *The Renaissance Idea of Wisdom* (Cambridge, Mass., 1958), p. 213.

Christ. In fact we are reviving that revolutionary and subversive strain in Christianity so well understood by those among its early followers who had elected to shun all civic involvement. The catastrophic consequences of such a course of action for European society, we have seen, were not overlooked by Vives. Hence his pitiless thunderings, despite his own aversion to violence, against the Anabaptists whom he considered to be Luther's natural offspring.

Such, in my view, is the substance of the *negotium* transacted in the gardens of the Belvedere between Democrates – scholar and sage, rich in learning and experience – and Leopoldus – young, idealistic, and afire with the limitless expanses seemingly promised by the Lutheran novelty. What is at stake in this dialogue, then, is the successful search for an alternative to the unbridled spiritualism which many observers foresaw bade fair to engulf Christendom in chaos. Inasmuch as the redoubt under siege was the frail *modus vivendi* which since Aquinas' time had preserved a relative balance between the apparatus of Aristotelian wisdom and Christian revelation, the options open to Sepúlveda are as plain as they are limited: either to strengthen and defend the orthodox solution *à outrance* or to modify it in such a manner as to accommodate the new imperatives while retaining the basic contours of tradition. A similar choice had been offered – or forced upon – Vitoria. The theologian, Thomist to his fingertips, had persevered in the master's efforts to stake out a sphere of dignity for metaphysics while preserving intact the hegemony of theology and retained Aquinas' resulting complementary dualism of heaven and earth, divinely ordained theological wisdom, with his own natural and transcendental orders; in fact, by partitioning the entire world of man into congenially autonomous bailiwicks Vitoria had extended this division to its farthest limits. In Sepúlveda, however, there is something new. Something less 'medieval' and more in line with what we might expect from an age which at times managed to show a considerable degree of originality. For one thing, the humanist, reared in a profoundly Peripatetic atmosphere of long standing, never felt constrained to understand Aristotle through the minds of the Schoolmen. For another, at no time does he feel compelled to reject any vital part of his own orthodoxy for the sake of the Aristotelian, Stoic, and civic humanist baggage with which he is burdened. And herein lies precisely a source of Sepúlveda's uniqueness: his ability to remain a theologian while retaining intact his humanist outlook, and vice versa. A striking characteristic which largely explains why he elects to ward off the threat of radicalism from the 'right' by means of a compromise which will retain a definition of wisdom capable of satisfying the most demanding Augustinianism, while leaving him free to elevate the moral virtues to the category of a functional wisdom naturally acquired and supreme in the order of secular life.

And yet, we may ask, is this not, together with the intrinsic superiority of contemplative wisdom which Sepúlveda willingly concedes, the old Thomist stab at striking a balance between heaven and earth? While on the one hand the answer is an affirmative one, on the other it must be remembered that in this age of transition it is the subtle distinctions which accompanying identical concepts characterize a man's thought as different from another's and give a measure of his own originality that are often most revealing. True enough, homage is rendered to a contemplative wisdom sinking its roots in divine illumination. But in the same breath we are told that the wisdom of Christianity and Aristotelian *sapientia* are tools of comparable efficiency in what concerns secular affairs and that both contain the formulae prescribed for good and right living; the moral virtues are identified with a prudence and justice keenly Aristotelian and savoring of that wisdom which elevated to an ethical category was indispensable to the Stoic *ars vivendi*. Finally, the moral virtues which deal with such things as 'customs and mores' constitute a species of wisdom unto themselves, specifically designed to guide and counsel man as he grapples with the complexities of temporal *negotium*, naturally acquired, and not necessarily related to Christianity.

If Sepúlveda is determined to resist the onslaught from the 'right', he is equally resolved to withstand the pressures from the 'left'; granted that worldly wisdom is not under Christian constraint, but neither is it necessarily unrelated to revealed *sapientia*. The unobtrusive bond which ties both, without in the least hindering the movements of either, is natural law. Aristotelian prudence is solidly anchored in natural law and nothing that natural law allows could possibly conflict with divine law and the wisdom of its vessel, revealed religion. Thus a permanent separation between contemplative and active wisdom becomes impossible in Sepúlveda.

In this general connection it would be useful to mention here one of the more important points of Rice's monograph: it is among French thinkers of the second half of the century that the secularization of wisdom was best realized. He suggests, moreover, that Budé and Le Caron concluded 'that wisdom as an intellectual virtue has no necessary relation with moral virtue and therefore does not guarantee the probity of the wise man'.[58] And with this last statement we find ourselves roundly back to Vitoria's old predicament – whether the good man is necessarily a good citizen as well – and also faced with a somewhat perplexing dilemma because in this conclusion of the French humanists seems to lurk the proposition that

[58] *Ibid.*, p. 155.

there lies an impassable barrier between two definitions of virtue best represented in their extremes by Luther and Machiavelli. Fortunately, Professor Rice himself comes to the rescue when he remarks that this and other criticisms were met by 'sixteenth-century humanists in Italy and the North...not by rejecting wisdom, but by redefining it, by transforming it from a knowledge of divine things or of divine and human things and their causes to a code of ethical precepts, indistinguishable from prudence, on how to live well and *blessedly*'.[59] Nothing could have summed up Sepúlveda's position better. His moral virtues will pave the way for man's *vivir bien*, while his contemplative wisdom enables him to live blessedly. And simultaneously, so that the wise citizen's probity is unquestionable. A denouement made possible by the denominator common to both natural and revealed wisdom: natural law. Reason, natural law's interpreter and inseparable companion, contemplates the truth supplied by the intellectual virtues and helps the moral virtues in their endless striving to give reality to the truth – the good – thus revealed. In this manner is the Lutheran emphasis on the superfluity of good works voiced by Leopoldus met. On the other hand, the Machiavellian gambit, the threat from the 'left', is equally well parried, for a sound citizen can only work for the welfare of the commonwealth after he has identified the good. The secularization of virtue, therefore, need not lead to Machiavellian immoralism. Sepúlveda's solution aims at reconciling ethical behavior with the demands of utilitarian politics or, in the terminology of seventeenth-century Spanish political thinking, at formulating a *verdadera razón de Estado*.

But, how does this differ from the vicious circle which had forced Vitoria to rely most heavily on the revealed order? The answer is that, in the last analysis, if we carry the polemic between reason and revelation to its rigorous conclusion it must be confessed that no sixteenth-century thinker, regardless of how far he goes in his secularization of wisdom, can refuse to acknowledge the supremacy of revelation. But to labor in such fields would be idle, for it implies demanding of the age something which it is not capable of yielding. We must not, then, look for absolutes but rather for more or less subtle variations on an as yet unique theme. Once this is understood it is not unreasonable to contend that Sepúlveda's secularization of wisdom offers him a freedom of action denied to Vitoria. Appreciation of temporal truth and with it the apprehension and eventual realization of secular good can be achieved equally well through Aristotle or Christ since the teachings of neither contradict natural law. The conclusion is simple: wisdom, that prudence indispensable to good citizenship is available to Christian and non-Christian alike. Naturally enough, the

[59] *Ibid.*, pp. 155–6. Italics mine.

Christian, out of pure convenience, chooses to reach the goal of civic perfection through Christian channels. The pagans of old achieved the same thing through Aristotle. Today's heathens, it is reasonable to expect, will follow an identical path guided by the counsels of their own sages. Unless, of course, they should happen to have none, in which case their evident ignorance of natural law would justify any impartial observer's questioning of their rationality, for, after all, what could be a more necessary and sufficient proof of man's humanity than his familiarity with natural law?

Needless to say, when Sepúlveda wrote the *Democrates primus* he did not have in mind the affairs of the New World. It is also true, however, that the ideas embodied in that treatise are the foundation on which his contribution to the American debate will stand. A fact which gives the Spaniard an excellent claim to uniqueness, for he, alone among the sixteenth-century humanists who contributed to the secularization of wisdom, descends from the realm of pure speculation into the arena of a most novel praxis to test the strength of his conclusions. These brief observations are worth remembering because in the past Sepúlveda's part in the American controversy has been judged solely on the basis of the *Democrates alter* (the *Apologia*, after all, is but a digest of the same tract). The results of ignoring the groundwork which prepared and gave cogency to the ideology on the Indians outlined in that dialogue have been lamentable in that they have created an interpretation of Sepúlveda which in my view is both incomplete and erroneous. And with these anticipatory remarks in mind we are now ready to study Sepúlveda's political ideas and his conclusions concerning the American Indians.

On civile *and* herile imperium

In the preceding pages I have, with some attention to detail, depicted Sepúlveda's conviction that the virtues demanded of Christians are in no way incompatible with those which actively involve them in the *negotium* of civil society. Activity and contemplation, as a result, emerged as substantive and praiseworthy forms of living essential to all men. Individuals have the choice of stressing one or the other freely; only the total rejection of both is deemed inadmissible. Under the circumstances the conclusion that Sepúlveda's entire political scheme rests squarely on the shoulders of this carefully laid foundation should not be unexpected. Naturally enough, a conspicuous segment of that scheme is the humanist's appraisal of the character, nature, and role of civil society; a subject actively touched upon in *De regno*. Man's many-faceted nature as disciple of Christ, socio-political being, and *homo economicus* is wholly there and its components proven to be mutually compatible and essential parts of the whole. Of the utmost import for this *totum* to exist at all is a society politically organized. And the 'state' is composed of men who must possess these prerequisites in harmonious balance. It is upon this essential bedrock that the state shall implicitly rest its function as the protector of society. What, then, is the state, and who may rightfully be adorned with the name of citizen?

In the brief introductory paragraphs used by Sepúlveda to dedicate *De regno et regis officio* to Philip II the humanist promises to deal first with 'some questions relative to government in general and each of its manifestations in particular'. Moreover, he further pledges, 'in this affair I shall follow Aristotle, whose doctrine in political and moral matters differs little or nothing from Christian teaching'.[60] Having once again acknowledged his debt to Aristotle, Sepúlveda goes on to identify the keystone on which the entire business of government, as everything else in nature, squarely rests: 'the dual principle of command and obedience'. The right to command naturally resides in that which is more perfect or of greater dignity; conversely, the less perfect by natural law obeys the former's empire. Such is the manner, for instance, in which the soul exerts its herile dominion over the body – as mistress over *servus* – and the mind or reason asserts civil suzerainty over the *appetitus*. When these two variants of natural regime are carried over into the realm of human affairs they are defined as follows: *civile imperium* is that manner of authority brought to bear upon men for their own benefit; *herile imperium*, by contrast, is the sovereignty exercised over *servi* for the profit of he who rules.[61]

In addition, Sepúlveda discovers that the moral virtues are an excellent standard for determining who among men must rule and who be ruled. The more highly endowed with virtue and prudence, the more perfect, a man is the stronger his claim to command; on the other hand, the coarser and less intelligent he is the greater his suitability for obedience.[62] Unfortunately the humanist's argument does not end here; instead, Sepúlveda elects to reinforce his thesis with an appeal to nature which will do little to clarify subsequent statements of great significance.

It happens that some men are born with an aptitude to command and others to obey which is said to be natural because it is exercised justly and usefully for both he who commands and he who obeys. In short, lord by nature (*natura dominus*) is he who excels in intelligence and *animus*, even though he may not be outstanding in strength; and *servus natura* the man who, while capable of fulfilling bodily tasks, is of faulty intelligence and slow mind.[63]

---

[60] Juan Ginés de Sepúlveda, *De regno et regis officio*, in *Opera*, iv, pp. 97–8. Cited hereafter as *DR*. See also A. Losada, *Tratados políticos de Juan Ginés de Sepúlveda* (Madrid, 1963).

[61] *Ibid.*, p. 98.   [62] *Ibid.*, p. 99.   [63] *Ibid.*

To all appearances the stress placed here on the natural origin of the moral virtues is in sharp contrast with Sepúlveda's earlier effort toward establishing a harmonious balance between nature and acquired *habitus* – education – on precisely the same question. Worse still, when the emphasis on nature is again insisted upon in the context of the forthcoming issue of the American Indians' rightful place in the universe of man the result is to open a Pandora's box largely responsible for those misinterpretations of Sepúlveda's position against which the author himself so loudly inveighed. Matters are improved, although by no means completely set aright, when the humanist, owning the existence of a third kind of man, implicitly reaffirms his belief in man's perfectibility.

All other men lie between these two categories [*domini* and *servi*]; they are outstanding neither by their prudence nor their intelligence, although they are by no means completely devoid of either; these men, the great mass of the people, are neither *natura domini nec natura servi*.[64]

Sharply on the heels of this threefold classification of man the author once more chooses to burden future developments with the weight of ambiguity by dividing the nations of the earth into two groups.

Just as within the *civitas* we can distinguish three kinds of men, we also find that a great difference separates nations; some are civilized and prudent; others, whose life and public mores depart from natural law, are held to be barbaric and uncivilized. The latter's condition dictates through natural law that they should obey the rule of the more cultured and civilized nations; in this manner they will be governed by the better laws and institutions created by the civilized nations. Should the barbarians, however, refuse the governance that is good for and beneficent to them, natural law commands that they be compelled to conform. Based upon this right the Romans subjugated the barbarians.[65]

What, then, have we so far learned that shall be of significance for the argumentation to follow? To begin with, there is as yet no evidence whatsoever to conclude that Sepúlveda is in any way advocating or even sanctioning natural slavery when he distinguishes as *servi natura* those born to obey from those born to command. To suggest differently is tantamount to implying that Sepúlveda (in the context of footnote 63) sees the world as irrevocably divided by natural law's caprice into masters and slaves, a patent absurdity of which a man of his learning and experience cannot possibly be guilty. It will not do, therefore, to equate 'those who rule' with 'master' and 'those who obey' with 'slave'. What we do find, however, is an emphatic elitism which unquestionably appreciates the superiority of intellectual accomplishments over the bodily gifts, necessary

64 *Ibid.*   65 *Ibid.*

as the latter no doubt are. We are offered, moreover, a refinement of this initial partition of mankind in the paragraph immediately following (see footnote 64). In it we are told that the majority of men fall somewhere between the two extreme categories defined above. This, in effect, will compel us to treat as a central theme of the ensuing analysis the following questions: does Sepúlveda view the American Indians as deserving membership in the extreme assemblage of *servi*, or does he include them among the amorphous mass of those who while not fit to command nevertheless do not deserve herile rule? In this context it would not be idle to remember for future reference Sepúlveda's belief that the nations of the world are divided into two groups. The point of significance here lies with the last sentence: 'Based upon this right the Romans subjugated the barbarians', and the manner in which the American case is related to the Roman example. It hardly needs reminding that Sepúlveda was well aware that Rome had not 'enslaved' the conquered barbarian nations, but had instead incorporated them into her political orbit and eventually had granted their inhabitants the full status and perquisites of Roman citizenship. A useful argument to which I shall later return.

Strictly speaking, the contents of the various passages cited above and the attendant comments have taken us beyond the boundaries of our immediate concern, for we are only interested at present in what happens within a single *civitas*, not in what sort of standards guide the relations among nations. But it was eminently relevant to introduce both subjects, briefly and simultaneously, at this point for two reasons: first, because the connection between 'cultured' and 'uncultured' nations will be extensively discussed when we come to the Indian question; second, because when the 'barbarian' states are incorporated into the institutional framework of a 'civilized' nation its members become parts of one single *civitas* – the Roman case. When dealing with the question of the American Indians, then, Sepúlveda will face a double task. On the one hand, he will have to prove that the Indian commonwealths are indeed in contravention of natural law – barbaric – and thus deserving of incorporation into the Spanish Crown; on the other, the humanist will be forced to explain what position the Indians, individually now, shall occupy within the Spanish *civitas*; and it is to answering this last question that Sepúlveda's task will ultimately reduce itself. As we shall see, it is in this last context that the axiomatic presence of a third category of men will become crucial.

Civil society: citizens and citizenship

But let us now return to our present concern: Sepúlveda's understanding of the nature of civil society. The city, we are informed, is composed of several parts. The household is the most basic among them. Next comes the settlement (*vicus*), in the manner of a colony derived from the household. The perfect association of several settlements creates the *civitas*. The latter, in turn, is said to be perfect when it is both self-sufficient and has at its disposal all the means to yield in abundance both the necessities of life and the imperatives of gracious living. The last condition is more important than it would seem at first sight, for Sepúlveda, in true humanist fashion, believes that commonwealths were brought into being not only for men to live but to live well (*recte vivere, bene vivere, bien vivir*).[66] According to one manner of distinction, he continues, 'the commonwealth is partitioned into *nobilitas* and *plebs*. Among the former we find those ennobled by riches; others by their illustrious lineage; some by the virtue of their deeds; while the rest are noted by their wisdom.' It is not without interest to note that this definition of nobility effectively cuts across traditional lines and is based, somewhat indiscriminately, on wealth, birth, accomplishment, and *sagesse*. The *plebs*, in turn, is a much more amorphous group comprising peasants, artisans, merchants, sailors, mercenaries, and others of similar ilk. Seemingly anxious to avoid misunderstandings Sepúlveda promptly adds that the mere and simple act of being a part of the commonwealth does not endow a man with the perquisites of citizenship.

Citizen is he who has the authority to judge and to deliberate on affairs of state. The act of judging, however, implies far more than merely placating controversy between two parties in conflict; it embodies the capacity of the citizens to designate the magistrates, thereby asserting with their vote their right to pass judgment on the dignity and merits of the candidates.[67]

To be a citizen, however, is but the first step; the apex of accomplishment is attained only when a man becomes a good citizen. In other words, he must be a virtuous citizen, for no man can be called good unless outstanding 'in some virtue'. Albeit admittedly vague and uncompromisingly dim at this point, to all appearances this distinction promises to be an important clue aimed at complementing the distinction made shortly before between those who are destined neither to obey nor to command and those who are natural rulers – a significant consideration, to be sure, toward the understanding of the role played by the Indians in civil society, for eventually Sepúlveda will admit that if a commonwealth is to survive it must offer some manner of political participation to those who hover between the two extremes of natural endowment. Moreover, the author proceeds, the *virtus* of the *bonus cives* cannot be the same in all forms of government; in fact, it varies according to whether the regime in question

[66] *Ibid.*, pp. 100–1.   [67] *Ibid.*, p. 101.

is democratic, aristocratic, or oligarchic. In general, however, it is possible to conclude that 'whatever faculty, potential, or power strives for the common good of the republic is said to be the virtue of the good citizen'.[68]

Fully realizing, however, that a casual reading of this statement may lead to Machiavellian results, Sepúlveda energetically proceeds to hedge his definition of the virtue of good citizenship. Whoever wishes to deserve the name of virtuous citizen, we are told, must be fully aware that it is not enough to toil for the well-being and prosperity of just any common-wealth; for in 'depraved regimes' the use of the word virtue is improper and deceitful. A citizen who lives in a republic where laws and custom sanction practices clearly contrary to natural law and reason is not a virtuous citizen but 'a vicious and monstrous criminal if he labors for the welfare and preservation of such a republic'. In short, warns Sepúlveda, we must beware of the habit, all too common, which defines as virtue 'that power or faculty inherent in a person which tends to achieve what-ever end'. The meaning is clear: no citizen can possibly be considered virtuous unless he first be a good man, for 'in just regimes, especially the aristocratic, that same virtue which denotes the *bonus vir* makes also the *bonus cives.*' Prudence, justice, fortitude, temperance, and all the minor attributes which accompany, complement, and enhance them make up and define the good man's virtue; similarly, they distinguish the good man and are the heart and soul of life in civil society.[69] Now as before the demand that man be an ethical being before he can be a sound citizen in no way must be construed as making the *cives'* behavior in the common-wealth conditional upon a previous acquisition of the Christian faith. After all, in matters of mores and custom Aristotle and Christ are equally competent authorities.

We may next properly ask: does education have a formative role in molding the citizen, or is he entirely wrought by nature? Regardless of the singleminded emphasis on nature displayed when depicting the political types which inhabit the earth in general and any commonwealth in particular, the preoccupation with education as the crucial influence in fashioning the virtues of those who rule exhibited in the *Democrates primus* is not in the least impaired.[70] The explanation lies with Sepúlveda's

[68] *Ibid.*, p. 102. [69] *Ibid.*

[70] *Ibid.*, p. 145. No discussion of kingship and the duties of the ruler could possibly omit the subject of the prince's education, especially when the writer is an intellectual trained in the humanist tradition. Sepúlveda, of course, considers the education of the future monarch to be a point of exceptional interest, for 'children, since the most tender age, must be accustomed to delight in virtue, to love goodness and hate turpitude'. *Ibid.* And yet, surprisingly enough, the fact remains that the humanist is disappointingly brief – devoting only one short article (XII) to the subject in question. The substance of its contents is this: since childhood the

understanding of the word 'nature'. He means a natural capacity or inclination, a spontaneous receptivity – a genetic propensity, if one wishes – to understand, accept, and practice all those things concomitant to the moral virtues. To put it in simple terms Sepúlveda, worshipper at the shrine of the intellect, believes that there are intelligent and stupid men. By virtue of their natural rational powers the former take to the civic virtues, after the educational preparation which is *de rigueur*, as the proverbial duck to the water. The latter do not. What it all means, if I may belabor the point, is that the moral virtues do not blossom in strong bodies but in stalwart minds. It is perhaps an elitist view; and I think that Sepúlveda, not feeling compelled to admire the mediocrity of the common man, would have accepted the label as a matter of course and without the slightest embarrassment. But it is not one necessarily dependent on birth or standing in life. Its members are the aristocracy of the intellect, not the partakers of a social class.

Again, we are here in the presence of an idea indispensable to the baggage of any humanist: reverence for the individual and the singularity of his accomplishments, the very theme which captivated Burckhardt's imagination, coupled with a profound disdain for the vulgar. And this is also the idea forever present in Sepúlveda's mind when he scrutinizes the accomplishments of the American Indians. Rightly or wrongly, he detects nothing admirably unique in their institutions, demeanor, culture, or leadership; no bold spirits capable of soaring above the banality of the common herd. On the contrary, he sees all members of the commonwealths discovered by the Spaniards as a grey mass universally sharing their approval of evil customs and even worse practices; no grandeur, no praiseworthy individualism, no admirable departure from a common norm which to all appearances is damnable can be detected among the benighted barbarians. It is no longer a question of class or social standing; it is rather a remarkably uniform incapacity on the part of a society to show or produce any spark of uniqueness.

On the other hand, it will simply not do to carry too far the conclusions seemingly implicit in the portrait just sketched. For one thing, humanist rhetoric is notoriously prone to one form of narcissism or another and it is often prudent to discard some of the more flamboyant flights of stylistic enthusiasm. For another, and of greater significance, Sepúlveda's vocabulary, even when shorn of its more florid accessories, still falls short of the mark. It lacks the flexibility needed to interpret a phenomenon which if

monarch must be trained in letters, arms, religion. As to his tutors, Sepúlveda lifts a page from the ancient Persians who were said to choose from among the entire population four mentors to the royal heir: the wisest, the justest, the strongest, and the most prudent.

not totally absent from the Old World experience has now become, on Sepúlveda's own interpretation of the facts, of overwhelming importance in the New. In other words, humanist rhetoric, by its own admission, sought to deal with great and singular deeds and events – one of the cardinal commandments of the age's historiography. Plainly, it considered it unworthy to deal with 'low' subjects, for the latter are the insipid province of the colorless vulgar. For this selective outlook to emerge and survive a society is needed composed of two distinguishable entities: an elite and a mass. It is in order to deal with all the richly varied aspects of the former that language is developed and nursed – a language not of the court, to freely paraphrase Cicero. The latter, by definition irrelevant, can be dealt with in the most general fashion by means of a terminology whose ambiguity and lack of precision is of little significance. Successful as this scheme undoubtedly was in the context of the western experience, it fell short of the mark when called upon to cope with the New World; for in America, or so Sepúlveda concludes, the Spaniards have encountered a society surprisingly uniform, a society of the common man. The all-important elite is absent; instead, it is the vulgar who reign supreme and the terminology available to deal with them is woefully inadequate. Sepúlveda, then, has discovered in the continent beyond the seas what Ortega y Gasset would four centuries later identify in the context of contemporary civilization: the *hombre–masa* and an entire society geared to his needs and requirements. What to do? Sepúlveda, as I see it, proceeds, to paraphrase a Spanish saying, in the manner of a blind man endeavoring to strike the unseen target with a stick: haphazardly and at random. As I will, again and more extensively, point out in the next chapter, it is in this light that such notorious phrases as *natura servi* should be understood.

7

Classical humanism on the American Indians: Juan Ginés de Sepúlveda (II)

Prudence, the ruler, and the laws

I have already remarked that among the traditional Stoic–Christian moral virtues justice holds pride of place in Sepúlveda's mind. He acknowledges two variations to the theme of justice. In the first justice 'is defined as the constant and perpetual will to give each his own'. In the second justice is taken in a much broader sense as aiming 'at the public good'. In this fashion Sepúlveda knits together good citizenship, justice, and the laws. The tapestry, however, is not complete until the basic role of the ruler is explained. According to Sepúlveda the specific virtue which typifies the good ruler is different from that which concretely adorns the good civil subject, although the remaining virtues are common to both.

The virtue proper to the good ruler is prudence, also known as the civil faculty, for both spring from the same habitual inclination...By prudence we understand the prevailing disposition to discern, according to reason, those things which are good for man from the bad ones; and the civil faculty is that same habit when applied to the governance of the commonwealth and its parts.[1]

Beyond question, with the identification of *prudentia* with the *facultas viro civilis* Sepúlveda brings the moral virtues fully within the social and political order inseparable from the *civitas'* scope.

But why should it be required that the ruler be a paragon of prudence? The first reason is not hard to find. We have already seen how the truly virtuous citizen must necessarily judge the virtue of the means by the justice of the end. This traditional teleological argument, whose truth only prudence can reveal, applies even more urgently to the ruler.

The virtue of the successful leader of pirates is really no virtue at all, but a criminal shrewdness, diligent and execrable audacity which imitates for evil

---

[1] *DR*, p. 102.

and unjust purposes the virtue and noble deeds of the just and prudent captain who wages a just war.[2]

The second reason is perhaps less obvious but certainly of no smaller import, for the ruler is also a legislator and this function rests on a foundation of prudence. Possibly the single most constant feature of Sepúlveda's thought is the relevance of the laws, the truest backbone of any commonwealth. The humanist is ready to understand and forgive the wretchedness of individuals who seemingly find their lives' fulfillment in trespassing against the laws of a well-organized commonwealth. What he will not countenance is a commonwealth ruled by faulty institutions and defective laws. Without excuse or exception the positive laws of any republic worth the name must perfectly dovetail with the demands of natural and eternal law; in short, positive law must be the incarnation of justice.

The laws are of two kinds. Some are called civil precisely because they depend on the city which promulgates them and which they rule. Others are known as common although, as they find their strength in natural law, they are also often called natural laws. These laws are not brought into being by the will and caprice of the legislator; God and nature carved them indelibly into the hearts of men. Even among less civilized peoples we find these laws in use; and this is the reason why they are so often referred to as the *jus gentium*. These precepts are as chapters and referential principles for all natural laws; and it is for this reason that the latter are counted among the laws divine: they derive from eternal law through human reason and the divine law imbedded in our hearts...If the governance of a republic is to remain healthy it must take care not to exclude from its midst any form of natural law. To do otherwise would be barbaric and contrary to that human nature which is held in high esteem precisely because of its reasoning powers.[3]

The bond tying the laws civil to natural law is self-evident. According to Gratian, Sepúlveda explains, 'natural law commands us to do only that which God wants to be done, and forbids us to do that which God does not want to be done'.[4] In the second *Democrates*, Sepúlveda, discoursing on war's just causes, explains the meaning of natural law. He points out, first of all, that all those laws known as natural have as their goal to keep men within the fulfillment of their duties, to preserve human society, and to make this life into a suitable stopover in man's journey toward eternal life. According to the philosophers, we are told, natural law is 'that which everywhere possesses the same strength, regardless of circumstances'. The theologians, albeit using different terminology, agree with the philosophers as to the meaning of natural law. To them it is the means whereby

[2] *Ibid.*   [3] *Ibid.*, p. 112.
[4] Juan Ginés de Sepúlveda, *Democrates alter*, ed. A. Losada (Madrid, 1951), p. 10. Cited hereafter as *DA*.

'creatures endowed with reason partake of God's law Eternal'. The latter in turn, according to Saint Augustine, is the 'will of God who demands the preservation of the natural order and forbids its perturbation'. Sepúlveda holds that man shares in this eternal law through his reason and his inclination toward virtue. In conclusion, *recta ratio*, acceptance of duty, and the obligations of virtue constitute what is known as natural law. And this law of nature (*recta rationis lumen*) enables the 'good man to distinguish goodness and justice from evil and injustice; and this is not only true of Christian man, but of any man who has not corrupted *recta ratio* with depraved behavior'.[5] On the basis of these premises Sepúlveda finds little difficulty in accepting the universal validity, for instance, of those injunctions which in Deuteronomy and Leviticus damn human sacrifices. 'Although these precepts are addressed to the people of Israel, God Himself has declared that they are not only divine law but also natural law applicable to all peoples.'[6]

But what of the civil or positive law which rules man's conduct within a given *civitas*? We already know one thing about it: it must conform to the canon of natural law. The validity of positive laws, then, stands or falls on the solid rock of this premise. There is, of course, more; and Sepúlveda begrudges positive laws none of their significance: 'The strength of the laws is such that should their authority vanish so would government disappear.' On the other hand, he is not blind to the limitations of human-made laws. For one thing, he realizes that they cannot possibly cover all eventualities.[7] For another, the laws are not immutable but must be wisely adapted to changing circumstances.[8] And here is precisely where the legislative function of the ruler, seated on a foundation

---

[5] *Ibid.*, pp. 11–12.   [6] *Ibid.*, pp. 40, 42.   [7] *Ibid.*, p. 117.

[8] *Ibid.*, p. 120. Sepúlveda – in common with the humanist tradition which had reasserted as one of the principles of its historiography the relativity of institutions – discovers that in the same manner as the laws are not universal they cannot be eternal. The reason is the same in both cases: 'the great variety of, and change in, man's behavior deprive the law of its perpetual character'. *Ibid.*, p. 152. We might pause, in this context, to reflect how remarkable it is that a man aware of the profound effect exerted by time on the usefulness and efficacy of the laws should have been unable to accept the validity of Indian customs in the same relative light. That such 'skeptical' outlook was at least tentatively possible in the sixteenth century is proven by the Christian humanist frantic search for an explanation to man's belligerence, Montaigne's mordant remarks on Indian mores reported below, Castrillo's anguished comments, or Las Casas' own passionate defense of the Indians' way of life. Be that as it may, however, Sepúlveda will confine his relativism within a context given by his understanding and interpretation of natural law. He concludes that the ruler–legislator and his advisers, if they are prudent men, will heed this inescapable fact. When a law, then, becomes obsolete it must be corrected and changed in accordance with the dictates of equity. *Ibid.*

of prudence, comes into play. A role, incidentally, which is not unlimited, for the ruler's legislative latitude is rigidly circumscribed by considerations of natural law, equity, and reason; all, in turn, normative aspects of God's eternal law.[9]

The next obvious question to be answered is: what is the best form of government? After the traditional fashion Sepúlveda lists three kinds of rule: by one, by a few, or by many; in principle 'they are all good when they look after the public weal and bad if their administration is solely aimed at the well-being and pleasure of the ruler'. *Regnum* is that manner of rule whereby a *civitas* or *gentes* is governed by one man, notable for his virtue, for the sake and welfare of his subjects. *Status optimatum* consists in administering the state through a few notable men (*paucorum optimorum virorum*) who rule with *summa potestas* for the common weal. Finally, '*Respublica vero, sive Timocratia* is the form of government in which the *populus* rules the community for the common good.'[10] Sepúlveda's preference is clear: the rule of one is the 'most natural, in that it imitates and sinks its roots in the administration of the household'.[11] Monarchy, then, 'is much superior to all other forms of government; with the understanding, of course, that the monarch be a king in the Aristotelian manner, namely, if he stands above all other men in prudence, virtue, and other civic qualities'.[12]

Sepúlveda, however, was well aware that his own preference was not universally shared. There were those who did not believe monarchy to be the best possible form of government. Their arguments are therefore carefully presented and systematically rebutted by the humanist who, in addition, goes on to discuss other matters pertinent to the rule of one man: the origins of kingly rule, whether elected monarchy is preferable to the hereditary type, the advantages and disadvantages of dynastic succession.[13] Of course, out of these extensive and detailed considerations there emerges the conclusion that, despite its possible shortcomings, the rule of one man is best for the commonwealth. It is important to understand, however, that although partial to monarchy Sepúlveda is not an advocate of absolutism. His ideal, in fact, is an aristocratic monarchy where the king is guided by the counsels of the sages of the republic (the aristocracy of talent) and the important public offices are occupied by men of proven ability.[14] In Sepúlveda's mind, then, the best form of government is one which brings together the advantages of the *regnum* and the *status optimatum*.

The duties of Sepúlveda's king are simple. He must, on the one hand,

[9] *Ibid.*, pp. 117–18.
[11] *Ibid.*, p. 122.
[13] *Ibid.*, pp. 121–36.
[10] *Ibid.*, pp. 102–3.
[12] *Ibid.*, p. 121.
[14] *Ibid.*, pp. 110, 125.

strive to cure whatever ills may afflict the realm and, on the other, preserve by all means whatever happiness the commonwealth may have attained. By happiness Sepúlveda means abundance, absence of foreign war and domestic conflict, freedom for the subjects to indulge in all manner of virtuous activities that through custom and innate habit they may find pleasure in good works. To achieve this end the ruler shall legislate wisely and encourage the citizens to live honorably. Here we discover a blend of Vitoria and Spanish Erasmianism: the strength of the laws and the ruler's normative role.[15] In short, Sepúlveda's version of his sovereign's duties is in no sense different from the recommendations found throughout the political literature of the age. But when we come to the question of how to select the right officials for public posts, Sepúlveda's commonplaces acquire particular relevance in that they will shape his later strictures on the proper course to be followed by the Spaniards in America. He begins by underscoring that the king must see to it that the administration of the many individual communities which compose the realm emulates the *status optimatum*.

In any kingdom of considerable extension we find not one city but many, as well as numerous municipalities and castles (*municipia et castella*). And it is the duty of the king to see to it that the administration of those communities (*communitatum*) shall emulate that of an aristocrat republic (*rempublicam optimatum aemuletur*), for, as taught by the Philosopher, the kingdom is akin to it. And it is proper of the *status optimatum* that the magistratures be confined to men called 'ingenuii', honest and prudent; by 'ingenuii' we mean those who are neither *servi* nor *libertini*; and by *servi*, in what refers to magistratures, the philosophers understand mercenaries and those who engage in sordid professions, whom they consider public *servi*. These same philosophers do not wish the magistratures bestowed upon merchants, whom they hold suspect of avarice and vanity.[16]

Certain segments of society, then, must be excluded from various positions of social and political responsibility – and for future reference the meaning given the word *servus* here should be remembered. Who, therefore, are fitting magistrates in Sepúlveda's commonwealth?

The realm's magistratures ought to be distributed in the following manner: the highest should go to those who meet with the king's – or his counselors' – approval; in the cities of minor importance and the hamlets which fall within the circumscription of the larger cities magistrates should be selected by popular election. It must be done, however, in such a manner that virtue and prudence not be subordinated to wealth; otherwise, the poorer citizens will be excluded.[17]

[15] *Ibid.*, p. 137.
[16] *Ibid.*, pp. 141–2.
[17] *Ibid.*, p. 142.

The rationality of the American Indians

Throughout the pages so far devoted to the study of Sepúlveda's political ideas we have had occasion, at one time or another, to identify many and varied elements greatly influential in the formation of the humanist's thought: activity, justice, reason, and natural law are but a few. When those elements are woven together they yield the foundations of a scheme which, clearly antedating the birth of Christ and being therefore the potential source of premises outside the Christian purview, neatly circumvents the difficulties inherent in a strictly Christian approach to the problem of the Indians. The rational and self-evident premises derived from such a universal program will be, of course, nothing short of first principles endowed with absolute validity. They are, in fact, the immanent notions implanted by God in all men, the stuff of natural law; and available to all men, Christian or not, for assessing the worth of social and political institutions. Under the circumstances, so runs Sepúlveda's argument, what could be more logical than to evaluate the *vita activa* of the American natives on the basis of those very universal principles which helped them, unless of course the Indians turn out to be barbarians, to set up that life of social activity. In its broadest outlines such is the program of the *Democrates alter*, the most notorious of all his works and the one singly responsible for the poor reputation enjoyed by the author among historians of early America. It is only fitting, then, that the remainder of this study should be overwhelmingly concerned with that treatise, the manner in which the ideas contained therein flow from his other political writings, and how these ideas fare in the context of his controversy with Las Casas.

The first question which Sepúlveda undertakes to explore in the *Democrates alter* is the one lying closest to the heart of the entire Indian question as viewed through Spanish eyes: are the American aborigines rational beings? Do they live rationally and in accordance with the principles of natural law? It is to be noted in this context that Sepúlveda's immediate objective is not to judge individual men; he recognizes and admits that even in the most accomplished of commonwealths men will be found who do unnatural deeds. Instead, his more pressing task is to determine whether an entire society (its 'positive laws and actual institutions of government') obeys natural law – an important point to bear in mind, for the author will answer his critics with the dictum that he does not judge men but the institutions they create. These institutions, specifically those of the Indians of 'New Spain and the province of Mexico' said to be among the most civilized, Sepúlveda finds to be 'almost all of them *seruilia et barbara*' because they permit, sanction, and encourage the rankest and most brutal violations of natural law. And if the public institutions of the Indians are unpalatable the humanist finds their religion execrable: 'What can I say of the impious religion and base sacrifices of those people who, worshiping the devil as if he were God, thought of no better way of placating him than by offering human sacrifices...and simultaneously feasting on the flesh of the victims?...To my judgment this is the gravest, most heinous crime and the most alien to human nature. The most shameful kind of idolatry is that of those who venerate the belly and the basest organs of the body as if they were God.' Although these are his strongest objections to the behavior of the Indians they are by no means the only ones. Absence of commerce, letters, money; even the cities they build are arguments used by Sepúlveda to prove the sorry plight of the natives. 'They do not know of letters; they do not preserve records of their history, and lack written laws...They wage endless war among themselves to satisfy their prodigious appetite for human flesh...they are cowardly and timid.' The claims of the aborigines of New Spain and Mexico to civilization the humanist dismisses as insubstantial, for 'the possession of houses, some rational manner of living, and commerce induced by natural necessity' means only that the Indians are not 'bears or monkeys completely lacking in reason'.[18] Finally, in *De regno*, Sepúlveda appraises the quality of Indian society in the following terms.

Here are the proofs of their savage life, comparable to that of the beasts: their execrable and prodigious immolations of human victims to demons, the eating of human flesh, the custom of burying alive the wives of prominent men with their dead husbands, and other similar crimes damned by natural law which, even though repugnant to the ears of civilized people, the Indians committed as if they were pious deeds and with public sanction.[19]

It might be argued that the last observations quoted above are no longer institutional criticisms but judgments aimed at the individual nature of the Indians. And such is undoubtedly the case. Assuming always that the laws and institutions of society ultimately emanate from the free consent of its members, Sepúlveda concludes that the rational powers of the Indians are faulty. For, after all, what man in full command of his faculties would willingly elect to defy the most fundamental of principles imbedded by God in his heart? In conclusion, the Indians are not fully rational and they do not live in harmony with the commands of natural law. Seeking to dispel possible doubts that he may have been influenced by religious considerations Sepúlveda is at pains to stress that he is evaluating the *vita activa* of the Indians and not judging their spiritual shortcomings. Thus

18 *Ibid.*, pp. 35–58.
19 *DR*, p. 100.

he points out that the natives' paganism is not the reason why they must
be ruled by the Spaniards.

If in the New World a people, cultured, civilized, and humane, were to be
found removed from idolatry and inclined by nature to worship the true God;
a people who would naturally, without explicit possession of the Law, do those
things that are of the Law even if they did not follow the evangelical teachings
and did not have faith in Christ, there would then be no reason for the
Christians to attack and punish that people with weapons in hand.[20]

Under the pressure of circumstances brought about by the expansion of
a hitherto local society Sepúlveda has sought common principles in
divergent customs; in an important sense his goal is to distinguish between
what is natural and universal, and what is merely conventional and local;
hence his willingness to let both the New Testament and Christ discreetly
fade from the picture and rest his argument solely on grounds unmistakably independent of the truths of Christianity. This conscious acquiescence
in dispensing with the more constraining teachings of the faith is by now
nothing new to us. It has crossed our path before, both during our discussion of Sepúlveda's evaluation of man's two *vitae* and in the context of
the problem of war. This incidental reminder is not untimely placed here,
for we shall presently see that the humanist is equally willing to forego a
strictly Christian point of view when dealing with the pivotal – to his
scheme – question of the justice of the war waged against adamant natives.
In addition, and this is the point of immediate interest to us, Sepúlveda's
self-appointed task suggests a parallel with that faced by the ancient Stoics:
'to define justice and good faith and fair dealing as general forms of
human relationships behind the particular duties imposed' upon local
societies by custom and convention.[21] Their efforts had resulted in an
ethical system which 'against unreasoning custom transmitted by blind
tradition and enforced by unreflecting use...sets the ideal morals of the
wise man, discovered by intelligence and enforced by the inherent
reasonableness of the ethical standard itself'.[22] Following the Cynics,

[20] *DA*, p. 44.
[21] Sabine, p. 11. It must be understood that I am not arguing here – and in what
follows – that Sepúlveda somehow managed to rise above the limiting circumstances
inherent in the mentality of his own age and definitely accomplished what others
had failed to do, or that he attempted to meet the challenges posed by America by
resorting to strictly secular parameters. Such contention would place him two
centuries ahead of his own time – and a radical precursor Sepúlveda was not. What
I do suggest, however, is that, fully partaking of a view not uncommon among
contemporaries, the humanist strove to understand the American puzzle in terms
as broad and universal as the traditions of the day and his own conservative inclinations permitted.
[22] *Ibid.*, p. 16.

although in theory only, the early Stoics had emphasized the relativity of all particular acts to circumstances. Zeno and Cleanthes, for example, 'argued that cannibalism and homosexuality are not wrong',[23] and pointed out that no matter of principle is violated when circumstances force upon us the eating of human flesh.[24] In the same vein Zeno defended incest and nudity, teaching that clothes should be worn for warmth and not simply to hide any part of the body.[25]

Ironically enough, however, Sepúlveda, heir to the compromises of the later Stoics and the teachings of Christianity, which often elevates convention to the realm of dogma, elects to outwardly identify the ethical standard with practices which the Early Stoa had viewed as conventions. The point is most aptly brought home by Montaigne in his essay *Of Cannibals* (1578–1580).

Now, to return to my subject, I think there is nothing barbarous and savage in that nation [Brazil], from what I have been told, except that each human calls barbarian whatever is not his own practice; for indeed it seems we have no other test of truth and reason than the example and pattern of the country we live in. 'There' is always the perfect religion, the perfect government, the perfect and accomplished manners in all things.[26]

It is Montaigne, then, who discourses most in the manner of the ancient Stoics – demonstrating at the same time a cultural relativism remarkably reminiscent of Las Casas' own.[27] He sees the inhabitants of French Antarctica (Brazil) as 'still very close to their original naturalness. The laws of nature still rule them.' And the absence of those very things which Sepúlveda wields as proof of their barbarity Montaigne holds in high esteem as examples of their natural state: 'no sort of traffic, no knowledge of letters...no riches...no clothes, no agriculture, no metals'. Their wars evidence courage and firmness. They do not eat their enemies 'for nourishment...it is to betoken extreme revenge'. They are at fault, yes, but not so much as ourselves.

I am not sorry that we notice the barbarous horrors of such acts, but I am heartily sorry that, judging their faults rightly, we should be so blind to our own. I think there is more barbarity in eating a man alive than in eating him dead; and in tearing by tortures and the rack a body still full of feeling, in

---

[23] Reesor, *The Political Theory of the Old and Middle Stoa*, p. 10.
[24] *Life of Zeno* 7. 121.   [25] *Ibid.*, 7. 33.
[26] M. de Montaigne, *The Complete Essays of Montaigne*, ed. D. M. Frame (Stanford, 1965), p. 152. Unless otherwise indicated all future references will be to this edition.
[27] See A. Losada's study of Las Casas' *Apologia* in 'La *Apologia*, obra inédita de Fray Bartolomé de las Casas: actualidad de su contenido', *BRAH*, clxii, 2, pp. 201–248.

roasting a man bit by bit, in having him bitten and mangled by dogs and swine (as we have not only read but seen within fresh memory, not among ancient enemies, but among neighbors and fellow citizens, and what is worse, on the pretext of piety and religion), than in roasting and eating him after he is dead. Indeed, Chrysippus and Zeno, heads of the Stoic sect, thought there was nothing wrong in using our carcasses for any purpose in case of need, and getting nourishment from them.[28]

Obviously Montaigne is not so much interested in appraising Indian life per se as he is in remonstrating against the brutalities of his own age, although in *Of Coaches* he will return to the subject, this time sketching an early portrait of the eighteenth-century 'noble savage' theme. His real grudge here, however, is against contemporary society. What right do we, cruel and irrational as our acts are, have to judge as barbarous the mores of alien peoples? Sepúlveda's argument, on the other hand, rests on the hope that as long as the institutions which govern society sink their roots into the fruitful soil of natural law the mores of man remain eminently perfectible. In my view what appears to be at stake here is a different interpretation of the meaning and substance of natural law. Sepúlveda's version is strictly in line with the traditional outlook. Montaigne, by contrast, offers an impressionistic translation leading to the conclusion that the barbarous character of the nations of the New World stems from the simple fact,

that they have been fashioned very little by the human mind, and are still very close to their original naturalness. The laws of nature still rule them, very little corrupted by ours; and they are in such a state of purity that I am sometimes vexed that they were unknown earlier...for it seems to me that what we actually see in these nations surpasses not only all the pictures in which poets have idealized the golden age and all their inventions in imagining a happy state of man, but also the conceptions and the very desire of philosophy. They could not imagine a naturalness so pure and simple as we see by experience.[29]

This conception of the law of nature Sepúlveda would plainly deem inadmissible, for Montaigne with it admits something that the Spaniard would hotly deny: that the laws and institutions of European commonwealths, by definition deemed well-ordered republics by Sepúlveda, can and do corrupt natural law. In short, for both authors the American 'nations' are 'barbarous' – for Sepúlveda because they violate the law of nature, for Montaigne because they are ruled by it.[30]

The imaginary controversy just related, of course, never actually

[28] Montaigne, *The Complete Essays of Montaigne*, pp. 153–5.
[29] *Ibid.*, p. 153.
[30] Sepúlveda's definition of barbarian is not disputed by Montaigne alone. In his own *Apologia*, Las Casas attacked the humanist's version of the word as included

happened. But it serves to illustrate some of the subtler aspects of one which did in fact take place between Las Casas and Sepúlveda. It also plainly hints at the unrealistic conclusions to which a skeptical view of contemporary life could lead. But Sepúlveda is no skeptic. As already remarked his faith in the soundness of the institutions which rule the existence of the Christian republics of his own day is unshakable. On the basis of that confidence and the principles which the compromises of Panaetius and the flexibility of Roman Stoicism had bequeathed European thought, the humanist asserts with dogmatic optimism the indubitable soundness of the nature–reason monism as the source for 'the perfect and accomplished manners in all things'. Montaigne mordantly pointed to the great chasm that separated the social relativism, perhaps the truest source of Stoic humanitarianism and certainly the strongest prop of its tolerance, of the Early Stoa from the self-delusions of his own age. Sepúlveda, on the other hand and in a manner not unlike the Cartesian search for first principles, sought for absolute and irrefutable premises, premises which the plasticity of Roman Stoicism and the manipulations of Christianity had made readily available.

Formerly, concludes Sepúlveda, the natives of the New World lived irrationally and under the rule of uncivil institutions; their society was not a true society, and their polities were not worth the name. But the arrival upon their shores of civil men (and the Spaniards, with certain qualifications which will shortly be made explicit, are obviously so) radically altered the situation. It is now possible for the Indians to cross over from chaos into the new social order offered by the Spaniards, a social order founded on reason and obedience to natural law.[31] From purely natural considerations it follows that the Indians must surrender politically to the new-comers in order to make their social integration possible.

in the *Apologia pro Democrates alter:* 'Barbarians, according to Saint Thomas, are those lacking in reason, either because of the climate in which they live and which causes man's atrophy or because of some evil custom responsible for turning men into beasts; men of such ilk must obey the more prudent and civilized in order that they may be ruled through better laws and institutions.' And, Sepúlveda adds, the barbarous nature of the Indians is precisely the first cause which justifies Spanish *imperium* over them or the war waged against them if they refuse to submit. '*Primum*: Because they are, or were before coming under Christian rule, all barbarians – some by virtue of their customs and practices, others by nature – with neither culture nor prudence, and soiled by innumerable vices. . .*Secundo*: These barbarians were implicated in the commission of most grievous sins against the laws of nature. . .*Tertio*: To save innocent men from a death full of indignity. . .*Quarto*: To mend the ways of men who dangerously err – be it through ignorance or in full conscience – and force them into the right path, even against their will, is of natural and divine law and a duty forced on all men.' *Apologia*, pp. 332–7.

[31] See Aristotle, *Politics* I. 2. 1252b25–1253a.

The Indians and civil society

Inasmuch, then, as the Spaniards are able to create a civil society in America, will the Indians who surrender to them and accept Christianity become civil beings? Sepúlveda's answer is an emphatic no, and the upshot is a gap, alien to Stoic ideology but not practically incompatible with Christianity, which separates the intellectual from the moral (now civic) virtues. Undoubtedly the subject is an important one meriting some attention. In what follows I will draw heavily on the substance of what was said in Chapter 6.

The separation in question is not new with Sepúlveda but goes back to Saint Augustine. The Bishop of Hippo did not accept the 'civic virtues' as true virtues, but only as quasi-virtues. Best embodied in the Roman yearning for glory, a subject amply discussed by Sepúlveda, they strictly remain vices for the great African because 'these actions were motivated by a desire to win the applause and good opinions of men, rather than God's blessing or the approval of conscience'.[32] The deeds of the Romans, then, approach the status of virtues only in comparison with the wretched conduct of other men.[33] Rigorously speaking, the full and true meaning of virtue, as far as Saint Augustine is concerned, is reserved for that Christian ethic which 'is clearly distinguished from any morality that is purely human or social, or from the conception that virtue resides in those actions and attitudes toward one's fellow men that are approved by individual reason or social tradition'.[34] This, of course, effectively undermines the strength of the pagan position which had founded the basic postulates of human conduct upon the bedrock of reason. Here and in his debate with Cicero (*The City of God*, Books II and XIX) on the latter's idea of justice Saint Augustine underlines the unbridgeable gap between Christian morality and a pagan ethic identical with the political good. Sepúlveda, and his humanist predecessors before him, ignores Augustine's formidable conclusions, choosing instead to start with an assumption that accepts the compatibility of the pagan and Christian purviews, to take the latter's presence for granted when all men have been converted (in this particular case the Indians), and to proceed from there to catalog the worldly characteristics that will define the goodness of a commonwealth.[35]

This is not to say, however, that Sepúlveda embraces without qualification the pagan side of the argument. The Stoics had maintained that moral idealism is attained by all men who follow the dictates of reason.

---

[32] Deane, *The Social and Political Ideas of Saint Augustine*, p. 51.
[33] *Ibid.*, pp. 267–78, n. 47.   [34] *Ibid.*, p. 80.
[35] *Ibid.*, ch. iii, iv, and pp. 122–3.

Armed with reason man is a pilgrim on the road to virtue living in a probationary state from which he will eventually emerge (although death may overtake him first). And 'as the Stoics were honestly bent upon the moral improvement of mankind, they came to concentrate their energies more and more upon the effort to initiate, encourage and continue in everyone, however ignorant and sinful, the idea, the hope and ardent desire of making progress. Indeed, this is the chief content of philosophy to later Stoics, such as Seneca and Epictetus.'[36] There is no doubt that, in Sepúlveda's mind, this is the justification for his demand that the Indians submit to the spiritual guidance of Christianity and the political rule of the Spaniards. True, then, Sepúlveda moves on a track in no essential sense different from the Stoics' (witness his desire to improve the general lot of the Indians) – with one important exception. He has discovered a group of men who, by all accepted standards, are not fully rational. When left to their own devices the Indians proved themselves short of wit and incapable of living in accordance with the simple and manifest dictates of natural law. It follows that the Stoic monism cannot be strictly adhered to in this instance.

Unquestionably, that side of the moral (here understood in the pre-Christian, Stoic sense of a whole embodying both activity and contemplation) teachings of Seneca and Epictetus which the advent of Christianity had narrowly and jealously associated with beatitude produced by transcendental contemplation will be ideally imparted to the Indians by the faith; that is, the aborigines, upon embracing Christianity, also acquire that manner of awareness, of truth, that only a form of spiritual contemplation transcending reason and solely nourished by revelation can give. Alas, reason is lacking; and prudence is likewise absent from the leadership of Indian society. The potential which only reason can actualize remains thus untranslated into reality. It inevitably follows that both the reason which the totality of Indian society lacks and the prudence foreign to its rulers must be borrowed from the Spaniards whose civic virtues, the realm of reason, enable them, in the presence of the will, to objectify the ultimate goals proper to a well-ordered commonwealth. Sepúlveda is thereby denying that a fool may become a sage, here understood as epitomizing a capacity for civility, through conversion to Christianity. A very interesting conclusion naturally flows from this: the Christian faith brings salvation, uplifts the soul, and bestows beatitude upon the believer; but it does not provide him with that essential ingredient – rational power – capable of bringing into being the intentions

---

[36] Hicks, *Stoic and Epicurean*, p. 89. A parallel idea is developed by Lionardo toward the end of Book II, in L. B. Alberti's *Della famiglia*, trans. R. N. Watkins (Columbia, S.C., 1969), pp. 132 *et sqq.*

inherent to the will. And reason is the *sine qua non* of civility. Even though not expressed in so many words the intent and purpose are clearly there: the sphere of influence of Christ's teachings must be restricted. The possession of Christian truth is not a prerequisite to the emergence of sound political institutions; in sharp contrast with the evangelical flavor of Christian humanism, only reason – a pre-Christian gift – is said to be indispensable. Thus far, then, Christian teaching has been effectively banished from two interrelated facets of man's existential totum: war and politics. Having made the pertinent deductions in our study of Vitoria – who, we remember, sounds an identical note – it would be idle to point out again that Machiavelli's conclusions, interpreted in this comparative light, no longer appear as radical departures from contemporary political theory.

The Indians and natural slavery

If not fully capable of civil status what, then, shall be the rightful place of the Indian in the emerging New World society? At this point it is often argued that Sepúlveda, on the basis of Aristotle as his sole authority, declares the American natives to be slaves by nature. I do not agree with this interpretation. Instead, I construe Sepúlveda's position, and the remainder of this chapter will be predominantly dedicated to proving my point, as one which denies the civility of the Indians while simultaneously rejecting the idea that they are naturally slaves.

To start with, it must be admitted that Aristotle had indeed conceived the society of the Greek *polis* as constituted of two parts – citizens and slaves – 'for that which can foresee by the exercise of mind is by nature intended to be lord and master, and that which can with its body give effect to such foresight is a subject, and by nature a slave'.[37] The insularity of the background supporting the Aristotelian idea of slavery and Aristotle's own contradictions made this theory of slavery untenable in the new cosmopolitan milieu of the Hellenistic world. As early as Chrysippus, for example, Stoicism had denied the doctrine of natural slavery, maintaining that 'no man is by nature a slave'.[38] The essence of this new world, Plutarch wrote, was that 'men should not live their lives in so many civic republics, separated from one another by so many different systems of justice; they should reckon all as their fellow-citizens, and there should be one life and one order (*cosmos*), as it were one flock on a common pasture feeding in common under one law'.[39] The point to remember in

[38] *Pol* I. 2. 1252a30–1252b.
[38] Quoted in Sabine, *A History of Political Theory*, p. 23.
[39] Quoted in E. Barker, *The Politics of Aristotle* (Oxford, 1958), LIX.

this connection is that even in antiquity Aristotle's view of slavery was by no means universally accepted. And we have already observed that although deeply influenced by Aristotle's philosophy Sepúlveda is by no means averse to treating rather eclectically the teachings of the master. It must be equally admitted, however, that the Stoic position does little to solve Sepúlveda's problem. And the schism introduced into the Stoic monism by Sepúlveda himself is responsible for that failure. In truth the humanist agrees that all men living according to reason and nature (or under institutions based on both) are equal and brothers (civil beings). But again, what is to be done when one finds, not individual outlaws defying the commands of just laws, but entire nations whose institutions are purposedly designed, it seems, to violate natural law?

Clearly, the Stoic flat denial of natural slavery is insufficient to resolve the issue faced by the humanist. To my knowledge, nowhere in his political treatises does Sepúlveda deal with the question of whether there is such a thing as natural slavery – unless we include Leopoldus' somewhat incidental comments on the subject, or Sepúlveda's own brief reference to Africans. The reason is simple: it is not Sepúlveda's aim to ascertain if nature has decided beforehand that some men be slaves. His goal is to determine the niche to be occupied by the Indians in the new scheme of things forced into being by the discovery of the New World. Under the circumstances, to maintain that Sepúlveda argues his own query by declaring the American aborigines to be slaves by nature is in my view both at variance with much of the evidence contained in the humanist's political writings (in fact, it is difficult not to be convinced that such an impression derives from reading Sepúlveda through Lascasian eyes) and an oversimplification which overlooks the subtler aspects of Sepúlveda's scheme.[40] Rather than confining myself to refuting this appraisal of Sepúlveda's conclusions, I have chosen to follow what appears to me to be a more productive path: namely, to study the question as part of a double inquiry of deeper content, broader implications, and more general signifi-

[40] Lewis Hanke, for example, writes that Sepúlveda fully intended to translate *servus* as slave. It must be pointed out, however, that this conclusion is based on a defective and incomplete edition of the *Democrates alter* – the only one available until recently. The work of A. Losada has brought to light the complete manuscript of this important treatise. Hanke's appraisal of Sepúlveda's intentions (see his *Aristotle and the American Indians*, Chicago, 1959), moreover, is not universally shared. Other scholars have concluded that *servus* may be taken to mean either slave or serf, and it was the latter meaning which Sepúlveda sought to convey. See R. E. Quirk, 'Some notes on a controversial controversy', *HAHR*, 34(1954), pp. 357–64. On the question of Aristotelian natural slavery and the problems of translating the word *servus*, see my 'Juan Ginés de Sepúlveda on the nature of the American Indians', *The Americas*, xxxi, 4(1975), pp. 434–51.

cance toward the understanding of Sepúlveda's political thought – what is the precise position occupied by the Indian as an individual entity within the universal brotherhood of man? What kind of rule has nature decreed be given to the Indians as a group?

In common with other sixteenth-century political thinkers Sepúlveda adopts the Aristotelian political nexus binding the household to the state.[41] Just as the father holds sway over a large and complex household, the king must exercise various forms of authority over his different subjects. In the household we find the sons and *servi seu mancipia*, as well as servants (*ministri conditionis liberae*). Just and humane the father lords it over them all; not in the same manner, but in accordance with the class and condition of each. So shall a good and just king rule. The Spaniards, who are naturally free, deserve the kind of rule that the father reserves for the sons (*regium imperium*) while 'those barbarians', being *servi natura*, shall be governed as free servants (*tamquam ministros, sed liberos*) with a mixture of herile and paternal authority as demanded by their condition and circumstances. Clearly, nowhere in this passage is there an indication either that the 'barbarians' are slaves by nature or that they should be treated as such. What immediately follows, moreover, is a strong, at least in appearance, assertion that despite the natural shortcomings underlined elsewhere the status and condition of the Indians are perfectible. 'Thus, in time, after they [the Indians] have become more civilized and, through our governance, probity in their mores and the Christian religion have taken firm roots, they must be given a treatment of greater liberty and liberality.'[42] The implications of this statement are tantalizing, and one wishes that Sepúlveda would have gone to greater lengths into an explanation of what he thinks the future should hold for the Indians who accept Spanish rule. Unfortunately he does not and the paragraph perforce remains isolated, leaving to the reader the task of reconciling its contents with other passages which appear to advocate the opposite. At this point Sepúlveda is only concerned with the various forms of *dominium* arising as a consequence of the appearance of the state, a subject which he had broached in the early pages of the *Democrates alter*. '*Dominium* is not always exercised in the same manner. Thus the authority of the father over the sons; the husband over the wife; the power that the lord enjoys over his slaves; the magistrate over the citizens; the king over his realms and the individuals subject to his empire: they are all of different juridical origin.'[43]

Plainly, then, the world is not simply divided into masters and slaves. The suggestion, on the contrary, is that within a well-ordered commonwealth there exists a complex hierarchy of jurisdictions. And the key to be

[41] *DA*, p. 120. [42] *Ibid.* [43] *Ibid.*, p. 20.

sought lies with the nature of those jurisdictions and the manner in which they bind some men to other men. The passage, for instance, clearly states that the authority exerted by the king over his subjects is different from the power enjoyed by the master over his slaves. A conclusion of importance, for the author invariably sees the Indians as subjects of the king of Spain. Thus when the practices of the American colonists brought the *encomienda* system down to a level hardly distinguishable from that defined by the master–slave jurisdiction, Sepúlveda points out that such conduct is a violation of the compact entered into by the individual *encomendero* and the Crown. For, as Sepúlveda views the theory of the *encomienda*, the obligatory character of Indian labor is justified only insofar as it aims at satisfying the physical needs of the man who has altruistically, in the best tradition of service to the state praised by Cicero, pledged to look after their educational and spiritual well-being. In other words, even when the toil of the Indian ministers to the needs of the *encomendero* it is in the latter's role as a public official, not a private lord.[44]

The strength of Sepúlveda's conviction that the Indians are the subjects of the king and not any man's property is again brought home when the author discusses the role of the multitude in the affairs of the republic. He begins by pointing out how pleased he is that 'the great philosophers who wrote about politics' should have taught that in a perfectly constituted republic not only prudent men of known probity but the multitude also should be considered for public office. The reason: good men are always few while the numbers of the multitude are great and against their will the rule of the former cannot maintain itself for long. 'It is wise and advisable, therefore, to grant to the mob the privilege of occupying minor posts.' Bringing this idea to bear in the American case, Sepúlveda concludes that the Spanish sovereigns would do well to keep in mind the wisdom of these Aristotelian counsels.

The kings of Spain and their advisers must remember the precepts of these philosophers because the nature of their governance over the barbarians must be such that the latter will not be given, through the granting of a degree of freedom unwarranted by their nature and condition, the opportunity to return to their primitive and evil ways; on the other hand, they must not be oppressed with harsh rule and servile treatment, for, tired of servitude and indignity, they may attempt to break the yoke to the peril of the Spaniards.[45]

Consequently, the Spanish rulers must at all costs avoid the error of the Thessalians and Spartans who, having treated the Penestae and Helots dishonorably and used them 'almost as *servi* to cultivate their fields', were

[44] *Ibid.*, pp. 122–3.   [45] *Ibid.*, p. 121.

rewarded with formidable rebellions.[46] Briefly, 'it is clear that it would be unjust as well as dangerous to treat those barbarians as slaves (*barbaros istos ut mancipia tractare*), except those who by their perfidy, cruelty, and pertinacity in waging war become worthy of such penalty and misfortune'.[47]

From all this it may be fairly inferred that the word *servus* cannot be here understood in the economic sense stressed by Aristotle, for Sepúlveda's *servus* is far more than a chattel: he is even *homo politicus* although never in the perfect civil sense of those fated by nature to rule. We meet again with the same theme in *De regno*, a treatise already removed in time from the author's feud with Las Casas, when Sepúlveda defines a herile form of government as that imposed by those chosen by nature to command, not for the benefit of the governed but for the profit of the rulers. In other words, the members of herile societies work and labor for the benefit of those whose nature makes them civil beings. But such is not exactly the position of the Indians (those of peaceful disposition, that is), for Sepúlveda's *servi* receive important benefits in return for their efforts in behalf of the state which are incompatible with an unqualified herile (servile) status. Instead, Sepúlveda postulates as the indispensable background governing the relations between Indian and Spaniard a political compact of mixed nature which unequivocally implies obligations mutually binding to both sides. The mutual dependence embodied in such a system bears little resemblance to Aristotle's conclusion, arrived at when discussing the nature of master–slave relations, that a 'possession may be defined as an instrument of action, separable from the possessor'.[48] Sepúlveda, on the contrary, is at pains to emphasize the reciprocal character of the unwritten compact established by nature between Indian and Spaniard.

True, he concedes, the Spaniards take gold and silver from the Indians, but, in return, they give them 'iron and bronze', metals which are of far greater intrinsic value to the needs of mankind. And that is by no means all. In exchange for those precious metals of no use to the natives, and of very relative value to civilized societies, the latter receive goods of much greater import: 'wheat..., horses, mules, sheep, goats, hogs, and many kinds of trees...' Above all, the Spaniards bring with them what Sepúlveda, good humanist and better Christian, prizes above everything else: the elements of European civilization, excellent laws and institutions, and 'the knowledge of God and of the Christian religion'.[49] These inseparable twins, European culture and the Christian faith, which more than compensate the Indian for the loss of his gold and silver, are the strongest and most important part of the bond which unites the Spanish Crown, through

[46] *Ibid.*, p. 122. See also *Pol* 2. 9.   [47] *DA*, p. 122.
[48] *Pol.* 1. 4. 1254a15 *et sqq.*   [49] *DA*, pp. 78–9.

its officials, to its charges, the Indians. And this is indeed that which has no parallel in the relations between master and slave as described by Aristotle, for the nature of the covenant requiring to give the Indians a Christian education inevitably lifts them above the level of mere chattels and establishes between the American aborigine and the Spanish administrator the important nexus of Christian *caritas*.[50]

In conclusion, the political barrier with which Sepúlveda surrounds the status of the Indians in society when he insists that the only authority over the natives is that of the Spanish Crown, and the emphasis on Christianity which so strongly conditions the manner in which the Crown (or its officials) may rightfully exercise this authority over its wards, give the relations between Indian and Spaniard a complexity and significance far beyond anything implied in the Aristotelian concept of slavery. To grasp correctly the full meaning and breadth of Sepúlveda's scheme, then, it would be useful to take into account other influences which may have shared in shaping that scheme. And in this context it is imperative to remember that although Aristotelian, Sepúlveda is no stranger to Saint Augustine. In fact, when it comes to delineating the distinctions separating the treatment accorded warlike Indians, on the one hand, and peaceful ones on the other (a point of pivotal importance to the entire question of natural slavery), Sepúlveda will find the doctrines of the Bishop of Hippo to be of considerable assistance.

On the nature and goal of the just war

To give substance and solidity to his scheme Sepúlveda turns to the theory of the just war. What is the nature and function of war? Should we be allowed but one sentence to answer the question it would still be possible to give an accurate definition of Sepúlveda's idea of the essence and purpose of war, for war is the mechanism chosen by the humanist to safeguard and preserve the hierarchy of the natural order decreed by God.[51] It is therefore not difficult to guess his reply to the most fundamental of all questions asked of all followers of Christ: are Christians permitted to wage war? Sepúlveda deals extensively with this age-old question in the *Democrates primus*, a dialogue, we have seen, 'devoted to discussing the compatibility of the military profession with the Christian religion'.

Leopoldus, by now a familiar figure, opens the discussion with a rather commonplace observation: by divine law Christians are forbidden to wage any kind of war.[52] To be sure, the Old Testament abounds in

[50] *Ibid.*, pp. 118–23.
[51] This and future remarks should be closely understood in the context of the ideas examined in Chapter 5.   [52] *DP*, p. 232.

examples in which God seemingly sanctions the waging of war; but what might have been permitted to the Hebrews is not necessarily allowed to Christians. It is also well-known that the Old Covenant is full of images and predictions. The latter have been made true by the coming of Christ whose teachings abolished the Old Testament and all its laws[53] – 'with the exception of the precepts of the Decalogue'. With this opening gambit Sepúlveda sets the board for his attack on those who based their opposition to war upon the superiority of the New Testament over the Old. The author's *alter ego*, Democrates, swiftly seizes upon Leopoldus' qualifying remark to ask rhetorically: 'Why are the Ten Commandments left untouched when everything else has been invalidated?' In truth, he answers, not everything in the Old Testament is imagery; we find in it potent laws whose very sturdiness testifies to their validity, usefulness, and natural origin.[54] And it is on this natural origin that Sepúlveda rests his argument. For, how could Christ abrogate natural law? 'Natural law must be counted among the laws divine and as such be timeless because it is clear that the laws of nature have their source in eternal law.'[55] Christ, then, did not abolish the Law but complemented it with His teachings. The thrust is unmistakable, if familiar by now: Christ's contribution was to make perfect matters which of themselves were already good and natural. It follows that by disregarding the Son's advice in such matters we do not sin, provided that we revert to the old precepts. We therefore have, on the one hand, laws such as those embodied in the Ten Commandments which rule man's active life, while on the other, those exhortations which, although not obligatory, are counsels conducive to a more perfect life. To this latter category, Sepúlveda holds, belong Christ's utterances on violence.

In a brief treatise published in Bologna (1529) exhorting the Emperor to undertake the Turkish war, Sepúlveda even more directly counters the arguments drawn from the New Testament which were commonly used as testimonies of Christ's pacifism: 'even though neither Christ nor the Apostles waged war, Christians are not necessarily prohibited from engaging in violence'. For, he continues, if we oppose no resistance to those who attack us, 'why not suffer thieves, murderers, poisoners, and parricides' as well? True, Christ opposes resistance to violence. But Paul's conduct proves that His words must not be taken literally or applied to all men and circumstances. Christ taught meekness not with the intention of binding men by those words as if they were laws, but to point the way of perfection to those who would be teachers of others in matters of mores and religion. After all, what is more contrary to nature than passivity in

[53] *Ibid.*, p. 234.   [54] *Ibid.*
[55] *Ibid.*, pp. 234–5.

the face of unjust attack, when not only *imperium* and dignity but salvation and life are all at stake?[56]

But it is in the first *Democrates* that the *ad naturam* flavor of Sepúlveda's stand on war is best defined. In the Old Covenant, we are told, the Hebrews were permitted to wage war when nature unambiguously decreed its necessity. The laws of nature are of divine origin and emanate from eternal law defined by Saint Augustine as the will of God, who decreed that the natural order should be preserved intact. It follows that whatever is done according to natural law is done with the full backing of God's authority. God, nature's First Cause, wants the order imposed by nature to be respected. Leopoldus protests. He accuses his friend of deviating from the main question and demands that the conversation return to the subject under discussion. Democrates begs Leopoldus' indulgence and asks: 'May war be waged under natural law?' As expected, his interlocutor answers with an uncompromising no: 'If we look back to the time of our earliest ancestors we find that in the beginning wars were provoked by cruel, ambitious, and unprincipled men; and down to the present we find no other reason for the waging of war. How can I agree that such a pestilential scourge of human life conforms to nature?' Democrates patiently asks one more question of his friend: 'Are we in agreement when I admit that those wars which are naturally just may be waged without violating natural law?' Leopoldus grudgingly acquiesces, although not without remarking that as far as he is concerned there is no such a thing as a just war.[57]

The very last sentence above is nothing more than the sum and substance of the question lying at the heart of the controversy on war among Renaissance thinkers: whether a war can be just at all. On this issue Sepúlveda's position leaves no room for doubt. What could be more natural than to defend one's own life and those of one's friends, or to prevent injustice from being done to ourselves, our friends, and the innocent?[58] What is more in accordance with natural law than to prevent those who would deny the hierarchy and order decreed by God from carrying out their wicked designs? War is not forbidden to Christians; on the contrary, they have the duty to serve in the army because all those who are a part of civil society have the natural obligation to defend that society and because war does not contravene divine law when it is waged for a just cause.

Evidently the question is no longer whether Christians may wage war

---

[56] Juan Ginés de Sepúlveda, *Cohortatio ad Carolum V, Opera*, IV, pp. 363–5. Cited hereafter as *Cohortatio*. See also A. Losada, *Tratados políticos de Juan Ginés de Sepúlveda* (Madrid, 1963).

[57] *DP*, pp. 234–5.   [58] *Ibid.*, p. 237.

but how to ascertain conclusively what is just according to nature. On the authority of Aristotle that which everywhere and at all times has the same force and not merely because it may be agreeable to some, that whose strength lies in itself independently of the decision or will of the law-giver, is just by nature.[59] Granted, Sepúlveda avers, that it is indeed difficult to select from among the many possibilities open to man that which is just; nevertheless, there exists one infallible rule of thumb. In distinguishing that which is good from that which is evil, the virtues from the vices, one must be guided by the judgment of good men, for virtue and those who enjoy it judge all things well.[60]

In retrospect these are but the barest preliminaries indispensable to any serious discussion of the ancient question of war. Having convinced himself both that Christians are permitted to wage war and that a just war is indeed a realizable possibility, Sepúlveda is ready to undertake an evaluation of the circumstances conducive to bringing about a war congruent with the principles of natural law. To that end he begins by borrowing a page from Saint Augustine: it would most assuredly be very desirable to live in perpetual tranquillity and peace; and he who wishes to root out war from the human mind in truth desires a good thing. But, and one recalls Luther's identical words, let him instruct the good and the just to lay down their weapons only when they have banished evil and injustice from the souls of the impious whose avarice, ambition, thirst for glory and fame can only be satisfied with the destruction of other men. Until such time arrives just men shall wage just wars.[61] The just war, never to be desired for its own sake, shall nevertheless be but a means to achieve a just peace. And that is precisely the one and only licit goal of a war said to be just: to enable men to live in peace, justly and virtuously. For peace is that which preserves human society best and to its defense civil life is oriented in a justly and wisely-ordered republic.[62] Understood in this sense peace is not an end in itself but merely a lofty means to a still higher good: to afford man the uninterrupted enjoyment of his Aristotelian capabilities as a social and political animal. The theme is clearly of Augustinian vintage but aptly modified to make comfortable room for the indispensable Peripatetic intrusion. Sepúlveda, moreover, discovers here a golden opportunity to tie the prince to war: it is the fundamental duty of the wise and just ruler not only to govern in peace but also to repel, with weapons in hand, the aggressive designs of evil men, be they citizens or strangers – a point well worth remembering, for it is the backbone of the argument whereby he will justify the war waged by the Spanish Crown against the Indians in America. Should in any given situation honesty

[59] *Ibid.*, p. 236.   [60] *Ibid.*, pp. 236–7.
[61] *Ibid.*, p. 247.   [62] *DA*, p. 4; DP, p. 243.

and gentle admonitions and counsels fail to dissuade the enemy, concludes Sepúlveda, the prince (only he has the power to declare and wage a just war) shall defend the freedom of the state with arms, supported by the authority of God and natural law.[63]

Having in this manner satisfactorily disposed of the important question concerning the just war's nature and objective, Sepúlveda next proceeds to consider under what conditions a war may be said to be just. To start with, no war may be called just unless it is waged, first, after the injured party has duly filed a claim for indemnity for the wrong received; and, secondly, after it has been formally declared. These two conditions must be met even if there is a just cause for undertaking the war. Immediately on the heels of this essential recommendation, Sepúlveda (in *De regno*) lists the just causes for war as three in number. First and most telling of all is that which seeks to repel injuries and avoid the loss of the commonwealth's liberty: 'This is the weightiest and most natural of causes because it demands the return of stolen property and it chastises unprovoked wrongs, for it is considered self-defense and the protection of one's own when the violence of those who injure is met with violence, punishment is meted out to the guilty, and restitution is made.'[64] The remaining two reasons which qualify a war as just are of great interest to us here because they establish important distinctions between the form of government best fitting 'barbarians' and that called for by the hopeless nature of benighted savages.

By means of a just war we also seek to establish *imperium* over those after whose welfare we care, so that the barbarians – once deprived of their license for sinning, their customs contrary to natural law uprooted, exhorted toward a more humane way of life through a *civil* form of government – be kept reasonably within the boundaries of their duties.[65]

On the basis of this very argument, we are reminded, Saint Augustine justified Roman dominion over the ancient world. It is to be noted that no mention is made of slavery; on the other hand, it is suggested that the barbarians be held under a civil governance. And this is in marked contrast with the third reason adduced as determining a war's justice.

The Philosopher adds to these reasons a third cause of just war; namely, to subject to herile rule those worthy of such condition. To this class belong those nations peopled by wicked men who must be controlled with an iron rod and kept away from mischief. We find this kind of men in Europe, but much more often in Asia; mortals for whom it is useful to obey better and more cultivated men so that with the latter's virtue and prudence and through fear –

---

[63] *DP*, p. 246.   [64] *DR*, p. 146.
[65] *Ibid.*, p. 146. (Italics mine.)

if no other solution remains – the fierceness, bestial mode of life, and lassitude of those people be transformed into a more civilized state beneficial to both sides.[66]

Concretely, Sepúlveda points out, this is the sort of relationship binding the Portuguese to African blacks. The inhabitants of the African coast, then, brought without injury into Christian servitude and Portuguese herile rule are clearly promised, either in the present or in the future, an infinitely better way of life than the one they lead in their own country. Such beneficial condition must, if necessary, be forced upon them, for, the theologians agree, no attention must be paid to man's evil desires; only to that which men should wish according to *recta ratio*.[67]

Sepúlveda's concern with war in *De regno* ends with some brief remarks on the correct manner of waging war drawn from the compulsory advice of Deuteronomy 20.10–15. According to the law therein contained, the humanist explains, 'it is plain that by the custom of nations and divine and natural law those who wage a just war are permitted to kill the enemy, deprive him of his goods, subject him to slavery, destroy his villages and cities, devastate his fields, and inflict all sorts of calamities upon him until such time as victory is assured; assuming, of course, that all these things are done with right intention and with peace as their goal'.[68] Such is the law. In practice, however, the magnanimous prince will temper his wrath in victory with humanity and equity and, subordinating his thirst for vengeance to the needs of the public good, will never show greater severity than the inflicted injury justly merits and is demanded by both the public tranquillity and a stable peace free from injustice. All men, by common agreement, concur that this is the end of all just wars.[69] Sepúlveda, however, carefully appends one basic condition to all this. Even though a war be just, he cautions, it does not follow that it is necessary. In other words, if a war, no matter how just, does not have as its end the forestalling of a present and immediate danger the prince must very carefully make certain that the enterprise he is about to undertake is not superior to his own strength. The reason is plain: a ruler who embarks upon a rash warlike enterprise will sooner or later be compelled to fatally weaken and oppress his own subjects. In short, the prince must be a shrewd assessor of the advantages and disadvantages accruing from a just war, for it befits madmen only to search after mediocre gains at the expense of great toil and danger.[70]

To Sepúlveda's mind an indisputable example of a just war is that waged against the Turks. In *Cohortatio ad Carolum* the humanist estimates that compared with the struggles of Christian against Turk all

[66] *Ibid.*, p. 147.   [67] *Ibid.*   [68] *Ibid.*, pp. 150–51.

[69] *DR*, p. 151.   [70] *Ibid.*, p. 148.

other wars pale. It is neither glory nor wealth that is at stake here but fatherland, home, liberty, salvation, and religion.[71] Under the circumstances the author does not hesitate to condemn the 'blindness and miserable insanity' of those who, unwilling to suffer the somewhat harsh rule of an occasional Christian prince, shout that it would be better to suffer the Turkish yoke. His argument is quite simple: from the depredations of a tyrant the oppressed will be freed in time; by contrast, those who moan under Turkish rule have no hope of reprieve.[72]

Democrates alter: *the just war and the New World*

Although, as we have seen, the question of war occupies a significant place in *Cohortatio ad Carolum, Democrates primus,* and *De regno,* it is in the sequel to the first *Democrates* that the subject is discussed specifically in the context of the American controversy. A measure of how central to the second *Democrates* the theme of war indeed was is given, first, by Soto's appraisal of the exchange between Sepúlveda and Las Casas in Valladolid: '[they] have in particular discussed if it is licit for His Majesty to wage war against the Indians. . .'; and second, by the very title which Sepúlveda chose to give his defense of the *Democrates alter* against the attack of Bishop Ramírez: *Apologia pro libro de justis belli causis* – the source, also, of Las Casas' acquaintance with Sepúlveda's ideas on the American question.

In the *Democrates alter* Leopoldus, Democrates' old friend and antagonist, renews – this time in Valladolid – the disputation which had absorbed the two scholars' attention ten years earlier in Rome. The young doubter still clings stubbornly to his doubts concerning the justice of war and the propriety of warlike activities for Christians; Democrates, on the other hand, handsomely reiterates his admiration for the altruism of those who yearn for lasting peace among men, and heartily concurs in their claim that nothing is more praiseworthy than human concord[73] – without, however, budging one inch from his conviction that Christians are not at all forbidden to wage war. In this conciliatory spirit Democrates points out, in answer to Leopoldus' charge that Christ compels His followers to refrain from acts of violence, that it is indeed of primary importance for us to distinguish between men who wage wars for just and necessary reasons, and those who find pleasure in discord regardless of the cause. 'War must never be desired for its own sake. . .even the best among princes, however, are oftentimes forced to accept it in order to reap important benefits. In the opinion of wise men war must never be any-

---

[71] *Cohortatio,* p. 359.
[72] *Ibid.,* p. 360.   [73] *DA,* p. 3.

thing else but a means to achieve peace.' In short, a war must only be undertaken after mature deliberation and for the most just causes.[74]

The matter, to all appearances, reduces itself to discussing the just causes for war. Leopoldus goes on record as denying their existence. Democrates, by contrast, believes that they are many and of frequent occurrence, although 'they are not born of man's goodness or pity but are an outgrowth of those crimes and passions which endlessly agitate human existence'. And because of this very human origin of war's just causes and the inextricable bond tying prince and war together, Sepúlveda once again elects to list briefly the qualities that should adorn the good ruler: 'The good and humane prince must never behave rashly or codiciously; he must exhaust all peaceful solutions whereby the passions of wicked men may be restrained without recourse to violence; and he shall forever devote his talents to enhancing the prosperity of the mortals confided to his care. Should his peaceful efforts, however, bear no fruit he will not hesitate to take cudgels against the unrighteous.'[75] Leopoldus remains unconvinced. Unimpressed by his friend's reasoning he asks: would the just ruler not behave with greater rectitude and more in agreement with Christian piety if he yielded to the injustice of the wicked, resignedly suffered their injuries, and subsumed human custom and laws to the evangelical commands of Christ? These words, identical to Erasmus' in his diatribes against war, sharply bring into focus the endless dialectic between the ethical contents of Christianity designed to rule individual man's life and his duty as a social being. They also serve to irritate Democrates who, chagrined by Leopoldus' obtuseness, reminds his young friend of the many times he has endeavored to convince him that 'sometimes the waging of war is not contrary to evangelical law'.[76] Somewhat crestfallen, Leopoldus assures the Greek scholar that their Roman conversations were highly enlightening and that he would like to hear his friend discourse more on the subject of war, but this time as it concretely applies to the case of the New World.

Evidently pleased by the young man's continued interest Democrates assents to his request and once more reaffirms: first, that what is done by natural law automatically follows both divine and evangelical law; and second, that Christ did not abolish natural law (according to which every man is permitted to meet force with force) with his exhortations meant to light the way toward apostolic perfection.[77] All these laws called natural which restrain our behavior, Sepúlveda continues, aim at forcing men to do their duty, preserving human society, and turning this life into a vessel suitable for man's journey to eternity. At the further request of his friend

[74] *Ibid.*, pp. 4–5.
[76] *Ibid.*, pp. 5–6.
[75] *Ibid.*, p. 5.
[77] *Ibid.*, pp. 7–8

Democrates once again explains the meaning of natural law with which
we are already familiar:[78] a form of divine legislation which, easily
comprehended through *recta ratio*, is within reach of all mortals whose
own nature has not been corrupted by depraved conduct. And this,
Leopoldus is informed, must be well remembered, for whatever judgment
we reach concerning natural law must be searched for not only among
Christian authorities but in the wisdom of pagan sources as well.[79]

Sepúlveda now feels confident that, with the indispensable foundations
firmly laid, the time is ripe to sketch the strict conditions ruling both the
justice of a war and the causes justifying it. These conditions, squarely
within the orthodox outlook depicted above in Chapter 5, demand: that
the causes themselves justify the war, a legitimate authority, *recta intentio*,
and moderation once undertaken.[80] The last prerequisite, a commonplace
in the traditional view, explicitly states that no harm shall come to the
innocent (if possible) and that care be taken not to punish the enemy
beyond his just deserts. All this follows smoothly from the self-evident
fact that the immediate goal of the just war is twofold: to deprive the
wicked of their capacity for mischief, and to insure a peaceful and tranquil
life for man. At this point in Democrates' discourse, Leopoldus raises a
question not frequently included, at least so explicitly, in contemporary
discussions: if, as Democrates claims, a necessary condition to be fulfilled
by any war is that it be waged for the profit of the commonwealth, would
it be proper for the ruler of an excessively constricted state to expand at
his neighbors' expense? Or, in modern parlance, is the search for *lebens-
raum* a just cause for war? Sepúlveda is categorical: 'Not at all, for such
would not be war but *latrocinium*. If the war is to be just the causes
themselves must be just.'[81]

As to the causes which label a war just Sepúlveda initially lists the three
most commonly cited by authorities. First and foremost is that which
allows man to repel violence with violence when no other alternative
remains. A second cause is the recovery of stolen goods, ours or our
friends'. Finally, it is licit to wage a war to punish the offender should
the proper authorities in the commonwealth of which he is a member fail
to do so.[82] This threefold formula, the encapsulated heart of the medieval
theory of the just war, although eminently acceptable, Sepúlveda finds
insufficient for his present purposes. He therefore hastens to add that
'other reasons may also justify the waging of a war'; reasons which
although perhaps of not so frequent application as those hallowed by
tradition are nevertheless 'just and founded upon divine law'. And one of

---

[78] *Ibid.*, p. 11.   [79] *Ibid.*, p. 12.   [80] *Ibid.*, p. 13.
[81] *Ibid.*, pp. 15–16.   [82] *Ibid.*, pp. 16–17.

them, perfectly applicable to 'those barbarians commonly called Indians', demands that 'those whose natural condition commands that they obey others shall be subdued by force of arms should they refuse the latter's *imperium* and no other recourse is left'.[83] For the moment Sepúlveda remains content with discussing the merits of this important reason. The others, three in number, are explicitly discussed much later (pp. 83 *et sqq.*). In the interest of convenience we might cite them here: ...'Secondly, to banish the horrible crime of cannibalism and devil worship...[Thirdly] to free from serious injury the innocent who are yearly immolated by these barbarians...Fourthly, to open the way to the propagation of the Christian faith and to facilitate the task of its preachers'.

It is the first reason for waging war against the American Indians which elicits Leopoldus' outraged protest against Democrates' 'strange doctrine'. After all, 'what else is to be by nature subject to someone else's *imperium* if not to be *natura servuum*?' Is it not, moreover, true that according to the jurists 'from the very beginning all men were born free and servitude is not naturally decreed but an innovation of the *jus gentium* instead'? Sepúlveda answers that his doctrine is not at all strange to those steeped in philosophy; for while the jurists rightly speak of civil servitudes, the philosophers choose to define a congenital intellectual inferiority which has little to do with the artificial legal postulates of man. (Compare this with Covarrubias; above Chapter 3). The message is unmistakable; Leopoldus pretends to understand Democrates' argument as one advocating civil servitude, that is, slavery, in which the relationship between the possessor and possessed is one of ownership. Sepúlveda flatly rejects Leopoldus' interpretation and stresses instead the word *dominium* as the one best embodying his intentions. As if to underline them the humanist once more treats the reader to a discourse on the natural need for the less endowed to submit willingly to the empire of their intellectual betters. The argument adduced and the examples which illustrate it we have already met. 'It is beneficial for the barbarians to be subjected to the *imperium* of nations or princes more humane and virtuous, the object being that through the latter's example of virtue and prudence the former embrace a more humane mode of life.'[84]

Just, then, is the war waged upon those Indians who refuse to submit to the authority of the Spanish Crown. Brutality, however, has no place in this war – a point driven home by Sepúlveda in the following quotation from Saint Augustine's letter to Vincentius: 'It is necessary to insist, even with those who resist correction, with a certain benign roughness...For even when the son is admonished with asperity paternal love remains

---

[83] *Ibid.*, p. 19.   [84] *Ibid.*, pp. 19–22.

present.'[85] For this reason and in view of the serious consequences potentially implicit in recognizing the legitimacy of the war waged against rebellious Indians, Sepúlveda proposes a rigid blueprint designed to keep development tightly under control. *Haec est igitur necessaria belli gerendi ratio*: first, the barbarians must be advised of the need to accept the empire of the Spanish king and the great benefits to be derived from their consent. Honesty and truth must rule these preliminaries. Neither threats nor deceit must be used; otherwise, should the outcome be war, its justice would be hopelessly compromised. Secondly, the natives must be given time to deliberate among themselves. If the Indians then submit in peace they shall be received within the Christian fold and be given 'conditions of just peace in conformity with their nature, so that, as it is written in Deuteronomy, they shall serve as tributaries *(sub tributo seruiant)*'.[86] This approach to war notwithstanding, warns Sepúlveda, it must be clearly understood that in truth the crimes of the Indians (cult of idols and human immolations) are so appalling in the eyes of nature that they might, in all justice as taught in the Old Testament, be summarily punished – submission or no submission – 'with the death of all sinners and the loss of their goods'. Clearly, this is not an attempt on Sepúlveda's part to sanction or justify the *desmanes* committed by the Spaniards in the New World, but an argument admitting that if the *laws* prescribed by the sovereign to deal with the natives had been as harsh as suggested above they would still have been in conformity with natural law. Only the magnanimity of the Spanish princes, born out of their respect for the counsels of the New Testament, is responsible for their desire not to punish the sins of the barbarians but instead to strive for 'the rehabilitation, salvation, and public well-being of the Indians'.[87] If the barbarians, however, compound their difficulties by rejecting what nature clearly demands, the Crown's *imperium*, war must be waged against them and 'once defeated, their persons and goods lawfully pass into the hands of the victor; and the latter shall freely decide their fate, in accordance with the norms applicable to the treatment of the vanquished'.[88]

But is it not true, questions Leopoldus, that the righteousness underpinning this argument has been undermined beyond redemption by the depredations of the Spaniards? Democrates' answer is worth reproducing in its entirety.

One should not conclude, Leopoldus, that he who sanctions a prince's or a republic's *dominium* over subjects and *clientes* flatly approves also of the sins committed by their prefects or ministers. And even though wicked and unjust

85 *Ibid.*, p. 22.   86 *Ibid.*, pp. 29–30. Deuteronomy 20. 10–15.
87 *DA*, p. 43.   88 *Ibid.*, p. 30.

men perpetrate crimes and acts of greed and cruelty, as I have heard is often the case, the righteousness of the cause defended by the prince and honest men is not at all impaired. Unless, of course, the latter – prince and honest men – through negligence and tacit consent provide the occasion for the commission of crimes, for then the rulers – as consenting parties – incur the same guilt as their ministers and should be punished by God's judgment in identical manner...If the war against the Indians is waged as you say, Leopoldus, it is impious and criminal and my opinion is that those responsible must be punished because it is useless to pursue a just end if the means themselves are not just.[89]

It is to be noted how the opening sentence of the above paragraph refers to *dominium* exercised over subjects and *clientes*. Assuming at this point that 'subjects' is presumably identical with the status of the sons within the family and thus exclusively reserved for the Spaniards, we are left with *clientes* as the status befitting the Indians – one by no means synonymous with natural slave but rather reminiscent of Roman precedent, 'the *dominium* of prudent, good and humane men over their opposite numbers is just and natural; no other reason sanctioned the legitimate empire of the Romans over other peoples'.[90] In addition, Sepúlveda uses the opening offered by Leopoldus' protest against the criminal behavior of Spaniards in the New World to state what, he will later complain, is the truth of his position which has been ignored and perverted by his enemies.

What is now under discussion is not the moderation or cruelty of rank and file or the leaders but the nature of this war and its relation to the just King of Spain and his just ministers. And I maintain that the said war is of such nature that, it seems, it may be waged with rectitude, justice, and piety. This war brings some benefits to the victor but much greater blessings to the vanquished ...If such an enterprise were confided to men both courageous and just, moderate and humane, it could easily be brought to a conclusion without transgression or crime.[91]

The very last sentences will shortly occupy our attention again, for they are the key to apprehending what status Sepúlveda seemingly had in mind for the Indians. For the moment let us return to the matter immediately at hand and attempt to isolate the implications of Sepúlveda's statements on the war against the American aborigines.

To my mind Sepúlveda has clearly identified two entirely different situations growing out of the twofold manner in which the natives may respond to the commands of nature. On the one hand, if the Indians submit willingly to their predestined fate they ought to be given the political status suggested in previous pages. On the other, those barbarians

[89] *Ibid.*, pp. 28–9. [90] *Ibid.*, p. 31. [91] *Ibid.*, p. 29.

who stubbornly refuse to comply with nature's will should be reduced to obedience by force of arms. And once recourse to arms has become inevitable the status of the Indians changes radically and their fate may then be decided in accordance with the laws of war. The reasons, explains Sepúlveda, are clear. First of all, in their rebelliousness the natives adamantly demonstrate their refusal to abandon those practices which clearly inflict injury upon God. In addition, when the barbarians resist the authority of the Spaniards they violate what, the reason of the philosophers tells us, is the explicit will of nature. Finally, refusal to accept Spanish rule inflicts the sort of injury on the Spanish Crown which, the jurists affirm, is punishable by human law. From all this, concludes Sepúlveda, it necessarily follows that the recalcitrant barbarians are not only *servi natura* but, as violators of civil law, also subject to those sanctions contemplated by human law and approved by the *jus gentium* (which Sepúlveda considers to be of natural origin); the rebellious Indians, then, may upon capture be subjected to civil slavery and the loss of their worldly goods.[92]

In the same page (p. 90) where Sepúlveda records this conclusion we read another statement which needs some clarification: 'I do not maintain as doctrine that the pagans are not true owners of the things they acquired through just means, for I do not believe that opinion to be true. What I hold is that they are worthy of being deprived of their goods by reason of the abuses they have committed and the idolatry with which they break the natural and divine laws.' True, Sepúlveda makes no distinction between warlike and peaceful Indians. All are guilty of heinous crimes, a stand no different from that reported earlier. But as remarked above the emphasis is on the theoretical existence of the right to deprive them of their goods (public or private) and not on the actual carrying out of that right. They *may*, in justice, be deprived of their possessions. In practice, we have seen, the Spanish kings, moved more by Christian charity than by legal considerations, will not enforce their rights. The exhortations of Christ, however, are not the only factor involved; shrewd pragmatism also plays a part and Sepúlveda is not slow in reminding his prince of what happened when Thessalians and Spartans ruthlessly insisted on their rights. In practice, then, with the Indians as with everything else moderation is by far the better policy.

Leopoldus, once again spokesman for Erasmian humanitarianism, refuses to be convinced that even those Indians who wage war against their natural ruler deserve civil slavery. His protest is no longer against natural slavery but against slavery by civil law. He is appalled at the prospect of condemning a man, any man, to the loss of property and self; after all, 'all men are born free'. In answer to his friend's objections Sepúlveda

[92] *Ibid.*, pp. 60, 90.

argues that sometimes two laws of natural origin may appear to be at odds with each other thereby compelling man to choose between two evils. Such is the source of that universal covenant which 'growing out of reason and natural need sanctioned by the tacit consent of all peoples empowers the victor to make his own the defeated and their property'.[93] The subject of slavery as the result of defeat in battle had traditionally been a delicate one among Christians, for it seemingly was at odds with the most basic tenets of the faith. It is not surprising, then, that Sepúlveda, sharply goaded by Leopoldus, should take pains to explain his conclusion at length and call to its support various and venerated authorities. Of more significance to our immediate purpose, however, is Sepúlveda's acceptance of man's natural freedom. Democrates, discoursing on the merits of civil slavery, does not refute – and thereby implicitly grants – Leopoldus' sweeping assertion concerning man's birthright of liberty – a rather incomprehensible attitude if we interpret Sepúlveda's ideas on natural servitude as slavery, for if the subject of the discussion are the Indians and they are naturally slaves, what is the object of this elaborate exchange aimed at explaining the juridical circumstances whereby transgressing natives may be lawfully enslaved? The answer is evidently a different one: the American natives are *servi natura* but not natural slaves. It follows that as it applies in practice the expression *servi natura* must be attributed a meaning different from the one heretofore given by some historians. Only when they refuse to meet their natural obligations do they become civil outlaws to be justly warred against. Sepúlveda himself fully appreciates the difference between the juridical position of the Indians who submit peacefully and that of those who resist.

The servitude contracted in a just war is legal, and the booty acquired becomes the rightful possession of the victor. But concerning these barbarians, the plight of the Indians defeated by Spanish arms in formally declared war is very different from the circumstances of those others who, through prudence or fear, delivered themselves to the authority of the Christians. Just as in the former case the victorious prince may determine, according to his will and right, the fate of the vanquished, in the latter both civil laws and *jus gentium* would rule unjust to deprive the natives of their goods and to reduce them to slavery; it is, however, licit to keep them as stipendiaries and tributaries (*stipendiarios et vectigales*) as befitting their nature and condition.[94]

---

[93] *Ibid.*, pp. 90 *et sqq.*

[94] *Ibid.*, p. 117. *Cliens, stipendiarius*, and *vectigalis* are words used by Sepúlveda to describe the position of the Indians in relation to the Spanish state – an indication of how clearly he keeps in mind the example of the kind of authority Rome exercised over her client states. In a letter to Francisco de Argote written before 1552, the author reiterates his position on the Indian question. 'I do not maintain that the barbarians should be reduced to slavery, but merely that they must be subjected

Sepúlveda has in this manner established the juridical foundations for the treatment of defiant Indians on the basis of the law of nations. But how shall these conclusions be applied in practice? In order to answer this question Sepúlveda feels compelled to embark upon a preliminary study of the problem of ignorance in war. Faithfully, Leopoldus provides the needed cue when he puts forth one of the queries lying at the heart of the doctrine of the just war: is it possible for justice to lie with both sides?[95] Democrates explains that under no circumstances can the opposing arguments which support the cause of two contending parties be simultaneously just. What may happen is that one of the warring factions, 'its understanding clouded by ignorance', shall be deceived into believing its cause to be just. And this is precisely what has taken place in the case of the Indians, for 'whereas the Spaniards (if their intentions were just) had a just cause to wage war the Indians also had a probable cause'. After all, '[they] knew neither justice nor truth, and could not learn about them merely on the Christians' word or a few days' time but only after prolonged contact with the reality of both truth and justice'.[96] A good prince, however, will put equity before his own right once victory has been attained. 'He will weigh the causes that brought the enemy to war and shall not be swayed in his judgment by hatred or greed.' Only when the interests of peace and the public welfare demand it may the prince treat the vanquished with the rigor allowed by the *jus gentium*.[97] Otherwise, the prince shall treat his enemies with equity and humanity. These, concludes Sepúlveda, are the cardinal principles which in practice must govern the treatment of the defeated Indians. After all, 'the most important aim of this whole affair is to pacify these barbarians, to introduce them to a more humane mode of existence, and to admit them to Christianity; and the more humanity the Christians show the barbarians the more easily that aim will be fulfilled'.[98]

To sum up, the American aborigines who willingly accept Spanish rule cannot, in justice, be treated as slaves. They are not slaves by nature and must not be subjected to a pure form of herile rule. Only when their pertinacious rejection of natural law forces the Spaniards to crush them in battle will the Indians forfeit (as any other men under similar circumstances) their juridical status as free men and lawfully become subject to the full rigors of herile government. Even then the provisions of the law

to our dominion; I do not propose that we deprive them of their goods. . .I do not say that we should hold herile empire over them, but regal and civil rule for their benefit.' Quoted in T. Andrés Marcos, *Los imperialismos*, p. 184. See also A. Losada, *Epistolario de Juan Ginés de Sepúlveda* (Madrid, 1966), Letter 53.

  [95] *DA*, pp. 100 *et sqq.*   [96] *Ibid.*, p. 118.
  [97] *Ibid.*, pp. 94–5.   [98] *Ibid.*, p. 118.

of nations shall be fully complied with only if their enforcement is compatible with the interests of the whole (Indians and Spaniards) commonwealth. To my mind these are unmistakable conclusions which the evidence of Sepúlveda's writings bears out. But it must also be confessed that this same evidence embodies nuances which must be carefully noted. In my view they go a long way toward clarifying the meaning of passages which, on the surface at least, suggest puzzling contradictions in Sepúlveda's outlook on the American question.

At the start of this study I proposed that the humanist's first care was to isolate a line of argument which would free his ideology from dogmatic dependence on Christianity. The outcome was to found upon the irreproachably impartial commands of natural law certain basic conclusions capable of guiding the steps of the perplexed along firm and unequivocal ground. On the basis of those conclusions, then, a dispassionate analysis of the Indians' circumstances would lead a sober observer to judge their crimes to be of such gravity as to merit drastic punishment. And this is the truth which Sepúlveda intends to ground with the firmest possible roots. In this fashion the humanist becomes the strict spokesman for natural law, the cold judge who bases his verdict on the stern harshness of the Old Testament. It is in this guise that he, as Democrates, dismisses Leopoldus' argument as irrelevant in law. Seen from the point of view of the law of nature alone – an eye for an eye and a tooth for a tooth – the catastrophic sins of the Indians deserve swift and harsh retribution. And to establish that fact beyond question Sepúlveda conducts his extensive disputation with those among his contemporaries – or their spokesman, Leopoldus – who sought to elevate Christ's counsels to the realm of dogma by branding all previous dicta as obsolete and irrelevant. But this is only one side of the coin. The other face becomes apparent only after Sepúlveda feels that he has carried the day and convinced his friend that under natural law strictly applied the position of the Indians is hopeless. Thus at one point he concedes that there may be circumstances under which 'out of two very just and natural laws nature itself may compel us to choose one over the other'.[99] Elsewhere and indirectly he is even more drastic: although it is in no sense unlawful to apply the tenets of natural law with rigor, neither is it against natural law to be merciful. In other words, there are times when it is sound to forego the meting out of well-merited punishment and show mercy instead. Indeed, upon occasion it is absolutely essential that the latter course be chosen over the former. Sepúlveda's reasons are two. The first one is of a purely practical nature and is clearly exemplified in his advice to the King of Spain to use with caution the

[99] *Ibid.*, p. 91.

righteous sword placed at his disposal by natural law. The second reason is, in the present context, more far-reaching in its significance because it involves the concept which Sepúlveda so arduously disputed over with Leopoldus – Christian *caritas*. It now turns out, at least implicitly, that Sepúlveda's objections to Christ's teachings were not pointed at the teachings themselves but aimed instead at those who insisted in viewing them as axiomatic and absolutely binding, a position which the humanist saw as absurd because in its impracticality he perceived a deadly threat to nature's order. Once this matter has been satisfactorily settled Sepúlveda sees no objection to applying the New Testament's counsels on mercy to the case of the Indians. It is now possible to give them something which the strictures of the law deny them: forgiveness. They shall in justice (the justice that only the New Testament makes possible and which is the unique contribution of Christianity) be given the opportunity to abandon their benighted ways. But Sepúlveda carries matters still further. If the natives decide to disregard the opportunity thus offered by Christian mercy they become culprits in the eyes of both the *jus gentium* and civil law. Their guilt is now doubly incontestable: by natural and civil law. Even under these circumstances, however, the humanist is not averse to leniency; and for reasons identical to those indicated above: expediency (the ultimate welfare of the commonwealth) and Christian charity.

On the basis of the evidence outlined above the following conclusion seems to me to be inescapable: Sepúlveda does not advocate natural slavery as the status befitting the Indians. On the other hand, the humanist appears to tell us clearly only what the Indians are not and must not become – slaves. When it comes to a positive definition of their political role within the new scheme of things whose birth he is conscious of witnessing, the Spanish humanist, disappointingly, wavers and refrains from drawing the conclusions which his forceful scholarship seems to warrant – a clear indication of the limitations, in the context of sixteenth-century reality, of the intellectual tradition which nourishes him. And it is perhaps this lack of boldness that in the last analysis has prejudiced his case in the eyes of posterity which forgetting the dangers besetting hindsight often unreasonably demands that the past adhere to its own canons of humanitarianism, for Sepúlveda, against his will, was drawn into a controversy with a man whose fiery character and passionate involvement sharply contrasted with his own tempered and academic outlook. It was thus in the nature of things that in a drama so forcefully dominated by Las Casas' heroic visions Sepúlveda, as he himself recognized in dismay, should have been cast in the role of the devil's advocate in *encomendero* garb.

The proto-civility of the American Indians

So far we know with precision only that the Indians are neither civil beings nor slaves. It must be reiterated that no similar certainty obtains when we attempt to answer the affirmative side of the question. And, again, no definite portrait should be expected to emerge Minerva-like from Sepúlveda's pen. Consistency and originality are not the characteristic virtues of Renaissance ideology, so fond of indiscriminately combining the ideas of one thinker with those of others; and if we are to assess the true measure of Sepúlveda's accomplishments we must not demand of him what is clearly beyond the powers of his age.

One more introductory remark is in order. What follows in this section will draw heavily on material presented in this and the preceding two chapters. The reason is simple. The concepts which give form to Sepúlveda's notion of the Indians' role in society, what I have chosen to call their proto-civil status, are scattered throughout his political treatises and have already been cited in other contexts. It is in the nature of things, therefore, that much of the material to be used in this section has been cited elsewhere. Under the circumstances what follows will be both an attempt to discuss the question of the Indians' proto-civility and a concluding summary of Sepúlveda's scheme.

Throughout the *Democrates alter* the author has gone to great pains to catalogue all those traits which brand the Indians as 'inferior'. But what are the claims of the Spaniards to the exalted throne of political supremacy? On the strength of his often repeated argument that it is both licit and just that those who by nature, the quality of their customs, and the strength of their laws, deserve to rule over the less gifted shall do so, Democrates informs Leopoldus that the Spaniards hold *dominium* over the barbarians with unquestionable legitimacy: 'in prudence, talent, all kinds of virtue, and human feelings [the Indians] are as inferior to the Spaniards as children to adults, women to men, the cruel and inhuman to the utterly meek, the intemperate to the moderate'. The talent and prudence of the Spaniards, continues Democrates as he gets down to cases, are a simple matter of record, for who can doubt the excellence of Lucan, Seneca, Saint Isidore, Averroes, Avempace, and Alfonso the Wise? As for their other virtues – fortitude, humanity, justice, religion – none doubts the Spaniards' lofty attainments. Democrates, however, sounds a note of caution of extreme importance to my argument:

I refer only to princes and those on whose aid and ability the former rely for the administration of the republic; and, finally, to those who have received a liberal education. For if some among the Spaniards are unjust and wicked their infamy in no way detracts from the reputation of their people which must be measured in terms of its enlightened and noble members and its customs and public institutions.

Clearly Sepúlveda sees the true quality of a nation as resting on its elite, an idea further emphasized by the author's own admission that there is an exception to the rule: 'Although there are certain virtues which are common to all classes.' The virtues in question are valor, frugality, religion, and humanitarianism.[100]

From these and similar passages already cited an idea of great significance emerges: whenever Sepúlveda glowingly reports on the cultural accomplishments of the Spaniards, whenever he unquestioningly accepts their capacity for civil life, he is not arguing for the superiority of *all* Spaniards. He is merely taking for granted what would have been tacitly understood by his contemporaries, untroubled as they were by any feelings of awe toward democracy as understood by our own age – namely, that a political philosopher worth his mettle would not waste a thought on the vulgar. By Spaniards, then, we must construe the elite, those who administer the admirable laws of the land and support the remarkable institutions of their country, the creative minds, in short, responsible for the splendid cultural accomplishments of which Sepúlveda speaks with pride. And it is precisely the failure of the Indian elite to live up to similar accomplishments (as rightfully demanded by natural law) which damns the Indian polities. With this in mind and remembering that for the humanist the backbone of civil society is reason, the following passage offers a clue as to the political role reserved for the Indians;

In a well-administered republic...it is not up to the vulgar in general to deliberate upon affairs of state...but to obey the order and decrees of the prince and high magistrates...for there where the vulgar arrogates the authority to ponder upon weighty matters of government we no longer have a republic but an aberration thereof; such form of government, known as 'popular', is both unjust and pernicious to the commonwealth.[101]

It is in the context suggested by these words, reflecting nothing more than the general distaste felt by the age toward democracy, that we must understand Sepúlveda's answer to the question of whether the American aborigines should be admitted to the same rights as the Spaniards.

There is nothing more opposed to the so-called distributive justice (*contra iustitiam distributivam appellatam*) than giving equal rights to unequal people; and to equate in favors, honors, or rights those who are superior in dignity, virtue, and merits to those who are inferior.[102]

[100] *Ibid.*, pp. 33–5.   [101] *Ibid.*, p. 110.   [102] *Ibid.*, p. 119.

To all appearances this is a broad declaration of unequal rights between Indians and Spaniards. And if we think of the New World as a land overwhelmed by the arrival of masses of disinherited from across the sea determined to carve a new and better life for themselves at the expense of the native inhabitants such a verdict may seem warranted. A close examination of the facts, however, appends important qualifications to this conclusion. For there is no reason to believe that Sepúlveda actually saw the New World as a land automatically open to all who desired to engage in what eventually came to be known as colonization. That such a thing, in a more or less modified form, came to pass by no means necessarily implies that Sepúlveda ever advocated or even contemplated it. On the contrary, I think that the evidence of the humanist's own testimony points to a different interpretation, one based on Sepúlveda's belief that the New World was a dependency of the Spanish Crown, its status in no significant way different from that of Aragon or Navarre, to be administered by royal officials. In the best classical tradition it is of course understood that those officials are to be strictly selected among those chosen by nature to rule: 'worthy, just, and prudent men of known and tested probity'. These are the men who modeling their lives after the Ciceronian ideal of public service and thus capable of understanding and carrying out the responsibilities and duties of the *vita activa* Sepúlveda would like to see in America. To these paragons of virtue, surely, the Indians are inferior.

The inferiority of the Indians is exactly the same as that of the Galicians or Sicilians, who are subordinated to the magistrates set above them by natural law for their governance, in all but one important respect: it is obvious that in the Old World provinces there exist aristocracies of service and talent fully capable of measuring up to the Ciceronian standards of public responsibility; not so, however, in the American 'province'. The Indian elite, and it should be clear by now that it is precisely this ruling class which Sepúlveda set out to judge and has found wanting, has proven its unfitness to rule. Whereas, then, in the Old World royal officials could cooperate on a parity basis with local notables and (in theory at least as proven by the case of the *corregidores*) rule jointly for the benefit of the ruled as fitting the definition of civil society, in the New World nothing stands between the Indians, now 'democratized' by the crushing canons of natural law, and the representatives of the Crown. To explain the form of government best adapted to them Sepúlveda has recourse to the already cited example of the Aristotelian household.

Just as the father holds sway over a large and complex household, the king must exercise various forms of authority over his different subjects. In the household we find the sons, and *servi seu mancipia*, as well as servants. Just and humane, the father lords it over them all; not, however, in the same manner, but in accordance with the class and condition of each. So shall a good and just king rule. The Spaniards deserve the kind of rule that the father reserves for the sons while those barbarians shall be governed as free servants with a mixture of herile and paternal authority as their condition and circumstances demand.[103]

What, precisely, is this 'mixture of herile and paternal authority'? No exhaustive reply to this question is ever forthcoming from Sepúlveda, but the last pages of the *Democrates alter* offer sufficient evidence to warrant the conclusion that the form of government recommended by Sepúlveda for the natives of the New World does not significantly depart from that recommended for the mass of the population in the Old. 'It is advisable to yield to the *plebes* control of public posts of minor importance and those whose nature require that they be occupied by many at the same time; if this counsel is ignored it is possible that through the opposition of the majority the stability of the commonwealth will be destroyed.' Such, argues Sepúlveda quoting from his own translation of Aristotle's *Politics* (Book III), are the recommendations of the master.

In this manner [explains Aristotle] could be resolved that controversy concerning the powers that should be placed in the hands of free men and those entrusted to the multitude lacking wealth and endowed with no distinguishing virtue. To entrust the latter with the important offices of the commonwealth is to invite mismanagement of the public affairs; to deny the mob all participation in the governance of the republic, on the other hand, courts disaster and civil war.[104]

On the redoubtable authority of Aristotle, finally, Sepúlveda earnestly entreats the Spanish rulers to avoid the fatal blunder of Thessalians and Spartans. Neither slaves nor fully civil beings, the Indians thus rightly belong in a political no-man's land reserved for the amorphous masses whose anonymity puts them beyond the purview of a humanist thinker trained only to understand and to appreciate singular deeds and individual accomplishments. When this is taken together with what has been said about Sepúlveda's views on the commonwealth, there emerge the outlines of a well-integrated society where slave (herile society), Indian and European vulgar in common (proto-civil society), and European ruling elite (civil society) occupy their naturally appointed places.[105] The fundamental

---

[103] *Ibid.*, p. 120.   [104] *Ibid.*, p. 121.

[105] It is to be noted, however, that the role apportioned to natural herile society is minimal. Only the natives of the African coast seem to deserve the status of natural slavery. And their case is mentioned only, and briefly, once. If slavery exists at all in Sepúlveda's social scheme it is for all practical purposes limited to the civil slavery brought about by the defeat, in a just war, of the unrighteous – and then only if the welfare of the commonwealth requires it.

justification for this hierarchy of social order is in Sepúlveda's eyes identical with that of ancient ethics: mankind's good life. Not surprisingly, the good life is not the same for all men because all men have not been endowed by nature with the same capabilities. But, the author concedes, within the strict boundaries drawn by nature's own relativism all men can achieve the good life. In truth, what matters is not so much what position we occupy in the socio-political hierarchy, only nature itself determines that, as the imperative need to be a part of the social scheme (in which the possession of Christianity guarantees the ultimate equality of all). This is why, in principle, the Indian can be as good and happy a social being as the *encomendero*, and the African slave as his Portuguese master.[106]

Moreover, in Sepúlveda's system the component social groupings proposed above are patently not of equivalent value. The reason is that his three social categories have political roles of unequal importance. As a result, we find an ascending hierarchy going from the rough and simple herile status to the sophisticated level of civil society occupied by those 'created by nature to rule'. Within this hierarchy the imperfect character of both herile and proto-civil society conditions their survival upon the existence of a perfect and just civil society. Only when he is fairly governed will the slave, Indian, and European plebeian, achieve the conditions of the good life to which he is entitled. And nowhere can this basic condition be better fulfilled than in a republic ruled by one man with the cooperation and support of the naturally fit few – in other words, in an aristocratic monarchy. The aristocratic bent of Sepúlveda's monarchical views stems, we have noticed above, from his conviction that very few men are capable of both comprehending and giving substance to what he feels is the fundamental duty of men in a well-ordered commonwealth: before he surrenders himself to the pleasures of *otium* a man must discharge his civic duties to the fullest.[107] A man's capacity for contemplation as derived from his belief in the faith of Christ entitles him to full status as a social being within the *respublica Christiana*, but only to a subordinate political

---

[106] This condition of harmony is not only a theoretical requirement but a practical imperative as well. See the Prologue to Alberti's *Della famiglia*.

[107] J. H. Parry has pointed out Sepúlveda's aristocratic convictions and the natural reaction of the Spanish government to them and their implications in the context of the New World. 'Sepúlveda wished to impose permanently between the Crown and the Indians a benevolent aristocracy, who might exercise at first hand a paternal authority which the Crown could not easily exert at a distance, and who would be entitled to use Indian labor in reward for their services. The feudal implications of this proposal in themselves made it unacceptable to the royal government always suspicious of aristocratic pretensions.' *The Spanish Seaborne Empire* (New York, 1971), p. 149. This goes a long way toward explaining the government's refusal to permit the publication of the *Democrates alter*.

Juan Ginés de Sepúlveda (II)

position if reason is lacking. Only the perfection yielded by the balance of faith and reason will carry him to the pinnacle of civility. And with this Aristotelian format which encloses a Christianized Ciceronian core we come back full circle to our starting point namely, the relation between the two *viae* open to man – the way of *otium* (and its close associate, the *via monastica*) and the path of *negotium*. A relationship which, in association with the assumptions implicit in the theory of natural law, lies at the foundation of Sepúlveda's political philosophy.[108]

[108] Among those publicists who may be considered precursors of Sepúlveda should be mentioned López de Palacios Rubios (1450–1524) and Matías de Paz (ca. 1470–1519). Their treatises on the subject of America – *De las Islas del mar Océano* and *Del dominio de los Reyes de España sobre los Indios*, respectively – have been translated by A. Millares Carlo (Mexico, 1954). The edition contains an excellent introduction by S. Zavala.

8

On princes, counselors, and councils: Charles of Habsburg, Antonio de Guevara, and Fadrique Furió Ceriol

The Carolinian instrucciones

Whatever significance in both practical and normative terms may be attached to the reflections of a political thinker or an entire school on the nature of the ruler's duties and the traits with which his character must be adorned will in the end solely be measured by his success in imbuing the prince with his teachings. We are fortunate in this respect to have a number of documents revealing to what extent the monarch whose reign encompasses most of the period under scrutiny here reflected the teachings in vogue among the thinkers who surrounded his person. Since to some extent we have already become acquainted with the political ideas sponsored by a few notable writers of the imperial age, I have chosen to introduce my future comments on their understanding of the prince's personality with a study of what the monarch himself has to say concerning his own duties as ruler and the qualifications that a good prince must possess or endeavor to attain. Or, to put the same thing in the form of a question, what does Charles V have to say on the subject of the attributes indispensable to the man whom God has chosen to guide His people?

The answer, I feel, can be found in the *instrucciones* or advice which at various times during his reign the Emperor addressed to his son for the benefit, edification, and guidance of the future ruler. There are four such *instrucciones*. The first one, dated Madrid November 5, 1539, was written when Philip was but twelve years old and its usefulness for our purposes is therefore very relative. About the last one (October 25, 1555) serious objections have been raised. E. W. Mayer, K. Brandi, and M. Fernández Alvarez consider this *instrucción* to be a fabrication. We are then left with two. Charles wrote the first one in the form of two letters: one open (May 4) and the other secret (May 6), from Palamós on the eve of his departure (1543) from Spain, an absence that was to last for eighteen years. The last *instrucción* (Augsburg, January 19, 1548) is often known as the Emperor's political testament. It was written under rather melancholy circumstances. The year before had witnessed the victorious conclusion, at the battle of Mühlberg, of his campaign against the Schmalkaldic League, and the ensuing disintegration of the coalition of Lutheran princes. Shortly afterward Charles became prey to a severe attack of the gout; fearing for his life 'he sent [to his son] through the Duke of Alba a long *instrucción de avisos* counseling him on how to rule, and whom to trust or distrust'.[1]

In the letter of May 4, 1543, Charles offers his son advice on two fronts: *cuanto al gobierno de estos reinos* and in what concerns the *gobierno de vuestra persona* – an interesting stab at systematization which seemingly promises to distinguish the virtues of the ruler from those of the man, a futile attempt, however, for as the points of counsel unfold it becomes clear that in practice it is impossible to separate the *persona regia* from the man. Indirectly a matter of some substance, for the Emperor, consciously or unconsciously, in this follows the path trodden by the conventional authors of *specula* before and immediately after Machiavelli: the perfect prince is also the perfect man (for how this should be qualified see below in the context of Furió Ceriol). Charles begins by informing his son that the inexperienced young ruler, for such was to be Philip's new office during his father's absence, who aspires to be a good one must do two things: first, he will keep God forever before his eyes and always willingly, for His sake, suffer the *trabajos* inevitably attached to the art of good governance; second, he shall trust and subject himself to *buen consejo*. Surely these two conditions, if fulfilled, will more than amply compensate

---

[1] On all this see the following works: R. B. Merriman, 'Charles V's last paper of advice to his son', *American Historical Review*, xxvii(1922–1923), pp. 489–91; and M. Fernández Alvarez, 'Las instrucciones políticas de los Austrias mayores', *Gesammelte Aufsäzte zur Kulturgeschichte Spaniens*, xxiii, pp. 171–88. The first *instrucción* has been published by F. de Laiglesia in *Estudios históricos (1515–1555)* (Madrid, 1918), i. That of 1555 can be found in B. Stübel, 'Die Instruktion Karls V. für Philipp II. vom 25 Oktober 1555', *Archiv für Österreichische Geschichte*, xciii (1905), pp. 181–284. For the *instrucción* of 1543 see Morel-Fatio, in *RecH* (1899); and J. M. March, *Niñez y juventud de Felipe II* (2 vols., Madrid, 1941). For that of 1548 we have three published versions: one in Laiglesia; another in *Papiers d'État du Cardinal Granvelle*, ed. C. Weiss, in *Collection de documents inédits sur l'histoire de France* (Paris, 1842), xliv, iii; a third version is that of Fray Prudencio de Sandoval, *Historia de la vida y hechos del Emperador Carlos V*, in Biblioteca de Autores Españoles (Madrid, 1956), 82, Part iii, bk. xxx, ch. v, pp. 323–37. B. Beinert, in 'El testamento político de Carlos V de 1548. Estudio crítico', *Carlos V. Homenaje de la Universidad de Granada* (Granada, 1958), has studied the relative merits of the three versions of the 1548 *instrucción* and prefers those of Sandoval and Weiss. The advice of 1543 will hereafter be cited as *Instrucción* (letter of May 4), and *Secreta* (letter of May 6) – both of them in the March edition. For that of 1548 I will use Sandoval's version and cite it as *Testamento*.

the youthful ruler for his lack of years and experience.[2] God is particularly recommended: never neglect to serve Him; be devout and fearful of giving Him offense; love Him above all things, give aid and comfort to His faith; never countenance heresy in your realms. We find identical concern in the *Testamento*: 'as principal and firm foundation of your governance you must acknowledge God's magnanimity, and submit your actions and desires to His will. Once this is done you shall enjoy His assistance and protection and in this manner judge what is best in matters of government'.[3] Once more the close dependence that must bind the good prince to God is recognized. If the king is to be favored with divine guidance, however, two conditions need be met. First, the true faith must be upheld and heresy stamped out; second, justice must be *favorecida*. In this spirit Charles admonishes his heir to obey the Church and show respect to Rome. With reference to the latter there is an important qualification: if on the pretext of the obedience owed to Rome abuses and excesses prejudicial to his realms were committed, Philip is urged to act – with reverence but also with firmness – bearing in mind only the well-being of his kingdoms and lordships. There is no question here as to where the ruler's priorities primarily lie.

Once God has been given his due Charles instructs his son on the importance of justice.

Son, you must always be just; command your magistrates to follow your example, never to be moved by *afición* or *pasión*, and to shun all corruption under penalty of punishment. Avoid at all costs giving the impression, particularly to your ministers, that passion moves you away from justice. Command nothing against justice; should you feel yourself at times caught in the grip of anger or *afición*, refrain from *ejecutar justica*, especially in criminal cases. For justice is the virtue which supports us all. It imitates that mercifulness shown by Christ to us. Mix them both in perfect proportions, for if used in excess either can turn from virtue into vice.[4]

The good prince must be temperate and a paragon of moderation, and never do anything in anger. He shall turn away from the advice of youths and avoid the bad counsels of his seniors. He must banish flatterers, a most dangerous species of man, from his presence – keeping by his side, instead, good men, praising and favoring them with largesse so that all will know that the ruler loves the good and abhors the bad. On this important question of counselors Charles takes further steps. The Emperor informs Prince Philip that in order to aid his son in carrying into effect his recommendations he has decided to leave behind all the councils of the monarchy together with detailed instructions to their members on how

---

[2] *Instrucción*, p. 13.   [3] *Testamento*, p. 324.   [4] *Instrucción*, pp. 13–14.

to serve and guide the new regent's steps. There also follow brief comments and short guidelines pertaining to the manner in which Philip must use the councils (State, Orders, War, Indies, Royal, Inquisition, *Cámara*, and Finance), appointment of *corregidores*, treatment of the Queen and Philip's own sisters, protection of frontiers, and *cosas de guerra*. The Church also comes in for a share of attention and Charles stresses how the new ruler must see to it that the bishops remain in their sees,[5] a question also discussed at the beginning of the *Testamento* when Philip is urged to distribute those ecclesiastical prebends which are his to give among men 'of letters, exemplary living, experience, and administrative acumen' who will govern their churches and benefices for the glory of God and the well-being of the souls of men.[6] One thing above all others, whether secular or ecclesiastical matters are concerned, Charles insists upon: the ruler must never promise anything *ni de palabra ni por escrito*.[7]

Wistfully and apologetically Charles reflects that circumstances are forcing Philip to mature before his age. They have compelled him, the father, to arrange an early marriage for his son and now to place the burden of government on his inexperienced shoulders. For this reason the Emperor fairly entreats his heir not to neglect his own education now that he has attained to supreme power – *no habéis de pensar que el estudio os hará alargar la niñez*. With penetrating insight and a happy phrase Philip is thus warned against the prejudice that formal learning is a matter for children. On the contrary, he explains in a paragraph that would have done honor to Erasmus, continued and ceaseless study

[w]ill make you grow in honor and reputation in such a fashion that even though of tender age you will be viewed as a man by all; for in order to become *hombre temprano* it is never enough to have the physical size, the desire to be one, or to think that you are one. Only sound judgment and knowledge on how to do those things proper to man are prerequisites for attaining manhood. But it is not enough to be a man; a ruler must also be a sound man: wise, sane, good, and honest. To attain to such a state study and examples are indispensable. And if this is true for all men it applies to you, son, even more; for you see how many lordships you must *señorear*, how different they are from one another, how far apart, and how separated they are by language barriers. And you, as their ruler, must understand those who live therein and be understood by them. To this end nothing is more essential than a good command of the Latin tongue. For this reason I entreat you to learn it.[8]

[5] *Ibid.*, pp. 16–17.
[6] *Testamento*, p. 324.
[7] *Instrucción*, pp. 16–17.
[8] *Ibid.*, p. 18. Philip, due largely to the weakness and the affection which his tutor, Siliceo, professed his royal charge, remained a notoriously poor linguist throughout his life.

For the sake of his new responsibility, moreover, the prince will now change his life style. Both the companions and the pleasures of youth must go. He will henceforth surround himself with mature and capable men, and shall take his leisure only moderately and not too often. 'There are those who for their own ends will seduce you away from *negocios* through all manner of entertainment, not all of it of an honest nature. Beware of such men.'[9] Although the Emperor next proceeds to close the contents of the open *instrucción* with brief remarks about counselors – especially one of them, Don Juan de Zúñiga, Duke of Béjar – it is in the secret letter which accompanied it (May 6) that he opens his mind to his son on the careful and often devious ways of truly using men to the ruler's best advantage. Here we see the Emperor at his best as a judge of men; the experienced ruler who puts to use a man's best qualities while skillfully neutralizing his shortcomings, a shrewd realist at work.

Charles begins his secret counseling by acknowledging the existence of a profound factionalism among his *criados*. From the start, then, Philip must make it clear to all that factions will be viewed with disfavor. He should, however, approach the problem with few illusions. It is no easy task to fathom accurately the depths of jealousy and animosity dividing the members of the royal entourage. The Emperor warns his son not to be deceived by the fraternal demonstrations of affection and show of harmony publicly displayed by his advisers: in private they will do precisely the opposite. With this in mind the father, it seems, decided to give his son a practical demonstration of the old divide-and-conquer principle: use your counselors' factionalism to your own best advantage. The Cardinal of Toledo (Juan Tavera), the President of the Council of Castile (Hernando de Valdés), and Francisco de los Cobos, were acknowledged *cabezas de bando*. Rather than leave the son under the sole influence of one of them, then, the father opted for bringing the three together and thus afford the new regent an opportunity to use all instead of being used by one. Concerning the formidable Tavera the Emperor urges his son to proceed as follows: 'the Cardinal of Toledo will make a humble and holy entrance; honor and trust him in matters of virtue, for on them he will counsel you well. Seek, moreover, his recommendation and aid in searching for good people to fill vacancies. In everything else be wary and do not place yourself in his hands, neither now nor in the future – nor, for that matter, in the hands of any other man – but listen to others as well.'[10] In these words can be detected the pragmatic leitmotiv of Charles' approach to his counselors: sift out their specialized talents and use them on a division-of-labor basis only.

[9] *Ibid.*, p .19.   [10] *Secreta*, p. 27.

There is no question that the Emperor's call to caution was fully justified, for there was indeed factionalism among his closest and most intimate advisers: personal ambition, jealousy, mutual likes and dislikes, were all contributing factors. Most important, however, were the ideological differences which roughly divided the ranks of those closest to the Emperor's person into two *bandos*. The two positions, most often clashing on matters of foreign policy, became best exemplified for this particular time in the context of the Peace of Crépy (1544). The provisions of this treaty which brought to a temporary halt Charles' struggle with France confronted his advisers, now Philip's, with a thorny situation which amounted to this: the matrimonial alliances compacted at Crépy seemed to demand that either Flanders or Milan be lost to the Habsburgs. Needless to say, the Council of State actively participated in the ensuing deliberations. Non-members, notably the President of the Council of Castile and the Vice-Chancellor of Aragón, were invited. The membership thus constituted promptly underwent the predictable alignment. One group, led by Tavera, embodied those who as Castilians viewed with great suspicion the foreign entanglements which they considered to be the result of Aragonese foreign policy aims inherited from Ferdinand's days and not of Castilian interests. These men – Tavera, Valdés, Zúñiga, the Count of Cifuentes, Fernando de Guevara – opted for yielding Milan. Ironically enough, in their traditional enmity toward the monarchy's Italian policy they were sealing with their approval the very Habsburg character of the Spanish monarchy which the strictly Castilian party of yesterday had fought against during the early years of Charles' reign. The other faction, led by Fernando Alvarez de Toledo, Duke of Alba, emphasized the strategic importance of the Italian duchy; its adherents – Alba himself, the Count of Osorno, the Vice-Chancellor of Aragón – perhaps more realistically agreed in considering Flanders expendable. Hovering between the two and leaning now to one side now to the other remained two state councilors: the Cardinal of Seville (García de Loaisa), and the imperial secretary Cobos. The clash between the two parties on the issue raised by the Treaty of Crépy was but one incident in the long struggle between the opponents of an 'Italian policy', created and vigorously defended earlier in the reign, and its supporters.[11]

This background is incidental to the central theme here discussed but – since all the personalities just named are, more or less extensively, examined by the Emperor for his son's benefit – it serves, first, to point out that the *bandos* mentioned by Charles V derived nourishment from high policy considerations as well as from more personal idiosyncrasies and ambitions; and second, it brings more clearly into focus the suspicion and dislike in

[11] F. Chabod, 'Milán o los Paises Bajos?', in *Homenaje de la Universidad de Granada*, pp. 331–71.

which the Emperor seems to have held the Duke of Alba. In his sketch of the grandee's character, Charles is merciless.

The Duke of Alba would like to have been counted among the above [Tavera, Valdés, and Cobos], not because he belongs to any *bando* but out of a desire to enhance his own position [the Duke was relatively young then; about thirty-six years of age]. I did not include him because in the governance of the realm the grandees must not be allowed to participate; my decision gave him considerable offense. After having him close to my person for some time I have come to recognize in him great ambition, although he was at first very humble and retiring. Your youth will expose you to danger from the duke. Both he and the other grandees must be kept out of the government. If he or the others win your favor – and they will try, even if it is *por vía de mujeres* – you will dearly pay for your weakness later...I employ him [Alba] *en lo de estado y guerra*. Honor him, favor him, and use him, for he is the best we now have.[12]

Charles' suspicion of the grandees' motives is not to be allayed. He considers them capable of resorting to every means to gain influence over the ruler – even to women, a weakness which he well knew could be effectively put to use in the case of Philip whose early years were not exactly dominated by a note of chastity. In general the Emperor's advice is clear: the ruler must always take the best of what a counselor has to offer without ever placing himself in his hands, a lesson which Philip would learn well indeed, as Alba's own case would prove. In disgrace in 1580 (his son had married without the king's approval), he was called back to court and placed in command of an army to enforce his sovereign's rights to the Portuguese throne – the best man for the task.

And Cobos? Cobos was the tireless clerk and capable financial administrator who from humble position had risen by dint of hard work to the post of secretary; he and Granvelle were probably the two most influential men in the Habsburg monarchy after Gattinara's death.

Covos I hold to be faithful: until now he has had little *pasión*; now he does not lack for it. He is no longer the hard worker he once was, probably due to old age, illness, and his wife's importunities...I have warned him against the last and I think that he will set matters aright. He has experience in all my affairs and is well-informed. I doubt that you will find a better person to advise you on those matters. I trust to God that his present troubles will not cause him to lose control. It would be advisable for you to use him as I do: a faithful executor of instructions, although he should never be the only one to be listened to. Give him your favor, for he has served me well and cleanly.[13]

Charles next briefs his son concerning Don Juan de Zúñiga, Philip's *Mayordomo Mayor*. The Duke of Béjar, the Emperor informs the prince,

[12] *Secreta*, p. 27.   [13] *Ibid.*, p. 28.

is a trifle harsh, something which should not be held against him because 'this harshness is born out of the love he has for you and his care that you should be endowed with all the necessary virtues. You must love, honor, and favor him.' In fact, Charles continues, his roughness should be doubly appreciated, for if he had been as indulgent as the other tutors were the results might have been disastrous. Béjar, however, is not free from short-comings. Charles viewed him as *algo apasionado* toward Cobos and Alba; he belonged to the party of the Cardinal de Toledo. Above all Charles understood Béjar to be jealous of Cobos, an upstart, for the favor shown the secretary. 'None of these things, however, should prevent him from advising and serving you faithfully. In short, better servants than he and Cobos you will hardly find.'[14] The Emperor concludes with a warmth unique in his appraisal of the men who are to aid his son. 'In what per-tains to virtue and the *gobierno de vuestra persona* no one is better and more faithful than don Joán [Béjar]. I beg of you, son, to believe and love him; not because he is your tutor but because he is a faithful and true servitor of yours and mine. Do not be offended or angered by his plain talk.' As final proof of Charles' high esteem Don Juan is referred to as Philip's *relox y despertador* (see below for Guevara's definition of the word).

The Bishop of Cartagena, Juan Martínez Siliceo, follows Béjar in this succession of portraits; and one can almost hear the Emperor chuckle: 'true [the Bishop] has not been the best influence in your life as concerns matters of learning'.[15] So much for the shortcomings. As for the Bishop's goodness and integrity the Emperor harbors no doubts. Short comments on the two remaining ecclesiastics, Loaisa and Valdés, follow; about the Count of Osorno the Emperor has only this brief but telling comment: 'the Count is skillful and not so straightforward in his dealings as he should be; he is *tan corto* in his speech that it is difficult to understand him – whether this is so because he wishes to offend no one or because he does not want to be understood, I do not know'.[16]

Advice on foreign policy and its tortuous conduct is certainly not absent from the *instrucciones* of 1543, but the subject is much more extensively scrutinized in the Emperor's political testament of 1548. And since foreign policy of necessity hinges on the double linchpin of war and peace Charles emphasizes throughout the theme of *conservar la paz*. Thus in the *Testamento* the Emperor shows himself convinced, and so lifts a prag-matic page from Valdés' musings on war, that God cannot be well-served unless in peace, to say nothing of the other multitude of problems caused by war. Consequently Philip must take great care and pains to avoid

[14] *Ibid.*, pp. 29–31.　　　　　　[15] *Ibid.*, p. 31.　　　　　　[16] *Ibid.*, p. 32.

discord by all ways and means available, and never undertake wars unless absolutely compelled to do so. But not only for the sake of God must wars be avoided. After years of clamorous complaints by his Castilian subjects that his extravagant foreign policy was ruining the country the Emperor appears to have learned his lesson. He cuts a slightly pathetic figure when he confesses that he has bankrupted Castile. 'Past wars have exhausted the realms of your inheritance, even though I have undertaken those wars in their defense. True, with God's favor I have succeeded in defending and adding to them; but at great cost, and so now they must be given a rest.'[17] Expounding further on the bond between endless war and economic disaster Charles concludes that his own experience has taught him how the latter inevitably follows the former. Moreover, insofar as wars can be avoided at all it must be in cooperation with one's neighbors whose good will need therefore be carefully cultivated.[18]

And there lies the rub. How can that wholesome end be achieved? To find the answer Charles unfolds a panoramically precise view of contemporary affairs which Philip must have found most instructive. Since the goal immediately at hand is to woo the monarchy's neighbors, the latter are studied individually with accompanying recommendations on how to insure at least their neutrality. The most essential step, Charles advises, is to keep on good terms with Ferdinand, the Emperor's brother and heir presumptive to the imperial crown. The friendship of the German princes must also be courted; the same applies to the Swiss. As far as the Pope is concerned Charles bitterly complains of his recent treachery. He encourages his son, however, to forget the past and to show 'greater respect for the papal office than the Pope himself has demonstrated by his actions'. Still, the Pope is old and should he die in the near future he, Philip, must endeavor to influence the papal election in the direction of Christendom's well-being. The remaining Italian potentates are well in hand and the Emperor foresees no serious difficulties from this quarter. The English friendship must be maintained and cultivated as a means of worrying and distracting the French from mischief. For it is at France that all this is aimed. To establish a *cordon sanitaire* around the Gallic troublemaker is the one solid guarantee for peace. Charles acidly complains that he has always sought to live in peace with a neighbor who 'as is notorious, has never honored either truces or peace treaties'. As in the case of Alba, the Emperor, often willing to see more than one face to the coin, admits very little that could be considered flattering to France. The death of the old king, Francis I, promises no respite, for his son, Henry II, bades fair to be a worthy chip off the old block. What to do, then, with France? In the past, he complains, I have done all I could to

[17] *Testamento*, pp. 324-5.   [18] *Ibid.*, p. 325.

live at peace with her, to the extent of sacrificing portions of my patrimony – Burgundy – for the sake of concord, and all to no avail. Today a wait-and-see policy seems to be the most appropriate stance. Offer peace to Henry for the sake of Christendom's tranquillity, if for no other reason. But, the Emperor urges, do not relax your vigilance. Be firm if he tries to worm his way out of his commitments and obligations, for otherwise whatever has been achieved in the past will have to be won all over again. Under the circumstances, he concludes, the best policy toward France is one of diligent watchfulness which while offering proof of your earnest desire to live by past treaties and agreements does not neglect preparations for possible aggression – *si vis pacem para bellum*.

On the basis of what has been said above, what conclusions can be drawn concerning the political ideology of the second Habsburg? The virtues of the accomplished ruler as seen by Charles V could perhaps be subsumed under three general categories: the prince must be a good Christian, just, and moderate. First and foremost, it is acknowledged that the ruler is God's deputy and responsible to Him for the well-being of the flock. And justice is the invisible mantle to be worn at all times by the representative of the divine authority – a cloak which shall thus cover any and all of the monarch's activities as governor of his people. In short, the sovereign's primary role is that of administrator of justice. Justice, on the other hand, must never be blind; clemency and Christian *caritas* shall forever mellow its harshness, an idea which fittingly introduces the concept of moderation – moderation, however, understood as applying not only to *negocios de Estado* but to the personal demeanor of the ruler as well. The man is also the ruler; his ability to control his own temper and leash his own passions is in no sense different from his skill in avoiding extremes of harshness or indulgence when acting as the master of affairs. But, how can a man be moderate if he is not honest? The prince's personal and private life, then, must be clearly above reproach and reflected for all to see in his conduct as husband and father. Above all the prince must be prudent, for prudence is the one gift embracing all the other desirable traits which a good ruler must both have and practice. And it is this very prudence which will compel the conscientious prince to seek the counsel of the best men, avoid flatterers and favorites, use his largesse and patronage worthily, prefer the weak to the mighty, curb the arrogance of the great, preserve intact his inheritance, and labor without rest for peace.

Following this somewhat extended exploration of what the most powerful practitioner of his age understood to be the *oficio* of ruler it would seem proper to attempt, at least implicitly, to tie up his idea of the good prince with the views on the same subject expounded by contemporary theoreticians. In past chapters we have had occasion to point out that any writer discoursing on matters of political theory will touch upon the nature of the qualities that must adorn the good ruler – Castrillo, Vitoria, Vives, Valdés, and Sepúlveda are no exceptions. I should like next, therefore, to examine panoramically the figure of the ideal prince as it emerges from the writings of the Spanish publicists of the Renaissance. In other words, to review the contribution of Castilian authors to the mirror-of-princes *genre*. It must be remarked, however, that no single publicist of the first rank seems to have written explicitly and exclusively on the subject of the ideal ruler – one would hesitate to consider Antonio de Guevara a first-rate political thinker. True, they all touch upon the question, and often they do so extensively, but always as a part of a larger and more all-embracing whole. It is only after Furió Ceriol's publication of *El concejo* that the *speculum principis* makes a consistent appearance to become, in the course of the first half of the following century, a veritable flood. The causes of this development lie clearly beyond the scope of this book in the changing and changed conditions of the reigns of the three Philips. Still, the following remarks may be appropriately made here.

Mirrors of princes: Renaissance and Baroque

The literature of mirrors of princes is both ancient and filled with famous examples and distinguished names. In the Middle Ages the subject of the virtues which go into the making of the accomplished prince, the nature of his personality, duties, and education, was frequently discussed in both general accounts of political theory and the specialized literature devoted exclusively to the matter. Among the most famous works of the period we find John of Salisbury's *Policraticus* (1159), Saint Thomas' *De regimine principum* (ca. 1265), and Egidius Romanus' *De regimine principum* (ca. 1287).[19] In medieval Spain the subject was not ignored and the

---

[19] On the general question of the *speculum principis* in Western European political literature, see L. K. Born, 'The *specula principum* of the Carolingian Renaissance', *Revue Belge de Philologie et d'Historie*, XII(1933), pp. 583–613; L. K. Born, 'The perfect prince: a study in thirteenth- and fourteenth-century ideals', *Speculum*, III (1928), pp. 470–504; L. K. Born, 'The perfect prince according to the Latin panegyrists', *American Journal of Philology*, LV(1934), pp. 20–35; and the same author's introduction to his edition of Erasmus' *Institutio*; J. Dickinson, 'The medieval conception of kingship and some of its limitations, as developed in the *Policraticus* of John of Salisbury', *Speculum*, I(1926), pp. 308–37; A. H. Gilbert, *Machiavelli's 'Prince' and its Forerunners* (Durham, N.C., 1938). For Italy, see C. Curcio, *La politica italiana del '400* (Florence, 1932); F. von Bezold, 'Republik und Monarchie in der italienischen Literatur des 15. Jahrhunderts', *Historische Zeitschrift*, LXXXI(1898), pp. 433–68; F. Gilbert, 'The humanist concept of the prince and the *Prince of* Machiavelli', *JMH*, IX(1939), pp. 449–83; D. Cantimori, 'Rhetoric and politics in Italian humanism', *JWI*, I(1937), pp. 83–102.

treatises of Saint Thomas and Egidius Romanus seem to have been highly influential. Among Spaniards who wrote on the subject, we may note: Francisco Eximenis (*Llibre de regiment de princeps*), Marqués de Santillana (*Doctrinal de privados*), Gómez Manrique (*Regimiento de príncipes*), Gómez Barroso (*Libro de los consejos e conseieros de los príncipes*), Arnaldo de Vilanova (*Allocutio christiani*), Cardinal Joan de Margarit (*Corona regum*), Diego de Valera (*Doctrinal de príncipes*). It was in the course of the sixteenth century, however, that works primarily or secondarily concerned with the prince as mirror of himself and as the ideal of his subjects began to appear with increasing frequency to become an impetuous torrent by the first half of the seventeenth. Castrillo, Guevara (see below), Valdés, Vitoria, Vives, Sepúlveda, all address themselves to the concept of the ruler, his rights and duties, the virtues needed to fulfill those duties, and his education in their writings on political theory. Concretely on the subject of the prince the Spanish Renaissance produced Francisco de Monzón's *Espejo del príncipe christiano* (Lisbon, 1544), characterized by Bataillon as 'not saying anything on politics'; Felipe de la Torre's *Institución de un rey christiano* (Antwerp, 1556); and, most significant of all, Furió Ceriol's *El concejo*. The proliferation of royal *espejos*, *instituciones*, *avisos*, and *regimientos* would be considerably stepped up after Ceriol's book to reach epidemic proportions in the following century.

If the fact that after 1559 there is a notable increase in the number of treatises *de regimine principum* is incontestable, the causes which might simultaneously explain their vogue both before and after that year cannot be discerned with the same incontrovertible clarity, notably because those common denominators applicable to, say, the period stretching from Alamos de Barrientos to the end of the seventeenth century may not always satisfactorily account for the age which is the province of this monograph. As far as the Renaissance is concerned the following generalizations could be put forward to account for its thinkers' concern with the prince's personality: the close proximity to the Middle Ages with its strong tradition of interest in the ruler's moral fiber; the influence of Italian humanism, itself an avid explorer of the prince's role on the stage of politics; the tacit identification of the ruler with the commonwealth's *potestas*; the sharp recrudescence of political moralism which makes its debut in the early 1520s; the appearance at this time of two masterpieces of *speculum* literature – Machiavelli's *Il principe* and Erasmus' *Institutio*. The presence of the former at this point, I might add, is a salutary reminder of the dangers implicit in drawing too sharp a distinction between the early and later periods in the history of Spanish mirrors of princes, for Machiavelli is one of the more serious influences in the development of post-1559 *espejo* literature. This is not to say, on the other hand, that the Spanish contribution to the *genre* hangs wholly on the Florentine's coat-tails; it is rather an admission of the undoubted weight of *Il principe*'s doctrine on the minds of the Spanish publicists of the Baroque.

After 1559 – and I use this date merely as a convenient cut-off point, the publication date of the last work which will be reviewed with some attention in these pages – a number of relatively novel factors come into play. First and foremost is the gradual realization of the enormous significance implied in the appearance of that tantalizingly imprecise phenomenon which often goes under the name of modern state. The notoriety of the terminological and conceptual deficiencies notwithstanding, a number of things were becoming progressively evident toward the end of the sixteenth century and would reach climactic proportions during the seventeenth. Foremost among them was the recognition that a critical confrontation had somehow and somewhere along the line occurred between the idea of the state conceived in the vague manner of traditional ideology, and the state's operative needs which, seemingly unbeknownst to all, had gradually crept in to present contemporaries with a sudden *fait accompli*. How complete the surprise was is testified to by Machiavelli. The Florentine failed to uncover the underlying essence of the state as warranted by the contemporary symptoms of what it had wrought and contented himself with speculating on the basis of its more superficial manifestations. But imperfectly as the true nature of the demands forced upon society by the Renaissance state was still understood in the later half of the century, there were those who noticed that accompanying those demands came an increasing depersonalization of the state, an impression which was to wax stronger as the state of the Renaissance evolved into its more sophisticated successor – the state of the Baroque – a successor which in turn gradually developed into an abstract entity finding its beginning and end, its *ragione*, within itself. It would not appear too far-fetched to propose that therein may precisely lie one explanation for the almost frantic tendency of Baroque thinkers to concentrate on the ruler: a desperate attempt to return to the familiarly reassuring anthropomorphism of the past as a means of both arresting the alienation of man from the creature of his creation, and making more manageable the task of understanding the creative and ever-expanding capacities of the creature itself.

The subtle entrance onto the stage made by the Renaissance state was responsible, as early as that initial period when Europeans were not quite conscious of what was actually taking place, for the appearance of two distinct approaches to the prince as the materialization of the state: on the one hand, the time-honored and tested perception of the prince in terms of his moral and ethical qualities, a piece designed to explain the observed but vaguely understood novelty of the times on the basis of distinctly medieval premises, and best exemplified by Erasmus' *Institutio*. On the other hand, Machiavelli's own manual for princes, the sole representative of an awareness, not fully grasped in all its implications as yet, as to what the state in its contemporary setting meant, demanded, and promised. The early sixteenth-century Spanish writers overwhelmingly toed one form or another of the Erasmian line; only with Furió Ceriol can we detect the beginning of a shift which notably conditioned by *Il principe* was to color the entire political product of the Spanish school during the Baroque along paths defined by Maravall in the following fashion: one leading to a root and branch rejection of Machiavelli; another trodden by some who to a degree came to accept the foundations of his ideology; and finally a third one aimed at achieving an integration of what is new in Machiavelli into the old familiar network of Christian morality.[20]

Perhaps the best way of bringing home the transformation wrought by the gradual realization that the emergence of the modern state had introduced a radically influential ingredient in the *ars gubernandi* is to indicate the subtle but crucial change undergone, as we move from Renaissance into Counter-reformation and Baroque, by the question to which the tracts on princes had addressed themselves since their inception. The Renaissance asked: what qualities must the prince possess to rule? The Baroque, by contrast, wanted to know the qualities needed by the prince to rule *in his own age*. The concern with the *hic et nunc* so characteristic of the Baroque is evidence that, among other things, the rise of the modern state had contributed substantially to the evolution of Europe's historical consciousness. A more immediate question, however, relates to whether this concern was totally absent in the Renaissance. Broadly speaking the answer must be an affirmative one in the context of the normative universalism of Erasmus, Vives, or Valdés. The same question, however, must be approached differently in the case of Sepúlveda as the humanist tries to adapt eternal canons of ethical conduct to concrete circumstances. Does this mean that Sepúlveda's care for specific realities turns him of necessity into a Machiavellian? Not at all, for as the Baroque amply illustrates in retrospect, pragmatism does not necessarily equate with Machiavellianism. What it unquestionably means, on the other hand, is that at least one Renaissance thinker (see also my concluding remarks on Furió Ceriol, below) reacted immediately to a novel reality which demanded that the fact of the Renaissance state's existence be faced without delay – the discovery of America. The uncertainty lies in another

[20] J. A. Maravall, 'Maquiavelo y maquiavelismo en España', *BRAH*, Oct.–Dec. (1969), pp. 183–218.

direction. Is Sepúlveda, for instance, aware that the Indian question is inseparable from the state conceived now, in its prerogatives and operative needs, in a way very different from the traditional manner still in vigor? I do not think so. Rather, Sepúlveda does what Machiavelli had done in the narrow province of *raison d'État* for the personality of the prince; he discovers one among the already multiple facets of the Renaissance state – exactly in the same fashion in which Vitoria may be said to have discovered still another: internationalism as a new operative need of the state – one, of course, implicitly denied by Machiavelli. But within those narrow confines and with all their shortcomings the contributions of Vitoria and Sepúlveda are as unique as Machiavelli's in that the three thinkers uncover three novel aspects of the state in its new setting. The ultimate problem, of course, lies in that the very nature of this new state demands more and more imperiously not a narrow and piecemeal form of analysis which stresses some of the state's facets while ignoring or denying others, but a systematic appreciation of all factors simultaneously. Something that the Renaissance was not equipped to accomplish.

The authors of Renaissance treatises dealing directly or indirectly with the subject of the prince's *espejo* failed to emulate Sepúlveda. They persisted instead in concentrating on the timeless moral gifts indispensable to the prince, an example not always followed by their Baroque brethren. In fact, at its best the school of the seventeenth century contributed one more link in the chain needed to view the state in all its concrete and contemporary aspects: the *raison d'economie* which complements and enhances the meaning of *raison d'État*. Living in a milieu beset by social ills, political failure, and, above all, economic catastrophe, the Spanish publicists of the seventeenth century had no choice but to abandon the dreams which had seemed so real to an earlier generation and face squarely the unsavory facts of life. It was in this frame of mind that Rodríguez de Lansina, viewing the immediate past from a vantage point as recent as 1687, argued that the Christian virtues are not enough. The prince must possess other faculties inseparable from good government. True, the Renaissance had spoken of similar needs; hence the accent on the import of prudence. But, how many Renaissance political writers had studied in detail the practical nature of this prudence? To my knowledge only Sepúlveda made a stab at rigor in this area – a paltry list indeed.

Faced with a reality unpalatable by any standards, the Spanish publicists of the Baroque are gripped by a pervasive sense of pessimism. This is the age of Spain's internal decay and foreign failure. It is the age of Olivares' catastrophic gamble. Politics continued to be viewed as the *arte de gobernar* and the prince, now more than ever, is its high priest. The earlier generation which lived through the rise of Castile to the position of first among the powers could understand both the art of ruling and its supreme practitioner in broad and sweeping terms, careless of the tribute inexorably exacted by *praxis*. It was an age, Erasmus himself at one time confessed, that promised the advent of the long-awaited Golden Age. And Valdés wrote as if the obstacles in his master's path toward final universal harmony were so many gnats to be easily swatted aside. But already during Philip's reign we hear the rumblings of discordant tunes. With his son the chorus was loud and clear, only to become deafening under Philip IV. In the age of pessimism the art of ruling became one about which timeless generalizations could not be made or sustained. The artist himself could no longer be induced to adopt an air of Olympic disdain toward life's realities. Instead, the *arte de gobernar* was now conceived as the art of dealing not in abstractions but with men, the art of the possible.

It is in this light that the emphasis placed by Baroque thinkers on prudence must be seen. Renaissance *specula* insisted on elevating the prince to be a paragon of Christian deportment. To a considerable extent, as a result, practical prudence, the art of ruling men, was left both unsystematized and free to fend for itself. And not without reason, for if the prince is in truth a Christian what else does he need in order to be a perfect ruler? The gradual differentiation of the contemplative and the active *viae* and the elevation of the latter's standing, an accomplishment of the Renaissance, contributed to break down a view of prudence stiffly conditioned by the moral standards of Christianity. We only have to remember Sepúlveda again. His Indian ruler remains politically incompetent even after he converts to Christianity, and will remain so regardless of the depth of his ethical endowment because he lacks the prudence which alone can resolve the uncertainties that a ruler must face. This prudence, the civic wisdom born out of the ability to apply *recta ratio*, implies on the other hand a background of virtue which only Christianity can give. Hence we find the Baroque authors of *espejos* endlessly engaged in bringing the two together in the person of the prince. And herein lies perhaps their most noteworthy contribution: to have endeavored to reconcile that pragmatic side of the ruler charged with meeting the demands of reality, his 'Machiavellian' face, with the other, the human side, which could only be concerned with behaving in accordance with the ethical standards of Christian deportment.

Valdés' perfect prince

Among those who wrote in the Erasmian tradition on the qualities of the good prince, Valdés was personally the closest to the Emperor. Elsewhere we discovered that the substance of the secretary's two dialogues cannot be separated from the figure of his master. It is but fitting, under the circumstances, that the remaining pages of this chapter, devoted to examining some examples of Renaissance *espejos*, should begin with Valdés' specific recommendations to the man who in truth wishes to be the 'shepherd of his people' as they are outlined in *Mercurio y Carón*.

After the terrifying nightmare experienced by the hitherto carefree and conventional ruler Polidoro, there awakened a new man and thus a new king. His first move is symptomatic of the important role attributed to counselors by Valdés, himself a royal adviser. 'It is more harmful for the realm to be burdened with a good king and bad counselors than with good ministers and a bad king.'[21] Polidoro, then, separates from his side those men noted, above all, for their 'viciousness, avariciousness, and ambition'. To some he gave posts away from the center of power – this is reminiscent of the early Habsburg's policy toward the great magnates. Others were sent to their estates, euphemistically *a reposar* – the case of Alba comes to mind. Finally, still others whose conduct had been plainly criminal were punished.

Having thus disposed of the dead and corrupt wood of the past the new king breathes freely and proceeds to surround himself with persons of proven worth, warning them that shortcomings in virtue will not be tolerated. The message is clear: the first care of a good prince is to find associates similarly endowed – an idea put across with equal forcefulness by Vitoria when the Dominican discusses the all-important question of war. Next, Polidoro sweeps the court clear of hangers-on (*truhanes, chocarreros,* and *vagabundos*), and reduces it to its bare functional essentials. *Ocio* is next banished from the court. 'Having reformed [my] house and court' – the Erasmian emphasis on self-reform is unmistakable – 'I proceeded to *reformar* my realms.' Ability and honesty were the twin conditions sought after by Polidoro as he filled the various governmental posts. 'The bishops I compelled to *residir ordinariamente en sus iglesias*', a phrase identical to that used by Charles in the *Instrucción* of 1543.[22]

With Polidoro, justice becomes a decidedly practical virtue embodied in the many changes he brings about at the bureaucratic and local levels. 'I reformed the laws, with the result that afterward few lawsuits lasted more than a year.' Lawyers who defended causes manifestly unjust were summarily punished, a suggestion of both the power of the ruler and his wisdom in ascertaining what is just and unjust, presumably despite the letter of the law. *Mercedes* were henceforth distributed on the basis of two criteria: some touched upon the republic's administration and were given solely with the *bien de la república* in mind; the others were personal rewards distributed by the king's largesse to those who had served him

21 *MC*, p. 169.   22 *MC*, pp. 169–70.

well and faithfully. Once again the reader receives the impression that behind the façade of moderation in Valdés' prince lies a boundless potential for despotic behavior. Indeed, the same sort of conviction is conveyed by the *Instrucción*: that in truth nothing can stop the ruler; that the only hope of the subject lies in his ruler's self-control. A case in point: Valdés informs us how Polidoro exercised clemency toward those who trespassed out of ignorance, and with what ruthlessness he punished those known to have erred through 'malice and with obstinacy'; there is implicit in that statement a tacit admission of a God-like quality to the prince: he *knows* that a lawyer's case is unjust, he *knows* that a man breaks the law out of ignorance, he *knows* that another acts with malicious intent. And in all cases the ruler is the authority who specifies the thickness of the disciplinary rod.

The catalog of reforms continues, further revealing the nature of the virtuous prince. Polidoro kept access to his person easy, particularly for the poor and those who came to complain against his ministers. He traveled extensively throughout his realm, always seeing to it that his presence yielded 'some fruit': building hospitals and bridges, giving away in marriage orphaned girls, rescinding burdensome taxes. He loved those who admonished and reprimanded him while loathing flatterers. Invariably he sought the advice of good and virtuous men of recognized devotion to the republic, and invariably chose their advice over his own. In short, and this is without exception both the beginning and the end of any mirror of princes in the Renaissance, Polidoro and those at court 'endeavored to live like Christians'.[23]

Guevara on the prince and his privado

Chronologically speaking, our next subject, Antonio de Guevara, belongs to the generation of Valdés and Vives. He was born in Treceño in or around the year 1480. At an early age he joined the court of Isabel and Ferdinand where his uncle was employed. In 1504 he became a Franciscan and through sketchy and incomplete information we know of the various posts which he occupied within the Order. The year 1520 finds Castile in turmoil and Guevara involved in various activities connected with the *Comunero* movement; his sympathies were clearly with the royalists and his correspondence fairly reeks with the contempt he felt for the rebels. Between 1525 and 1529 he was associated with the Inquisition's business among the Valencian Moriscos. He was also one of the company of theologians gathered to examine Erasmus' writings. In 1535, already for some time employed as imperial chronicler, Guevara joined Charles V and the

[23] *Ibid.*, pp. 171–3.

imperial expedition against Tunis. After extensive travels in Italy he returned to Spain becoming Bishop of Mondoñedo in 1537. He died in 1545.[24]

As a literary figure Antonio de Guevara was enormously popular in his own day, both in Spain and abroad. He is also unique among the authors surveyed here, Sepúlveda excepted, in that he had numerous detractors whom, in an age of unbounded trust in the wisdom of antiquity, he scandalized by his unhibited fabrication of dicta, events, and even personalities, to suit the immediate needs of his peremptory arguments and florid rhetoric. No question about it: Guevara was a charming literary rogue who cheerfully seems to have made his own the frame of mind of the pious medieval forgers – if it was not said or done, it should have been. But we are not concerned here with the virtues or shortcomings of his literary enterprises. Rather, we are interested in certain aspects of his political thought, concretely, in what he has to say about the virtues of the good prince and the competent counselor. Three of Guevara's works are of particular significance in this context: *El despertador de cortesanos* (Valladolid, 1539); *Una Década de Césares* (Valladolid, 1539); and *Vida del famosísimo Emperador Marco Aurelio* (Seville, 1532).[25]

In the *prólogo* to the *Despertador* the Bishop of Mondoñedo suggests that the prince's *privado* (favorite, minion, counselor) would do well to keep in mind ten *consejos*: do not disclose all your thoughts, flaunt all that you possess, take all that you desire, say all you know, nor do all you can; in what pertains to your own person, honor, possessions, and conscience, do not unduly trust fortune; beware, moreover my lord, of trusting others to come to your aid in time of need; refrain from meddling in another's affairs, and as for your own never force the hand of time; be sure to choose among your friends those who help you to remain standing rather than those who will succor you after you fall; be as heedful of your

---

[24] On Guevara's life, see R. Costes, 'Antonio de Guevara', *MLR*, XLVI(1951), pp. 253–5, and *Vida de Fray Antonio de Guevara* (Valladolid, 1960). See also Lino G. Canedo, 'Las obras de Fr. Antonio de Guevara. Ensayo de un catálogo completo de sus ediciones', *AIA*, VI(1946), pp. 441–603; M. R. Lida, 'Fray Antonio de Guevara. Edad media y siglo de oro español', *RFH*, VII(1945), pp. 347–88; J. A. Maravall, *Carlos V*; R. Menéndez Pidal, 'Fr. Antonio de Guevara y la idea imperial de Carlos V', *AIA*, VI(1946), pp. 331–8; F. M. Ros, 'Guevara auteur ascétique', *AIA*, VI(1946), pp. 338–404; A. Uribe, 'Guevara, inquisidor del Santo Oficio', *AIA*, VI(1946), pp. 185–281. For an extensive bibliography on Guevara, see his *Una Década de Césares*, ed. J. R. Jones (Chapel Hill, N.C., 1966), pp. 56–9.

[25] The following editions have been used here: *El despertador de cortesanos* (Paris: Michaud, n.d.), cited hereafter as *Despertador*; *Una Década de Césares*, ed. J. R. Jones (Chapel Hill, N.C., 1966), cited hereafter as *Década*; *Vida del famosísimo Emperador Marco Aurelio, con el Relox de príncipes* (Seville, 1532), cited hereafter as *Vida*.

soul as you are of your honor; do good and shun evil; in the matter of distributing favors and adjudicating offices see to it that good Christians are given priority over your friends; banish passion from your mind as you counsel for or against anything; never be uncompromising in your commands; if you wish not to err in your counsel, suffer failure, or fall from grace, honor those who tell the truth and detest the sycophant.[26]

Guevara warns his subject not to despise the book on account of its brevity, for the excellence of a work lies not with its size but in the quality of its contents. In addition, he makes a distinction between the courtier and the *privado*, one of import to us because unless forewarned it will not be difficult to confuse the one with the other. 'This work is divided into two parts. The first ten chapters deal with the manner in which the courtiers shall conduct themselves at court.' In other words, we have in the first part a true guide for the perfect courtier as he must be if he desires to triumph at court. 'The remaining eleven chapters treat of those matters that will enable the *privado* to remain in the prince's *privanza*. I am certain that the former [the courtier] will derive pleasure from reading it; as for the latter it will not be harmful for the *privado* to act upon its contents.'[27] This statement of purpose gives us a clear view of the distinction between the simple courtier, accessory and seemingly necessary – but not essential – adjunct to the regal apparatus, and the *privado*, indispensable cog in the royal machinery. In short, the courtier is a social cosmetic, the *privado* a political instrument. Needless to say, in what follows we shall be concerned with the latter.

As promised, Guevara returns, in the eleventh chapter, to the *privado*. He begins with some maxims of general advice. In the first place, the affairs of the court are by their very nature susceptible of arousing restlessness and passions. The *privado* must be wary of this and preserve his equanimity, remembering all the while that the disappointed petitioner will not blame the prince who denies the favor but curse the *privado* who fails to obtain it. It would be the height of folly and self-delusion for the man who enjoys the confidence of the ruler to believe that in doing many a good turn he will arrest gossip, envy, and rumors against his person. Do not trust, Guevara advises the favorite, either the favors that you have bestowed nor the friends you have made through them, for it is in the very nature of things that he who is not *privado* will be the *privado*'s enemy. Under the circumstances the first counsel of Guevara to the *privado* is to ignore the gossip and murmurs that will inevitably be raised against him. Living in an atmosphere where every hand is potentially raised against him the *privado* must refrain, for instance, from associating himself with any side should dissension break out in the kingdom. The

[26] *Despertador*, pp. 33–5.   [27] *Ibid.*, p. 37.

favorite who takes sides endangers his person, property, and position. A *privado*, on the other hand, who in his political behavior is neither *apasionado* nor *aficionado* will be feared and served by all. It is to be noted that Guevara approves of this behavior as best fitting the role of the *privado*. Fear is stressed but love is not mentioned.

Skepticism toward friendship and gratitude; carefully guarded impartiality; princely disregard of rumors as long as they remain exercises of the tongue and not actions; healthy realization that the very nature of his status breeds enemies; coolness under the incessant barbs of envy; evenness of temper, for only so will the favorite instill a salutary fear in his inevitable enemies while simultaneously being served by all – such is the general advice given by Guevara to the *privado* who wishes to survive.

Once the general tenor of the favorite's frame of mind has been agreed upon, the Bishop of Mondoñedo proceeds to the details of a good *privado*'s tenure and administration. In Chapter XII the twin subjects of how to expedite the public business and supervise the *privado*'s own subordinates are dealt with. To start with, Guevara warns, involvement in affairs which must be transacted at court is tantamount to navigating uncharted seas with faulty instruments – all this accompanied by an hilarious account of the misadventures faced by the unfortunate who must conduct his business at the courts of princes. The purpose is clear: the *privado* must transact the public affairs with dispatch – it is useful to remember in this and future contexts that the twin notorious characteristics of Renaissance bureaucracy were dilatoriness and venality. At this point, moreover, Guevara elects momentarily to leave the *privado* and with uncharacteristic brevity formulates some of the virtues indispensable to the good prince's baggage. He must be: easy to talk to, a good listener, cautious in his answers, clean in his living, and prompt in the conduct of business. In addition the ruler will not show himself inexorable to those who implore, sour to those who petition, ungrateful in what he gives, or careless toward those who counsel him. It is further essential that the prince consider not only what he gives but how much he gives and how he gives. The ruler who disregards these truths will find in the republic neither willingness to serve nor yearning to love. Returning once more to the *privado*, Guevara bids him to choose wisely when surrounding himself with subordinates, taking care that they be: free in their condition, meek in their deportment, accurate in their writing, skillful with their pen, and honest in their dealings. After all, the life and fate of the man who commands lie in the hands of those who serve him. Dissoluteness, insolence, dishonesty in the servant are often automatically attributed to the master as well by public opinion.

From the accursed vice of arrogance, says Guevara in the next chapter, the *privado* must guard himself. And nowhere is the Bishop more emphatic than when he inveighs against *soberbia*. From the heights of most vices men may descend; from the precipice of arrogance he is bound to fall. Nothing is more harmful in the princely courts than presumption because it seals the prince's disfavor and awakens the people's ire. A commonwealth may well put up with the *privado*'s surrender to the flesh, bad temper, gluttony, envy, or sloth; it will never tolerate an arrogant one. But what does this *soberbia* consist of? Aside from the meaning commonly associated with the word, in a *privado* arrogance means the refusal to accept criticism or to admit failure, unwillingness to share with others the prince's favor, and an insistence on receiving total trust from the prince and absolute obedience from the republic. In brief, Guevara warns the *privado* against becoming a tyrant. At the very least such conduct will excite the jealousy of the ruler and so seal the favorite's fate. If the *privado* truly wishes to succeed, the author suggests, let him give the appearance that he is serving and not commanding. The substance of power he will enjoy completely if only he takes pains to appear not to have it – *el camino mas seguro es que el privado se precie de ser criado y no el que el criado se alabe de ser privado*. Shrewdly appraising one of the cardinal rules of Spanish royal policy, Guevara encourages the favorite never to forget that it was the king who elevated him.

The remaining chapters are more remarkable for their ever-increasing barrage of classical quotations and examples – their authenticity seems to bother Guevara not in the least – than for their concern with the *privado*. In general the Bishop of Mondoñedo contents himself mostly with cataloging recommendations which he has already listed for the *privado*'s benefit: shun avariciousness and favor magnanimity, gladly agree to share the king's confidence with other *privados*, steer a course clear of the company of women of ill-repute, avoid gluttony. In particular a *privado* must not lie to his prince. 'A favorite who lies to his master after the latter has taken him into his confidence commits a supremely treasonable act.'[28]

On the whole Guevara's treatise seems to be more concerned with the manner in which the courtier and *privado* must deport themselves in the rather unsettling atmosphere of the court. Beyond a few remarkable insights into the duties of both *privado* and prince nothing substantive appears to have been added to an already well-stocked arsenal of advice on the qualities necessary to the prince and his closest counselor, the *privado*.

Una Década de Césares seems to have been Guevara's second book. It was published, together with other works, in Valladolid, 1539. As in the case of the *Despertador*, the *prólogo* to the *Década* – addressed to Charles V – makes very useful reading for our purposes because Guevara

28 *Ibid.*, p. 265.

condenses in its pages much of what he will extensively discourse upon concerning the attributes of princes in the ensuing ten biographical sketches. *Grandeza y nobleza* are attributes placed by the author at the head of the list. With his *grandeza* the prince strengthens the awesome quality of his authority. The possible deleterious effects of the sovereign's *grandeza* – it may deteriorate into arrogance – can be avoided by culti-vating a plainness of manner designed to allay the subjects' fears. The matter is neatly clinched in Guevara's picturesque style: *con la grandeza pongan espanto y con la llaneza quiten el miedo.* Accessibility and happy demeanor are equally important qualities in the prince; the rectitude of a ruler's justice inspires salutary fear, his cheerful demeanor instils love in his subjects. This quality of humanity, equally necessary to prince and counselor alike, is according to Guevara inseparable from good rule. On the grounds that familiarity breeds contempt, however, the prince is warned to prudently restrain this needed affability. Thus the ruler's good nature should not be so extreme that it encourages abuse, particularly in the *privado*. Harmonious balance, then, is the secret – a desirable means whose effectiveness will be enhanced if the prince remembers the selfless-ness which must be the distinguishing mark of his governance. 'All must live off the prince's *merced* as the prince himself must subsist on the commonwealth's love.'

Although Guevara does not mention it by name the next group of attributes proper to the prince fall within the general meaning of prudence. To start with the Bishop of Mondoñedo insists, the prince must have his political acumen honed to a fine edge because if he fails to foresee the totality of his goals he will never carry them completely to fruition. Before he undertakes anything the ruler must weigh all the factors involved. The reason, Guevara states, is simple: the mistakes of a private individual affect none but himself; the errors of the ruler bring grief to the entire republic. A logical outcome of these demands made upon the ruler is the imperative need that he be informed. Part and parcel of this necessary quality is that intuitive skill which enables him to ferret out and ignore the counsels of flatterers and rumor mongers. The next piece of advice offered by Guevara is a flat reversal of Machiavelli's own order of priorities: love your subjects and be beloved of them, for much greater is the effort of the man who labors through love than the toil of the man who merely serves. Love shall be repaid with love.

The art of ruling is of such nature that it cannot be practiced by one man in isolation. The prince, then, is forced by the very essence of his task to ask the aid of others – his *privados*. And in the selection of his close advisers the prince must display the utmost sagacity. Granting that in distributing *mercedes* the prince may at times show poor judgment, in the choice of *privados*, however, he cannot afford to err. Woe to the king – and his kingdom – who elevates an unworthy man to the position of *privado*! Endeavoring to summarize the various virtues sketched so far Guevara, in his own unabashed way, attaches to Plato's teachings the following six attributes of princes. To be a good ruler the sovereign must yield his heart to the republic, give *mercedes* to those who serve him, surrender his desires to the gods, unveil the secrets of his office to the *privado* alone, and devote his time to affairs of state. The prince who in this 'Platonic' manner shares his person among all will find, in return, that all are united in him.

All these recommendations, Guevara informs the Emperor, remain mere vanities unless the prince practices them, for there is no better way of persuading others to virtue than through one's own example. With this maxim in mind Guevara emphasizes that whoever wishes to convince a prince of virtue's convenience should appeal to the example of those rulers who in the past have practiced the prince's virtues: great deeds, moderation, magnanimity, sobriety, among them. By the same token nothing should convince a prince to steer clear of vices more effectively than the wretched behavior of some among his peers in the past; for even though a prince can do what he wishes and his authority is absolute and boundless, he must refrain from transferring that freedom from constraints into tyranny – a perfect instance, incidentally, of the pragmatic role attributed to history by the humanists. For these twin reasons, Guevara concludes, 'I have translated and gathered together the lives of ten Roman princes... The goal of such arduous task has been to say with my pen what my tongue could not express without inhibition.'[29] This is a variant of the theme which Guevara was to stress throughout his writings; one which is couched in the following terms in *Menosprecio de corte y alabanza de aldea*: 'What I have always counseled the Emperor my lord in my writings, preached to him in my sermons, and told him by word of mouth, is that he be always open to advice and intelligence (*aviso*); the former will profit him in what he must do, the latter in what he must avoid.'[30]

The Vida del famosísimo Emperador Marco Aurelio, con el Relox de príncipes

From the strict point of view of his contribution to political literature Guevara's first book (or books if we consider the *Relox de príncipes* a separate work),[31] *Vida del famosísimo Emperador Marco Aurelio, con el*

---

[29] *Década*, pp. 61–70.   [30] Edition of Clásicos Castellanos (Madrid, 1952), p. 19.
[31] For an explanation of this, see R. Foulché-Delbosc's introductory notes to his edition of Guevara's *Libro áureo*, in *RecH*, 169(June, 1929), pp. 1–319.

Relox de príncipes, is the most significant. The Bishop of Mondoñedo was – with Vives, Mexía, Valdés, and Ulzurrum – a partisan of the imperial idea. So much so, in fact, that Menéndez Pidal credited him (and not Gattinara) with the responsibility for having inspired Charles V's early political ideology. Maravall has further characterized the learned bishop's *ideario político* in the following terms: 'His imperial vision consists in gathering the politico-moral topics accumulated by European thought toward the end of the Middle Ages and presenting them as the mission to be carried out by the Emperor',[32] which is precisely the essence of the theme presented here as embodied in the catalog of princely virtues drawn from the medieval mirror literature.

In the general introduction Guevara sketches the broad outlines of the work's purpose.

This dial for princes is no hour-glass, sundial, or clepsydra. It is a clock of life. Other timepieces are useful for knowing the time of day or night; this one, however, teaches how each hour of our daily life must be occupied and in what manner our existence should be regulated. The ultimate purpose that justifies the possession of *reloxes* is the republic's regulation; but this particular *relox* teaches how to improve men's lives. For, after all, it is of little consequence that the *reloxes* be in harmony if men are entangled in strife and dissension.[33]

The central theme of the *Vida*, then, is not aimed at formulating a viable condition for the republic, but for man – and one man above all others, the prince. A thoroughgoing political moralist, Guevara wastes no time on institutions; his only preoccupation is the one concrete reality under the heavens from which everything else in the commonwealth flows: man himself. His logic is simple. If the members of the commonwealth learn to conduct their lives along paths of virtue the well-being of the republic itself is irrevocably assured, a commonplace but essential component of humanist ideology. In the process Guevara catalogs mankind's monumental shortcomings: the misery that is man's by inheritance, the fatal weakness of his will, his lasting servitude, the flaws in his nature. The Golden Age was noted not for its abundance in sages but for the dearth of evil men who tarnished its glint. Our own, the age of iron, owes its ferrous quality not to its lack of wise men but to its excess of malicious ones.[34] Man is assuredly cursed. Without rhyme or reason he forever strives to change fame into infamy, justice into injustice, rectitude into tyranny, truth into lie, and despising what he owns greedily dies for what belongs

[32] J. A. Maravall, 'La visión utópica del imperio de Carlos V en la España de su época', in *Homenaje*, pp. 42–58.
[33] *Vida, prólogo general*, fo. VI r.
[34] *Prólogo* to *Libro áureo*, in Foulché.

to others.[35] Seen without passion, man is nothing. Only two things of value he possesses: his reason, and the promise of eternal life. All else is vanity and a mirage; in all else man is inferior to the animals. The only hope for man is that he will exercise his only two attributes to temper the anguish which eternally agitates his existence. Only through reason and his God-given immortality may man hope to derive the strength needed to search for and attain to a state of harmony with himself and his fellows. Guevara's treatise, then, is an interminable litany of recommendations aimed at all men, but particularly at those who by reason of their authority occupy positions of responsibility within the commonwealth, to shun all vices and embrace all virtues. The catalog is a commonplace listing of the traditional Christian virtues: munificence, justice, prudence, honesty, moderation, steadfastness, incorruptibility, clemency, piety, sobriety, generosity, humility – all opposing their corresponding vices: greed, cruelty, venality, gluttony, arrogance, tyranny, injustice, dishonesty, con-cupiscence.[36]

It is against this background in which man's will endlessly battles against his corrupt nature that Guevara's prince emerges as the figure bearing the brunt of the conflict. Time and again the Bishop of Mon-doñedo warns his prince to view his office not as a desirable sinecure but as a burden, a position of supreme responsibility setting him painfully aside from other mortals. Moreover, the full significance attributed by the author to the role of the ruler, and so the qualities that he must possess to play that role best, makes complete sense only when taken within an even more total context: Guevara's vision of the origins, causes, and meaning of political authority.

There was a time, Guevara begins, when all men lived in peace and contented harmony – the Golden Age. Each man cared for his lands, derived sustenance from them, and raised his children. Because all lived off their own toil there was no strife.[37] But man is naturally a political animal, which means that he craves the company of other men.[38] And this fact alone was responsible for introducing in the midst of mankind the deadliest of *novedades*: the decision to live together in society. Evidently, in his understanding of man's social and political evolution Guevara differs little from Castrillo, including the latter's fear and hatred of *nove-dades*. On the other hand, whereas Castrillo paradigmatically speaks of the bees Guevara uses the example of the ants to thrust home the point that man must perforce function in association with the group. Again in agreement with Castrillo – and Erasmus – the Bishop feels that mere

[35] *RecH* (Foulché), pp. 120–21.
[36] This spirit permeates the entire work. See ch. xxxii, xxxix, xxxx.
[37] *Vida*, fo. xxxvii r.   [38] *Ibid.*, fo. xxxv v.

yearning for company was not the sole reason for the emergence of structured human gatherings. Fear was also a compelling motive. As the world's population increased, man's wits sharpened and tyrants appeared to oppress the poor, thieves to despoil the rich, troublemakers to disturb the meek, murderers to kill the peaceful, parasites to live off the toilers. This state of affairs compelled good men to band together for protection.[39] Alas, this turned out to be something quite different from the panacea sought after by mankind, for the company thus achieved served to compound the evil which it tried to ward off. 'Man's *compañía* engenders envy and the latter gives birth to discord.'[40] The ultimate result of this seemingly inevitable sequence of cause and effect, Guevara concludes, was the advent of political servitude among men. Its first exponent was the tyrant Nimrod. A sobering thought, the author warns, which should not be lost to princes and great lords: their lordship had its origin not among virtuous men but stems from the ambition of evil ones.[41] But this is not all. True, the immediate responsibility for the imposition of servitude on mankind lies with Nimrod; but the ultimate culprit is man. Man who forever dissatisfied with what he possesses yearns to navigate uncharted seas in search of additional bounty. According to Guevara, then, it is mankind which brought about its own ultimate political doom in the form of *servidumbre*.

So far the author has traced and accounted for the origin of political authority. But it all lies in the misty past. What is the situation prevailing in his own day? Guevara is under no illusions. Man's thirst for *novedades* has not slackened. If anything, it has increased, and with not foreseeable hope of reprieve. 'It is an undeniable truth that as long as we live in the flesh the yoke of servitude will never be lifted.'[42] The end result is a foregone conclusion. If under these conditions man is to survive at all he has to accept two things: political authority, and the rule of one man. On the second imperative Guevara is absolutely uncompromising. The discord which man's social nature and his search for company in his peers inevitably creates is part of a chain reaction that brings about war, tyranny, the corruption of the republic, and even the demise of the latter's inhabitants. To avoid this succession of misfortunes it is essential that in all manners of human association the many be ruled by one, for no republic will be well governed that is not ruled by one good man. True, Guevara concedes, there are those who disagree. It is clear, however, 'that men who do not want a king at the commonwealth's helm are but drones who while refusing to toil still gulp the beehive's honey'. No greater enemy has the republic than the man who wishes many to rule it.[43]

[39] *Ibid.*, *prólogo general*, fo. v r.   [40] *Ibid.*, fo. xxxv v.
[41] *Ibid.*, fo. xxxvii.   [42] *Ibid.*, fo. xxxvi r.   [43] *Ibid.*, fo., xxxv v.

Having in no uncertain terms expressed his preference for monarchy Guevara does not hesitate to go even further. It is clear, he states flatly, that once the greatest *novedad* in the history of mankind – for one to command and all others to obey – became an established fact there was no alternative but to understand the role of the ruler in divine terms. 'Princes are created by God's hand to rule. It is our obligation, therefore, to obey them in everything; there is no greater pestilence for the republic than to disobey the prince...Since political servitude came into the world by reason of sin the princes have their authority by divine commandment, for He said "by me the king rules and by me the prince administers justice".'[44] Guevara's departure from tradition is notable in that he does not even bother to compare the various alternative forms of government open to the men of the commonwealth. Monarchy is not only dogmatically affirmed to be the best. It is also the only sane one, a monarchy clearly defined as divine in origin and endowed with all the absolutist perquisites deemed indispensable by the political literature of the Baroque. With one exception, however, because no seventeenth-century publicist would seriously propose what the good Bishop rather blandly does not hesitate to assert: 'God wishes that one Emperor alone be monarch and lord of the world.'[45] For the most part Guevara's contemporaries did not share his boldness. We have heard Vitoria, for instance, categorically state that neither by divine, natural, or human law, is the Emperor lord of the whole world. And not even Sepúlveda, faced with imperatives far more universal than the medieval idea of empire ever produced, countenanced his king's claims to sovereignty over the New World in those terms. It would not do, on the other hand, to overestimate Guevara's emphasis on the significance of the imperial dignity, for the Bishop of Mondoñedo quite openly acknowledges also the rightful existence of princes independently ruling their own realms. Instead, it would be closer to the mark to interpret Guevara's statements as exemplifying Castile's peculiar political position and the enthusiasm it elicited in some intellectual quarters during the halcyon days immediately following the crushing of the *Comuneros*. If we behold Guevara's politics within this particular context it is certainly no coincidence that throughout his *Vida* the author should have sketched a portrait of the prince alternately composed of general reflections on princely behavior and concrete recommendations made for and by an emperor, Marcus Aurelius.

Guevara, moreover, does not rest content with the conclusion that monarchy is the form of government ordered by God. Additionally reflecting on the subject he judges that over and beyond the divine will lie causes of a purely natural character which conclusively prove that it is

[44] *Ibid.*, fo. xxxviii v.   [45] *Ibid.*, fo. xxxiv v.

essential in the commonwealth for one to command and the rest to obey –
tan antigua novedad. The first reason, explains the author, is that in any
mixture of natural origin one of the elements is invariably of greater
weight than all the rest put together. A second one derives from the
relationship that body and soul bear to each other: when in harmony the
soul rules as mistress and the body obeys as *siervo.* In addition, it is but
natural that wise men should lord it over all others, for it would be monstrous if those of simple mind were to rule the commonwealth. Finally, it
is merely just that so many men who are more bestial than the beasts
themselves should be ruled by men of wisdom.[46]

In a passage purporting to embody Plutarch's advice to Trajan, Guevara,
with unquestioned imagination and skill, summarizes the views just outlined on the origin and nature of political authority, and sketches the
personality of the good prince, this last the very subject which will occupy
us immediately below.

You and your empire are but a mystic body after the fashion of the human
body...the head...is the prince who has authority in all things. The eyes...are
the republic's good men whose example we follow. The ears...are the subjects
who do as we command. The tongue...are the sages from whom we hear laws
and doctrines. The hairs on the head...are the injured who demand redress of
the king. The hands and the arms are the nobles who oppose the enemy. The
feet are the husbandmen who feed all others. The bones...are the learned men
who bear the republic's burden. The hearts...are the *privados* who advise in
the secret council. The throat...is the love of the king and the realm which
make the republic what it is...In the same manner as the head rises above all
other parts of the body so the authority of the king is greater than that of all
other members, for whereas only the prince may command all others must
obey...If it were up to men to create princes they would also have the power
to depose them. On the other hand, if it is true – and it is – that God alone
makes the prince it also follows, in my view, that only God can deprive him of
his authority...Just as the kingdom has its beginning in the king so does the
king have his beginning in the kingdom...because the laws are given by the
king to the kingdom and not by the kingdom to the king. Largesse and gifts
flow from the king into the realm; they do not come into the king from the
kingdom. To the king's majesty alone belongs to order and command; it is the
republic's province to *autorizar* and obey...the king who is not beloved of his
kingdom cannot live in peace, and the kingdom which is not feared by its king
cannot be well governed. I say that the well-being of both king and realm is
assured if the king surrounds himself with good men and banishes the wicked
from his presence...the king must truly love his kingdom...he must treat his
subjects as he would his own children...he need be just in his commands...
defend his subjects...hold the republic in peace.[47]

[46] *Ibid.*, fo. xxxiv v.   [47] *Ibid.*, fo. xliii v–fo. xliv r.

As Guevara sees it, then, everything hinges on the prince. His ideal monarchy is not contractual but absolute. His ruler makes the law and administers justice. He governs responsible only to God. This, of course, makes the task all the more difficult, for the greater the power the more telling the responsibility and the more immediate the threat of tyranny. The awesome nature of the king's responsibility lies in that the shepherd shall eventually render detailed account of his management to the supreme master of the flock. And so, Guevara concludes, a prince cannot be like other men.

If we were to ask a prince born, raised, and living like other men although he rules all other men, for what purpose God gave him the power to command; and if he were to answer that he only knows that he was born into that power, then we could easily judge how unworthy that king would be. Because unless a man knows beforehand what justice is he will be manifestly incapable of administering it. . .when [God] decided to create kings and lords he did so on condition that they would be better than other men. . .if a lord is to be obeyed by all in all it is imperative that he be the first to give example.⁴⁸

And in what does that supreme goodness indispensable to the prince consist? Clearly Guevara's *Vida* is entirely devoted to answering that question. The ultimate aim, moreover, is directed toward Charles V, the supreme arbiter of man's destinies in Guevara's own age. In this manner the Bishop of Mondoñedo creates what Maravall has called the utopia of the good shepherd. *Fiet unum ovile* is the motto and Charles shall be the supreme and peerless shepherd. The most immediate matter in hand, however, is to define the nature of the prince's task within the commonwealth.

I wish to say to you all, oh princes and great lords, a word about what the good lord and ruler shall do in the republic. A prince from whose mouth nothing but the truth flows, who is openhanded with *mercedes*, whose ears are closed to lies and heart open to clemency, is blessed. . .He who is true prince has made you ruler of the world so that you shall be a nemesis to heretics, a father to orphans, a friend to sages. . .a headsman to tyrants, a scourge to the wicked, a shield to the church, a warden to the republic. Above all you are the executor of justice; a task which you shall begin first in your own house and person, for inequality may be tolerated in all things except justice which shall be the same in the prince as in the commonwealth.⁴⁹

To that end the prince must have an intimate knowledge of the commonwealth he rules.

As head of the public body it behooves the prince to know everything. . .for it can hardly be expected that the prince will rule well his kingdom if his

⁴⁸ *Ibid.*, fo. xli r–fo. xlii v.   ⁴⁹ *Ibid.*, fo. xlii v–fo. xliii v.

acquaintance with it is not complete. It is necessary that the prince know the good in order that he may honor them...the wicked so as to admonish them... the wise to seek their counsel...the clever to encourage them into teaching others...the poor to help them...the presumptuous and malicious to humiliate them...the peaceful to guard their rest...the faithful servitors to recompense them...the murmurers to discount their whispers...the truthful to love them.[50]

Guevara dedicates an entire chapter (XX, Book I) to show how, among all men, the prince must more than anyone else depend on God, trust in God, pattern his life after God, draw his power from God, and finally, render account to Him. The essence of these obligations the Bishop of Mondoñedo subsumes under a number of reasons which are said to compel the ruler to be virtuous.

First, princes must fear, honor, and serve God, for He is their only superior... Second, princes must be better Christians than other men because they enjoy supreme authority...Third...When princes do not fear God and His commandments their realms and subjects are invariably bad Christians.[51]

Clearly, not every man is fit to be prince. In Chapter XXI (Book I) Guevara attributes to an ancient philosopher ten laws or conditions which a commonwealth must see to it the ruler fulfills before he is elevated to the republic's supreme magistrature. No one, counsels the philosopher, should be elected to the post unless he be at least forty years of age. This is the optimum age: neither too young to be inexperienced nor too old to successfully bear the burden of authority. If a man is not universally acknowledged as a good man he should not be elected prince, for anyone who in the eyes of at least some of his subjects is held to be wicked will not be obeyed. Since no greater pestilence can engulf the commonwealth than an ignorant ruler lacking in prudence, no one should be elected who is not a learned man. The prince-elect must have experience in war, at least of ten years' standing. After all, only he who has experienced the travails of war at first hand can comprehend the need to preserve peace. No man noted for his cruelty must be permitted to govern, for cruelty inevitably leads to tyranny. The prince must not break the commonwealth's ancient laws; there is nothing worse than the introduction of new laws and the violation of time-honored customs. The supreme magistrate ought to be worshipful of the gods, for a man who lacks reverence toward them cannot possibly dispense justice. Finally, if a prince is elected by the commonwealth it must be on condition that he be content with the realm as it is given to him and refrain from undertaking wars to enlarge it.[52]

Perhaps the single item pertaining to the art of ruling on which Guevara lavishes the most careful attention is justice and its executors, the *ministros*

[50] *Ibid.*, fo. xlv.   [51] *Ibid.*, fo. xxii r–fo. xxiii v.   [52] *Ibid.*, fo. xxv.

de justicia. Thus Chapters I to XI of Book III are largely concerned with justice and those to whom its administration should be entrusted. The teachings of all men of worth from poets to princes, Guevara begins, seek to impress upon us how indispensable justice is to the life of the republic. A commonwealth devoid of justice is prey to the same corruption which devours a soulless body. To say that a people can survive without justice is to argue that fish can live out of the water.[53] Having established the need for justice on unquestionable grounds Guevara proposes first to find out *que cosa es justicia.* Accordingly, he proposes the following traits essential to the correct dispensing of justice. 'The task of good judges is to defend the common weal, protect the innocent, bear with the ignorant, admonish the guilty, honor the virtuous, aid the orphans, help the poor, restrain the greedy, humble the ambitious; finally, each must be given according to his deserts and those who unjustly own must be dispossessed forthwith.'[54] And what is to be said of those entrusted with the administration of justice? First the prince, the highest of earthly judges:

To give added credibility to the ruler's justice it is imperative that the prince's own private life be spotless because it is impossible to expect justice from a man incapable of setting his own house in order, much less when that man is responsible for an entire commonwealth...The entire quality of justice stands or falls on the prince's personal honesty, the care he lavishes on his own affairs, the zeal he displays toward his republic, and the sensitivity of his conscience.[55]

Above all, the prince shall forever bear in mind that whereas it is within his power to distribute *mercedes* as he sees fit God remains the only absolute lord of justice. In this respect alone the prince is but a trustee, an administrator. Justice, then, is not a *merced* to be capriciously given or withheld and must not be treated as such. 'Princes in all things are called lords except in what pertains to justice, for in this respect they are but ministers.'[56] Great as the prince's authority in matters of justice is, however, he cannot properly administer it without the aid of subordinates – his own ministers of justice. It follows that the said *ministros* must be faithful reflections of the prince as the latter is himself but an image of God. In consequence, Guevara earnestly entreats the prince to choose for the post only the best among men.

We ask of the princes that they provide the commonwealth with good ministers of justice...of what advantage is it to the republic that the prince be honest if the judge who administers his justice is dissolute...a liar...a drunk...a butcher...a thief...lazy and vicious?...it is not enough for the princes to be

[53] *Ibid.*, fo. cxxxvi v.   [54] *Ibid.*, fo. cxxxvi r.
[55] *Ibid.*, fo. cxxxvii v.   [56] *Ibid.*, fo. cxxxviii.

just, they are also obliged to *hacer justicia*...If the princes themselves do not want or are not able to rule the republic we beg of them to search for good ministers of justice...It is not a matter of voluntary choice; it is rather an essential question that the ministers of justice be very judicious, very stable, and very honest...for good judges must patiently listen to others and afterward sentence justly...If a judge is to feel that he in truth is the republic's caretaker it is not enough that he be peerless in his administration of justice; the entire republic must also be cognizant of that fact, for then none will dare to request unseemly things of him...Judges must not be avaricious, for greed and justice are hardly compatible. Those whose task it is to rule peoples or judge lawsuits must take care not to be corrupted by gifts.[57]

Although it is in the all-important context of justice that the figure of Guevara's prince emerges in its most accomplished form, the Bishop of Mondoñedo speaks also at length on the manner in which the prince must expedite the *negocio* of war and peace (Book III, Chapter XII). Following in the footsteps of contemporary Erasmianism, Guevara does not hesitate to throw the weight of his authority on the side of peace. Doubtless, he grants, a prince who is magnanimous, sober, honest, and meek truly deserves to be loved by all. But if in addition he preserves the republic in peace such a prince truly deserves that his subjects pray to God for his life. For without peace, continues the author, none may enjoy his goods, eat without alarm, sleep restfully, travel without fear, or trust his neighbor. It is unconditionally true, grants Guevara, that the prince should cleanse the realm of thieves, blasphemers, gamblers, and other undesirables. 'But, I ask, of what good is it that the ruler banish all manner of vice from the commonwealth if, on the other hand, he keeps the republic submerged in war? For the truth of the matter remains that in time of war princes have the time neither to uproot vice nor to punish the vicious.'[58]

Guevara convincingly makes his own the Christian humanist argument that if only the prince fully understood what calamities war brings to his realm he would undoubtedly desist from engaging in discord. And it is primarily up to the prince's advisers to make their master realize the truth of that statement. 'Those who counsel their princes to search for peace, to love peace, and to preserve peace, must be listened to, loved, and believed. Whoever encourages a prince to undertake war on a flimsy pretext, on the other hand, is either a wrathful man or he lacks a con-science.'[59] Borrowing a page, although not their style or systematic method of argumentation, from his Neoscholastic countrymen, Guevara com-minates the prince who is about to embark upon a warlike enterprise first to consult with God and heed his counselors' views on its propriety. 'Matters pertaining to war must be examined with a great deal of prudence

[57] *Ibid.*, fo. CXLIV–fo. CXLV.   [58] *Ibid.*, fo. CLI r.   [59] *Ibid.*

. ...General questions concerning his governance the prince may safely discuss with his *privado* alone but the facts of war he must investigate with God's aid, for otherwise his cause will never be victorious.'[60] On the question of responsibility Guevara does not mince words. He urges those whose business it is to decide on war or peace to bear in mind that if an unjust war is declared the onus of its harm rests squarely on their consciences. So dearly must men love peace, declares the Bishop, that whoever has voting privileges in the council of war should undergo the same sort of self-examination demanded of the priest who is about to say Mass. Guevara is more than willing to understand the prince's position. After all, he is a man and as such subject to human weaknesses – the desire to revenge an injury, for example. But it is precisely to counterbalance the imperfections of the ruler's character that his advisers exist. The latter, the prudent men who compose the prince's council, must be precisely the ones who will mitigate the prince's ire and defuse the violence of his passion.[61]

Insofar as the reasons for declaring and waging a war are concerned Guevara is openly skeptical. There is no war, he declares, so just that it can absolutely erase all reservations in the prince's conscience about its righteousness. The situation is even more patently clear-cut when the reasons themselves are of dubious justice. Thus, continues the author, if the prince initiates war merely to augment his own greatness he is chasing after a hopeless dream, for more often than not the prince comes out of it with greater losses than gains. If, on the other hand, the war is begun to avenge an injury the results are equally disastrous: all too often those who enter into discord with one injury emerge from it with many. Equally useless is a war waged by a prince who merely seeks to win honor because the fortunes of war are too unpredictable to trust our honor, possessions, and life to their doubtful favor. Finally, if the goal of the warlike ruler is to leave a permanent imprint in ages to come let him remember this lesson clearly taught by history: far more numerous are the rulers who earned infamy from their wars than the princes who came back from the battlefield with an enhanced reputation. In brief, Guevara concludes, let a prince be content with the enjoyment he can find in his land without casting covetous eyes on the precarious pleasures he may derive from owning his neighbors'.[62]

Having in the preceding pages reviewed some of Guevara's salient opinions on the republic, the prince and his virtues, it is not difficult to agree with Maravall's conclusion that 'Guevara sought to insert into an idealized portrait of the Emperor and articulate into a utopian vision the whole of the *loci communes* which since the time of Petrarch have been

[60] *Ibid.*, fo. CLII v. [61] *Ibid.* [62] *Ibid.*, fo. CLII.

part and parcel of moralizing and Senequist humanism.'[63] Perhaps no-where is this better illustrated than at the end of the *Libro áureo* when Marcus Aurelius, in his deathbed, gives his son Commodus a written list of princely 'dos' and 'don'ts'. They are the brief and complete expression of Guevara's ideal prince, his *espejo* and *relox*. They are a short *vade mecum* with which fittingly to close this study of Guevara's political ideas.

I never elevated the rich tyrant nor abhorred the just poor. I never denied justice to the poor for being poor nor forgave the rich because of his wealth. I never recompensed solely on the grounds of affection nor punished merely because of my wrathful mood. I never left evil without punishment nor good without reward. I never applied clear justice to others while inflicting vague standards on myself. I never denied justice to those who requested it nor mercy to him who deserved it. I never punished while irate nor promised favors when in a happy mood. I never grew careless in favorable times nor desperate in adversity. I never did evil through malice nor committed villany through avarice. I never welcomed flatterers nor listened to rumor mongers. I always endeavored to be loved by the good and feared by the wicked. Finally, I favored the poor who were weak and was in turn favored by the gods who were mighty.[64]

The life and times of Furió Ceriol

In the introduction to this monograph I spoke of the two constitutional crises which were responsible for molding the course of Spanish Renaissance political thought. At the very close of our period a third crisis, more subtle and enduring, which had struggled in vain to assert itself since the early years of the Emperor's reign began to take the upper hand. Even though its existence, pertinence, and influence on the course of Spanish history are undeniable, its contours remain still imperfectly delineated. It was a crisis of the mind, of the spirit, and of the soul. Without attempting to go into the dangerously polemical topic of the two Spains, the fact remains that in its intensity and life-span the crisis – at the time by no means confined to Spain alone – affected Spanish life with particular virulence, an admission which in no way prejudices my view that to use historical hindsight to elevate this fact to the realm of axiomatic truth which explains all of Spain's real or imaginary difficulties since cannot be justified. To insist on understanding Spanish history in the context of an eternal battlefield where 'native' and 'foreign' values are endlessly pitted against one another and labeling the phenomenon as peculiarly Spanish is to forget that as long ago as the Peloponnesian War Thucydides discovered that the struggle between the old and the new is the stuff of

[63] Maravall, 'La visión utópica', p. 49.   [64] *RecH* (Foulché), p. 192.

history and rooted in man's very nature. In short, the age of Trent, in Spain as elsewhere, marked the beginning of the end for an epoch noted for its openness and plasticity. In Spain the future was to be particularly bleak, for the crisis of the spirit would shortly be followed by a military, political, and economic one. A combination of circumstances which could not but profoundly affect the mood of the Spanish intelligentsia. It is at the beginning of this period that Furió Ceriol writes his *El concejo* – a book which combines the best in the Erasmian tradition with the imperatives of the future.

In the words of Bataillon, 'between 1556, the year of Charles' retreat to Yuste, and 1563, the year marking the close of the Council of Trent, Spain's spiritual climate changed rapidly and profoundly'. This change, all agree, was not for the better. On the contrary, the flexibility and 'openness' of the Carolinian period gave way to the rigidity, progressive intolerance, and inward retrenchment of spiritual and intellectual life commonly associated with the age of Philip II. On the whole, the phenomenon was a European malady best represented outwardly by the comparative eclipse of Lutheranism as a decisive spiritual and political force in European affairs, the rise of militant Calvinism, on the one hand, and the uncompromising stance of a rejuvenated Tridentine Catholicism, on the other. How important the influence of Geneva's missionary work was to be in unleashing the tide of Spanish orthodox reaction, ready since the early 1520s to do battle with suspect Erasmianism, is recognized by Bataillon. 'A decisive circumstance in the transformation suffered by Spain toward 1558 was the attraction exercised by Geneva and the use of the Genevan presses for evangelical propaganda in Spain. For the first time Spanish Illuminism was seen as the close associate of international Protestantism.'[65]

The circumstance in question was the discovery, toward the end of 1557 in Seville and at the beginning of 1558 in Valladolid, of heterodox communities which although branded as Lutheran at the time appear in reality to have been groups of *alumbrados* influenced by Protestant ideas. The Inquisition, headed since 1547 by the unsavory Fernando de Valdés, acted swiftly and with unprecedented severity. The leaders were tried by the Inquisition and executed or died in prison. Among them were Constantino Ponce de la Fuente, canon of Seville and Charles V's former confessor; Juan Ponce de León, a distinguished member of Seville's aristocracy; Agustín Cazalla, canon of Salamanca and court chaplain; Domingo de Rojas, a member of the influential Dominican Convento de San Esteban; and Antonio de Herrezuela, a lawyer from Toro. The Suprema's offensive did not stop here. Since the advent of Erasmianism it

---

[65] *EE*, pp. 199, 704.

had waged relentless war against anything it considered a deviation from the strictest orthodoxy. During the years before 1558, however, its heavy hand had been stayed by the liberal influence of men like Alonso Fonseca, Archbishop of Toledo, and the Inquisitor General, Alonso Manrique, both open supporters of Erasmus. After 1558 the climate and the personalities changed radically; neither the Inquisitor General Valdés nor his theological adviser, Melchor Cano, were disposed toward leniency. Carranza was arrested in August, 1559, and in succeeding years many other notable members of Spain's intelligentsia came, in varying degrees, under Inquisitorial scrutiny: Fray Luis de Granada, Francisco de Borja, Juan de Ávila, Sánchez de Brozas, Alonso Gudiel, Fray Luis de León, and Juan de Mariana. The case of the last four, however, proves something that is often forgotten: the Suprema was not an irresistible juggernaut from whose clutches escape was impossible; on the contrary, it was not uncommon for the individual pitted against the institution to emerge ultimately victorious – especially when the Inquisition was headed by stern but fair-minded men like Gaspar de Quiroga. Still, on the whole, there is no denying that the activities of the Tribunal had a severely deleterious effect on the intellectual and spiritual climate of Spain. Far more devastating than the Inquisition's actual measures against individuals was its capacity to create an atmosphere of uncertainty and mistrust among those whom it never touched; the awareness of its ever-present vigilance was sufficient to inhibit free examination of the day's important issues, particularly in the Scriptural field. 'The Spanish Church of the Counter-Reformation proved incapable of assimilating creative speculation in these [Biblical and theological] fields and could only tolerate a barren and lengthy repetition of old knowledge, with the result that original thought was confined to security and the Counter-Reformation lost one of its most promising assets.'[66] As fitting corollary to persecution the Inquisitor General Valdés published, 1559, a new Index of prohibited books which considerably enlarged its predecessor of 1551.

It would be wrong to place the entire responsibility for the demise of toleration in Spain on the shoulders of the Inquisition and the intransigent supporters of orthodoxy. It must be shared by the secular authorities. Upon hearing of the events in Seville and Valladolid, Charles advised his daughter Juana, acting as Regent in her brother's absence (away in Brussels), to act with inflexible rigor. One result of this counsel may have been the *pragmática* of September 1558. Since the spiritual troubles of Castile were attributed to foreign influence it was decided to isolate the patient from the source of contagion. The import of foreign books was prohibited and those printed in Spain could be published only after

66 J. Lynch, *Spain Under the Habsburgs* (2 vols., Oxford, 1964), I, p. 248.

permission had been granted by the authorities. During the same month the Emperor died. In August of the following year, 1559, a few months after concluding the Peace of Cateau–Cambrésis with France, Philip II left his dominions in Flanders. Shortly after his arrival in Castile another *pragmática* was issued (November, 1559) forbidding Spaniards to study abroad. As in the case of the Inquisition's activities the resolutions embodied in both *pragmáticas* were far more formidable on paper than they were in reality; Spaniards did not stop going abroad, and foreign books were shipped to America in Spanish ships. Nevertheless, the intention to isolate Spain from the contagion of foreign – and therefore dangerous – influences was as clear in the case of the secular power as it was in that of the religious authorities.

The break with the past, however, could not be complete. In the political field, for example, Cateau–Cambrésis underlined what Augsburg had already suggested: the demise of Charles' imperial conception and the emergence of a monarchy headed by a thoroughly Spanish king, based on Spanish sources, and directed toward Spanish goals – *un rey, un imperio, una espada*. Even so, the history of Philip II's reign was to prove that the commitments inherited from the imperial age could not be easily shrugged off. In the same vein, the year (1559) center of that period (1556–1563) witnessing the third and final crisis with the early phase of which we are concerned in this study, the crisis of Spain's intellectual and spiritual life, also saw the publication (Antwerp, 1559) of *El concejo y consejeros del príncipe*, a political treatise written by a man whose credentials included that Erasmian background now so sharply under attack and the enmity of the Inquisition, from which he had only been saved by the intervention of his royal patrons.

Little is known, beyond the broadest outlines, of the life of Fadrique Furió Ceriol. He was born in Valencia, probably in 1527, of noble parents. After an initial course of studies at the University of Valencia, Furió, like his countryman Vives before him, went to Paris where he studied under Omar Talon and Peter Ramus. Shortly afterward we find him with the imperial army besieging Metz (1552). Around 1553 he went, again following Vives' footsteps, to the Univeristy of Louvain where he became embroiled with Jean de Bononia, the Rector of the University, on the question of translating the Bible into the vernacular. It was around this time that Furió became attached to Prince Philip's court – on the initiative, it seems, of the Emperor. Sometime after the publication of *El concejo* he began his extensive travels through Europe, presumably in the service of Philip II. He died in 1592.[67]

[67] For further details on Furió's life and works see the following. Nicolás Antonio, I, p. 363; M. Bataillon, *EE*, pp. 552–4, 630–31, *passim*; J. Bécker, *La tradición*

It is in the context of his exchange with Bononia that Furió entered the lists in the virulent controversies which engaged the theologians of Louvain and the partisans and followers of Erasmus. The issues at stake and under discussion are, strictly speaking, beyond the province of this book. They are of some interest to us, however, because they reveal the Erasmian inclinations of Furió Ceriol. The central theme of *Bononia* (Furió published his conclusions in Basel, in 1556, under a title which is the name of his chief opponent at Louvain) is simple. Against the judgment of the supporters of the traditionalist position who argued that to offer the sacred writings of the faith in the vernacular amounted to inviting dangerous speculations by the untutored vulgar, the author reasons that the truths of Christianity are plain and evident enough to be grasped by all. Furió's position on this delicate issue seems to have been shared by other Spaniards both in Louvain and in Spain itself. In the end, however, orthodoxy once more won the day and the Bible remained the exclusive preserve of professional theologians. It is not through *Bononia*, then, that Furió came to occupy an important part in the intellectual history of Renaissance Spain. His claim to fame rests with a treatise conceived as part of a never completed larger work: the *El concejo y consejeros del príncipe*

El concejo y consejeros del príncipe: *the prince*

Seemingly determined to waste no time on useless preliminaries Furió goes to the heart of the matter from the start. A prince, he writes in a prologue addressed to Philip II, is a composite of almost two persons. One of them is the result of nature's own work insofar as through it he shares the same attributes with other men. The second is unique to the prince; it is a 'gift of fortune and favor from heaven' created to rule and to look after the public well-being, which is the reason we call it public person.[68]

política española (Madrid, 1896); D. W. Bleznick, 'Los conceptos políticos de Furió Ceriol', *REP*, 149(1966), pp. 25–45, and *Fadrique Furió Ceriol, Political Thinker of Sixteenth-Century Spain* (Unpublished dissertation. Columbia University, 1954); J. M. Castro y Calvo, *El arte de gobernar en las obras de don Juan Manuel* (Barcelona, 1945); J. A. Maravall, *La philosophie politique espagnole au XVIIe. siècle*, trans. L. Cazes and P. Mesnard (Paris, 1955), *passim*; J. M. Semprún Gurrea, 'Fadrique Furió Ceriol, consejero de príncipes y príncipe de consejeros', *Cruz y Raya*, 22(1935), pp. 9–89; C. Viñas Mey, 'Doctrinas políticas y penales de Furió Ceriol', *Revista de Ciencias Jurídicas y Sociales*, IV(1921), pp. 67–83.

[68] Fadrique Furió Ceriol, *El concejo y consejeros del príncipe* (Antwerp, 1559), fo. 1 r; cited hereafter as *Concejo*. There is a modern edition of three of Furió's works by D. Seville Andrés, *El concejo y consejeros del príncipe y otras obras* (Valencia, 1952). The folios of the *prólogo* are not numbered. For referential purposes I have assigned them Roman numerals.

After a fashion, then, it is possible to distinguish the prince 'almost' from two distinct points of view: as a ruler and as a man. As a man the prince is endowed with both body and soul, and the better the former is taken care of the more efficiently it will serve the latter. As for the soul, it should be carefully instructed in all those arts essential to the prince in his role as ruler. Furió leaves no room for ambiguity on this issue; a prince who lacks the adequate instruments – the *artes de governar* – is doomed to hopeless failure in anything he undertakes in the commonwealth's behalf.[69] That explains, continues the author, why so many excellent men have always striven with all their might to instill in the prince the art of ruling, for on the prince's adequate or faulty education hangs the welfare and life of human society.[70]

At this point Furió confesses his intention to abandon the beaten path, a pledge not unlike Machiavelli's under similar circumstances. Those men who heretofore have sought to teach the prince, he explains, have gone about it in the wrong manner. Such teachers, it is true, correctly discovered the twofold nature of the prince's personality; but in the actual matter of their teachings they hopelessly confused the two components of that personality. According to the humanist the source of that misunderstanding has been the failure of the royal preceptors to grasp a simple truth: all disciplines (*artes*) are like the links of a chain; each has its boundaries and preserves its own individuality while simultaneously remaining a part of the larger whole. Thus of necessity those disciplines must be taught independently, as self-contained entities. At the same time it happens that in the course of human affairs sooner or later they must all come together, an incontrovertible truth which few understand and fewer still have ever put into practice.[71] We see how often, explains Furió, the prince is taught such subjects as theology, natural and moral philosophy, law, mathematics, and medicine, among others. But in this his teachers are at fault because when they so instruct the prince they solely aim at his human side, neglecting to emphasize the relevance of those disciplines to the ruler part of his personality.[72]

Granted, then, that the education of princes, a most important landmark in the development of a sound ruler, has suffered in the past from misinterpretations as to the correct fashion in which it should be conducted. Does Furió have a better way? Most definitely, and this is precisely what he means when he vows to tread paths hitherto left virgin by previous educators. To educate a prince as one would an ordinary sage is not enough, for the royal pupil is more than a sage; he is a ruler and the ruler needs a kind of expertise which cannot be found in treatises devoted

[69] *Concejo*, fo. II r.   [70] *Ibid.*
[71] *Ibid.*, fo. III v.   [72] *Ibid.*, fo. III.

solely to imparting abstract knowledge. It is that expertise, the body of knowledge enabling the prince to meet the demands of praxis, which Furió stresses and undertakes to explain for the benefit of the man in whose hands lies the commonwealth's fate. According to the humanist, then, the education (*institución*) of the prince – *qua* ruler – consists in giving him a body of maxims or rules (*regla, precetos o avisos*) of such quality and breadth that will both teach and enable him to be a good prince.[73] On the surface the solution is simple; but appearances are deceptive. And Furió understands it to be so.

These words, 'good prince', are comprehended correctly by very few. As a result we read many explanations on the subject; all sound in appearance but vain and out of context in reality. Because the authors invariably think that a good prince is a man who is good, and vice versa. In truth I must agree that the most important piece in the princely harness is goodness. On the other hand, one cannot explain singularly skillful rule merely in terms of goodness understood in the sense applicable to ordinary affairs. In affairs of government a very different terminology prevails. The kind used when we speak of a good diamond, a good horse, a good painter, a good pilot, a good physician. We say, for instance, that a musician is good when he is perfectly acquainted with his profession, and this regardless of whether he personally is a knave.[74]

In this fashion, the author proceeds, the good prince is defined as he who both knows his job perfectly and uses this knowledge shrewdly and prudently. The good ruler knows, through industrious prudence, how to preserve himself and his subjects from harm, expand his dominions, and triumph over his enemies under any and all circumstances – a man fully capable of rising up to the demands of reality.

There can be little doubt that when Furió's formulation of the good prince is viewed against the background which on the same subject has so far been sketched in this and preceding chapters, we find ourselves in the presence of a new conception of the prince, or at the very least a much expanded one. How this came to happen is not easy to trace in detail. Surely, the influence of Machiavelli cannot be discounted. The greatest share of the responsibility, however, should unquestionably go to the very circumstances which gave birth to the Florentine's role as revolutionary teacher of princes. As far as the Spanish theorists here surveyed are concerned Valdés, Vives, and Guevara cling to the old panacea that if we create a good man first the good prince will inevitably follow. Within the formalistic framework of Neoscholasticism we saw how Vitoria tried to establish some sort of independence for the prince *qua* governor through a separation of the natural and supernatural orders – and how he failed.

[73] *Ibid.*, fo. III r.   [74] *Ibid.*, fo. III r–IV v.

Sepúlveda, and with him we are already entering the second half of the century, without doubt remains a staunch partisan of the prince's Christian endowment. But his willingness (more or less manipulated by circumstances) to deal with a pragmatic situation allowing little room for moralizing fantasy is a fact which cannot be discounted when interpreting some among his more ruthlessly realistic utterances. It is only with the advent of Furió Ceriol that we meet an unprecedented, in that it is explicitly admitted, recognition of an inescapable dichotomy in the nature of any ruler. It remains for us to see how this dichotomy affects – or better still, conditions – Furió's political ideas, for they are unquestionably based on the figure of the prince and the men who surround him.

The subject of counselors is introduced with rare skill by the author while still fully occupied with the ruler's personality, an early indication of how inseparable the prince and his advisers are in Furió's scheme. Summarizing what he has so far said on the ruler's goodness Furió concludes that 'good is the prince who knows how to rely on his own counsel and use that of others and putting both to work in accordance with the imperatives dictated by the time, place, people, and nature of the affairs under consideration, he brings the republic's *negocios* to their successful conclusion'.[75] The parallel with Charles V's *instrucciones* is unmistakable. The Emperor had earnestly admonished his son to give God his due, and nothing could better epitomize the good man than his compliance with the divine mandates. Something which Furió does not fail to do, for he also admits the important role played by goodness in the prince's armor. But Charles had then proceeded to devote the more considerable portion of the two documents to the task of enlightening his son on the paths, often devious ones, to be trodden by the sound ruler. Precisely, Furió maintains, what the prince should be taught. The question of the prince's 'own counsel' introduced above is used by Furió as a springboard to emphasize how essential it is that the prince know his own mind. On this subject the author concludes that there are three kinds of intellects. Some men understand, comprehend, and know on their own, without help or aid from anyone else; others have to be taught or counseled; still others belong to neither category. These last, the humanist argues, are useless and were naturally born into perpetual slavery; the second manner of intellect, on the other hand, is both good and satisfactory. But the first is truly divine in that men endowed with it were born to rule. Evidently Furió does not believe that the first category is a very realistic one in human terms, for he concentrates on the nature of the middle one: the *entendimiento* which he has classified as good. He begins by redefining it as gifted with the ability to differentiate between good and evil. And upon

75 *Ibid.*, fo. IV r–v v.

this natural prerequisite it is possible to build solidly. True, the imagination of such an intellect may not be scintillating or overwhelming but a man thus gifted is discerning enough to accomplish a crucial task: separate the good advisers from the bad and act accordingly. How important this ability is in the ruler is demonstrated, according to Furió, if by contrast we look at what happens to a commonwealth ruled by a diffident or incompetent prince. 'Woe to the kingdom whose prince says to his council: "examine the business at hand and act as you see fit, for I leave the decision in your hands"! Such a kingdom shall inevitably be prey to misrule because there will be no unifying force at the helm; councilors will go their separate and individual ways looking after their own.' Invariably this state of affairs is the result of the ruler's ineptitude. In short, the prudence and good governance of the council depend on the prince, and not the prince's on the council. 'For all these reasons I reiterate that a good prince is one capable of following both his own counsel and that of others, adopt one or the other as demanded by time and circumstances, and gloriously guide the republic's paths to its goal.' It follows, therefore, that

The *institución* of the prince is no other than the art of good, true, and proven *avisos* drawn from long experience, forged by the intellect of the most illustrious men, confirmed by the words and deeds of those who by their true rule and memorable exploits deserved the title and renown of good prince. Such *avisos*, for the prince who reads them and puts them into effect, are a guide and safe path leading certainly and by easy stages to the pinnacle of power and glory.[76]

The concejo

Perhaps the single most telling argument used by Furió Ceriol in behalf of his claim that his princely pedagogy is radically innovative lies with the author's explanation to King Philip of the kind of work that should be written on the subject. The education – *arte o institución* – of the prince, claims Furió, will be correctly imparted when it is divided into five distinct categories; each the subject of one *tratado*. The first shall be divided into three books: 'one explaining what the prince is, how and why he came to be; what power he possesses, who gave it to him, and who may deprive him of it. The second book shall discourse on those *artes* which necessary to the governance of the body politic are to be learned by the prince. The third book lists the moral virtues most necessary to the ruler, and how to use them – a subject which is little understood even though it is the hinge of good government.'[77] The second *tratado* Furió dedicates to the *crianza*

[76] *Ibid.*, fo. VI–VII r.   [77] *Ibid.*, fo. VI r–VII v.

of the prince: his teachers, tutors, servants, friends, and *privados*. In the third volume two basic subjects, one book to each, must be discussed: one concerning the subjects' duties to the prince, and the other explaining the obligations of the prince toward his subjects. In this manner, the author points out, it will be possible to differentiate between loyal and treacherous subjects, prince and tyrant. In the next tome the prince shall be shown how to rule, overcoming whatever difficulties he may find in his path. This delicate subject, continues Furió, cannot be properly taught unless it is clearly understood that each kingdom is unique and that the manner of ruling it must be considered to be so as well. And nowhere is the individuality of the realm better embodied than in the way in which it was acquired. There are in fact four distinct means whereby the prince may have come to rule his kingdom: inheritance, election, force, or cunning. It follows, then, that the fourth volume must be divided into four books. Finally, since the prince cannot possibly hear, know, be a part of, and provide for, everything that pertains to the business of ruling it is imperative that a fifth *tratado* be added to the others on the subject of the council and councilors needed by the prince.[78] Needless to say, the first book of the fifth treatise – the book concerned with the prince's council and his *consejeros* – was the very one offered by Furió to his sovereign.

In his characteristic straightforward manner Furió opens his discussion of the council with a sober and incisive definition. 'The Council of the Prince is a congregation or gathering of people chosen to advise him on all matters of peace and war. The object is that in this fashion the prince will be in a better position to remember the past, know the present, provide for the future, achieve success in his enterprises, and steer clear of difficulties or, since the last are often impossible to avoid, reduce their potential for harm as much as possible.'[79] The council, continues the author, is akin to the prince's senses: his understanding, memory, eyes, ears, voice, hands, and feet. Indeed, both the prince and the council are God's lieutenants on earth. It follows that a good council gives perfection to the ruler; it sustains and ennobles his people. By contrast, the bad council demolishes the prince and destroys the commonwealth; the bad council and the prince, far from being God's ministers, become then vassals of the devil. Such is the importance of this question 'that I doubt there is anything that can surpass its significance'. Obviously, concludes Furió, princes must move earth and heaven in their anxiety to find a good council.[80]

Furió next argues that for best results it is often required that the council be divided into several parts. He does not object to this necessary division of labor as long as the various parts of the whole continue to be directed by a single head – the monarch. With this matter of principle out of the

[78] *Ibid.*, fo. VII v–VIII r.   [79] *Ibid.*, fo. 1 r–2 v.   [80] *Ibid.*, fo. 2 r–3v.

way Furió proceeds to point out that whoever is to write on matters concerning the king's education cannot limit his concern to sanctioning the need for the council in broad terms. He, on the contrary, has the duty to discourse on the more prosaic matters of the council's organization, membership, and obligations. For his part the author is perfectly willing to meet that responsibility. And the first step taken in this direction must be to determine the number of councils needed to aid the prince effectively in the governance of his realm. Furió decides that seven is the ideal number – 'neither more nor less'. The seven councils must be totally specialized to meet the commonwealth's various needs and as such should be different from one another in all respects: jurisdiction, membership, and authority. The seven councils proposed as indispensable by Furió are: Finance (*Hacienda*), Peace (*Paz*), War (*Guerra*), Subsistence (*Mantenimiento*), Justice (*Leyes*), Punishment (*Castigo*), and Grants (*Mercedes*).

In Furió's scheme the Consejo de Hacienda oversees the collection, preservation, guarding, and enlarging of the prince's ordinary and extraordinary income. Taxes, of course, are the peculiar province of this council: to increase them if possible and necessary; to reduce or eliminate them if injurious. In either case the compelling reason should be the public well-being – naturally the one overriding concern of Furió's ideology. The prince's own expenditures in times of war and peace are also the concern of the Council of Finance. Perhaps bearing in mind contemporary fiscal policies, invariably aimed at squeezing money out of the country, Furió stresses that the function of this council is twofold: to seek means to increase the prince's income, and to find means of reducing his expenses. In brief, the author conceives the Consejo de Hacienda as the public fist holding the purse's strings; precisely the role, it was already clear by this time, that the Cortes of Castile had failed to monopolize. In this sense an important characteristic of Furió's conciliar system emerges: the council is not the prince's creature but the guardian of the public interest.[81]

The second council in Furió's hierarchy is the Consejo de Paz. The humanist views it as the equivalent, in the context of the Spanish conciliar structure, of the Council of State. However, in Furió's mind this council is far from merely fulfilling the honorary role of its Spanish counterpart. He envisions it, rather, as the nerve center of the civil government. Its functions are broad and important: to see to it that all officials (both for peace and war), from viceroy to castellan, fulfill their duties. It shall, moreover, decide who is fit to fill a vacant post in the administration and who unfit. The Consejo de Paz is also empowered to pay the king's bills, in 'time of peace and war'. Just as the Consejo de Hacienda monopolizes the collection of public monies, only the Consejo de Paz is authorized to

[81] *Ibid.*, fo. 4 r–5 r.

spend them. Its attributions also embrace matters of foreign policy, for it partakes of the prerogatives and responsibilities attached to making peace and declaring war, undertaking alliances and initiating presumably hostile actions. In short, concludes Furió, the Consejo de Paz 'shall be at the head of all the other councils'.[82]

Next is the Consejo de Guerra. Not unexpectedly, all aspects of warfare are said to fall within its purlieu. More surprisingly there emerges as well the suggestion of an elaborate structure of remarkable complexity. Fortification and upkeep of strategic strongholds, defense of the frontiers, and training of soldiers, are some of the predictable tasks assigned to the council. In addition, however, the council is expected to study thoroughly ancient methods of warfare and compare them with those of the age, and know those nations that are renowned for their infantry and which for their cavalry; it will keep careful tally of what forces are available to the ruler, those of his enemies, and the strength of potential allies; it must also have readily available complete information concerning the wars waged by the prince and his predecessors, how they were conducted, how they were brought to a conclusion; identical records should be available concerning the warlike history of the prince's enemy, and the latter's friends and foes. The benefits to be derived from this mass of accumulated data are truly Machiavellian, for Furió points out that in this manner 'if we find the forces at the enemy's disposal to be greater than our own we shall opt for peace; if contrariwise we shall decide for war'. If, moreover, careful study reveals 'our' forces to be inferior the next task to be immediately undertaken by the council is an exhaustive assessment of the factors, causes, and remedies applicable to the situation. Under the circumstances the significance of the war council is manifest, and Furió rightly concludes that in its absence both the commonwealth and the prince face a somber future.[83]

The Consejo de Mantenimiento has as its primordial goal to insure the steady flow of provisions and victuals into the principality both in 'times of war and peace'. And as was the case with the preceding councils the fourth's task is anything but simple. If *Mantenimiento* is to keep the realm well stocked with munitions of peace and war a host of complex details must be conscientiously taken care of: abundant articles and those in short supply have to be identified and cataloged in detail; which are imported; whether the latter come in by land or by sea and how is their distribution effected once they have arrived; as far as exports are concerned they must be strictly controlled by the council. As Furió sees it, if the said council does its job properly the kingdom shall suffer from want neither in war nor in peace. Moreover, a realm well provisioned through

[82] *Ibid.*, fo. 5 r–6 r.   [83] *Ibid.*, fo. 6 r–9 v.

the foresight of an effective conciliar machinery will be able to share its bounty with those whose friendship 'we find it advisable to cultivate'. Conversely, if a principality lacks a Consejo de Mantenimiento or if the latter is ineffective the painful results are soon felt: each province endures grievous vicissitudes; the malice of a few speculators abundantly feeds on the want of the many; our friends abroad are left without our succor; military campaigns must be brought to an ignominious conclusion; disadvantageous peace, truces, and alliances are inevitably forced upon the prince whose council has failed to achieve a degree of autarky: the prince, as a result, loses the trust of his allies and the friendship of his subjects. In brief, an improvident prince cannot preserve his people's respect if he fails – and he will unless he has a good Council of Subsistence to advise him – to provide two things most necessary to his subjects: protection from their enemies, and alliance with those nations with whom commercial intercourse is essential.[84]

The fifth administrative body proposed by Furió is the Consejo de Leyes. 'It shall behoove this council to concern itself with the posts, magistrates, governors, and officials indispensable to the governance of the principality, as well as the power and authority vested in each. . .It will moreover play a legislative role, making and promulgating new laws and invalidating obsolete ones.' Furió views this council as the 'father of the laws', seeing to it that they will be kept and obeyed *limpiamente*. What happens, then, when a kingdom lacks such a legal watchdog? All kinds of evils are visited upon the republic. The magistrates forget the public welfare; posts are multiplied, often with contradictory prerogatives; endless scandals, infinite lawsuits, *bandos* and thievery without number ensue that more often than not end in conspiracies which in turn bloody the prince's hands. The ultimate consequence of this state of affairs is not hard to predict: the prince loses his principality.[85]

The Concejo de Pena is summarily dealt with by the humanist. 'This council shall look into everything pertinent to criminal matters. . .it shall inform itself on and pass sentence upon – according to the laws of the land – all the crimes and iniquities committed in the realm'.[86]

The seventh and last member of Furió's conciliar system is the Concejo de Mercedes. Its province is rather broad and amorphous – one is reminded of the Consejo de Cámara – for it deals with the king's largesse. How important a part of the structure and practice of the Renaissance state the latter was is illustrated by Furió's willingness to control it by means of a council. *Mercedes* will concern itself with the 'merits and demerits of all; the manner of living, customs, ability, and services of those who, although never asking reward, deserve it in consideration of their rare and excellent

[84] *Ibid.*, fo. 9 v–10 v.   [85] *Ibid.*, fo. 10 r–11 r.   [86] *Ibid.*, fo. 11 r.

virtues'. Whatever favors the prince may see fit to bestow must first pass the scrutiny of the council, and without its recommendation no favor shall be granted anyone. Wherever such a council fails to be organized the entire meaning of the *merced* is perverted. Favors go to undeserving wretches and the good and faithful remain unheard, unknown, and unrewarded.[87]

Such, concludes Furió, is the conciliar structure indispensable to any well-governed republic. A prince thus aided will be free from the vexing importunities attendant to the need for wasting precious time and effort in matters of detail. One thing above all others need the prince avoid as he organizes the membership of his councils: under no circumstances must any counselor be permitted to belong to more than one council. Any relaxation of this rule would mean that the councils would rapidly be reduced in number from a theoretical seven to an effective one. The consequences would be to plunge the realm into the dangers which the conciliar system is precisely designed to ward off.

The consejero

So far Furió Ceriol has extensively discoursed on the prince and the councils. Both, the author has emphasized throughout, are intimately linked to each other by one of the most important cogs in the governmental machinery: the *consejero*. The author immediately offers the reader a formal definition: 'The *consejero* is a fully endowed (*suficiente*) person selected for membership in one of the above-mentioned councils. Two conditions must the *consejero* fulfill. First, the *consejero* must be fully equipped (*suficiencia*) with all the attributes required by the post. Second, the *consejero* must be elected.'[88] One important terminological item surfaces from the author's definition. The word *consejero* as used by Furió clearly applies to a man as a member of a council; he, therefore, is not a mere adviser or *privado* in the sense studied in the context of Guevara. He is a functionary with a specific task and belonging to a specific bureaucratic structure. For this reason it will hereafter be translated as 'councilor' rather than as 'counselor'; the latter term will, as heretofore, be reserved to denote the more general and ambiguous role of adviser – or *privado*, meaning an intimate adviser.

Furió further proposes to pay particular attention to two concepts closely associated with the councilor: his *suficiencia* and his election. The latter, the exclusive prerogative of the prince, is a thoroughly crucial one because since the councilor must be a specialist the prince will emerge as a man of almost limitless wisdom capable of judging the abilities of indi-

[87] *Ibid.*, fo. 11 r–12 r.   [88] *Ibid.*, fo. 15 v.

viduals who, each in his own field, are the greatest experts available. It follows that the two concepts must be studied in strict order, and Furió therefore begins with the *consejero*'s *suficiencia* – his expertise.

'A man's *suficiencia* is to be understood in two ways: *suficiencia* in what refers to the soul, and *suficiencia* in what pertains to the body. . .I shall at present concern myself with the former.' As far as the soul is concerned, then, Furió believes that a man's *suficiencia* comprises a grand total of fifteen perquisites or *calidades*. *Ingenio* (talent, creative or inventive faculty) is the first. It is the beginning, middle, and end of any endeavor with a claim to greatness. Such is the import of this *calidad* that in its absence all the other virtues lose their potency and are reduced to nothing. Experience, moreover, teaches that without *ingenio* books, tutors, *avisos*, and counsels signify very little; on the other hand, *un grande ingenio* will need little in the way of artificial improvement to achieve great results. '*Ruin* (low, base) *ingenio* is akin to a naturally sterile field which regardless of care and effort will forever yield scanty and poor fruit.' The parallel with Sepúlveda in the latter's discussion of education is remarkable and reminiscent of Castiglione's own *paideia* with its emphasis on nature and art: without the gift of the former nothing can be accomplished by the latter. Needless to say, then, *grande ingenio* is an innate and capital prerequisite in the councilor. One which, Furió insists, the prince must be able to identify through his own experience instead of relying on the report of others. This point is so important that the author decides to give the prince some pointers on how to develop his 'experience' so as to recognize *grande ingenio* in a man. To begin with, the ideas of a man of talent are often most unusual; his conceptual approach is very different from other men's and his conclusions are correspondingly unique and frequently unexpected. Other singular traits make the *grande ingenio* unmistakable: clever speech, punctuality, easy understanding, clear and resolute teaching, wit, seriousness. The man of talent never follows the crowd; he is not colloquial in his speech and is never a bore; his reasoning always avoids confusion; he holds no prejudices against other nations or peoples – whether Jews, Moors, Gentiles, or Christians – because he recognizes that good and bad can be found everywhere. The deeds of talented men are always sharp, alive, because so is their author: active, curious, diligent; anxious to know the past, understand the present, and foresee the future; proficient in many *artes* he endlessly strives to know more than others.[89]

From what follows it is quite clear that the other qualities of the good counselor are explicit instances of the many facets implicitly considered in the author's definition of the *grande ingenio*. It is of interest, on the other

[89] *Ibid.*, fo. 15 r–18 v.

hand, to examine them briefly because *in toto* they constitute the educational baggage of the councilor. Furió's second *calidad* is knowledge 'of the *artes* of good speech; because men are different from the beasts in their ability to speak and reason'. The very nature of the counselor's duties compels him to be excellent in rhetoric. It is not unusual, for instance, for the prince to send a councilor abroad in delicate diplomatic errands. An inarticulate man can very easily embarrass himself and his prince with the concomitant strain in relations. It is important, therefore, that the prince be able to ascertain the forensic skill of his councilor. The method to achieve this, Furió points out, is easy enough: the councilor should be often called into the prince's presence and given the opportunity to speak at length, narrate stories, and expound on varied and sundry subjects. If the councilor has written something the prince ought to examine it; if not, the councilor should be required, on the spot and without previous warning, to compose a letter or some other form of written exercise.[90]

The next quality demanded of the councilor by Furió is that he be a polyglot. Special knowledge of the tongues spoken by the prince's friends and enemies is particularly recommended. In the concrete case of the king of Spain a councilor should be conversant in Latin, Italian, Arabic, French, and German; the assumption being, of course, that he is a Spaniard. The reason proposed by Furió is identical to that used by Charles V in his *instrucciones* to his son: the subjects must understand and be understood by their rulers.[91] To this gift of languages a good councilor must add that of *grande historiador*, a man steeped in the reading of ancient and modern history, particularly that of his own prince, his allies, his friends, and his enemies.

Furió's reflections on the usefulness of history are interesting in the extreme, mirroring as they do a remarkably pragmatic approach to the subject. What the author finds fascinating about history is its incomparable value as a tool for the councilor. Thus a man capable of truly reaping history's fruits 'becomes, I dare say, a perfect councilor highly experienced in all affairs pertaining to the realm's government, for history is nothing but the bringing together of the manifold experiences of all ages and many men. Give me a man well versed in historical lore and capable of drawing lessons from it, and I will show in him greater expertise in affairs than another who has twenty years' practice behind him.' To prove his point Furió uses the example of a veteran commander. At most he has taken part in a few battles, encounters, mutinies, sieges, truces. A historian, by contrast, can boast his participation in an infinitude of such events. And as far as effectiveness in inculcating experience there is no

90 *Ibid.*, fo. 19 v–20 r.   91 *Ibid.*, fo. 20 r–22 r.

comparison between the few in number and the infinite many. And what is self-evident in matters of war, argues Furió, is equally true in all affairs pertaining to the commonwealth's governance. 'To bring stability to a republic, rule a principality, wage a war, keep a state, increase one's power, seek after the good, and flee from evil, what better means is there than history?' Alas, complains the author, this simple lesson is ignored by many. Few man in positions of responsibility read works on history; and if they do their reading is superficial, without any serious attempt at putting its deeper lessons to use. History, says Furió, is not a pastime; it is instead a tool which enables a man with political responsibilities to gain time, to understand in one day what would otherwise take a lifetime to learn. 'History is a portrait of human life, a brief for all *negocios,* a model for man's customs, the infallible and definitive source for experience in human actions, prudent and faithful counselor in all questions, teacher in peace, general in war, north star at sea, haven for all men. And how few understand all this! For these reasons I want the councilor to be a *grande historiador.*'[92]

The sixth gift of the soul with which the councilor should be adorned is a rather subtle one: he must be thoroughly capable of estimating with accuracy the end, the substance, and the outward appearance of each virtue. Above all, he must competently discern their respective boundaries. It is common among the vulgar, explains Furió, to mistake the goats for the sheep, and vice versa. Thus among the untutored the man of violent temper is called strong, the lazy or ignorant is praised as straightforward, the superstitious is held in awe as holy, while the prodigal passes for generous. Understandably, from this 'diabolical' practice which confuses the virtues with their respective vices the councilor must be absolutely free.[93]

A most important prerequisite for a sound councilor is that he be *político.* By *político* Furió means profound expertise in the affairs of war and peace. The author reiterates that the prince's twin obligations are *gobierno y protección.* Specifically, the former refers to the affairs of peace while the latter pertains to matters of war. And if the councilor is not professionally competent in both, his usefulness to the prince will be nil. It is therefore essential that the councilor first of all be aware that the republic – man's society brought together into a community of living – is composed of body and soul. The republic's body comprises its physical aspects: general location, climate, strategic features, street planning in its cities, buildings, etc. Of all this the councilor must be cognizant so that he may change or manipulate these conditions as dictated by circumstances. As concerns the soul of the republic Furió understands it to be its government,

[92] *Ibid.,* fo. 22 r–26 r.   [93] *Ibid.,* fo. 26 r–28 r.

of which there are three pure forms – monarchy ('king'), aristocracy ('nobles'), and polity ('plebeians') – and four mixed ones resulting from the combination of the pure three: king and nobles; king and plebeians; nobles and plebeians; king, nobles, and plebeians. It is to be noted that Furió considers the government of Castile as belonging to the first category, that of pure monarchy, while Aragón is said to have a form of government akin to the last of the mixed. Regardless of the format adopted by any commonwealth for its government Furió insists that the councilor must be thoroughly versed in all its aspects, precisely what best defines him as *político*. And the prince who wishes to have the best *político* as councilor must test, first hand, his knowledge on all substantive matters pertaining to the body and soul of the republic.[94]

The perfect councilor must also be a man of the world and experienced traveler – not after the fashion of a common vagabond but in the manner of an observer bent on acquiring a large store of knowledge, and Furió would have it as detailed as possible, for here as elsewhere the *consejero* is to be no dilettante but an accomplished professional, about his own and foreign lands to be placed at the service of his prince.[95]

The eighth *calidad* of the *consejero* rests with his complete knowledge 'of the strength and power of his prince, and those of his allies, enemies, and neighbors'. And, again, this knowledge must not be superficial or cursory but painstaking in its thoroughness as befits a true expert. The remaining seven *calidades* with which the efficient *consejero* ought to be endowed lose some of the pragmatic flavor which characterized the first eight and come closer to the broad Christian quality that we have identified in Guevara. Thus the *consejero* is urged to forget his own reputation and profit for the sake of the public well-being. He is advised, moreover, to sacrifice the duties of friendship, family, and *bando* in the altar of the public interest. The councilor must 'belong to all, listen to all, and favor all without distinction; but he will favor more those excellent in reason and virtue and less those who are mediocre in the practice of both'. The eleventh *calidad* is justice. As expected Furió places a special emphasis on justice: 'among all qualities justice occupies such an exalted place that without it the other virtues are worth little'. Generosity, strength of character, accessibility to all, affability, meekness, evenness of temper, clemency: such are some among the more common attributes associated by Furió with the last few *calidades* of the councilor's soul.[96]

The qualities of the councilor *en cuanto al cuerpo* occupy only a fraction of the space devoted to the *consejero*'s spiritual baggage. Contrary to what one might expect Furió does not intend to produce the ideal athlete who combining bodily perfection with intellectual greatness and moral excel-

[94] *Ibid.*, fo. 28 r–32 v.   [95] *Ibid.*, fo. 32 v–35 r.   [96] *Ibid.*, fo. 35 r–55 v.

lence will emerge as the paragon of bureaucratic efficiency. The author
has something else in mind; he believes that the physical appearance of the
consejero is a superb clue toward ascertaining the man's potential. 'It will
suffice for our purposes to know that just as there are ways of determining
whether a plot of land is fertile or sterile, a horse good or bad, it is quite
possible to tell from certain bodily signals the composition of a man's
soul.' These physical pointers are precisely what Furió views as the *calidades
en cuanto al cuerpo* – a grand total of five. The first is age: neither younger
than thirty nor older than sixty. During that thirty-year span men 'are
neither too green nor too dry', possess all their faculties in harmonious
balance, and have the *humores templados*. The second *calidad* Furió calls
complissión: 'there are some temperaments which naturally possess
hability, *suficiencia*, and luster; others, by contrast, are unskilled, *in-
suficientes*, and obscure. The former, perfected by *arte y diligencia*, improve
by the hour. The latter are hopeless in their clumsiness. I conclude, then,
that the most promising councilor is one of sanguine or choleric *complissión*, for those endowed with this mixture of temperaments are
ingenious, of good memory, know how to discourse, possess sound judgment, are just, loving, affable, loyal, magnificent, magnanimous, strong,
healthy, agile...Above all, the prince must take care not to chose for
councilors men of phlegmatic and melancholy temperaments, for they are
naturally incompetent in matters pertaining to governing and counseling.'[97]
   The councilor's size is also a good indicator of his *suficiencia*. Neither
too tall nor too short, nor too thin, nor too fat: such is the ideal. He must,
it follows, be well-proportioned. Furió here reflects the age's widespread
belief that physical deformities are indications of spiritual shortcomings –
muy malas señales del alma. 'Those who are born gibbous, lame, one-
eyed, or otherwise marked by excess or defect are invariably, as proven by
Galen and Hippocrates, plagued by innumerable shortcomings of the
mind and mores.' Finally, Furió suggests a fifth *calidad*: the *consejero*
should have a good face and graceful demeanor. A curious portrait follows
describing the facial features which the author presumably considered to
be the acme of manly beauty, and one which also brings to an end Furió's
extensive analysis of the councilor's spiritual and physical virtues.[98]
   In the following chapter Furió undertakes to answer a question suggested by his insistence that the responsibility for selecting the councilor
rest entirely with the prince: what guidelines does the prince have at his
disposal when he seeks to find the best man for the post? The matter is
not an idle or trivial one, for Furió stresses that at stake are the prince's
honor, his future, and that of the commonwealth. The first thing to bear
in mind, continues the humanist, is that commonly the prince's own

[97] *Ibid.*, fo. 55 r–59 v.   [98] *Ibid.*, fo. 60 v–64 v.

abilities are judged on the basis of the qualities of his councils. In other words, the reputation of the prince stands or falls on his Council. And this is Furió's first *aviso* on the subject. The second is that 'the prince stands in more need of a good councilor than he does of the bread he eats'. The councilor, it is in the nature of things that it should be so, has access to public opinion in ways barred to the prince. Furió's third *aviso* is probably born out of the cosmopolitan character of Philip's dominions; 'a prince who rules many and diverse realms must have councilors from all of them'. It is the only hope that the prince can entertain of being attuned to the needs and desires of his subjects. A further *aviso* counsels the ruler not to be content with electing the councilors from his immediate entourage; he, on the contrary, ought to search far and wide for the right men. The fifth and sixth *avisos* are aimed at convincing the prince that the selection of *consejeros* must be a slow and gradual process, and that although the prince shall listen to all who have something to say for and against a given candidate the ultimate decision must remain his and based on his own appraisal of the evidence. Under no circumstances, so goes the next *aviso*, should the prince name a *consejero* without first exhaustively examining his credentials. The standard for the test lies at hand – Furió's own twenty *calidades* – and one which obviously places a formidable burden on the shoulders of the prince, for he now becomes, so to speak, the expert among experts. The examination concluded, the winner shall be summoned to the prince's presence and told of his success; a brief talk shall follow to impress upon the new *consejero* the burdens, responsibilities, and perils of his office – such is the substance of the eighth *aviso*. The ninth and last instructs the prince on how to give the councilor the oath of office. The *consejero* thus vows to be a good subject and excellent magistrate; to seek nothing but the honor of his prince; to sacrifice friends, family, and his own personal interests for the sake of justice.

Conclusion

What general conclusions can be drawn from this extended description of Furió Ceriol's conciliar system? Although in this instance it would perhaps be best to let the evidence speak for itself it may not be too impertinent or without purpose to suggest a few concluding remarks. And the first one which comes to mind concerns a matter that we have often encountered in our survey of Renaissance Spanish political thought: Furió's search for those principles underlying a political order capable of giving life and reality to the ideal state as measured by contemporary standards. Despite his unquestionable pragmatism at no time does the author seem to feel the need for any compromise which for the sake of the former may impair the integrity of the latter. One result is that Furió is able to retain the ethical monism of traditional political thinking which Machiavelli felt compelled to break. He will, however, articulate its unity along two directions corresponding to the double personality of the prince himself: the public and the private *persona*.

The crucial question, of course, is whether these two princely facets may at any one time come into conflict in such a manner as to force the sacrifice of one for the sake of the other – the very essence of the Machiavellian dilemma. In truth the matter is never explicitly broached by Furió. Presumably it should have been touched upon in some portion of the total *opus* needed to explain the *arte o institución del príncipe* – one, incidentally, which Furió at no time promises to undertake. This last is an important point to remember, for it deprives *El concejo* of that haunting flavor associated with unfinished works: *El concejo* is not an incomplete work.

After listing the monumental gifts that must accompany the sage who attempts to write exhaustively on the prince's *institución*, Furió openly declares his intention to offer Philip his thought on the first book of the eight which shall compose the fifth and last part of the total work – no more and no less. At the very outset of the dedication to the king, Furió in fact gives every indication of an unwillingness to commit himself irrevocably even to a permanent schism of the prince's personality; and so he speaks of the prince as being made *almost* of two persons, a fact duly emphasized by various commentators. On the other hand, a little later Furió – now discussing the incompetence of those who having discovered 'as I [did] two distinct and different persons in the prince' still failed to come up with a fitting educational scheme – apparently decides to throw caution to the wind and accept the fact of the ruler's double self. But although it may be possible to argue that Furió finally bows to the inevitable there is still no discussion of the possible conflicts (much less their outcome) resulting from the coexistence of two different persons in the same being. And so the matter stands, never satisfactorily resolved.

In the absence of hard and fast evidence, then, the reader can only guess what Furió's ultimate answer to the riddle might have been if he had in fact undertaken to write on all aspects of the king's *institución* – a most perilous procedure by any standards. Nevertheless, the existing evidence leaves room for some cautious speculation. For one thing, the perquisites which the author demands of the sound *consejero* leave no doubt as to the fact that the latter must be a thoroughly competent professional. The case for the councilor's 'goodness' is admittedly less strong; we have seen that although explicitly mentioned, the emphasis on the strictly Christian attributes of the *consejero* suffers in comparison with the

intensity which accompanied the discussion of his practical virtues. But it
is nevertheless there. And the bond, the prince's power of election, established by Furió between the ruler and the *consejero* is a secure foundation
from which to conclude, first, that the prince must be at least as competent as any counselor, and second that he need also be at least as 'good'
a man as his subordinate. Rather than approaching the question as a harsh
dilemma where the prince has no alternative but to choose between his
political duties and his human ethic, then, I am inclined to believe that
Furió elects to follow a milder course and view the problem as a choice
between an active and a contemplative course of action. This interpretation, I think, has certain positive features. For one thing, it fits well with
the general flavor of Spanish political thinking before and after Furió.
For another, it is one by no means foreign to the age as we have had
occasion to observe in the case of Sepúlveda.

   This last I hold to be especially important, for if we re-examine Sepúlveda's extensive discoursing on the relative merits of the active and contemplative ways we find little with which the other humanist, Furió,
would seem to disagree. We have seen, for example, how Furió explains
that the last two books of the first treatise of the *opus* dealing with the
prince's *institución* shall deal, respectively, with the disciplines necessary
to the republic's proper governance, and with 'the most necessary among
the moral virtues, and – a subject understood by few – how to use them,
for it is on such that government hinges'. Understood in this manner,
Furió would emerge not as a disciple of Machiavelli but, rather, as a
pragmatist to be classed among the contributors to the Renaissance
secularization of wisdom. Such, I think, is the tenor of *El concejo*.
Implicitly, he makes the distinction between the contemplative (Christian)
and active (moral virtues) manners of living as sharply as Sepúlveda does
explicitly, and with the same result. Furió's prince *qua* private man
indulges in the pleasures of *contemplatio*; *qua* prince he is forced to
concentrate on *actio*. Often they cannot be practiced simultaneously and
although the caliber of the former is unquestionably superior life's imperatives at times force the latter to take the upper hand. The crucial point is
that there is never an inevitable or insoluble clash; merely a smooth
periodic shifting of priorities.

   Granted that this interpretation is not irrevocably sanctioned by the
explicit evidence of Furió's words, it nevertheless seems to commend itself
as a middle-of-the-road alternative to explanations which attempt, on
equally shaky foundations, to reveal Furió's strong leanings toward
Machiavellianism. Regardless of how similar some passages of *El concejo*
may seem to be to portions of *Il principe* the crucial ingredient is missing:
the open acknowledgment that Christian virtue and political action are

mutually exclusive. The ambiguous statements of the dedication notwith-standing, one thing remains clear: Furió never makes the choice or even proposes that a choice is needed – pragmatic approach to the *ars guber-nandi*, yes; Machiavellianism, no. Pragmatism is indeed a trait that cannot be denied Furió, a point quite explicitly made in his dedication to Philip II. What could be more pragmatic than the goal of the treatise itself, to surround the prince as ruler with a ring of experts? Furió's *consejero* and his prince are both unquestionable professionals. We know little about the prince's practical education – that *tratado* was never written – but we know the *consejero* and we are also told that the prince must easily encompass both the depth and the breadth of his counselor's exper-tise, a not inconsiderable piece of evidence indicating that the purely pragmatic side of the ruler's education has to be one of rare intensity.

When the various utilitarian aspects of government explicitly or implicitly discussed by Furió are taken into a total context, the general impression derived is one of overriding concern with the need to systema-tize the prince's government, to do away with mere dilettantism in the higher echelons of the state bureaucracy and to thoroughly professionalize the public administration from top to bottom. Since Furió chooses a conciliar structure as the basic desirable organization it is not unwarranted to conclude that his goal is to sharpen the contours and more effectively tighten the working conciliar system of his own day. Professionalism, however, ought not to be read to mean businesslike narrowness, for Furió's bureaucrat is anything but narrow or myopic in his expertise. Conceived by the mind of a humanist, Furió's public functionaries – both prince and *consejero*, in their respective spheres – are bred by a humanist education attuned to the demands of praxis – one stressing breadth through the study of rhetoric and history, and emphasizing as well a depth acquired through experience. As we move from Guevara to Furió it becomes clear that a generation has gone by. The Bishop's prince and *privado*, like Erasmus', are above all good men; Furió's are both good men and superlative bureaucrats.

We may conclude here by pointing out that in common with all the publicists of the Renaissance, Furió conceives order and stability to be the *summum bonum* of the republic. And this desirable end can only be attained when certain prerequisites are present. The first, if implicit, is the presence of those Christian gifts which correctly mold the private side of the ruler and his *consejero*. It is no coincidence, as Sevilla Andrés points out, that 'it would be possible, without inflicting irreparable harm on the truth, to reduce the *consejero's calidades del alma* to the four Christian virtues', for practical as those fifteen *calidades* for the most part are they rest on the assumption that the *consejero* is a man of Christian deportment.

The second is the one which explicitly occupies the author's attention: the virtues that an efficient councilor must possess. The third is the emphasis on reason (perfected by education) as the essential point of departure of all the *calidades*. The fourth is the goal to which all the gifts and activities of the *hombre político* must be aimed: the common well-being. For without the latter the republic cannot survive.

Bibliography

I. PRIMARY SOURCES

Agrippa, C. *Of the Vanitie and Uncertaintie of Artes and Sciences*, trans. J. Stanford (London, 1575).

Alberti, L. B. *Della famiglia*, trans. R. N. Watkins (Columbia, S.C., 1965).

Aristotle. *Politics*, Jowett edition.

Augustine, Aurelius. *The City of God*, trans. M. Dods, in 'A Select Library of the Nicene and Post-Nicene Fathers of the Christian Church', ed. P. Schaff (14 vols., Buffalo, 1887; and New York, 1907), II.

The Free Choice of the Will, trans. R. P. Russell (Washington, 1967).

The Letters of Saint Augustine, in 'A Select Library of the Nicene and Post-Nicene Fathers of the Christian Church', ed. P. Schaff (14 vols., Buffalo, 1887; and New York, 1907), I.

Reply to Faustus the Manichaean, in 'A Select Library of the Nicene and Post-Nicene Fathers of the Christian Church', ed. P. Schaff (14 vols., Buffalo, 1887; and New York, 1907), IV.

Cajetan. *Commentaria in IIam IIae Summae Theologicae St Thomae Aquino*, Editio Leonina of St Thomas' Works (Rome, 1895), VIII.

Casas, B. de las. *In Defense of the Indians*, ed. and trans. S. Poole (De Kalb, Ill., 1974).

Castiglione, B. *The Book of the Courtier*, trans. C. S. Singleton (New York, 1958).

Castrillo, A. de. *Tractado de república* (Madrid, 1958).

Cicero, M. T. *De finibus*, Loeb edition.

De legibus, ed. W. D. Pearman (Cambridge, 1881).

De officiis, Loeb edition.

On the Commonwealth, ed. and trans. G. H. Sabine and S. B. Smith (Columbus, 1910).

Clichtove, J. *De bello et pace* (Paris, 1523).

Covarrubias y Leyva, D. de. *Regulae peccatum, de regulis Iuris lib. 6 Relectio* (Salamanca, 1558).

Textos jurídico-políticos, ed. M. Fraga Iribarne, trans. A. Río Seco (Madrid, 1957).

Diogenes Laertius. *Life of Zeno*, in *Lives of Eminent Philosophers*, Chapter 7.

296 *Bibliography*

Erasmus, D. *The Complaint of Peace*, trans. T. Paynell, ed. J. W. Hirten (New York, 1968).

The Education of a Christian Prince, ed. and trans. L. K. Born (New York, 1968).

Erasmus Against War, ed. J. W. Mackail (Boston, 1907).

Obras escogidas de Erasmo, trans. L. Riber (Madrid, 1964).

Opera omnia, ed. J. Clericus (10 vols., Leiden, 1703–1706).

Opus epistolarum Erasmi, ed. P. S. Allen and H. M. Allen (Oxford, 1906–1958).

Scarabaeus aquilam quaerit, in *Adages of Erasmus*, trans. M. M. Phillips (Cambridge, 1964).

Utilissima consultatio de bello Turcis inferendo, in *Opera omnia* (10 vols., Leiden, 1703–1706), v.

Furió Ceriol, F. *El concejo i consejeros del príncipe* (Antwerp, 1559).

El concejo y consejeros del príncipe y otras obras, ed. D. Sevilla Andrés (Valencia, 1952).

Galilei, G. *Dialogues Concerning Two New Sciences*, trans. H. Crew and A. de Salvio (New York, 1952).

Dialogues of the Two Chief Systems of the World, trans. S. Drake (U. of California Press, 1953).

Guevara, A. de. *Aviso de privados o despertador de cortesanos* (Paris, 1912).

Libro áureo de Marco Aurelio, ed. R. Foulché-Delbose, in *Revue Hispanique*, LXXVI (June, 1929), pp. 1–319.

Menosprecio de corte y alabanza de aldea (Madrid, 1952).

Una década de Césares, ed. J. R. Jones (Chapel Hill, N.C., 1966).

Vida del famosísimo Emperador Marco Aurelio, con el Relox de Príncipes (Seville, 1532).

López de Palacios Rubios, J. *De las Islas del Mar Océano*, trans. A. Millares Carlo (Mexico, 1954).

Paz, M. de. *Del dominio de los Reyes de España sobre los Indios*, trans. A. Millares Carlo (Mexico, 1954).

Menno Simons, *The Writings of Menno Simons*, ed. J. C. Wenger, trans. L. Verduin (Scottdale, Penn., 1956).

Montaigne, M. de. *The Complete Essays of Montaigne*, ed. D. M. Frame (Stanford, 1965).

More, T. *Utopia*, ed. E. Sturz (New Haven and London, 1968).

Palmieri, M. *Della vita civile* (Florence, 1529).

Porta, G. della. *Natural Magick* (London, 1659).

Rabelais, F. *Gargantua and Pantagruel*, trans. J. Le Clerq (New York, n.d.).

Ronsard, P. de. *Oeuvres complètes*, ed. G. Cohen (Paris, 1950), II.

Sandoval, P. de. *Historia de la vida y hechos del Emperador Carlos V*, in Biblioteca de Autores Españoles (Madrid, 1956), v. 80–82.

Santa Cruz, A. de. *Crónica del Emperador Carlos V* (5 vols., Madrid, 1920–25).

Sepúlveda, J. Ginés de. *Democrates alter*, ed. A. Losada (Madrid, 1951).

Epistolario de Juan Ginés de Sepúlveda, ed. A. Losada (Madrid, 1966).

Opera (4 vols., Madrid, 1780).

Proposiciones temerarias, escandalosas y heréticas que notó el doctor Sepúlveda en el libro de la conquista de Indias, in A. M. Fabié, *Vida y escritos de don Fray Bartolomé de las Casas* (2 vols., Madrid, 1897), II.

Tratados políticos de Juan Ginés de Sepúlveda, ed. and trans. A. Losada (Madrid, 1963).

Soto, D. de. *De justitia et jure,* trans. M. González Ordoñez (5 vols., Madrid, 1967–1968).

Fray Bartolomé de las Casas. *Controversia con el doctor Sepúlveda acerca de los Indios,* in Biblioteca de Autores españoles (Madrid, 1857), v. 65.

Seyssel, C. de. *La Monarchie de France,* ed. J. Poujol (Paris, 1961).

Suárez, F. *De legibus,* ed. and trans. J. R. Egillor Muniozguren (6 vols., Madrid, 1967).

Valdés, A. de. *Alfonso de Valdés and the Sack of Rome,* trans. J. E. Longhurst (Albuquerque, N.M., 1952).

Diálogo de las cosas ocurridas en Roma, ed. J. F. Montesinos (Madrid, 1928).

Diálogo de Mercurio y Carón, ed. J. F. Montesinos (Madrid, 1929).

Vitoria, F. de. *Comentarios a la Secunda secundae de Santo Tomás,* ed. V. Beltrán de Heredia (5 vols., Salamanca, 1932–1935).

De Indis et De jure belli relectiones, ed. E. Nys, trans. J. P. Bate, in The Classics of International Law, gen. ed. J. Brown Scott (Washington, 1917), III.

Las relecciones De Indis y De jure belli, ed. J. Malagón Barceló (Washington, 1963).

Les leçons de Francisco de Vitoria sur les problèmes de la colonisation et de la guerre, ed. and trans. J. Baumel (Montpellier, 1936).

Obras. Relecciones teológicas, ed. T. Urdánoz (Madrid, 1960).

Relecciones teológicas, trans. J. Torrubiano Ripoll (3 vols., Madrid, 1917).

Relecciones teológicas, ed. and trans. L. A. Getino (3 vols., Madrid, 1933–1936).

Relectio Concerning Civil Power, trans. G. L. Williams, in J. Brown Scott's *The Origin of International Law. Part I: Francisco de Vitoria and his Law of Nations* (Oxford and London, 1934).

Relectio de Indis, ed. L. Pereña Vicente (Madrid, 1967).

Vives, J. L. *De communione rerum,* in *Opera omnia* (8 vols., Madrid, 1780), v.

Obras completas de Juan Luis Vives, ed. and trans. L. Riber (2 vols., Madrid, 1948).

Opera omnia (8 vols., Valencia, 1784).

II. SECONDARY WORKS

Adams, R. P. *The Better Part of Valor* (Seattle, 1962).

Albertini, Q. *L'oeuvre de Francisco de Vitoria et la doctrine canonique du Droit de la guerre* (Paris, 1903).

Arquillière, H.-X. *L'Augustinisme politique* (Paris, 1955).

Atkinson, W. C. 'Luis Vives and Poor Relief', *The Dublin Review,* CXCVII (July–Sept., 1935).

298 *Bibliography*

Allen J. W. *A History of Political Thought in the Sixteenth Century* (London, 1928).

Allevi, L. 'Francesco de Vitoria e il Rinascimento della scolastica nel secolo XVI', *RFN*, xix (1927), pp. 401–441.

Alvarez, J. L. 'Sobre Maquiavelo en España', *RDP*, iii (1934), pp. 155–60.

Alvarez Gandín, S. *Doctrinas políticas de Vitoria y Suárez* (Oviedo, 1950).

Andrés Martín, M. *Historia de la Teología en España (1470–1570)* (Rome, 1962).

Arco y Garay, R. *La idea del imperio en la política y literatura españolas* (Madrid, 1944).

Antonio, N. de. *Bibliotheca hispana nova* (2 vols., Madrid, 1788).

Andrés Marcos, T. *Los imperialismos de Juan Ginés de Sepúlveda en su Democrates alter* (Madrid, 1947).

Bainton, R. H. *Christian Attitudes toward War and Peace* (New York, 1960).
'The Early Church and War', *HTR*, 39 (1946), pp. 189–211.

Barcia Trelles, C. *Francisco de Vitoria, fundador del Derecho internacional moderno* (Valladolid, 1928).
Interpretación del hecho americano por la España universitaria del siglo XVI. La escuela internacionalista del siglo XVI (Montevideo, 1949).

Barker, E. *The Politics of Aristotle* (Oxford, 1958).

Baron, H. *The Crisis of the Early Italian Renaissance* (Princeton, 1966).
'Secularization of Wisdom and Political Humanism in the Renaissance', *JHI*, xxi 1 (1960).

Bataillon, M. 'Alonso de Valdés, auteur du *Diálogo de Mercurio y Carón*', in *Homenaje ofrecido a Menéndez Pidal* (2 vols., Madrid, 1925).
'Autour de Luis Vives et d'Iñigo de Loyola', *BH*, xxxii (1930), pp. 97–113.
'Erasme et la chancellerie impériale', *BH*, xxiv (1924), pp. 27–34.
Erasmo y España, trans. A. Alatorre (Mexico, 1966).
'J. L. Vives, réformateur de la bienfaisance', *BHR*, xiv (1952).
'L'idée de la découverte de l'Amérique chez les Espagnols du XVIe. siècle (d'après un livre récent)', *BH*, lv (1953), pp. 23–55.

Batllori, M. 'Lignes fondamentales de l'humanisme dans la Péninsule Ibérique', Congrès International des Études Humanistes, in *Revue de Littérature Comparée* (Paris), xxx 4 (1956).

Baumel, J. *Les problèmes de la colonisation et de la guerre dans l'oeuvre de Francisco de Vitoria* (Montpellier, 1936).

Beaufort, D. *La guerre comme instrument de secours et de punition* (The Hague, 1933).

Becker, J. *La tradición política española* (Madrid, 1896).

Beinert, B. 'El testamento político de Carlos V de 1548. Estudio crítico', in *Carlos V. Homenaje de la Universidad de Granada* (Granada, 1958).

Bell, A. F. G. *El Renacimiento en España* (Zaragoza, 1944).
Juan Ginés de Sepúlveda (Oxford, 1925).
Luis de León (Oxford, 1923).

Beltrán de Heredia, V. 'Doctrina de Vitoria sobre las relaciones entre la Iglesia y el Estado y fuentes de la misma', *CT*, 56 (1937).

'El maestro Domingo de Soto en la controversia de Las Casas con Sepúlveda', *CT*, xlv (1932), pp. 35–49; pp. 177–93.

'Final de la discusión acerca de la patria del Maestro Vitoria. La prueba documental que faltaba', *CT*, xlv (1953), pp. 275–89.

Francisco de Vitoria (Barcelona, 1939).

'La Teología en nuestras Universidades del Siglo de Oro', *Annalecta Sacra Tarraconensia*, xiv (1942).

Las corrientes de espiritualidad entre los dominicos en el siglo XVI (Salamanca, 1941).

Bender, H. S. 'The Pacifism of Sixteenth-Century Anabaptists', *MQR*, 30 (1956), n.1, pp. 5–19.

Beneyto Pérez, J. *Ginés de Sepúlveda, humanista y soldado* (Madrid, 1944).

Los orígenes de la ciencia política en España (Madrid, 1949).

Textos políticos españoles de la baja Edad Media (Madrid, 1944).

Benito, E. *Toledo en el siglo XV* (Madrid, 1961).

Bense, W. F. 'Paris Theologians on War and Peace, 1521–1529', *CH*, June (1972), pp. 168–85.

Beuve-Méry, H. *La thèorie des pouvoirs publics d'après Francisco de Vitoria* (Paris, 1928).

Bigongiari, D. *The Political Ideas of Saint Thomas Aquinas* (New York, 1960).

Bleznick, D. W. *Fadrique Furió Ceriol, Political Thinker of Sixteenth-Century Spain* (Unpublished Dissertation, Columbia University, 1954).

'Los conceptos políticos de Furió Ceriol', *REP*, 149 (1966), pp. 25–45.

'Spanish Reaction to Machiavelli in the Sixteenth and Seventeenth Centuries', *JHI*, xix (1958), pp. 542–50.

Boas, M. *The Scientific Renaissance* (New York, 1962).

Boehmer, E. *Bibliotheca Wiffeniana. Spanish Reformers of Two Centuries from 1520* (3 vols., Strasbourg and London, 1874–1904).

Bonet, A. *La filosofía de la libertad y las controversias teológicas en la España del siglo XVI* (Barcelona, 1932).

Bonilla y San Martín, A. *Luis Vives y la filosofía del Renacimiento* (3 vols., Madrid, 1929).

Born, L. K. 'Erasmus on Political Ethics', *Political Science Quarterly*, xliii (1928).

'The Perfect Prince: a Study in Thirteenth- and Fourteenth-Century Ideals', *Speculum*, iii (1928), pp. 470–504.

'Some Notes on the Political Theories of Erasmus', *JMH*, ii (1930).

'The *Specula principum* of the Carolingian Renaissance', *Revue Belge de Philologie et d'Histoire*, xii (1933), pp. 583–612.

Braudel, F. *La Méditerranée et le monde méditerranéen* (2 vols., Paris, 1966).

'La politique imperiale de Charles-Quint', *Annuaire du Collège de France*, lix (1959).

Brière, Y. de la. 'La conception de la paix et de la guerre chez Saint Augustin', *Revue de Philosophie*, Nouvelle Sèrie, i (1930), pp. 557–72.

La conception du Droit international chez les théologiens catholiques (Paris, 1929).

Le Droit de juste guerre (Paris, 1938).

'Les étapes de la tradition théologique concernant le Droit de juste guerre', *RGDIP* (1937).

Brock, P. *The Political and Social Doctrines of the Unity of the Czech Brethren* (The Hague, 1957).

Brufau Prats, J. 'El pensamiento político de Domingo de Soto y su concepción del poder', *AS* Derecho IV 3 (1960).

Buisson, F. *Dictionnaire de pédagogie et d'instruction primaire*, lère partie, pp. 2435–39, 'Education de princes', bibliography (Paris, 1882–1887).

Bullón Fernández, E. *El concepto de soberanía en la escuela jurídica española del siglo XVI* (Madrid, 1935).

Burtt, E. A. *The Metaphysical Foundations of Modern Physical Science* (New York, 1960).

Caballero, F. *Alonso y Juan Valdés* (Madrid, 1875).

Cadoux, C. J. *The Early Christian Attitude Toward War* (London, 1919).

Caldwell, W. E. *Hellenic Conceptions of Peace* (New York, 1919).

Cameron, R. 'The Attack on the Biblical Work of Lefèvre d'Etaples, 1514–1521', *CH*, 38 (1969).

Cánovas del Castillo, A. 'Sobre las ideas políticas de los españoles durante la Casa de Austria', *Revista de España*, VI–VII (1868–1869).

Cantimori, D. 'Rhetoric and Politics in Italian Humanism', *Journal of the Warburg Institute*, I (1937), pp. 83–102.

Carro, V. 'El Emperador Carlos V ante las controversias teológico-jurídicas de Indias', *Cuadernos Hispanoamericanos*, 107–108 (1958), pp. 262–83.

La 'Communitas orbis' y las rutas del Derecho internacional según Francisco de Vitoria (Santander, 1962).

La Teología y los teólogo-juristas españoles ante la conquista de Indias (Seville, 1945).

'Las controversias de Indias y las ideas teológico-jurídicas que las preparan y explican', *CT*, LXVII (1944), pp. 5–32.

Las controversias teológico-jurídicas en el siglo XVI (Salamanca, 1950).

'Los fundamentos teológico–jurídicos de las doctrinas de Vitoria', *CT*, LXXII (1947), pp. 95–122.

'The Spanish Theological–Juridical Renaissance and the Ideology of Bartolomé de las Casas', in *Bartolomé de las Casas* (De Kalb, Ill., 1971), eds. J. Friede and B. Keen, pp. 236–75.

Caspari, F. 'Erasmus on the Social Functions of Christian Humanism', *JHI*, VIII (1947).

Cassirer, E. *The Individual and the Cosmos in Renaissance Philosophy*, trans. M. Demandi (London, 1963).

The Philosophy of the Enlightenment, trans. F. C. A. Koelln and J. Pettegrove (Princeton, 1951).

Castro y Calvo, J. M. *El arte de gobernar en las obras de Don Juan Manuel* (Barcelona, 1945).

Ceñal, R. 'Anti-maquiavelismo de los tratadistas españoles de los siglos XVI y XVII', in *Umanesimo e scienza politica* (Milan, 1951).

Cepeda Adán, J. 'El gran Tendilla, medieval y renacentista', *Cuadernos de Historia*, I (1967), pp. 157–68.

En torno al concepto del Estado en los Reyes Católicos (Madrid, 1956).

Cereceda, F. 'El diálogo Menéndez Pidal–Brandi–Rassow sobre la idea imperial de Carlos V', *RF*, cxxxiv (1936), pp. 411–27.

Chabod, F. 'Milán o los Países Bajos', in *Carlos V. Homenaje de la Universidad de Granada* (Granada, 1958).

Chaunu, P. *L'Espagne de Charles-Quint* (2 vols., Paris, 1973).

Chossat, M. *La guerre et la paix d'après le droit naturel chrètien* (Paris, 1918).

Church, W. F. *Constitutional Thought in Sixteenth-Century France* (New York, 1969).

Cohn, N. *The Pursuit of the Millennium* (New York, 1961).

Colish, M. L. 'The Mime of God: Vives on the Nature of Man', *JHI*, 23 (1962), pp. 3–20.

Collingwood, R. *The Idea of Nature* (Oxford, 1945).

Corona, C. E. 'España desde la muerte del Rey Católico hasta la llegada de Don Carlos', *Universidad* (Zaragoza), xxxv 3–4 (1958), pp. 343–68.

Corts Grau, J. 'La doctrina social de Juan Luis Vives', *EHSE*, II (1962), pp. 65–89.

Los juristas clásicos españoles (Madrid, 1948).

Costa y Martínez, J. *Apuntes para la historia de las doctrinas políticas en España* (Madrid, 1884).

Costes, R. *Vida de fray Antonio de Guevara* (Valladolid, 1960).

Crombie, A. C. *Augustine to Galileo* (London, 1952).

Medieval and Early Modern Science (2 vols., New York, 1959).

Robert Grosseteste and the Origins of Experimental Science (Oxford, 1953).

Curcio, C. *La politica italiana del '400* (Florence, 1932).

Danvila y Collado, M. *Historia crítica y documentada de las Comunidades de Castilla* (6 vols., Madrid, 1897).

Davis, D. B. *The Problem of Slavery in Western Culture* (Ithaca, N.Y., 1966).

Deane, H. *The Social and Political Ideas of Saint Augustine* (New York, 1963).

Delboz, L. 'La notion éthique de la guerre', *RGDIP*, xxiv (1953), pp. 16–39.

Desdevises du Dezert, G. 'Les institutions de l'Espagne', *RH*, lxx (1927), pp. 26–146.

'Luis Vives d'après un ouvrage récent', *RH*, xii (1905).

Devine, F. E. 'Stoicism on the Best Regime', *JHI*, 31 (1970).

Díaz-Jiménez y Molleda, E. *Historia de los Comuneros de León y de su influencia en el movimiento general de Castilla* (Madrid, 1916).

Dickinson, J. 'The Medieval Conception of Kingship and Some of its Limitations, as Developed in the *Policraticus* of John of Salisbury', *Speculum*, I (1926), pp. 308–37.

Difernán, B. *El concepto del Derecho y justicia en los clásicos españoles del siglo XVI* (Madrid, n.d.).

Dijksterhuis, E. J. *The Mechanization of the World Picture*, trans. C. Dikshoorn (Oxford, 1961).

Domínguez Ortiz, A. *The Golden Age of Spain 1516–1659*, trans. J. Casey (London, 1971).

Duhem, P. *Le système du monde* (Paris, 1954).

Eguiagaray, F. *Los intelectuales españoles bajo Carlos V* (Madrid, 1965).

Elbe, J. von. 'The Evolution of the Just War in International Law', *American Journal of International Law*, xxxiii (1939), pp. 665–88.

Elías de Tejada Spinola, F. *Notas para una teoría del Estado según nuestros autores clásicos (siglos XVI y XVII)* (Sevilla, 1937).

Elliott, J. H. *Imperial Spain, 1469–1715* (New York, 1966).

The Old World and the New, 1494–1650 (Cambridge, 1970).

Eppstein, J. *The Catholic Tradition of the Law of Nations* (London, 1935).

Febvre, L. *Le problème de l'incroyance au XVIe. siècle: la religion de Rabelais* (Paris, 1947).

Fernández Alvarez, M. 'Bibliografía de Carlos V', *Cuadernos Hispanoamericanos*, 107–108 (1958), pp. 448–81.

Carlos V (Madrid, 1966), in *Historia de España*, ed. R. Menéndez Pidal.

'La paz de Cateau-Cambrésis', *Hispania*, xix 77 (1959), pp. 530–44.

La sociedad española en la época del Renacimiento (Madrid, 1970).

'Las instrucciones políticas de los Austrias Mayores', *Gesammelte Aufsäzte zur Kulturgeschichte Spaniens*, xxiii, 171–88.

Política mundial de Carlos V y Felipe II (Madrid, 1966).

Fernández de la Mora, G. 'Maquiavelo visto por los españoles de la Contrarreforma', *Arbor*, xiii 43–44 (1949), pp. 417–49.

Fernández de Velasco, R. *Referencias y transcripciones para la literatura política en España* (Madrid, 1925).

Fernández del Corral, J. M. 'Algunas ideas sobre la guerra de un canonista español del siglo XVI: el Doctor navarro Don Martín de Azpilcueta', *REDI*, vii 1 (1954), pp. 145–64.

Fernández-Santamaria, J. A. 'Erasmus on the Just War', *JHI*, xxxiv 2 (1973), pp. 209–26.

'Juan Ginés de Sepúlveda on the Nature of the American Indians', *The Americas*, xxxi (April, 1975).

Festugière (ed.), A. J. *Corpus Hermeticum* (4 vols., Paris, 1945 and 1954).

La révélation d'Hermès Trismégiste (4 vols., Paris, 1950–1954).

Fitzgerald, A. *Peace and War in Antiquity* (London, 1931).

Folgado, A. 'Los tratados *De legibus* y *De iustitia et iure* en los autores españoles del siglo XVI y primera mitad del XVII'. *CD*, clxxi 3 (1959), pp. 275–302.

Fontaine, J. 'Christianity and Military Service in the Early Church', *Concilium*, 7 (1965), pp. 107–19.

Fontán, A. 'Introducción al humanismo español', *Atlántida*, iv 22 (1966), pp. 443–54.

Fraile, G. 'Francisco de Vitoria, norma y síntesis del Renacimiento ortodoxo de nuestro siglo de oro', *CT*, l (1934), pp. 15–26.

Galán y Gutiérrez, E. 'Esquema historicosistemático de la teoría de la escuela española del Siglo de Oro acerca de la esencia, finalidad y legitimidad titular, por Derecho natural, del Poder político', *Revista General de Legislación y Jurisprudencia*, xxv (1953), pp. 57–91.

La teoría del Poder político según Francisco de Vitoria (Madrid, 1944).

Galino Carrillo, M. A. *Los tratados sobre educación de príncipes (siglos XVI y XVII)* (Madrid, 1948).

García Gallo, A. *Curso de historia del Derecho español* (2 vols., Madrid, 1950).

García-Pelayo, M. 'Juan Ginés de Sepúlveda y los problemas de la conquista de América', *Tierra Firme*, ii (1936), pp. 227–58.

García Villoslada, R. *La Universidad de Paris durante los estudios de Francisco de Vitoria* (Rome, 1938).

'Luis Vives y Erasmo; sus relaciones personales y doctrinales', *AAFV*, ii (1931), pp. 277–309.

Garín, E. *La cultura filosofica del Rinascimento italiano* (Florence, 1961).

Medioevo e Rinascimento (Bari, 1961).

Gero, S. '*Miles gloriosus*: The Christian and Military Service According to Tertullian', *CH*, 39 (1970), pp. 285–98.

Getino, L. A. *El maestro Francisco de Vitoria y el renacimiento teológico del siglo XVII* (Madrid, 1941).

Gilbert, A. H. *Machiavelli's 'Prince' and its Forerunners* (Durham, N.C., 1938).

Gilbert, F. 'The Humanist Concept of the Prince and *The Prince* of Machiavelli', *JMH*, xi (1939), pp. 449–83.

'Political Thought of the Renaissance and Reformation', *HLQ*, 4 (1941), pp. 443–68.

Gilmore, M. P. 'Erasmus and Alberto Pio, Prince of Carpi', in *Action and Conviction in Early Modern Europe*, eds. J. Siegel and T. Rabb (Princeton, 1969).

Gomis, J. B. 'El Nuevo Mundo en Luis Vives', *VV*, i (1943), pp. 332–69.

Gounon-Loubens, J. *Essais sur l'administration de la Castille au XVIe. siècle* (Paris, 1860).

Graf, P. *Luis Vives como apologeta: Contribución a la historia de la apologética*, trans. J. M. Millás Vallicrosa (Madrid, 1943).

Grant, E. 'Late Medieval Thought, Copernicus, and the Scientific Revolution', *JHI*, xxiii (1962), pp. 197–220.

Green, O. H. 'A Note on Spanish Humanism: Sepúlveda and His Translation of Aristotle's *Politics*', *Hispanic Review*, viii (1940), pp. 340.

Spain and the Western Tradition (4 vols., Madison, 1963–1966).

Gutiérrez, C. *Españoles en Trento* (Valladolid, 1951).

Guy, A. *Esquisse des progrès de la spèculation philosophique et théologique a Salamanque au cours du XVIe. siècle* (Paris, 1943).

Haines, C. G. *The Revival of Natural Law Concepts* (Cambridge, 1930).

Hale, J. R. 'Sixteenth-Century Explanations of War and Violence', *Past and Present*, May 1971.

'War and Public Opinion in the Fifteenth and Sixteenth Centuries', *Past and Present*, 22 (1962), pp. 18–35.

Hall, A. R. *The Scientific Revolution 1500–1800* (Boston, 1960).

Hamilton, B. *Political Thought in Sixteenth-Century Spain* (Oxford, 1963).

Hanke, L. *All Mankind is One* (De Kalb, Ill., 1974).
Aristotle and the American Indians (Chicago, 1959).
Las teorías políticas de Bartolomé de las Casas (Buenos Aires, 1935).
'More Heat and Some Light on the Spanish Struggle for Justice in the Conquest of America', *HAHR*, XLIV, pp. 293-340.
The Spanish Struggle for Justice in the Conquest of America (Boston, 1965).
Hartigan, R. S. 'Saint Augustine on War and Killing: The Problem of the Innocent', *JHI*, 27 (1966), pp. 195-204.
Haydn, H. *The Counter-Renaissance* (New York, 1960).
Heredia y Larrea, P. 'Ensayo sobre le evolución de las ideas políticas en España', *Revista de Archivos Bibliotecas y Museos* (1918).
Hicks, R. D. *Stoic and Epicurean* (New York, 1910).
Hillebrand, H. J. 'The Anabaptist View of the State', *MQR*, XXXII 2 (1958), pp. 83-111.
Huizinga, J. *Erasmus and the Age of the Reformation* (New York, 1957).
Jover Zamora, J. M. *Carlos V y los españoles* (Madrid, 1963).
'Panorama of Current Spanish Historiography', *CHM*, 6 (1960), pp. 1023-38.
Sobre los conceptos de monarquía y nación en el pensamiento político español del siglo XVI (Buenos Aires, 1950).
Keen, M. H. *The Law of War in the Late Middle Ages* (London, 1965).
Koyré, A. *Etudes galiléennes* (Paris, 1939).
Mystiques, spirituels, alchemistes (Paris, 1955).
Kristeller, P. O. *Renaissance Thought II* (New York, 1965).
Kuhn, T. *The Copernican Revolution* (Cambridge, Mass., 1957).
The Structure of Scientific Revolutions (Chicago, 1962).
Labrousse, R. *Essai sur la philosophie politique de l'ancienne Espagne: politique de raison, politique de la foi* (Paris, 1937).
Lange, C. L. *Histoire de l'internationalisme* (2 vols., New York, 1919).
Larequi, J. 'Del "jus gentium" al Derecho internacional. Francisco de Vitoria y los teólogos españoles del siglo XVI', *RF*, 83 (1928), pp. 21-37.
'El Derecho internacional en España durante los siglos XVI y XVII', *RF*, 81 (1927), pp. 222-32.
Laven, P. *Renaissance Italy* (New York, 1967).
Lewy, G. *Constitutionalism and Statecraft during the Golden Age of Spain; A Study in the Political Philosophy of Juan de Mariana* (Geneva, 1960).
Lissarague, S. *La teoría del Poder en Francisco de Vitoria* (Madrid, 1947).
Losada, A. *Fray Bartolomé de las Casas* (Madrid, 1970).
Juan Ginés de Sepúlveda a través de su Epistolario y nuevos documentos (Madrid, 1949).
Lynch, J. *Spain Under the Habsburgs* (2 vols., Oxford, 1964).
Maier, A. 'Ergebnisse der Spätscholastischen Naturphilosophie', *Scholastik*, XXXV 2 (1960), pp. 161-87. Reprinted in *Ausgehendes Mittelalter* (Rome, 1964).
Maravall, J. A. *Antiguos y Modernos. La idea del progreso en el desarrollo de una sociedad* (Madrid, 1966).
Carlos V y el pensamiento político del Renacimiento (Madrid, 1960).

'El descubrimiento de América en la historia del pensamiento político', *REP* (1952).

El humanismo de las armas de Don Quijote (Madrid, 1948).

La teoría española del Estado en el siglo XVII (Madrid, 1944).

'La visión utópica del imperio de Carlos V en la España de su época', *Carlos V. Homenaje de la Universidad de Granada* (Granada, 1958).

Las Comunidades de Castilla (Madrid, 1963).

Los factores de la idea del progreso en el Renacimiento Español (Madrid, 1963).

'Maquiavelo y Maquiavelismo en España', *BRAH*, Oct.–Dec. (1969), pp. 183–218.

'The Origins of the Modern State', *CHM*, vi 4 (1961), pp. 789–808.

March, J. M. *Niñez y juventud de Felipe II* (2 vols., Madrid, 1941).

Marcos Rodríguez, F. 'Don Diego de Covarrubias y la Universidad de Salamanca', *Salmanticensis*, vi 1 (1959), pp. 37–85.

Margolin, J.-C. *Guerre et paix dans la pensée d'Erasme* (Paris, 1973).

Marín López, A. 'El concepto del Derecho de gentes en Diego de Covarrubias y Leyva', *REDI*, vii 2–3 (1954), pp. 505–28.

Martin, R. 'Augustine's Two Cities', *JHI*, 33 (1972), pp. 195–216.

Mattingly, G. *Renaissance Diplomacy* (Baltimore, 1964).

McIlwain, C. H. *The Growth of Political Thought in the West* (New York, 1932).

McKenna, C. H. *Vitoria and His Times* (Washington, 1932).

Menéndez Pidal, R. 'Carlos V y las Comunidades vistas a nueva luz documental', in *El P. Las Casas y Vitoria* (Madrid, 1958).

'Fr. Antonio de Guevera y la idea imperial de Carlos V', *Archivo Ibero-Americano*, vi (1946), pp. 331–38.

La idea imperial de Carlos V (Madrid, 1955).

Menéndez-Reigada, I. G. 'El sistema ético–jurídico de Vitoria sobre el Derecho de gentes', *CT*, xxxix (1929), pp. 307–30.

Menéndez y Pelayo, M. *Historia de los heterodoxos españoles* (2nd ed., 7 vols., Madrid, 1911–1932).

Merriman, R. B. 'Charles V's Last Paper of Advice to His Son', *American Historical Review*, xxvii (1922–1923), pp. 489–91.

The Rise of the Spanish Empire in the Old and in the New (4 vols., New York, 1918–1934).

Mesnard, P. *L'Essor de la philosophie politique au XVIe. siècle* (Paris, 1952).

Monceaux, P. 'Saint Augustin et la guerre', in *L'Eglise et le Droit de guerre* (Paris, 1920), ch. ii.

Mónica, M. *La gran controversia del siglo XVI acerca del dominio español en América* (Madrid, 1952).

Monsegú, B. *Filosofía del humanismo de Juan Luis Vives* (Madrid, 1961).

'Los fundamentos filosóficos del humanismo de Juan Luis Vives', *VV*, xii no., pp. 47–8.

Montesinos, J. F. 'Algunas notas sobre el *Diálogo de Mercurio y Carón*', *Revista de Filología Española*, xvi (1929), pp. 225–66.

Moody, E. E. 'Empiricism and Metaphysics in Medieval Philosophy', *The Philosophical Review*, LXVII (1957), pp. 145-63.

Naszalyi, E. *El Estado según Francisco de Vitoria*, trans. I. G. Menéndez-Reigada (Madrid, 1948).

Nauert, C. G. *Agrippa and the Crisis of Renaissance Thought* (Urbana, Ill., 1965).

Newman, W. L. *The Politics of Aristotle* (2 vols., Oxford, 1887).

Nussbaum, A. *A Concise History of the Law of Nations* (New York, 1953).

Nys, E. *Le Droit de la guerre et les précurseurs de Grotius* (Brussels, 1882).

Le Droit des gens et les anciens jurisconsultes espagnols (The Hague, 1914).

Les origins du Droit international (Brussels, 1894).

'Quatre utopistes du XVIe. siècle', *Revue du Droit International*, XXI (1889).

Parry, J. H. *The Spanish Seaborne Empire* (New York, 1971).

The Spanish Theory of Empire in the Sixteenth Century (Cambridge, 1940).

Payne, S. G. 'Jaime Vicens Vives and the Writing of Spanish History', *JMH*, XXXIV (June, 1962), pp. 119-34.

Pereña Vicente, L. 'Diego de Covarrubias y Leyva, Maestro de Salamanca', *REDC*, XI 31 (1956), pp. 191-99.

'El concepto del Derecho de gentes en Francisco de Vitoria', *REDI*, V 2 (1952), pp. 603-28.

'La Universidad de Salamanca, forja del pensamiento político español en el siglo XVI', *AS* (Historia de la Universidad), I 2 (1954)

'Melchor Cano, discípulo de Francisco de Vitoria en Derecho internacional', *CT*, LXXXII (1955), pp. 463-78.

Misión de España en América, 1540-1560 (Madrid, 1946).

Pérez, J. *La révolution des Comunidades de Castille* (Bordeaux, 1970).

Pinta Llorente, M. de la; and Palacio, J. M. de. *Procesos inquisitoriales contra la familia de Juan Luis Vives* (Madrid, 1964).

Puigdollers Oliver, M. *La filosofía española de Luis Vives* (Madrid, 1940).

Quintanilla, M. 'El episodio de las Comunidades', *Estudios Segovianos*, VI (1954).

Quirk, R. E. 'Some Notes on a Controversial Controversy', *NAHR*, 34 (1954), pp. 357-64.

Randall, H. R. 'The Development of the Scientific Method in the School of Padua', *JHI*, I (1940).

Real Academia de la Historia. *Cortes de los antiguos reinos de León y Castilla* (5 vols., Madrid, 1861-1903).

Recasens Siches, D. L. 'Las teorías políticas de Francisco de Vitoria', *AAFV*, II (1931), pp. 165-222.

Redonet, L. 'Comentarios sobre las Comunidades y Germanías', *BRAH*, 145 (1959), pp. 7-87.

Reesor, M. E. *The Political Theory of the Old and Middle Stoa* (New York, 1951).

Regout, R. *La doctrine de la guerre juste de Saint Augustin à nos jours* (Paris, 1935).

Reidy, S. J. *Civil Authority According to Francis de Vitoria* (River Forest, Ill., 1959).

Riber, L. 'Erasmo y Luis Vives', *BRAE*, 24 (1945), pp. 193–224, and 26 (1947), pp. 81–135.

Rice, E. F. *The Renaissance Idea of Wisdom* (Cambridge, Mass., 1958).

Rodríguez Aranda, L. 'El racionalismo en el pensamiento político español', *REP*, 119 (1961), pp. 117–46.

Rolland, L. *Les fondateurs du Droit international* (Paris, 1904).

Rosen, E. *Three Copernican Treatises* (New York, 1939).

Russell Major, J. 'The Renaissance Monarchy as Seen by Erasmus, More, Seyssel, and Machiavelli', in *Action and Conviction in Early Modern Europe*, eds. J. Siegel and T. Rabb (Princeton, 1966).

Ryan, E. A. 'The Rejection of Military Service by the Early Christians', *Theological Studies*, 13 (1952), pp. 1–29.

Sabine, G. H. *A History of Political Theory* (New York, 1959).

Sala Balust, L. 'La espiritualidad española en la primera mitad del siglo XVI', *Cuadernos de Historia*, 1 (1967), pp. 169–87.

Salvá, A. *Burgos en la Comunidades de Castilla* (Burgos, 1895).

Sánchez Agesta, L. *El concepto del Estado en el pensamiento español del siglo XVI* (Madrid, 1959).

'La definición de los derechos naturales del hombre y el descubrimiento de América', *EA*, XVII 94–5 (1959), pp. 1–23.

'Ordine medievale e pensiero politico moderno', *Jus* (Università Cattolica del Sacro Cuore, Milano), VI 1 (1955), pp. 65–78.

Scott, J. B. *The Discovery of America and Its Influence on International Law* (Washington, 1929).

The Spanish Conception of International Law and of Sanctions (Washington, 1934).

The Spanish Origen of International Law (Washington, 1928).

Seaver, H. L. *The Great Revolt in Castile* (Boston, 1928).

Semprún Gurrea, J. M. 'Fadrique Furió Ceriol, consejero de príncipes y príncipe de consejeros', *Cruz y Raya*, 20 (1934), pp. 9–65.

'Fadrique Furió Ceriol. La pica en Flanders', *Cruz y Raya*, 22 (1935), pp. 9–89.

Shaetzel, W. 'La teoría de la guerra de Francisco de Vitoria y la moderna guerra de agresión', *Anales de la Universidad de Murcia*, XII 3–4 (1953–1954), pp. 407–24.

Silió Cortés, C. *Maquiavelo y su tiempo* (Madrid, 1946).

Stapfer, L. 'Idées de Rabelais sur la guerre', *Bibliothèque Universelle et Revue Suisse*, Nov. (1888), pp. 367–79.

Sturzo, L. 'La communauté internationale et le Droit de la guerre', *Cahiers de la Nouvelle Journée*, 18 (1931).

Sugranyes de Franch, R. 'Les études humanistes en Espagne et au Portugal', Congrès International des Etudes Humanistes, in *RLC*, XXX 4 (1956).

Tate, R. B. 'Italian Humanism and Spanish Historiography of the Fifteenth Century. A Study of the Paralipomenon Hispanae of Joan de Margarit, Cardinal Bishop of Gerona', *BJRL*, XXXIV 1 (1951), pp. 137–65.

'Nebrija the Historian', *BHS*, XXX 3 (1957), pp. 125–46.

Throndyke, L. *History of Magic and Experimental Science* (6 vols., New York, 1923–1941).

Tierno, E. 'De las Comunidades o la historia como proceso', *Boletín del Seminario de Derecho Público* (Universidad de Salamanca), May–Oct. 1957, n. 16–19.

El tacitismo en las doctrinas políticas del Siglo de Oro español (Murcia, 1949).

Tooke, J. D. *The Just War in Aquinas and Grotius* (London, 1965).

Truyol Serra, A. *Los principios del Derecho público en Francisco de Vitoria* (Madrid, 1946).

'Razón de Estado y Derecho de gentes en tiempo de Carlos V', in *Karl V. Der Kaiser und seine Zeit. Kölner Colloquium*, eds. P. Rassow and F. Schalk (Köln, 1960).

Vanderpol, A. *La doctrine scolastique du Droit de guerre* (Paris, 1919).

Le Droit de guerre d'après les théologiens et les canonistes du Moyen Age (Paris, 1911).

Vernon Arnold, E. *Roman Stoicism* (New York, 1958).

Vega, P. de (ed.). *Antología de escritores políticos del Siglo de Oro* (Madrid, 1966).

Vicens Vives, J. 'Estructura Estatal en los siglos XVI y XVII', XIe. Congrès International des Sciences Historiques. *Rapports*, IV (Stockholm, 1960), pp. 1–23.

Vicens Vives, J. et al. 'L'Espagne aux XVIe. et XVIIe. siècles. L'Epoque des souverains autrichiens. Tendences, problèmes et perspectives de travail de la recherche historique en Espagne', *RH*, ccxx 447 (1958), pp. 1–42.

Vilar, P. *Spain: A Brief History* (Oxford, 1967).

Vollenhoven, C. van. *The Law of Peace*, trans. W. Carter (London, 1934).

Walker, D. P. 'Orpheus the Theologian and the Renaissance Platonists', *JWI*, xvi (1953), pp. 100–20.

Spiritual and Demonic Magic from Ficino to Campanella (London, 1958).

Walters, L. B. *Five Classic Just-War Theories: A Study in the Thought of Thomas Aquinas, Vitoria, Suárez, Gentili, and Grotius* (Unpublished Dissertation, Yale University, 1971).

Watson, F. 'J. L. Vives and St Augustine's "Civitas Dei"', *The Church Quarterly Review*, LXXVI (1913).

Williams, G. H. *The Radical Reformation* (Philadelphia, 1962).

Wright, H. F. *Vitoria and the State* (Washington, 1932).

Yates, F. A. 'Charles Quint et l'idée de l'Empire', in *Fêtes et cérémonies au temps de Charles-Quint-Les fêtes de la Renaissance*, IIe, Congrès de l'Association Internationale de Historiens de la Renaissance (Paris, 1960), pp. 57–97.

Giordano Bruno and the Hermetic Tradition (Chicago, 1964).

Zanta, L. *La Renaissance du Stoicisme au XVIe. siècle* (Paris, 1914).

Zavala, S. *Servidumbre natural y libertad cristiana*, Publicaciones del Instituto de Investigaciones Históricas, LXXXVII. Universidad de Buenos Aires (Buenos Aires, 1944).

Index

Activity (active life), 173, 174, 175, 177, 178, 188
see also under Sepúlveda
Adrian of Utrecht (Pope Adrian VI), 17, 50, 52, 163
Alamos de Barrientos, Baltasar, 248
Alba, 3rd duke of, Fernando Alvarez de Toledo, 238, 242, 243
Alberti, Leon Battista, 184
Albornoz, Gil de, Cardinal, 163
Alcalá, University of, 4, 50, 163
Aldus Manutius, 163
alumbrados, 272
Ambrose, St, 94
America, discovery of
and change, 59
and Christianity, 60
problem, 60
and Christian humanism, 60
and humanism, 60
jus communicationis, 61
and law of nations, 61
and Renaissance state, 61
and law of war, 62
see also under Vitoria, Sepúlveda
Anabaptists, 122, 130, 156, 185; *see also* Menno Simons and Vives on war
Aquinas, St Thomas, 3, 64, 67, 90, 92, 96, 98, 106, 107, 118, 129, 160, 185, 247
Argote, Francisco de, 227 n.94
Arias Barbosa, 88
Arias Montano, Benito, 88
Aristotle, 67, 88, 94, 160, 174, 175, 177,

178, 185, 187, 189, 209, 210, 211, 212, 213, 234
Athenaeus, 170
Augsburg, Peace of, 274
Augustine on war
definition, 123–4
in antiquity, 124
kinds of war, 124–5
pacifism, 125
New Testament, 125–6
the just war, 126
goal of the just war, 126–7
unjust peace, 127
defeat of the just, 128
defensive war, 128–9
definition of peace, 127, 138
doubts about war's justice, 129
Augustine, St, 3, 94, 109, 158, 159, 160, 178, 198, 207, 217, 218
on justice, 104–5
definition of commonwealth, 105
Avila, Juan de, 273

Baroque, age of the, 249, 251, 252
Bataillon, M., 63, 248, 272
Beda, Noel, 143 n.77
Béjar, duke of, Juan de Zúñiga, 241, 243–4
Bender, H. S., 156
Berges, Antoine de, 50
Béza, Theodore, 155
Bigongiari, D., 107 n.22
Bodin, Jean, 1, 5, 62
Bologna, University of, 163, 164
Bononia, Jean de, 274

Borja, Francisco de, 273
Brandi, K., 37, 237
Bruni, Leonardo, 184
Budé, Gillaume, 186
Burgos, 19, 20

Cajetan, Cardinal (Tommaso da Vio), 90, 133, 134
Calvin, Jean, 155
Cambrai, Peace of, 36
Cano, Melchor, 5, 95–6, 273
capítulos, 22
Carpi, Prince of, Alberto Pio, 163, 165
Carranza, Bartolomé de, Cardinal Archbishop of Toledo, 95, 273
Carro, V., 4 n.2
Casas, Bartolomé de las, 95, 167, 168, 174, 186, 201, 206, 220
Castiglione, Baldassare, 154–5, 154 n.122, 285
Castrillo, Alonso de
  on foreigners, 15
  and *novedades*, 15
  and *comunes*, 16
  art of ruling, 16
  origin of political authority, 23, 24
  origin of society, 23, 24
  on monarchy, 24
  opposition to imperial idea, 25
  and *Comunero* movement, 25
  on medieval constitutionalism, 25, 30–4
  on social hierarchy, 27
  on citizens and citizenship, 26, 28, 30
  on the nobility, 27, 28, 30
  and the middle class, 27, 28, 29
  on the people, 28, 29
  and private property, 28–9
  on wealth and greed, 28, 29
  on the ruler, 29
  and the *Comunero* radicals, 25, 30
  on Castile's woes, 30
  on temporary rule, 30–1
  on government irresponsibility, 31
  on constitutional monarchy, 32
Castro, Alfonso de, 88
Cateau-Cambrésis, Peace of, 274
Catherine of Aragon, 17
Cazalla, Agustín, 272
Charles v, 35, 238, 273, 278

arrival in Castile, 12
and advisers, 13
disaffection of Castile, 13
and imperial election, 13
and *Perdón*, 35
political ideology, 36, 37, 245–6
crowned at Bologna, 37
Madrid speech, 37
see also under Valdés
Charles v's *instrucciones*
  the inexperienced ruler, 238
  the ruler and God, 239
  the ruler and the Church, 239
  the ruler and justice, 239
  the ruler and flatterers, 239
  the ruler and counselors, 240, 241
  education of the ruler, 240
  the ruler and foreign policy, 244–5
  the ruler and war and peace, 244–5
  the good ruler, 246
Charles viii of France, 147
Charron, Pierre, 184
Chelchitzky, Peter, 129, 130, 156
Chrysippus, 209
Church, W. F., 21 n.17
Cicero, 94, 171, 172, 173, 207
Cifuentes, Count of, 242
Cisneros, Francisco Jiménez de, Cardinal Archbishop of Toledo, 12, 163
Cleanthes, 204
Clement vii, 163, 166
Clichtove, Josse, 134
Cobos, Francisco de los, 241, 242, 243
College of Saint Jacques, 63
College of San Antonio de Sigüenza, 163
College of San Clemente (University of Bologna), 163
College of San Gregorio, 63
Commonwealth
  see under Community
Comunero movement
  in political literature, 14
  see also Comunidades, Castrillo, and Constitutionalism
Comunidades
  antecedents of the war, 11
  background of the revolt, 17
  and the *servicio*, 17
  and the *procuradores*, 17, 18, 20, 22, 25

and the Santa Junta, 17, 18, 19, 22
ideology of the movement, 18
and the *Provisión*, 18
and the Royal Council, 18, 22
and Burgos, 19
and the *capítulos*, 20, 21, 22
and constitutionalism, 20, 22
and the Cortes, 21
and royal power, 21, 22
consequences of their failure, 23
consejero
  see Furió Ceriol
Concejo
  see Furió Ceriol
Concord, 120
  see also under Vives
Constitutionalism
  in Castile, 11
  in France, 33
  and *Comunero* movement, 33
  French and Castilian, 33, 34
  see also under Castrillo
Contemplation (Contemplative life), 173,
  174, 175, 177, 188
  see also under Sepúlveda
Cortes of Castile, 11, 12, 13, 17, 20, 22
Council of Castile, 88
Council of Justice, 22
Council of State, 242
Covarrubias, Diego de
  life and works, 88
  on political authority, 89
  on the just war, 90 *et sqq.*
  causes for just war, 90, 91, 92
  on slavery caused by war, 92, 93
  on natural law, 92, 93
  and the law of nations, 93, 94
  on the law of war, 93 *et sqq.*, 94
  on Aristotle's natural servitude, 93-4
  on natural servitude and war, 94
  on natural freedom, 94
  on civil slavery, 94
  and origin of slavery, 94
Crépy, Peace of, 242
Crockaert, Peter, 63
Croy, Gillaume de, 13, 50
Cynics, 203

Dante, 49
Discord

see under Vives
Domínguez Ortiz, A., 13
Dorp, Martin, 50

Eck, Johannes, 90
Egidius Romanus, 247
Elton, G. R., 5 n.4
encomendero, 212
encomienda, 212
Epictetus, 208
Erasmianism, Spanish, 4, 6, 35, 36
Erasmus, age of, 2, 4, 33, 113, 120, 158,
  171
Erasmus, Desiderius, 1, 3, 4, 5, 35, 37,
  38, 39, 40, 42, 49, 50, 56, 63, 64,
  121, 122, 130, 250, 252
  man as social and political animal,
  114
  the importance of the ruler, 114-15
Erasmus on war
  the nature of war, 130
  and the survival of society, 131
  differences with Neoscholasticism, 131
  and Christians, 132
  the New Testament, 134
  causes, 135, 137
  and its evils, 136
  and arbitration, 138
Evangelical humanism
  see under Valdés, Vives, Erasmus
Eximenis, Francisco, 248

Ferdinand of Aragon, 11, 12, 18, 242,
  254
Fernández Alvarez, M., 237
Fonseca, Alonso, Archbishop of Toledo,
  273
Fortitude, 177
French constitutional thought, 33
Furió Ceriol, Fadrique
  life and works, 274
  the ruler's twofold nature, 276
  the ruler's education, 276-7, 278-9
  the good ruler, 277
  on the ruler's prudence, 277
  pragmatism, 278
  on counselors, 278
  on the ruler's intellect, 278
  on kingdoms, 280
  the ruler's council, 280

Furió Ceriol, Fadrique (*cont.*)
  purpose of the council, 280
  the council and the ruler, 280–1
  organization of the council, 281–4
  number of councils, 281
  functions of the councils, 281–4
  Council of Finance, 281
  Council of Peace, 281–2
  Council of War, 282
  Council of Subsistences, 282–3
  Council of Justice, 283
  Council of Grants, 283–4
  definition of *consejero*, 284
  the *privado*, 284
  qualities of *consejeros*, 284–90
  on history, 286–7
  selection of *consejeros*, 289–90
  the ruler's public and private personality, 291–2
  on activity and contemplation, 292
  on expertise in government, 293–4
  the republic's stability, 293–4

Galileo, 117–18
Gattinara, Mercurino, 37, 243
Gayangos, Diego de, 15
Gómez Barroso, 248
Gómez Manrique, 248
Gonzaga, Ercole, 163
Gracián de Alderete, 50
Granada, Luis de, 273
Granvelle, Antoine Perrenot de, Cardinal, 243
Gratian, 197
Gudiel, Alonso, 273
Guevara, Antonio de
  life and works, 254–5
  on the *privado*, 255–6, 257, 258
  on the ruler, 257, 259, 260, 262, 264, 265, 266, 267, 269–70
  mirror for a prince, 261
  on man's nature, 261–2, 263
  man as social and political being, 262–3
  on monarchy, 263–4, 266
  origin and nature of political authority, 264–5
  justice, 268–9
  on war and peace, 269–70
  on the ruler and war, 269–70

Guevara, Fernando de, 242
Guicciardini, Francesco, 178

Habsburg, dynasty, 12, 36
Hale, J. R., 159 n.130
Hanke, L., 210 n.40
Henry iv of Castile, 32
Henry viii of England, 50, 55
Herrezuela, Antonio de, 272

Illuminism, Spanish, 272
Innocent, the
  see Erasmus, More, Sepúlveda, Vitoria on war
Inquisition, the, 272, 273, 274
Instrucciones, 237
  see also under Charles v
Isabel of Castile, 6, 11, 12, 18, 31, 254
Isabel of Portugal, 36
Isidore of Seville, 129

Juana of Castile, 12, 18
Junta of Valladolid, 95
Justinian, 94

Koenigsberger, H. G., 37

Laínez, Diego, 5
Law
  see law as positive, natural, of nations, of war, under the various authors
Lefèvre d'Étaples, Jacques, 143 n.77
León, Luis de, 88, 273
Loaisa, García de, Cardinal Archbishop of Seville, 242, 244
Lombard, Peter, 3
López de Palacios Rubios, Juan, 236 n.108
López Zúñiga, Diego, 164
Louvain, University of, 50, 274
Lull, Ramón, 129
Luther, Martin, 155, 164, 187

Machiavelli, Niccolò, 2, 5, 47, 62, 103, 106, 109, 110, 115, 122, 130, 187, 248, 249, 250, 251, 276, 277, 292
Madrid, Treaty of, 36
Magnanimity, 177
Manetti, Giannozzo, 184
Manrique, Alonso, Archbishop of Seville, Inquisitor General, 273
Maravall, J. A., 36, 37, 250, 261, 270

Margarit, Joan de, 248
Mariana, Juan de, 273
Marsilius of Padua, 101, 112
Mary Tudor, 50
Martínez Siliceo, Juan, Cardinal Archbishop of Toledo, 166, 243
Martire d'Anghiera, Pietro, 38
Mayer, E. W., 237
Maximilian of Habsburg, 13
McIlwain, C. H., 113
Menéndez Pidal, R., 37, 261
Menéndez-Reigada, I. G., 100
Mexía, Pedro, 14, 21
Miranda, Sancho de, 163
Mirrors of princes, 247
Molina, Luis de, 88
Moncada, Hugo de, 155
Montaigne, Michel de, 204–5, 206
Monzón, Francisco de, 248
More, Thomas, 40, 153
Mülhberg, battle of, 238

Naszalyi, E., 71, 107
Nebrija, Antonio de, 50
Neoscholasticism, 4, 60, 61, 62, 63, 64, 72, 87, 115, 116, 130, 131, 132, 277
Núñez, Hernán, 88

Olivares, conde duque de, Gaspar de Guzmán, 251
Ortega y Gasset, J., 195
Osorno, Count of, 242, 244
Oxford University, 50

Páez de Castro, Juan, 160
Palmieri, Matteo, 184
Panaetius, 170, 172, 206
Paris, University of, 50, 63, 274
Parry, J. H., 235 n.107
Paul, St, 182
Paz, Matías de, 236 n.108
Pérez, J., 23 n.20
Petrarch, Francesco, 270
Philip of Habsburg, Archduke, 4, 12, 30
Philip II of Spain, 13, 88, 166, 189, 237, 239, 244, 252, 274, 275, 279
Philip IV of Spain, 252
philosophia Christi
    see under Valdés, Vives

Plato, 94
Plutarch, 209
Ponce de la Fuente, Constantino, 272
Ponce de León, Juan, 272
Posidonius, 170
privado
    see under Furió Ceriol, Guevara
procuradores
    see under *Comunidades*

Quiñones, Francisco de, Cardinal of Santa Cruz, 164, 166
Quiroga, Gaspar de Quiroga, Cardinal Archbishop of Toledo, 273

Rabelais, François, 151, 152
Ramírez, Bishop, 220
Ramus, Peter, 274
Regout, R., 129
Rice, E. F., 184, 186, 187
Rodríguez de Lancina, Juan, 251
Rojas, Domingo de, 272
Royal Council, 18, 37
Russell Major, J., 33 n.57

Salamanca, School of, 3, 4, 5, 60, 113, 122, 123, 131
    see also under Spanish school
Salamanca, University of, 4, 5, 63, 87, 88
Salisbury, John of, 247
Salmerón, Alfonso, 5
Sánchez de Brozas, Francisco, 273
San Esteban, Convento de, 272
Santa Junta
    see under *Comunidades*
Santillana, Marquis of, 248
Schmalkaldic League, 238
Scholasticism, 3, 4
Science, 116, 117–19
Scott, J. B., 80
Seaver, H. L., 13
Seneca, 208
Sepúlveda, Juan Ginés de, 94, 95, 159–60, 251, 278
    life and works, 163–7
    controversy with Erasmus, 165, 167–9
    controversy with Las Casas, 167, 168
    universal society, 171, 172

Sepúlveda, Juan Ginés (*cont.*)
  on justice, 180, 196
  on prudence, 180, 181, 189, 196
  on virtue, 180–1, 183, 207
  on reason, 181
  activity, 181, 183, 233, 236
  contemplation, 181, 183, 236
  wealth, 182
  theologian and humanist, 185
  secularization of wisdom, 187
  Aristotle and Christianity, 187
  natural law, 188, 197, 198, 205, 206, 215–16, 229
  speculation and *praxis*, 188
  on civil society, 189, 191–2, 234–5
  on the state, 189
  servus, 190, 213
  elitism, 190, 194, 195, 231–2, 233
  definition of nobility, 192
  virtues of good citizenship, 192–3
  on education, 193
  on the law, 197, 198
  on monarchy, 199, 200
  on war, 208–9
  on natural servitude, 209 *et sqq.*, 226–8, 229, 230
  on herile rule, 211, 213, 228, 234–5
  on the law of nations, 230
  see also Stoicism
Sepúlveda on the American Indians, 191
  as rational beings, 201–2, 208
  Indian society, 202, 203
  and natural law, 202, 203, 210
  and activity, 203
  as civil beings, 207
  and their status, 211–12, 214, 232–3, 234, 235
  and civil servitude, 225–9, 230
  and natural servitude, 228, 229, 230
Sepúlveda on war
  the just war, 214, 216, 218, 219, 221, 222, 223
  and Christians, 214
  and Christ, 215–16, 230
  and natural law, 216, 217, 221
  and the ruler, 217, 221
  and peace, 220–1
  and moderation, 222
  and the innocent, 222

  and the Indians, 223–4, 228
  and civil servitude, 225–9, 230
  and ignorance, 228
Sessa, Dukes of, 164
Seyssel, Claude de, 24 n.26, 26 n.29, 27 n.33, 27 n.37, 31 n.55
Simmons, Menno
  on war, 157–8
Slavery
  see such titles as Indians, natural law, servitude, war, etc., under the following authors: St Augustine, Aristotle, Cano, Covarrubias, Sepúlveda, Soto, Vitoria
Soto, Domingo de, 5, 61, 94, 95, 220
Spanish imperialism, 14
Spanish political philosophy, 2
Spanish school, 1, 2, 3, 106, 121, 134, 158
  see also under School of Salamanca
Stoicism, 169, 170, 171, 172, 203, 207, 208, 209, 210
  Roman, 170, 206
Suárez, Francisco, 61, 132–3, 135

Talon, Omar, 274
Tavera, Juan, Cardinal Archbishop of Toledo, 241
Tertullian, 130, 132
Thucydides, 271
Toledo and the *Comunidades*, 17, 19
Tordesillas, 18, 22
Torre, Felipe de la, 248
Trastámara, dynasty, 11, 36
Trent, 88, 95
Turrecremata (Juan de Torquemada), 94

Ulzúrrum, Miguel de, 14

Valdés, Alfonso de
  version of the battle of Pavia, 36
  life and works, 38
  Mercurio y Carón, 39 *et sqq.*
  the state of Christendom, 39, 40, 41
  evangelical humanism, 39
  Charles v, 40
  as moralist and reformer, 40
  on education, 40, 46
  on man's nature, 40
  on the good prince, 43–5, 253–4

and political reform, 44–5, 47
and Erasmus' *Institutio*, 45, 46
dynasticism, 46
and Machiavelli, 46
Church and state, 48
philosophia Christi, 48
on war, 151, 152, 153–4
Valdés, Hernando de, Inquisitor General, 241, 244, 272
Valencia, University of, 49, 274
Valera, Diego de, 248
Valladolid, *Comunero* radicals, 17
Valldaura, Margaret, 50
Vico, Giambattista, 184
Vilanova, Arnaldo de, 248
Villalar, battle of, 14, 17, 23
Vitoria, Francisco de
Spain in America, 62, 80 *et sqq.*
life and works, 63
origin of society, 65
Aristotelian teleology, 70
international law, 70, 99
the common good, 70–1
rationality of the Indians, 78, 86–7
the Emperor is not lord of the world, 81
illegitimate titles for conquest, 81–4
legitimate titles for conquest, 84–7
law of nations, 98, 99, 100, 108, 112, 113
the orders, 97–8, 100 *et sqq.*, 101, 102, 103, 110, 111–12
see also under Vitoria and the state
justice, 103, 109, 110
on law and justice, 107 *et sqq.*
natural right and natural law, 107–8
Vitoria's system, 108–9
good man and good citizen, 109
alternative to Machiavelli, 110
Vitoria on political authority
origin, 66
legitimacy of, 66
and natural law, 66–8
universal, 67
and human law, 68
and the ruler, 72
and the origin of monarchy, 72
and the community, 73, 74
the ruler as legislator, 75
see also Vitoria on the state

Vitoria on the state
its function, 68–9
as regulator of violence, 69
its sovereignty, 69, 76
authority to declare war, 69
and the origin of war, 70
the perfect community, 75–6
definition, 77
and Indian communities, 78–9, 111
and transcendental order, 102
and its moral autarchy, 105
and its end, 108
Vitoria on war
definition, 69–70
origin, *see* under Vitoria on the state
as coercive organ, 100
as instrument of justice, 110
the just war, 112, 113
and the ruler, 131, 138–9, 139–40, 140–1
and Christians, 132–3
offensive war, 133
New Testament, 134
Old Testament and natural law, 134
causes, 135–6
its conduct, 135, 136
the innocent, 136–7
arbitration, 139
and its ethics, 142
Vives, Juan Luis, 36, 121
Erasmian program, 37
life and works, 49–51
imperial idea, 51
De concordia, 52
philosophia Christi, 52
the Emperor's role, 52–3, 54
politics and the state, 53, 54, 55
political Augustinianism, 54
and Christianity, 54
on education, 55
on love, 55–6
on change, 56
and Valdés, 56
and teachings of Christ, 56–7
dignity of man, 56–7
Vives on war
concord, 51–2, 53, 54, 55, 57, 144–5
discord, 52, 145
and the ruler, 54
the state and concord, 146

Vives on war (*cont.*)
  and property, 146
  and vengeance, 146–7
  and honor, 147
  and forgiveness, 147–8
  and the state, 148
  as destroyer, 148–9
  and the Anabaptists, 149

War, 3, 64, 121
  and political thought, 64, 158–9
  just, influence in sixteenth century,

Augustinian influence, 121
as every man's responsibility, 121
and Christ, 122
goal of just war, 133
see also the authors studied under
  war, just war, discord, law of war
Wycliffe, John, 129

Zeno, 170, 172, 204
Zúñiga, Alonso de, 18 n.10
Zurita, Jerónimo de, 160
Zwingli, Ulrich, 155